The Complete Latin Course

Second Edition

G. D. A. Sharpley

Routledge
Taylor & Francis Group

LONDON AND NEW YORK

First published 1994 by Bristol Classical Press under the title "Latin: Better Read than Dead"

First published as *Essential Latin* in 2000 by Routledge

This second edition published 2014 by
Routledge
2 Park Square, Milton Park, Abingdon, Oxon OX14 4RN

and by Routledge
711 Third Avenue, New York, NY 10017

Routledge is an imprint of the Taylor & Francis Group, an informa business

British Library Cataloguing in Publication Data
A catalogue record for this book is available from the British Library

Library of Congress Cataloging in Publication Data
Sharpley, G. D. A., author.
The complete Latin course / G.D.A. Sharpley. — Second edition.
  pages cm
Includes index.
1. Latin language—Textbooks. 2. Latin language—Grammar. I. Title.
PA2087.5.S525 2014
478.2'421—dc23
2013044721

ISBN: 978–0–415–60389–8 (hbk)
ISBN: 978–0–415–59645–9 (pbk)
ISBN: 978–0–203–83445–9 (ebk)

Typeset in Baskerville
by RefineCatch Limited, Bungay, Suffolk.

MIX
Paper from
responsible sources
FSC® C013056
www.fsc.org

Printed and bound in Great Britain by
TJ International Ltd, Padstow, Cornwall

Contents

Acknowledgements

There have been many contributions to both editions of this course, from colleagues, teachers, students and my own teachers, whose lasting enthusiasm has been inspirational. Mark Espiner, David Miller, Niall Rudd and Philip Smiley helped to steer it first time around; and Pauline Nugent of Missouri State University and Susan Edgington of Queen Mary, University of London, have been generous with their comments on the current edition. My students from the University of Bristol and Gloucester Cathedral have contributed in all sorts of ways, and so too Yürg Beyeler, Olivia Cockburn, Conrad Donaldson, Arthur Easton, Paul Pritchard, Charlotte Whiting, Steve Wright, and all those involved in film projects at the Latin Qvarter: there isn't much conversational Latin here, but sound still matters, especially for the verse. Lingua (UK) has given much practical help and embraced within the family of languages this aged relative, sharing broader linguistic values and perspective I hope to mutual benefit. My thanks to the illustrator, Doreen Hebron, and to Andrea Hartill, Anna Callander and Isabelle Cheng at Routledge, and to my daughters, Becca, Meg and Flora, for their humour and fun, and of course to Sarah for all that and more.

quod spiro et placeo, si placeo, tuum est.
Horace, *Odes* 4.3.24

Introduction

Latin and the world of Rome

This course is a much enlarged version of what was first published in 1994 under the title *Latin: Better Read Than Dead* and then six years later as *Essential Latin*. The 13 chapters in the previous editions are now 26, and will provide enough material for students taking Latin for a year or more. The principle of this course, now as then, is to learn the language by reading the ancient authors themselves. The quotations illustrate a narrative of the historical and social background of ancient Rome, which in turn puts the quotations in their context and throws some light on the lives of the writers and their contemporaries. It is hardly possible to read authors from a different time and not be curious about their world.

Henry of Huntington, a twelfth-century chronicler, once wrote that an interest in the past is one of the characteristics which distinguished humans from animals.[1] As I sit in the garden and watch our cat making cautious inquiries into who or what has recently been in his domain, the chronicler's line between us and the animal world fades before my eyes. Our tools of enquiry may be more sophisticated, and our scope for enquiry broader and deeper than that of my four-legged friend, but his instinct for historical research is fresher and more vital. Our sense of smell is not what it was. In turn we have created something potent and enabling in our academic lives, 'historical studies', which can though seem a little remote, half-hidden in a room full of specialists. All of us want to enter that room at some point, following a particular interest or need, and I suspect that history will forever remain a primal curiosity, for it informs us, shapes us, defines us, stirs up passions, misleads us, entertains us, and warns us in all sorts of ways.

The historical survey here is only a sketch, subject to inevitable distortions: my selective process skips far more than it includes, and leaves a good deal unsaid; also missing is the ancient writing which did *not* survive and might well tell a story differently; then there is all the material which has survived but cannot be included here, because it was written in Greek; and lastly a note of caution about the writers themselves, who are subject to wobbles of accuracy or partiality or tinted specs (aren't we all). The written evidence cannot always be taken as solid fact, which presents the student today with an opportunity: to learn how to weigh up all that we read and hear in our own time which claims to report the truth.

---

1 *Historia Anglorum* (A History of the English) by Henry of Huntington: 'The knowledge of former events . . . forms a main distinction between brutes and rational creatures.'

Learning the language

The readings in the first half of the course sketch the history of early Rome and tell the story of the end of the Republic and rise of Augustus. The second half looks more at the social and cultural background of Rome, what people got up to, their jobs, education, and religious beliefs. The Latin is taken from ancient writers themselves. There is minor editing here and there to clarify a context or simplify the Latin a little, and where words have been omitted, the introductory sentences should make up for any gap in the meaning. The editing though is negligible. The words are the Romans' themselves and make little allowance that by the end of Chapter 2 you have only covered nouns like **puella** and **servus**. The support is there in the notes to help you complete the meaning.

There is a similarity here with learning to speak a modern language in an immersion environment, for instance French: you cannot wait until you have covered the grammar of reflexive pronouns before you learn to say what your name is (*je m'appelle* . . .) or object pronouns before you learn to respond to someone saying 'thank you' (*je vous en prie*). When French learners come to the detail of these expressions they already have examples to engage with the theory. Thus in general the grammar is taught descriptively not prescriptively, and the learning inductive not deductive. But it is not that black and white and nor does it need to be.

A key part of the approach here is the reappearance of texts in later language topics. New points of grammar and syntax are illustrated by the passages you have already read. So if some of the minutiae pass you by first time around there are many opportunities later to refocus. The Index of examples (p. 364) will point you to all the reappearances of any given sentence, which are listed, for example, as [10.4] to refer to Chapter 10, sentence 4. There is also the Index of grammar (p. 367) to help you with words such as verb, noun, voice, mood, and so on.

Latin has an elaborate grammar and in the readings there is plenty to analyze and decode. However, Latin is not as 'logical' as it is sometimes made out to be: you will meet ambiguity and inconsistency in this language as in any other – and meaning will only come if you look for it. Of course there will be times when you get the wrong end of the stick, when you think you nearly have it and then a word appears which throws all into confusion. How you learn to step back and retrain your efforts will be the making of you as a reader.

So from the very first chapter expect the readings to present a challenge, and prepare to cling on to your hat as the boat sets sail. Don't feel too frustrated if you fail to place every last ending. Many of these gaps will be filled as you progress through the course. If that sounds indulgent, then here is the deal: if we say that half-success with the readings is a cup half-full, then the approach to the exercises should be less forgiving. These are set to reinforce the language covered and test your learning. Half-success in the exercises is a cup half-empty!

If you are a beginner and ready for a challenge, the course I hope will prove engaging, fulfilling and even bring some joy.

Teachers' notes

The Complete Latin Course is intended to meet the requirement of beginners' courses lasting one academic year. I recommend you allow at least two hours' class-time a week for each chapter: in class, cover the grammar, take the practice exercises, and then the Latin readings; and add your own extras, tests, quizzes and any other activities as you feel it right. For home study I suggest you give one or both sets of exercises, and encourage students to read the introduction to the following chapter's readings and to make what headway they can into the texts. The online resources include full vocabulary lists for you to make use of in your own activities, and additional exercises for further examples, practice or testing.

I have tried to present a clear step-by-step unfolding of the rules of the language. The learning path is rapid enough, and I recommend teachers resist the temptation to explain grammar prematurely. How resistant will depend on the level and appetites of your students; but in my experience those who feel sold short by a word or word-ending left unexplained are usually those who know it already. Too much grammatical detail before time will dismay beginners.

Online support

Various additional supports are available online, including answers and translations. It is not essential to have access to these supports unless you are a class teacher or are studying without teacher support. See p. 393 for details.

The sound of Latin

Two thousand years on, all we have left of the Latin language is what has survived in writing. This gives the misleading impression of a language which lives only on paper, written or read silently. In fact Latin was a very vocal language, written to be heard, prose as well as verse. When someone like Cicero spent an evening 'reading', more often than not he would be listening to one of his readers. So to ignore the sound of Latin would be to miss a vital part of it.

I suggest you start by listening to your teacher read sentences aloud. For a guide to the sound of individual letters see p. 352. There are recordings of some of the readings (see below), and an introduction to verse metres which appear in the course is available with the other online supports.

Recordings

Selective readings of the texts are available online (see p. 393).

The Latin alphabet

The English alphabet is based upon the Latin alphabet with one or two additions. The English letters which were not a part of the ancient Latin one are in brackets:

A B C D E F G H I (J) **K L M N O P Q R S T** (U) **V** (W) **X Y Z**

The Romans themselves wrote everything in capitals (e.g. **IVLIVS** for Julius). The convention today is to use lower-case, and in many texts (as here) capitals do not even begin sentences: only proper nouns (i.e. names) start with capital letters.

V served as both the consonant 'v' (or 'w' – see p. 352 for the pronunciation of individual letters) and the vowel 'u'. When written today, in lower-case, it always appears as a 'u' if a vowel (**puella**); while as a consonant you will find it written either as a 'v' (as in this course, **servus**) or as a 'u' (**seruus**).

I is another letter which may be either consonant or vowel. Until relatively recently the practice was to write the consonantal **I** as a 'j', e.g. **jacet** for **iacet** (*lies*). The current (and ancient) convention is to use **I** for both uses of the letter (**Iulius**).

K is rare, and likewise **Y** and **Z** which appear chiefly in words borrowed from other languages.

Macrons

You will see that some vowels show macrons (e.g. **ā**). This means that the vowel is 'long' as opposed to 'short' (no macron). This 'length' or 'quantity' refers to the duration of its sound. There are slight changes in quality between short and long vowels but the principal difference is in the time taken to say it. For examples see p. 352.

Macrons do not appear in Latin texts, only in coursebooks as a guide for students. Thus if you do not include macrons in exercises where you write Latin it is not incorrect, but you may wish to include them all the same.

— 1 —

Myth, legend and history

Nouns and verbs

A noun is a 'thing', like *paper, butter* or *happiness*. We often use *the* or *a* before a noun. Names are also nouns (but we don't normally put *the* or *a* in front of names, except for a plural like *the Smiths*). Many nouns are solid things, which you can see or touch. Some are abstract, like *happiness, injury* or *debt*. Abstract nouns are not so solid but we may feel them keenly enough.

A verb describes the action, what is done by the nouns, e.g. *have, run, speak*. Some English nouns are used as verbs, as in <u>*paper*</u> *over the cracks*, or <u>*butter*</u> *the toast*.

Practice 1a
Identify two Latin nouns and a verb in this sentence:
agricola taurum fugat
the farmer chases/is chasing the bull

Nouns: subjects and objects

The Latin verb **fugat** appears at the end of the sentence above. *The farmer*, **agricola**, is the active one, the person doing the chasing, and so this noun is the subject. *The bull*, **taurum**, is the object, because he is on the receiving end, i.e. the one being chased.

Now subject and object are swapped:

> taurus agricolam fugat
> *the bull chases/is chasing the farmer*

The endings of the two nouns have changed: **agricol<u>am</u>** (*the farmer*) is now on the receiving end of **fugat** (*chases*) and so is the object, while **taur<u>us</u>** (*the bull*) is the subject, the one who is doing the chasing.

farmer as subject is	**agricol<u>a</u>**
and as object	**agricol<u>am</u>**
bull as subject is	**taur<u>us</u>**
and as object	**taur<u>um</u>**

Negative

Here are some more nouns. The presence of the negative (**nōn** = *not*) does not alter the endings. Grammatically there is still an action being described, if negatively:

puella servum **nōn** fugat
the girl is not chasing the slave

servus agricolam **nōn** amat
the slave does not like the farmer

taurus puellam **nōn** fugat
the bull is not chasing the girl

There are many nouns like **agricola** and **puella** which have the same endings, and there is another group like **taurus** and **servus**:

	farmer	*girl*	*bull*	*slave*
as subject	agricola	puella	taur**us**	serv**us**
as object	agricol**am**	puell**am**	taur**um**	serv**um**

Articles *the* and *a*

There are no Latin words for 'the' or 'a', so add them to your English translation as you feel it right: **taurus** = *a bull* or *the bull*.

Practice 1b

Fill the gaps with nouns with the right endings:
(a)   taurus . . . . {*a farmer*} fugat.
(b)   . . . . {*the farmer*} taurum nōn amat.
(c)   puella . . . . {*a bull*} nōn fugat.
(d)   servus . . . . {*the girl*} amat.

Word order

In English we rely on the position of the words to know who is doing what to whom. The subject is almost always first, then the verb, followed by the object (*the farmer chases the bull*). Mix them up and we're in a muddle. In Latin the status of subject or object is made clear by a word's ending, not by its position. So the word order is more flexible

Practice 1c

Translate:
(a)   puella taurum amat.
(b)   taurum puella nōn fugat.
(c)   servum taurus nōn amat.
(d)   taurus nōn amat servus.
(e)   servus fugat taurus.

and variable. The subject typically appears before the object, with the verb at the end – but by no means always.

The 'object' of est

The verb **est** (*is*) does not govern an object as most other verbs do:

> Brūtus **agricola** est
> *Brutus is a farmer*

Like **Brūtus, agricola** has the subject ending (**agricola**, not **agricolam**). The noun **agricola** describes **Brūtus**. It is not an object as such but a description of the subject. So the 'object' of *to be*, sometimes called the 'complement', has a subject ending:

> agricola nōn **servus** est
> *the farmer is not a slave*

Verbs

The verbs listed are in the present tense. The action is happening now or within the present period. English has different ways of expressing the present tense:

> **fugat** = *chases*
> *does (not) chase*
> *is chasing*

fugat	*(s/he) chases/is chasing* *
amat	*(s/he) loves*
laudat	*(s/he) praises/is praising*
habet	*(s/he) has, owns*
timet	*(s/he) fears*
contemnit	*(s/he) despises*
est	*(s/he, there) is*

* Latin does not need **est** to represent '*is* chasing'.

Some verbs exist chiefly in just the one form, e.g. we say 'it matters', not 'it is mattering'. In the short exercises it does not matter which you use. In longer ones usually only one or other will make a good English translation.

Practice 1d

Translate:
(a)   agricola taurum habet.
(b)   servus taurum timet.
(c)   agricola puellam laudat.
(d)   puella taurum nōn contemnit.

'and'

There is more than one word for 'and' in Latin: **et, atque** and **ac** all mean 'and', and so too the enclitic **-que** ('enclitic' is from the Greek word for 'lean on'): **-que** should be taken *before* the word it leans on:

> agricola tauru**que**   (the equivalent of 'agricola **et** taurus')
> *the farmer and the bull*

> **Practice 1e**
> Rewrite each, using **et** in place of **-que**:
> (a)   puella servusque.
> (b)   agricola puellam servumque laudat.
> (c)   agricola servum taurumque habet.

Cases

The technical name for the different endings of a noun is 'case'. Each case has a particular function. The subject ending is called the nominative case, and the object ending is called the accusative case.

The nominative case

This indicates the subject of the verb:

> **agricola** taurum timet
> *the farmer fears the bull*

The accusative case

This is used for the object of the verb:

> agricola **taurum** timet
> *the farmer fears the bull*

> **Practice 1f**
> Identify the case of each underlined word:
> (a)   taurus **agricolam** fugat.
> (b)   **puella** servum nōn habet.
> (c)   agricola nōn est **servus**.
> (d)   agricola **taurum** amat et nōn timet.
> (e)   puella in **forum** venit.

The accusative case is also used as an object of movement:

> agricola in **forum** venit
> *the farmer comes into the forum*

English pronouns to add in translation

Where no subject noun appears, the subject is implied in the verb-ending, in English represented by *he, she* or *it* (and later when we see the plural verb-ending *they*):

> taurum **timet**
> *he/she fears the bull*

An object noun may only appear once when it is in fact the object of two verbs, as with **puellam** below, in which case you add the relevant pronoun to your English version (*him, her, it, them*):

agricola **puellam** nōn amat sed contemnit
the farmer does not like <u>the girl</u> but despises <u>her</u>

et	and
numquam	never
sed	but

His, her or their in place of the/a

Sometimes in English we put *his, her* or *their* in place of *the* or *a*, where it seems obvious or the English is awkward without it. In the absence of other information we take **fīlium** below to be the son of the **agricola** and so say 'his':

agricola **fīlium** laudat
the farmer praises <u>his</u> son

Later you will meet Latin words for *his* or *her*, which are used for the sake of clarity or emphasis.

Practice 1g
Translate:
(a) agricola numquam fīlium laudat sed contemnit.
(b) Romulus agricolam contemnit sed taurum timet.
(c) puella servum amat et laudat.
(d) Brūtus nōn servus sed agricola est.
(e) puella servum nōn contemnit sed agricola.

Vocabulary 1
Start your own vocabulary notebook or file. Allow at least a page for nouns like **agricola** and another page for nouns like **taurus**. Add the nouns below to the correct list:

agricola	farmer	**dominus**	lord, master	**puella**	girl
Ascanius	Ascanius	**equus**	horse	**Rōma**	Rome
Britannia	Britain	**fīlia**	daughter	**Romulus**	Romulus
Brūtus	Brutus	**fīlius**	son	**rosa**	rose
dea	goddess	**Lāvīnia**	Lavinia	**servus**	slave
deus	god	**poēta**	poet	**taurus**	bull
domina	lady, mistress	**populus**	people		

Exercises 1a

1.   Fill each gap with the correct Latin word:

[*Check with your teacher whether you need to include macrons* (**ā**, **ē**, *etc*) *in your Latin answers. See* p. xiv]

(a)   puella . . . . {*her master*} nōn amat.

(b)   Romulus nōn est . . . . {*a god*}

(c)   dea . . . . {*the girl*} nōn laudat.

(d)   Romulus . . . . {*his son*} amat.

2.   Translate:

(a)   deum deamque laudat agricola.

(b)   dominus taurum equumque fugat.

(c)   servus dominum et dominam laudat.

(d)   puella nōn dominum sed Romulum amat.

(e)   Ascanius numquam dominam laudat, sed deam timet.

3.   Can you think of any English words whose shape or ending depends on whether they are subject or object?

4.   Fill each gap with the correct Latin word, and translate:

(a)   . . . . {*The goddess*} rosam amat.

(b)   puella . . . . {*a horse*} habet.

(c)   Ascanius . . . . {*the goddess*} timet.

(d)   servus . . . . {*the girl*} nōn timet.

(e)   dominus . . . . {*Lavinia*} amat.

(f)   populus . . . . {*Romulus*} laudat.

Myth, legend and history

The 'origins' of something are usually defined for us by the limits of what we can see. Rome emerges from obscurity as a collection of villages which grow together and become a satellite of Etruria, a powerful culture to the north. The traditional date of the expulsion of the last king, Tarquin, the break with Etruria, and the beginning of the Republic is 509 BC. The king was replaced by a pair of elected leaders (consuls), whose length of office was restricted to one year. Romans in authority or close to it did not like the idea of power concentrated in one individual, and this shared sense of unease guided the politics of the Republic for some hundreds of years, before it eventually gave way to the single control of Augustus and the emperors who followed.

Reading notes

If you haven't already, read 'Learning the language' in the Introduction (p. xii).

Unfamiliar endings appear in the readings, which are not like those of **puella** or **taurus**. Where so, the case will be given with the meaning, and it is up to you to figure out why the case is used in that sentence. As the course progresses you will return to many of these words when you meet others like them.

There is a guide to pronunciation on p. 352.

The beginning of the Republic was a much-heralded moment for later Romans. We might say that it was much like any other political struggle and ousting of those in authority followed by a compromise of power-sharing between the leaders of the victorious faction. But this perspective was too prosaic for Roman historians. They worked within a different set of conventions from those of our time. In a world without novels, films, television, internet, anything electronic, historians were expected to entertain as well as inform. Our notion of history – an informed and balanced interpretation of dependable facts – would have left the ancients feeling sold short. The first two books of Livy's *History of Rome* interweave fact with legend and myth, which is how his readers wanted to see the beginning of their era.

A myth is by definition untrue, while a legend has factual origins which are distorted in the telling and retelling of the story. There is a clear difference in meaning, as the hapless newspaper editor discovered, who in an obituary of a local dignitary described the man's kindness as mythical when he meant legendary. One might say that the stories of the poet Virgil are myths, while the stories of the historian Livy are mostly legends.

Myths, though untrue, are not always meant to mislead. They are valuable as symbols or moral paradigms, and can be an articulate if implausible way of perceiving the world. Greek writers had already borrowed the theatre's tendency to make a metaphor of life, not simply hold up a mirror. But factual accuracy had mattered to the Greeks. The Athenian historian Thucydides, who wrote an account of the war in the latter part of the fifth century between Athens and Sparta, set standards of accuracy and impartiality which Roman historians acknowledged and tried to emulate. There were later Greek historians who didn't reach the heights attained by Thucydides and whose primary objective was to tell a good story, capped with a clear moral. Romans absorbed these conventions too and added their own taste for biography with its natural inclination to extremes. And they raised the moralizing element to the grander level of national interest, public duty and Rome.

1. The poet Virgil introduces his poem the *Aeneid*, the story of Aeneas, the most famous of Rome's ancestors, who escapes from Troy after the city has fallen to the Greeks:

arma virumque canō.

Virgil, Aeneid 1.1

arma [acc.: for unfamiliar endings see Reading notes above]   *arms, war*
virum [acc.]   *man*
-que   *and* (see p. 4 above)
canō   *I sing of, celebrate (in song)*
Use the Index of examples on p. 364 to see where a Latin quotation reappears as an illustration of a point of language (not essential at this stage for beginners, but it may prove helpful later)

2. After a perilous journey westwards, including a shipwreck on the coast of Dido's Carthage, Aeneas and his companions arrive in Italy. His destiny is to build a settlement there.

urbem Rōmam condidērunt Trōiānī.

Sallust, Conspiracy of Catiline 6.1

urbem [acc.]   *city*
Rōmam [acc.]   *(of) Rome*

condidērunt   *(they) founded*
Trōiānī [nom.]   *Trojans*

3. There was resistance to this foreign prince. The local tribes send out their warriors
    against him. The two armies . . .

    ## . . . clāmōre incendunt caelum.

    Virgil, *Aeneid* 10.895

clāmōre   *with noise, shouting*
incendunt   *(they) set fire to, inflame* (here, metaphorical)
caelum [acc.]   *sky, heaven*

4. Camilla, the leader of a troop of female fighters, kills a number of Aeneas' men before
    she herself dies in battle.

    ## linquēbat habēnās / ad terram nōn sponte fluēns.

    Virgil, *Aeneid* 11.827–8

linquēbat   *s/he let go*
habēnās [acc.]   *reins* (ignore '/', which marks a linebreak in the poem)
ad [followed by a noun in the accusative]   *to, towards*
terram [acc.]   *ground, earth*
nōn   *not*
sponte   *of one's own accord, voluntarily*
fluēns [the subject of 'linquēbat' is doing this]   *sliding*

5. Turnus, the principal warrior against Aeneas, pleads for his life in the closing lines of the
    poem. He surrenders his claim to marriage with Lavinia, daughter of Latinus, king of
    the Latin people:

    ## 'tua est Lāvīnia coniūnx.'

    Virgil, *Aeneid* 12.937

tua coniūnx [nom.]   *your wife*
est   *is*
Lāvīnia [nom.]   *Lavinia*
tua . . . coniūnx: grammatically both *your wife is Lavinia* and *Lavinia is your wife* are correct,
    though one is better than the other here

6. When Aeneas eventually died his son Ascanius was still too young to rule.

    ## nōndum mātūrus imperiō Ascanius erat.

    Livy, *History of Rome* 1.3

nōndum   *not yet*
mātūrus [describes a noun in the nominative]   *ready*
imperiō   *for power*

Ascanius [nom.]   *Ascanius*
erat   *(s/he, it) was*

7. When Ascanius grew up he left Lavinia to look after the existing settlement and himself
    built a new one close by.

urbem novam ipse aliam sub Albānō monte condidit.

Livy, *History of Rome* 1.3

urbem [acc.]   *city* (the city of Alba Longa was about 13 miles south-east of Rome)
novam [describes a noun in the accusative]   *new*
ipse   *he himself*
aliam [describes a noun in the accusative]   *other*
sub Albānō monte   *beneath the Alban hills*
condidit   *(s/he) founded*

8. Romulus, a descendant of Aeneas, is equally well known to us as a founder of
    Rome. The legend has it that as babies he and his twin-brother Remus were suckled by
    a she-wolf, but later as young men came to blows. Romulus killed his brother when
    Remus mocked the walls he was building. As sole leader he appointed a group of
    advisers.

Romulus centum creat senātōrēs.

Livy, *History of Rome* 1.8

Romulus [nom.]   *Romulus*
centum   *hundred*
creat   *(s/he) appoints*
senātōrēs [acc.]   *senators*

9. Romulus invited neighbouring peoples to visit the new settlement. The Sabines arrived
    with their families, including their many daughters.

Sabīnī cum līberīs ac coniugibus vēnērunt.

Livy, *History of Rome* 1.9

Sabīnī [nom.]   *Sabines*
cum līberīs ac coniugibus   *with their children and wives*
vēnērunt   *(they) came*

10. Romulus had a darker design, motivated by a shortage of women in Rome. While the
    guests were being shown around, his comrades leapt out and carried off the Sabine girls
    by force. This sparked a conflict which the women themselves resolved. For some time
    thereafter Rome was ruled by a line of kings.

urbem Rōmam ā prīncipiō rēgēs habuērunt.

Tacitus, *Annals* 1.1

urbem [acc.]   city
Rōmam [acc.]   *(of) Rome*
ā prīncipiō   *from the beginning*
rēgēs [nom.]   *kings*
habuērunt   *(they) had, held*

Exercises 1b
In the 'B' exercises at the close of each chapter you will meet words and phrases from the chapter's readings.

1.   Translate:
(a)   agricola Romulum Remumque laudat.
(b)   tuus est Romulus dominus.
(c)   tuus est Ascanius filius.
(d)   domina nova Ascanium fugat.
(e)   Romulus urbem novam laudat.
(f)   servus centum senātorēs nōn creat.

2.   Identify the Latin words above (as they appear in the text) for:
(a)   *city*
(b)   *sky*
(c)   *ground*
(d)   *wife*
(e)   *ready*
(f)   *new*
(g)   *mountain*
(h)   *hundred*
(i)   *kings*

3.   Translate:
(a)   tua est Clōdia domina.
(b)   Romulus mātūrus imperiō est.
(c)   agricola taurum nōn fugat, ad terram nōn sponte fluēns.
(d)   dea filium Ascaniumque amat.
(e)   novam dominam sub Albānō monte laudat poēta.

4.   Find Latin words in this chapter which are ancestors of *creative, fluent, imperial, regal, spontaneous* and *virile*.

— 2 —

The Republic

The genitive case

The nominative case is used for a subject, and the accusative for an object. Now there are four more cases for you to look at. First, the genitive case. The English preposition *of* is used to translate the genitive case:

dominus **puellae**
the master of the girl (the girl's master)

fīlia **servī**
the daughter of the slave (the slave's daughter)

	girl	slave
Nominative	puella	servus
Accusative	puellam	servum
Genitive	**puellae**	**servī**

The genitive is often used to show possession. If so, an English equivalent phrase might leave out 'of' and use an apostrophe instead: 'the girl's master'. Centuries ago English nouns had cases too. The 'e' of the English genitive ending '-es' has since given way to the apostrophe.

Practice 2a
Translate into Latin (two words per answer):
(a) the son of a goddess
(b) the mistress of Rome
(c) Romulus' slave
(d) Lavinia's daughter

The dative case

The dative case is used to show an indirect object. The English prepositions *to* or *for* can often be used in an equivalent English expression:

Romulus **puellae** rosam dat
Romulus gives a rose to the girl

Lāvīnia vīllam **servō** ostendit
Lavinia shows the villa to the slave

est **dominō** fīlius
there is a son for the master (i.e. the master has a son)

	girl	slave
Nominative	puella	servus
Accusative	puellam	servum
Genitive	puellae	servī
Dative	**puellae**	**servō**

The dative can also show possession: it appears in harness with a verb, especially a verb like **est**, when the emphasis falls on the thing possessed rather than the possessor (dative):

est **servō** coniūnx
there is a wife for/to the slave (i.e. *the slave has a wife*)

Practice 2b

Fill each gap with the right Latin word, and translate:

(a)   dominus rosam . . . . {*to Lavinia*} dat.
(b)   Romulus Rōmam . . . . {*to his son*} ostendit.
(c)   deō . . . . {*a bull*} dat Ascanius.
(d)   fīlius . . . . {*for the goddess*} est.

Some more verbs
dat   *(s/he) gives* *
ostendit   *(s/he) shows*

* also *is giving*: only the simple form will be shown

The ablative case

The usual words which translate the ablative are *in, on, with, from* and *by*:

agricola cum[1] **servō** venit
The farmer comes with the slave

servus ā **puellā** rosam accipit
the slave receives a rose from the girl

dominus **Rōmā** venit
the master comes from Rome

domina in **lectō** sedet
the mistress sits on the bed

in **vīllā** est puella
there is a girl/a girl is in the villa

puella equum ē **vīllā** fugat
the girl chases the horse from the villa

Brūtus ā **populō** creātus est
Brutus was appointed by the people

	girl	*slave*
Nominative	puella	servus
Accusative	puellam	servum
Genitive	puellae	servī
Dative	puellae	servō
Ablative	**puellā**	**servō**

---

1 Sometimes separate Latin prepositions appear with the ablative case, sometimes they do not.

Practice 2c

Fill each gap with one Latin word, and translate:

(a) cum .... {*with Ascanius*} sedet Lāvīnia.

(b) in .... {*in Italy*} est dominus.

(c) dominus cum .... {*with his son*} venit.

(d) agricola ē .... {*from the villa*} taurum fugat.

(e) cum .... {*with the master*} in vīllā est domina.

accipit	*(s/he) receives*
sedet	*(s/he) sits*
venit	*(s/he) comes*

Prepositions

In, on, with, from, by, at, of, for and *to* are all prepositions. They are used with nouns to say where something is, or when, or who or what we do it with, or who it was done by.

In Latin, case-endings give the value of many English prepositions (e.g. **puellae** = *of the girl*), but there are also separate Latin prepositions which help clarify the meaning. Some Latin prepositions are used with a noun in the accusative, some with a noun in the ablative.

The accusative is used as an object of movement:

in vīllam   *into the villa*
ad terram   *to, towards the ground*

and the ablative for a fixed point:

in vīllā   *in the villa*
in terrā   *on the ground*

One or two prepositions, like **in**, are used with both cases.

The accusative and the ablative are the two cases most used with prepositions. The dative is the '*to* . . .' case, but seldom as the object of a journey (**ad** or **in** + accusative).

with accusative
ad   *to, towards*
in *   *into, onto*

with ablative
ab (ā #) *by, from*
cum   *with, together with*
ex (ē #) *from, out of*
in *   *in, on*

* used with both cases
\# before some consonants

Practice 2d

Give the case of the underlined words, and translate:

(a) puella in **terrā** sedet.

(b) dominus cum **dominā** in **lectō** sedet.

(c) Lāvīnia rosam ab **Ascaniō** accipit.

(d) servus in **vīllam** venit.

(e) dominus ē **vīllā** servum fugat.

(f) fīlia ad **vīllam** venit.

Same endings for different cases

The same endings occur for different cases (e.g. **puellae** – genitive or dative, and **servō** – dative or ablative). And where macrons are not used, the ablative of **puella** will look the same as the nominative. Thus the case system is not entirely distinct, and there will be grey areas for you to resolve with help from the context.

Practice 2e
Give the case of the underlined word, and translate:
(a)   fīlius **Lāvīniae** in vīllā est.
(b)   poēta rosam **dominae** dat.
(c)   poēta fīliam **dominī** laudat.
(d)   servus taurum **agricolae** timet.
(e)   poēta nōn **dominō** sed **puellae** rosam dat.

The vocative case

The vocative case is the form used when a person is being addressed. You will recognize it easily enough when it appears, usually but not always preceded by **ō** or **mī/mea** . . . (*my . . .*).

Most forms of this case are identical to the nominative ending, except notably for nouns like **servus** or **dominus**, which end **-e** (and a few words **-ī**) in the vocative singular:

ō domine, taurus in vīllā est
sir, a bull is in the villa

mī fīlī, Ascanius in vīllā est
my son, Ascanius is in the villa

Practice 2f
Translate:
(a)   ō dea, puellam amat Ascanius.
(b)   ō domina, agricola in vīllam servum fugat.
(c)   et tū, Brūte?
(d)   ō Collātīne, in lectō sedet Sextus.

---

est **and** sunt

The Latin verb **est** means *is*. It can be *he is*, *she is*, *it is*, or *there is*:

servus in vīllā **est**
a/the slave is in the villa   or   *there is a slave in the villa*

The plural of **est** is **sunt**, which can mean _they are_ or _there are_:

centum senātōrēs in vīllā **sunt**
there are a hundred senators in the villa/a hundred senators are . . .

Summary

Latin nouns change endings according to their function in the sentence. These endings are called cases.

There are five types of noun altogether, of which you have met the first two. These types are called 'declensions'. Nouns like **agricola** or **puella** belong to the 1st declension, and those like **servus** to the 2nd declension:

Case	Function	1st decl. **puella** _girl_	2nd decl. **servus** _slave_
Nominative	subject	puell**a**	serv**us**
Vocative	person addressed	puell**a**	serv**e**
Accusative	object	puell**am**	serv**um**
Genitive	_of_	puell**ae**	serv**ī**
Dative	_to, for_	puell**ae**	serv**ō**
Ablative	_in, on, with, from, by_	puell**ā**	serv**ō**

Vocabulary 2

Which of these nouns belong to the 1st declension and which to the 2nd? List them in your vocabulary notebook accordingly:

amīca	_friend (female), girlfriend_	**lectus**	_bed, couch_
amīcus	_friend (male)_	**Lucrētia**	_Lucretia_
annus	_year_	**mēnsa**	_table_
Brūtus	_Brutus_	**Porsenna**	_Porsenna_ *
fēmina	_woman_	**prōvincia**	_province_
gladius	_sword_	**puer** #	_boy_
Horātius	_Horatius, Horace_	**rēgīna**	_queen_
Ītalia	_Italy_	**Rōma**	_Rome_
Tarquinius	_Tarquin_	**vīlla**	_villa_
terra	_ground, land_	**vir** #	_man, husband_

* Most personal names ending **-a** (i.e. belonging to the 1st declension) are female: **Porsenna** is one of a handful which are male: **Caligula, Sulla**, etc.

Add **vir** and **puer** to nouns like **servus** (i.e. the 2nd declension).

Vir (*man, husband*) has lost its ending **-us** in the nominative, if it ever had one, just possibly to avoid confusion with the Latin ancestor of our word 'virus' (**vīrus** = *poison, slime*). The same for **puer** (*boy*): other than the nominative and vocative singular all the case-endings are regular.

	man/husband	boy
N.	vir	puer
V.	vir	puer
A.	virum	puerum
G.	virī	puerī
D.	virō	puerō
Ab.	virō	puerō

Exercises 2a

1.   Translate:
(a)   puella in vīllam venit.
(b)   servus Ascaniō vīllam ostendit.
(c)   puella cum puerō in mēnsā sedet.
(d)   fēmina in lectō Tarquiniī est.
(e)   fīlius agricolae equum taurumque habet.
(f)   Antōnius cum rēgīnā in lectō sedet.

2.   Think of an English word from
(a)   amīcus
(b)   annus
(c)   gladius
(d)   terra

3.   Give the case of the underlined word, and translate:
(a)   agricola fīliam **Lāvīniae** amat.
(b)   gladius in **mēnsā** est.
(c)   Horātius deō **taurum** dat.
(d)   in prōvinciā est vīlla **Brūtī**.
(e)   rēgīna **agricolae** gladium dat.
(f)   Lucrētia gladium **Sextī** nōn timet.
(g)   ō **domina**, puella fīlium Lucrētiae nōn amat.
(h)   Brūtus, amīcus Lucrētiae, in **terrā** sedet.

The Republic

The kings of Rome were replaced by a government of two elected consuls sharing power, for one year only, with a more influential role from the senate than under the monarchy. Records of the past begin to have a more factual feel to them, though the history of the early Republic is still enlivened with many a legendary tale, good stories all. A narrative of virtuous or vicious acts engaged readers and served up moral paradigms. Killing your father (or revelling in his death as Tullia does below) was a shocking impiety. But killing members of your own family might have its virtues. Brutus, who executes his own sons (no. 9), shows how far a true patriot will go for his country. The other side to this of course, for people routinely entertained by butchery in the amphitheatre, is the fresh excitement of a father killing his own children.

Reading notes

You will see that in the notes beneath each passage some of the Latin is explained without a complete breakdown of individual words and endings. This is necessary while you gather the relevant skills and knowledge. Many sentences will return in later chapters to provide examples of points of language, and by the end of the course you will be able to revisit texts and recognize much more of the detail.

A text beginning with three dots (. . .) is not a complete sentence.

1. Tarquin, the last of the kings, seized power after plotting with his wife Tullia against her father, Servius, the reigning king. Tarquin called a meeting of senators, into which rushes Servius:

'quā tū audāciā patrēs vocās?'

Livy, *History of Rome* 1.48

quā [take with a noun in the ablative]   *with what*
tū [nom.]   *you*
audāciā [has endings like 'puella']   *presumption*
patrēs [acc.]   *fathers, senators*
vocās   *you call, summon*

2. Tarquin picked up Servius and hurled him out into the forum, where he was finished off by accomplices. A short while later the dead king's daughter, Tullia, arrived in a chariot determined to show support for her husband. Her horrified driver points out Servius' body:

dominae Servium trucīdātum ostendit.

Livy, *History of Rome* 1.48

Servium: with endings like 'servus'
trucīdātum [describes a noun in the accusative]   *murdered, butchered*
ostendit   *(s/he) shows*

3. Tullia ordered him to drive the horses and chariot over her father's dead body, a notably shocking incident which Livy tells us gave the name to a street in Rome, *Vicus Sceleratus* ('Wicked Street'). Livy's stories of intrigue and rivalry for kingship foreshadow later events in imperial housholds. Women are often in the frame – though never with official authority – either scheming mischief and malice or as models of virtue and courage. Such was Lucretia, the wife of Tarquin's nephew Collatinus, who attracted the unrequited attention of Tarquin's son, Sextus Tarquin. As a guest in her house, and while Collatinus was absent, Sextus forces himself upon her, threatening her with a knife:

'tacē, Lucrētia. Sextus Tarquinius sum; ferrum in manū est.'

Livy, *History of Rome* 1.58

tacē   *keep quiet*
Lucrētia: with endings like 'puella'
sum   *I am*
ferrum [looks like an accusative but is in fact nominative; more on p. 23]   *knife*
manū [abl.]   *hand*
est   *(s/he, it or there) is*

4.   In despair Lucretia took her own life, but not before making Collatinus and his kinsman Lucius Junius Brutus swear vengeance:

'vestīgia virī aliēnī, Collātīne, in lectō sunt tuō.'

Livy, *History of Rome* 1.58

vestīgia [nom.pl.]   *traces*
virī [gen.]   *man*
aliēnī [describes a noun in the genitive]   *other, strange*
sunt   *(they, there) are*
tuō [with a noun in the ablative]   *your*

5.   This sparked a struggle to overthrow Sextus's father, Tarquin, who turned out to be the last *rex* of Rome. *Superbus* (proud, arrogant), as he was now called, was forced into exile by Brutus and Collatinus, and these two were together appointed consuls.

Tarquinius Superbus rēgnāvit annōs quīnque et vīgintī. duo cōnsulēs inde creātī sunt.

Livy, *History of Rome* 1.60

rēgnāvit   *(s/he) ruled*
annōs quīnque et vīgintī   *for five and twenty years*
duo   *two*
cōnsulēs [nom.]   consuls
inde   *then*
creātī sunt   *were appointed*

6.   Tarquin remained a threat to the new Republic for he had the support of Porsenna, king of the Etruscans, the principal power in the north of Italy. Porsenna sent an ultimatum to the Romans to take back Tarquin, which they refused, and so he . . .

. . . ingentīque urbem obsidiōne premēbat.

Virgil, *Aeneid* 8.647

Where the Latin begins with dots take it as an incomplete sentence dependent on the introduction

-que: take *and* as the first word (*and he . . .*)
ingentī [describes a noun in the ablative]   *huge, immense*
urbem [acc.]   *city*
obsidiōne [abl.]   *siege, blockade*
premēbat   *(s/he) pressed*

7.   Rome's defence was remembered for many acts of patriotism. Horatius Cocles stood alone on a bridge resisting Etruscan advances while his comrades dismantled it behind him. The bridge would have fallen to the enemy . . .

. . . nī ūnus vir fuisset, Horātius Cōcles.

Livy, *History of Rome* 2.10

nī   *if not*
ūnus [nom.]   *one*
vir [nom.]   *man*
fuisset   *had been*

8.   Cloelia was one of several Roman girls taken hostage by the Etruscans. She helped her comrades to escape and led them back to Rome.

Cloelia Tiberim trānāvit sospitēsque omnēs ad propinquōs restituit.

Livy, *History of Rome* 2.13

Tiberim [acc.]   *River Tiber*
trānāvit   *(s/he) swam across*
sospitēs [acc.]   *safe*
omnēs [acc.]   *everyone*
propinquōs [acc.]   *relatives*
restituit   *(s/he) restored*

9.   All eyes were on the new consul Brutus when he had his own sons publicly executed for conspiring to bring back the former king.

stābant dēligātī ad pālum cōnsulis līberī.

Livy, *History of Rome* 2.5

stābant   *(they) stood*
dēligātī [describes a noun in the nominative]   *tied, bound*
pālum [acc.]   *stake*
cōnsulis [gen.]   *consul*
līberī [nom.]   *children*

10. The monarchy gave way to government shared between aristocratic families, from which consuls and other magistrates were elected. These families were 'patrician' and access to the senate was blocked to 'plebeian' ones. By Caesar's time this distinction had faded and there were many wealthy and powerful plebeians in the senate. Lucius Sextius was the first plebeian consul in the fourth century BC:

prīmus ex plēbe cōnsul Lūcius Sextius creātus est.

Livy, *History of Rome* 6 (Summary)[1]

prīmus   *first*
plēbe [abl.]   *plebeians*
cōnsul [nom.]   *consul*
creātus est   *(he) was appointed*

Exercises 2b

General vocabularies (Latin to English and English to Latin) appear towards the end of the book. There are additional exercises online (see p. 393).

1.   Identify the case of each underlined word:
(a)   quā tū **audāciā** patrēs vocās?
(b)   **dominae** Servium trucīdātum ostendit.
(c)   tacē, **Lucrētia**. Sextus Tarquinius sum.
(d)   vestīgia **virī** aliēnī in lectō sunt tuō.

2.   Translate:
(a)   vir ē vīllā venit.
(b)   Cloelia cum amīcā Tiberim trānāvit.
(c)   Ascanius cum Lāvīniā in urbem venit.
(d)   servus taurum ad agricolam restituit.
(e)   rosa in manū dominae est.
(f)   Brūtus vīllam ingentī obsidiōne premēbat.
(g)   stābat dēligātus ad pālum Brūtī fīlius.

3.   Fill each gap with a single Latin word, and translate:
(a)   Brūtus . . . . {*to Collatinus*} fēminam trucīdātam ostendit.
(b)   fīlius . . . . {*of a goddess*} ad lectum tuum venit.
(c)   vestīgia equī in . . . . {*on your table*} sunt tua.
(d)   in . . . . {*on the horse*} est servus Lāvīniae.

4.   Find Latin ancestors in this chapter of *alien, incarcerate, ligament, unify* and *vocal*.

---

1 Summaries, or 'Periochae', of the books of Livy's *History* were added by later editors. In some cases only these summaries survive and the books themselves are lost.

— 3 —

Carthage

Singular and plural: nominative and accusative

Much as English nouns change their endings to show a plural (*farmers*, *children*), so do Latin nouns. However, as you may have guessed, the Latin ones have more than one plural ending. There is a plural ending for each of the cases:

Nominative plural:

>**puellae** amīcam amant
>*the girls love their friend*

>**servī** taurum timent
>*the slaves fear the bull*

Accusative plural:

>puella **amīcās** amat
>*the girl loves her friends*

>servus **taurōs** timet
>*the slave fears the bulls*

	singular	plural
Nominative	puella	**puellae**
Vocative	puella	**puellae**
Accusative	puellam	**puellās**
Nominative	servus	**servī**
Vocative	serve	**servī** *
Accusative	servum	**servōs**

* the vocative plural is identical to the nominative plural for all nouns.

The ending of the verb also changes if the <u>subject</u> is plural:

>**puella** amīcās **amat**
>*the girl loves her friends*

>**puellae** deam **timent**
>*the girls fear the goddess*

a verb ending	**-t** has a singular subject
	-nt a plural subject

In English too a singular/plural subject will dictate the number (i.e. singular or plural) of the verb (e.g. *he <u>lives</u>, they <u>live</u>*). Note that the object, singular or plural, has no bearing on the ending of the verb. It is only the subject which influences this.

Practice 3a

1. Translate:
    (a) in vīllā sunt centum taurī.
    (b) agricolae taurōs ē vīllā fugant.
    (c) dominus centum servōs habet.
    (d) populus[1] tribūnōs nōn timet.

2. Fill each gap with the correct Latin word, and translate:
    (a) puella Lāvīniam . . . . {*loves*}.
    (b) servī rēgīnam nōn . . . . {*fear*}.
    (c) puellae Tarquinium nōn . . . . {*love*}.
    (d) Ascanius . . . . {*the gods*}
         . . . . {*and goddesses*} timet.

Genitive, dative and ablative plural

Genitive plural:

> amīca **puellārum** in vīllā est
> *the friend of the girls is in the villa*

> puella dominum **servōrum** nōn amat
> *the girl does not like the master of the slaves*

Dative plural:

> agricola **puellīs** equum dat
> *the farmer gives a horse to the girls*

> agricola **servīs** equum nōn dat
> *the farmer does not give a horse to the slaves*

Ablative plural:

> rēgīna cum **puellīs** in lectō sedet
> *the queen sits on the couch with the girls*

> rēgīna cum **servīs** in lectō nōn sedet
> *the queen does not sit on the couch with the slaves*

	singular	plural
Nominative	puella	puellae
Vocative	puella	puellae
Accusative	puellam	puellās
Genitive	puellae	**puellārum**
Dative	puellae	**puellīs**
Ablative	puellā	**puellīs**
Nominative	servus	servī
Vocative	serve	servī
Accusative	servum	servōs
Genitive	servī	**servōrum**
Dative	servō	**servīs**
Ablative	servō	**servīs**

---

1 **populus** is treated as a singular noun despite referring to more than one person, as with collective nouns in English (*herd, troop*, etc).

Practice 3b

1. Translate:
    (a) Cloelia cum puellīs Tiberim trānāvit.
    (b) Hannibal amīcīs Ītaliam ostendit.
    (c) domina cum centum rosīs in vīllam venit.
    (d) vestīgia taurōrum in vīllā sunt.

2. Fill each gap with one Latin word:
    (a) puella cum . . . . {*with her friends*} sedet.
    (b) agricola taurōs . . . . {*to the slaves*} ostendit.
    (c) servus . . . . {*the friends*} . . . . {*of the farmers*} timet.
    (d) dominus . . . . {*of the slaves*} in vīllā est.

Gender

By now you will have seen that nouns of the 1st declension are listing towards the female gender (**puella, dea, domina, fēmina, fīlia, rēgīna**, etc). Most 1st declension nouns are indeed feminine, even those we think gender-free, like **mēnsa, terra** and **vīlla**.

There are a few exceptions. Women certainly worked in the fields, but a farmer, **agricola**, is masculine. If women shone at poetry we don't know about it because almost all surviving poems were authored by men: **poēta** (*poet*) is masculine. And there are men's names ending **-a** which are masculine: **Catilīna, Porsenna, Sulla**.

If 1st declension nouns are mostly feminine, almost all 2nd declension nouns like **servus** are masculine. Some are obviously male: **deus, dominus, fīlius, servus, taurus**. Other **-us** nouns are masculine too: **annus, gladius, lectus, populus**.

Neuter nouns

The 2nd declension (nouns like **servus**) are mostly masculine. But there is also another gender of noun which belongs to this declension: a neuter noun, like **vīnum** (*wine*):

servus **vīnum** nōn habet
the slave does not have the wine

vīnum in mēnsā est
the wine is on the table

	singular	plural
Nominative	**vīnum**	**vīna**
Vocative	**vīnum**	**vīna**
Accusative	**vīnum**	**vīna**
Genitive	**vīnī**	**vīnōrum**
Dative	**vīnō**	**vīnīs**
Ablative	**vīnō**	**vīnīs**

domina **vīnō** ēbria est
the lady is drunk with wine

Many endings of **vīnum** are the same as those of **servus**. The vocative endings are the same as nominative and accusative ones.

One characteristic of *all* neuter nouns is there is no difference between nominative and accusative endings, whether singular or plural. That means the ending of a neuter noun will not tell you whether it is subject or object. You need help from the other words to resolve that.

Here, **ferrum** (a noun like **vīnum**) is nominative:

ferrum in manū est
there is a weapon in (my) hand [from Chapter 2, no. 3]

In the plural the same applies, with no distinction between the nominative and accusative. In fact there is a simple rule for *all neuter endings* in the nominative and accusative plural: they all end **-a**. Below, **arma** is accusative plural:

arma virumque canō
I sing of weapons (i.e. a war) and a man [1.1][1]

Practice 3c
Translate the underlined word(s) into one Latin word:
(a)   he keeps many wines
(b)   drunk with wine
(c)   she drinks the wine
(d)   a love of wines
(e)   the wine is sweet.

Summary: puella, servus **and** vīnum

Case	Function	1st declension feminine *girl*	2nd declension masculine *slave*	2nd declension neuter *wine*
singular				
Nominative	subject	puell**a**	serv**us**	vīn**um**
Vocative	person addressed	puell**a**	serv**e**	vīn**um**
Accusative	object	puell**am**	serv**um**	vīn**um**
Genitive	*of*	puell**ae**	serv**ī**	vīn**ī**
Dative	*to, for*	puell**ae**	serv**ō**	vīn**ō**
Ablative	*in, on, with, from, by*	puell**ā**	serv**ō**	vīn**ō**

---

1 Words taken or adapted from the reading sentences and shown as examples will be listed by their chapter number first then the sentence number.

plural				
Nominative	subject	puell**ae**	serv**ī**	vīn**a**
Vocative	person addressed	puell**ae**	serv**ī**	vīn**a**
Accusative	object	puell**ās**	serv**ōs**	vīn**a**
Genitive	*of*	puell**ārum**	serv**ōrum**	vīn**ōrum**
Dative	*to, for*	puell**īs**	serv**īs**	vīn**īs**
Ablative	*in, on, with, from, by*	puell**īs**	serv**īs**	vīn**īs**

Latin nouns are shown in dictionaries in their nominative and genitive forms. Thus **puella, puellae; servus, servī**; and **vīnum, vīnī**; which may be abbreviated to **puella,-ae; servus,-ī**, and **vīnum,-ī**.

Declensions which you have now seen, i.e. nouns like **puella, servus** and **vīnum**, from here on will be listed in vocabularies in their nominative and genitive forms, with their gender added: [m.], [f.] or [n.]. Thus **rosa,-ae** [f.] is a feminine noun like **puella**; **bellum,-i** [n.] is a neuter noun like **vīnum**; **ventus,-ī** [m.] is a masculine noun like **servus**; and **Rōmānī,-ōrum** [m.] is like **servus** in the plural.

Practice 3d

Fill each gap with *two* Latin words:
(a) cum . . . . *{with a horse and with a bull}*
(b) . . . . *{of the girl and of the boy}*
(c) . . . . *{the wine of the gods}*
(d) cum . . . . *{with the girlfriend of Horatius}*
(e) . . . . *{the mistress of the villas}*
(f) . . . . *{with wines of the master}*

Endings are listed on p. 356. The online support provides additional grammar tables with a choice of USA or UK listing of the cases (see p. 393).

Vocabulary 3

Add the genitive forms to the 1st and 2nd declension nouns already listed in your vocabulary notebook.

Start another page for 2nd declension neuter nouns like **vīnum**. Add these nouns to their correct lists:

arma,-ōrum [n.; used only in the plural]
  weapons, forces
auxilium,-ī [n.]   *help, aid*
bellum,-ī [n.]   *war*
caelum,-ī [n.]   *heaven, sky*
captīvus,-ī [m.]   *captive, prisoner*
cōnsultum,-ī [n.]   *decree, resolution*
dōnum,-ī [n.]   *gift*
elephantus,-ī [m.]   *elephant*
exemplum,-ī [n.]   *example, precedent*
ferrum,-ī [n.]   *iron instrument, knife, sword*
forum,-ī [n.]   *forum*
gaudium,-ī [n.]   *joy*
habēna,-ae [f.]   *rein, strap*
imperium,-ī [n.]   *power, empire*
incendium,-ī [n.]   *fire*
lacrima,-ae [f.]   *tear*

littera,-ae [f.]   *letter (of the alphabet)*
litterae,-ārum [plural of the above]
  letter (missive), literature
numerus,-ī [m.]   *number*
patria,-ae [f.]   *country (one's own)*
praeda,-ae [f.]   *loot, plunder*
praemium,-ī [n.]   *reward, prize*
proelium,-ī [n.]   *battle*
rēgnum,-ī [n.]   *kingdom*
silva,-ae [f.]   *wood*
tribūnus,-ī [m.]   *tribune*
unda,-ae [f.]   *wave*
ventus,-ī [m.]   *wind*
verbum,-ī [n.]   *word*
vestīgium,-ī [n.]   *trace, footstep*
victōria,-ae [f.]   *victory*

Exercises 3a

1. Translate each into two Latin words:
(a) the tears of the captives
(b) the victory of the people
(c) the plunder of the tribune
(d) weapons of war
(e) the joy of power
(f) the mistress's wine
(g) the number of letters
(h) the literature of Rome
(i) the gifts of Horatius
(j) with/by the help of the tribunes
(k) the words of the master
(l) with/by the reins of a horse
(m) traces of an elephant
(n) by decree of the queen.

Subject:	she, he, it . . .	they . . .
beg(s)	ōrat	ōrant
chase(s)	fugat	fugant
come(s)	venit	veniunt
despise(s)	contemnit	contemnunt
fear(s)	timet	timent
flee(s), escape(s)	fugit	fugiunt
give(s)	dat	dant
has, have	habet	habent
hear(s)	audit	audiunt
is, are	est	sunt
lead(s), bring(s)	dūcit	dūcunt
love(s), like(s)	amat	amant
make(s), do(es)	facit	faciunt
praise(s)	laudat	laudant
receive(s)	accipit	accipiunt
see(s)	videt	vident
send(s)	mittit	mittunt
sit(s)	sedet	sedent
wander(s)	errat	errant

2. Fill each gap with the correct verb from the list, and translate:
(a) captīvī tribūnum . . . . *{beg}*
(b) servī ē vīllā . . . . *{flee}*.
(c) domina in silvā . . . . *{wanders}*.
(d) agricola equōs taurōsque . . . . *{sees}*.

(e)   tribūnī populum in forum . . . . {*lead*}.
(f)   domina ā poētā dōna . . . . {*receives*}.
(g)   agricola ad tribūnum praedam . . . . {*sends*}.
(h)   tribūnus in equō . . . . {*sits*}.

Carthage

Rome's development from small city-state to a centre of importance in the Italian peninsula was the result of both military successes and also of less aggressive diplomatic alliances and protective ventures. Her growing influence in the south of Italy presented a threat to Carthage, a city in north Africa with strong trading links and a powerful navy to protect them. Rome was competition Carthage could do without. From the early third century BC the two cities were locked in a military struggle which lasted for about a hundred years. For much of that time Rome was fighting on the back foot. First the Romans had to build a navy and learn how to use it, and then later survive the fifteen years of defeats Hannibal inflicted on them while camped in Italy. History relates how he arrived in Italy not by ships in the south but, to the surprise of his enemy, over the Alps with his elephants. If his peers in Carthage had given him their full support, he probably would have completed what he set out to do.

Reading notes

Reading Latin is not just a word-by-word decoding exercise. For example, the shared case-endings (e.g. **servī** – genitive singular or nominative plural) leave you with a decision to make. So as well as unpicking individual words it helps to build the context, to look for the overall meaning. Try to predict, guess even. And don't be afraid to find yourself down the wrong alley: the more you practise the easier it will become.

A word with an ending you have not yet seen will be given in the notes. If the ending can represent more than one case you will be given a choice, e.g.

mīlitibus [dat. pl./abl. pl.] *soldiers*

It is over to you to decide whether it is dative or ablative in that particular sentence.

Hannibal's eventual defeat signalled the end for Carthage, and greatly empowered Rome. In the west there were Spanish territories – previously under Carthaginian influence – to be annexed and controlled. And just as inviting were opportunities in the east across the Adriatic. Rome already had some cultural and diplomatic contact with the cities in Greece, which had once been independent states before falling under the rule of Macedonia in the fourth century. Many Greeks were hopeful that their new friends in Italy would help them win back their independence.

Virgil's story of Dido and Aeneas is one of the most celebrated in literature. Romans of Virgil's day (nearly two hundred years after Hannibal) would not have missed the underlying symbolism of the two cities fated to come into conflict and Rome's ultimate victory: Aeneas and his men escape from Troy and are washed up on the shores of north Africa, where Dido, the queen of Carthage, gives them shelter. Dido and Aeneas fall in love; he rests, gathers his strength and even helps with the building of her new city; then, as suddenly as he arrived, he prepares his fleet for departure. Dido fails to dissuade him; she is distraught, and after he sails away takes her own life.

Aeneas had a divine excuse for his behaviour: reaching Italy was his destiny, planned by the gods. The gods are physically involved in the plot: Venus and Juno orchestrate their falling in love and Mercury relays Jupiter's message to Aeneas to pack up and set sail for Italy. *Italiam non sponte sequor*, pleads Aeneas before he leaves (no.11). Historically any other conclusion was unthinkable, in fact impossible. *Delenda est Carthago* (Carthage must be destroyed) was Cato's famous phrase, half a century after Hannibal, and the ghost remained.

But the story has a purely human momentum too, and the gods' involvement serves as a metaphor as much as manipulator of human feelings. Like other great narratives of divine interference, human behaviour can be seen in a purely human dimension. Virgil manages to combine an inflexible and predictable plot – Aeneas' inescapable destiny to settle in Italy – with the challenges of human life and the confrontation of none-too-easy moral decisions.

1.   Livy reflects upon the significance of the war against Hannibal's Carthaginians:

bellum maximē omnium memorābile erat.

Livy, *History of Rome* 21.1

maximē   *most*
omnium [gen.]   *of all*
memorābile [describes a neuter noun in the nominative or accusative]   *memorable*
erat   *(s/he, it) was*

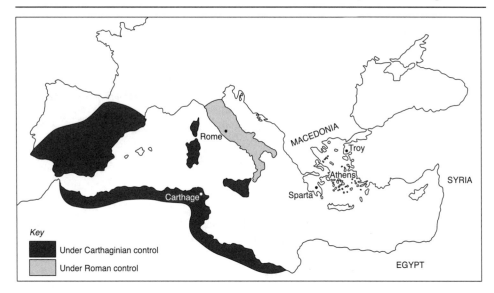

Map of the Mediterranean, c. 270 BC

2.   Hannibal led his army across the Alps.

nōnō diē in iugum Alpium vēnit.

Livy, *History of Rome* 21.35

nōnō [with a noun in the ablative]   *ninth*
diē [abl.]   *day*
iugum,-ī [n.]   *summit, ridge*
Alpium [gen.]   *Alps*
vēnit   *(s/he) came* ('venit' without the macron is present, *s/he comes*, and with the macron
    is past)[1]

3.   Faced with harsh mountain conditions and hostile tribesmen, Hannibal tries to lift
     Carthaginian morale by pointing out the land ahead of them.

Hannibal mīlitibus Ītaliam ostendit.

Livy, *History of Rome* 21.35

mīlitibus [dat. pl./abl. pl.]   *soldiers*
Ītalia,-ae [f.]   *Italy*
ostendit   *(s/he) shows*

---

1 Macrons are used today to help students to distinguish between long and short vowels. To the Romans, the present
   and past looked the same: **venit**. But they had different sounds (much as 'read' in English can be present or past).
   For more on macrons see p. xiv, and for pronunciation p. 352.

4. The Romans were not expecting war in Italy. Several defeats cause confusion and panic
    in the city:

cum ingentī terrōre ac tumultū populus in forum fugit.

Livy, History of Rome 22.7

ingentī [describes a noun in the dative or ablative singular]   *huge, great*
terrōre [abl.]   *terror, fear*
ac   *and*
tumultū [abl.]   *noise*
fugit   *(s/he) flees, escapes* (not to be confused with 'fug<u>a</u>t')

5. Despite an overwhelming victory at Lake Trasimene, Hannibal avoids a quick assault on
    Rome and camps in hills close to the city.

Hannibal in montibus manet.

Cornelius Nepos, Hannibal 5

montibus [dat. pl./abl. pl.]   *mountains*
manet   *(s/he) remains*

6. The next year, 216 BC, Hannibal inflicted even worse losses on the Romans at the battle
    of Cannae in southern Italy. Following the battle thousands of corpses lay scattered
    around.

iacēbant tot Rōmānōrum mīlia, peditēs passim equitēsque.

Livy, History of Rome 22.51

iacēbant   *(they) lay (on the ground)*
tot   *so many*
Rōmānī,-ōrum   *Romans*
mīlia   *thousands*
peditēs [nom.pl./acc.pl.]   *footsoldiers, infantrymen*
passim   *everywhere*
equitēs [nom.pl./acc.pl.]   *cavalry*

7. The defeats by Hannibal caused Rome to appoint a single dictator, Quintus Fabius
    Maximus, with emergency powers for six months. Fabius used his time well: by avoiding
    Hannibal altogether he allowed Rome some breathing space and earned himself the
    sobriquet '*Cunctator*' (Delayer).

ūnus homō nōbīs cūnctandō restituit rem.

Ennius, Annals (Fragments)

homō [nom.]   *man, person*
nōbīs [dat./abl.]   *us*
cūnctandō   *by delaying*

restituit   *(s/he) restored, recovered*
rem [acc.]   *thing, matter, situation* (as in *state of affairs*)

8.   Carthage remained in people's thoughts long after Hannibal's eventual defeat. Virgil's story of Dido and Aeneas symbolized the conflict. Under the influence of the gods, Dido, queen of Carthage, falls in love with the shipwrecked Aeneas. He lives with her for a while and helps to build her city. But the god Mercury is sent by Jupiter to remind Aeneas of his destiny to found Rome, not Carthage.

'tū nunc Karthāginis altae / fundāmenta locās?'

Virgil, Aeneid 4.265–6

'/' marks a linebreak in the poem
nunc   *now*
Karthāginis [gen.]   *Carthage*
altae [take with a noun in the genitive]   *high, towering*
fundāmentum,-ī [n.]   *foundation*
locās   *you lay, put in place*

9.   Aeneas prepares to go, uncertain whether to tell Dido; but she finds out:

at rēgīna dolōs (quis fallere possit amantem?) / praesēnsit.

Virgil, Aeneid 4.296–7

at   *but*
dolus,-ī [m.]   *trick, deception* (translate the plural as a singular)
quis [nom.]   *who*
fallere   *to deceive*
possit   *is able*
amantem [acc.]   *lover*
praesēnsit   *(s/he) felt in advance, had an early sense of*

10.   She pleads with him to stay:

'ōrō, sī quis adhūc precibus locus – exue mentem.'

Virgil, Aeneid 4.319

ōrō   *I beg you, please*
sī   *if*
quis [nom.]   *any* ('quis' usually means *who* or *which*, but can also mean *any(one)* or *some(one)*)
adhūc   *still, yet*
precibus [dat.pl./abl.pl.]   *prayers, entreaties*
locus,-ī [m.]   *place*
sī . . . locus: you have to supply the verb 'is' to your translation
exue   *lay aside, cast off*
mentem [acc.]   *mind, purpose*

11. Aeneas tries to calm her:

'dēsine mēque tuīs incendere tēque querēlīs.
Ītaliam nōn sponte sequor.'

Virgil, Aeneid 4.360–1

Word order for translation of the first line: 'dēsine incendere tēque mēque tuīs querēlīs'
dēsine   *stop, cease*
mēque tēque [acc.]   *both me and you*
tuīs [with a dative or ablative plural]   *your*
incendere   *to inflame* (i.e. *stop inflaming*, not *stop to inflame* which would suggest a cigarette
      break or act of arson), *to distress*
querēla,-ae [f.]   *complaint, wailing*
sponte   *by choice*
sequor   *I follow, make for*

12. Dido realizes Aeneas will not change his mind:

'neque tē teneō, neque dicta refellō.
ī, sequere Ītaliam ventīs, pete rēgna per undās.'

Virgil, Aeneid 4.380–1

neque . . . neque   *neither . . . nor*
tē [acc.]   *you*
teneō   *I keep, hold*
dicta [nom.pl./acc.pl.]   *the things (you) said*
refellō   *I refute, challenge*
ī   *go!*
sequere   *follow! make for!*
ventus,-ī [m.]   *wind*
sequere Ītaliam ventīs   *make for Italy with (the help of) the winds*
pete   *seek!*
rēgnum,-ī [n.]   *territory, dominion*
per [+ acc.]   *through, across*
unda,-ae [f.]   *wave*

13. Aeneas sails away, and Dido takes her own life. Later in the poem Aeneas meets her
     spirit in the underworld:

Dīdō / errābat silvā in magnā.

Virgil, Aeneid 6.450–1

errābat   *(s/he) was wandering*
silva,-ae [f.]   *wood* (word order for translation: 'in magnā silvā')
magnā [with a feminine noun in the ablative]   *great, large*

14. She has nothing to say to him.

inimīca refūgit.

Virgil, *Aeneid* 6.472

inimīca [take with a feminine subject]   *hostile, unfriendly*
refūgit   *(s/he) fled back, away*

Exercises 3b
1.   Identify the case and number (singular or plural) of each underlined word:
(a) Hannibal **mīlitibus** Ītaliam ostendit.
(b) dēsine mēque tuīs incendere tēque **querēlīs**.
(c) pete **rēgna** per **undās**.
(d) Dīdō errābat **silvā** in magnā.

2.   Translate:
(a) gaudium in forō est.
(b) rēgīna cum centum servīs sedet.
(c) captīvī gladium Tarquiniī vident.
(d) vestīgia servōrum in tuō lectō sunt.
(e) praeda in silvā est.
(f) equōs servus ad vīllam dūcit.
(g) tribūnus querēlās captīvōrum audit, lacrimās videt.

3.   Choose the correct form of each verb, and translate:
(a) populus tribūnum . . . . {laudat/laudant}.
(b) Lāvīnia in silvā cum Ascaniō . . . . {errat/errant}.
(c) domina ā tribūnō dōna . . . . {accipit/accipiunt}.
(d) dominus nōn servīs vīnum . . . . {dat/dant}.
(e) deae vestīgia in vīllā . . . . {est/sunt}.
(f) servus cum dōnīs dominae . . . . {fugit/fugiunt}.

4.   Find Latin ancestors in this chapter of *error, fundamental, maximum, military* and *querulous*.

— 4 —

Greece

Questions

Some questions begin with an interrogative word (as in English, e.g. *who. . .?, what. . .?, where. . .?*):

> **quis** est tribūnus?
> *who is the tribune?*

If there is no interrogative word introducing the question, the first word of the question ends **-ne**:

> taurum**ne** agricola fugat?
> *is the farmer chasing a bull?*

In English we can ask a question by expressing a statement in a questioning tone (e.g. *You're driving home tonight?*). Similarly the suffix **-ne** does not always appear and so a Latin question may look like a statement until you reach the question mark:

> taurum tribūnus fugat?
> *is the tribune chasing a bull?*

Practice 4a
Translate:
(a)   suntne servī in vīllā?
(b)   ubī est rēgīna?
(c)   quis in silvā est cum deā?
(d)   cūr cum taurīs errat servus?
(e)   quid dominae poēta dat?

---

quis?	who?
quid?	what?
cūr?	why?
ubī?	when?/where?

Adjectives: bonus, bona, bonum

Adjectives are words which describe nouns, lend them extra detail or qualify them in some way:

> in **magnā** silvā
> *in a large wood*

An adjective may appear as the complement of a verb, usually *to be*:

silva est **magna**
the wood is <u>large</u>

Practice 4b

We may know what an adjective means, but this meaning has no value unless it is applied to something or someone. Match the adjectives *amoral, demanding, fizzy, loyal* and *rusty* to these nouns:
(a) a car; (b) a friend; (c) a glass of wine; (d) your teacher; (e) a thief.

Adjective have endings so that we can identify which noun the adjective is describing, as here with the adjective **īnsānus** (*mad, raging*):

tribūnum **īnsānus taurus** fugat
the <u>raging bull</u> chases the tribune

tribūnus īnsānus taurum fugat
the <u>mad tribune</u> chases the bull

An adjective can appear before or after the noun it describes.

Look again at the endings of **puella, servus** and **vīnum** in the previous chapter, and compare them with the endings below of the adjective **bonus** (*good*). The masculine endings of **bonus** are identical to those of **servus**, the feminine to **puella**, and the neuter to **vīnum**:

	masculine	feminine	neuter
singular			
Nom.	bon**us**	bon**a**	bon**um**
Voc.	bon**e**	bon**a**	bon**um**
Acc.	bon**um**	bon**am**	bon**um**
Gen.	bon**ī**	bon**ae**	bon**ī**
Dat.	bon**ō**	bon**ae**	bon**ō**
Abl.	bon**ō**	bon**ā**	bon**ō**
plural			
Nom.	bon**ī**	bon**ae**	bon**a**
Voc.	bon**ī**	bon**ae**	bon**a**
Acc.	bon**ōs**	bon**ās**	bon**a**
Gen.	bon**ōrum**	bon**ārum**	bon**ōrum**
Dat.	bon**īs**	bon**īs**	bon**īs**
Abl.	bon**īs**	bon**īs**	bon**īs**

Agreement of an adjective and noun

A Latin adjective is said to 'agree with' the noun it describes. It must share the same case, gender and number (singular or plural):

> **domina bona** servō vīnum dat
> *the good lady gives the wine to the slave*

> domina **bonō servō** vīnum dat
> *the lady gives the wine to the good slave*

> domina servō **bonum vīnum** dat
> *the lady gives the good wine to the slave*

benignus,-a,-um	*kind*
bonus,-a,-um	*good*
contentus,-a,-um	*contented, satisfied*
ēbrius,-a,-um	*drunk*
īnsānus,-a,-um	*mad, raging*
magnus,-a,-um	*great, large*
malus,-a,-um	*bad*
meus,-a,-um	*my*
multus,-a,-um	*much, many*
novus,-a,-um	*new*
optimus,-a,-um	*best, very good, excellent*
prīmus,-a,-um	*first*
saevus,-a,-um	*harsh, cruel*
tuus,-a,-um	*your (s.)*

Practice 4c

Translate:

(a) domina īnsāna in forō errat.
(b) ubī est meus servus novus?
(c) deī rēgīnae nōn benignī sed saevī sunt.
(d) sunt-ne in vīllā multī servī novī?
(e) tribūnus magnus est et multō vīnō ēbrius.
(f) domina contenta est multīs rosīs.
(g) dominus in vīllam venit prīmus.
(h) quis malō servō tuō vīnum dat?

Not all Latin adjectives are like **bonus**, and not all nouns are like **servus, puella** or **vīnum**. So there will be adjectives which agree with nouns and correspond in case, number and gender, but do not share the same final letters:

> **estne agricola bonus?**
> *is the farmer good?*

Practice 4d

Fill each gap with one Latin word:
(a)   . . . . {*mad*} tuus est vir!
(b)   domina nōn contenta est poētā . . . . {*with a drunken*}.
(c)   Brūtus, vir . . . . {*excellent*}, patriam amat.
(d)   Hannibal amīcīs est . . . . {*kind*}.

2nd declension nouns ending -er

On p. 16 **vir** and **puer** appeared, which are 2nd declension nouns like **servus**, except for a clipped nominative and vocative singular. There are one or two others like this, both nouns and adjectives.

The nouns shown here have the ending **-er** instead of **-us**, and also drop the 'e' in the other cases (unlike **puer** which keeps it). These nouns are all masculine.

	book	*master/teacher*	*field*
N.	liber	magister	ager
V.	liber	magister	ager
A.	librum	magistrum	agrum
G.	librī	magistrī	agrī
D.	librō	magistrō	agrō
Ab.	librō	magistrō	agrō

	plural		
N.	librī	magistrī	agrī
V.	librī	magistrī	agrī
A.	librōs	magistrōs	agrōs
G.	librōrum	magistrōrum	agrōrum
D.	librīs	magistrīs	agrīs
Ab.	librīs	magistrīs	agrīs

In classical Latin, **magister** is 'master' in the sense of someone who presides over something, a director or leader or teacher, whereas **dominus** is generally less formal, a boss or owner, although there is a degree of overlap. **Dominus** survives in Italian/Spanish *don*, our university 'dons', 'domineering', etc. From **magister** English has taken 'master' and less formal 'mister', via German *meister*, and French has *maître*, and Italian/Spanish *maestro*. **Magister** is one of the words suspected of having a fading 'g' sound – see the pronunciation guide on p. 352.

Vir,-ī (*man*) has very few words like it. **Triumvir,-ī** (*triumvir*) is one.

Practice 4e

Give the case of the underlined word:

(a)   cūr triumvir **<u>magistrum</u>** īnsānum amat?
(b)   agricola poētam ē vīllā in **<u>agrōs</u>** fugat.
(c)   in mēnsā est **<u>liber</u>** meus.

The same clipped ending occurs with a few adjectives, which in most of the cases are like **bonus,-a,-um**. Only the masculine nominative (and vocative) singular is different.

Some keep the **e** (**miser, līber, tener**), others drop it (**noster, vester**).

	masculine	*feminine*	*neuter*
N.	**miser**	misera	miserum
V.	**miser**	misera	miserum
A.	miserum	miseram	miserum
	etc		
N.	**noster**	nostra	nostrum
V.	**noster**	nostra	nostrum
A.	nostrum	nostram	nostrum
	etc		

Practice 4f

Translate:

(a)   ego nunc sum līber!
(b)   puella tenera magistrum ēbrium nōn timet.
(c)   cūr errat noster magister miser in vestrīs agrīs?
(d)   puella librum rosāsque multās accipit ā poētā miserō.

miser,-era,-erum	*wretched*
līber,-era,-erum	*free*
tener,-era,-erum	*tender, soft*
noster,-tra,-trum	*our*
vester,-tra,-trum	*your* (pl.)

Adjectives as nouns

An adjective will sometimes appear without a noun, as in English: 'the ways of the <u>wicked</u>' (i.e. wicked people). If a Latin adjective appears without a corresponding noun then we treat the adjective as a noun:

Mārcus nōn **superbōs** amat   [accusative masculine plural]
Marcus does not like <u>the arrogant/arrogant men</u>

tribūnus **multa** dīcit   [accusative neuter plural]
the tribune says many things/much

Practice 4g

Translate:
(a)   multī in forō sunt.
(b)   in vīllā nostrā nōn est locus saevīs.
(c)   tribūnus in amphitheātrum miserōs mittit.

Vocabulary 4

Review the two lists of adjectives which appear earlier in this chapter (like **bonus,-a,-um** and **miser,-era,-erum**). Start a list of these in your notebook.

From **līber,-era,-erum** (*free*) comes the noun **līberī,-ōrum**, in the masculine plural only, meaning (freeborn) children. It is easy to confuse these with **liber, librī** (*book*) and also **lībertus,-ī** (*freedman*).

You have already met a number of words with fixed endings. These include all those words which are *not* nouns, adjectives, verbs or pronouns. Here are a few to start your list:

at *but*	**neque . . . neque** (or **nec . . . nec**) *neither*
atque (or **ac**) *and*	. . . *nor*
cūr? *why?*	**nihil** *nothing*
et *and* (occasionally *even,*	**numquam** *never*
and also, and . . . too)	**nunc** *now*
et . . . et *both . . . and*	**quia** *because*
etiam *also, even*	**sed** *but*
iam *now, already*	**semper** *always*
neque or **nec** *and not, but not*	**sī** *if*
	ubī? *where? when?*

The adjective **prīmus,-a,-um** (*first*) is like **bonus,-a,-um**. From this adjective two adverbs have been created: **prīmum** meaning *at first, first, in the first place, in the beginning*, and very similar **prīmō** meaning *at first, at the beginning, first, firstly* (particularly of time). If you find these words alone take them to be adverbs, but where they appear in agreement with a noun they mean '*the first . . .*'.

More adjectives which appear in this course can be found online.[1]

---

1 See p. 393 for access to the online resources.

Exercises 4a

1. Translate:
(a) cūr triumvirī semper tribūnum īnsānum fugant?
(b) taurusne noster, ō amīcī, in vestrā vīllā est?
(c) centum taurī in nostrīs agrīs sunt.
(d) magistrī multōs librōs poētārum habent.
(e) poētane dominam teneram audit?
(f) lībertusne librōs miserīs līberīs dat?

2. Fill the gaps (one word), and translate:
(a) librī in vīllā . . . . {*our*} sunt.
(b) servī miserī nōn sunt . . . . {*free*}.

3. Translate:
(a) multī līberōs tuōs laudant.
(b) prīmum lībertīs benigna est domina.
(c) quis novum dominum contemnit?
(d) Crassus multa habet sed poēta nihil.
(e) Brūtus, vir optimus, lacrimās fīliōrum nōn videt.

4. Add two words to each sentence:
(a) rēgīna cum . . . . {*with the excellent poet*} in agrīs errat.
(b) . . . . {*the mad farmer* } taurum in vīllam fugat.
(c) domina cum . . . . {*with her new husband*} in lectō sedet.
(d) dea . . . . {*my many*} lacrimās . . . . videt.
(e) vestīgia . . . . {*of the drunken teacher*} in forō sunt.

Greece

In the past few years trends of enquiry in classical scholarship have concentrated on the 'reception' of the classics in later cultures; in other words how others have interpreted and recreated the ancient world in their time. At the top of the list of 'receptive' cultures has to be Rome itself, for the literary and artistic achievements of Rome were a deliberate and comprehensive reception of Greece.

In the third century BC Romans started to consume Greek culture as hungrily as they annexed new territories. Their own artistic and literary output was explicitly measured against Greek predecessors. For such an apparently bullish people it is perhaps surprising that Roman writers do not boast they will outdo their illustrious neighbour's model. They proclaim that they will live up to it, yes, and be considered alongside it, but not as something better. The achievements of classical Greece were regarded with awe, something to be re-ignited in Italy and the Latin language. But not all things Greek were held in such high esteem. Rome's sense of cultural inferiority added spice to the contrasting irritation felt towards Greeks of their day: full of rhetorical puff, disingenuous, and worse – clever and skilful.

The period we call Classical Greece spans the fifth century and the first part of the fourth century BC. Greece at that time was not a single unified country, but a collection of separate city-states who cooperated from time to time, notably to resist Persian advances, and who

Reading notes

English **word order** generally has the object appearing after the verb, and this is what we anticipate as we read or listen:

the bull . . . chases   . . . . .   ***the farmer? the tribune?***

In Latin the verb is more likely to come at the end of a sentence or clause,[1] and so it is the verb's action, not the object which we are predicting:

the bull . . . the farmer   . . . . .   ***chases? tramples on? admires?***

One reading method which has stood the test of time is to scan ahead and identify the verb before turning back to the other words. The eye darts back and forth through the sentence in order to understand the structure. This is the method most of us use where the meaning is elusive. It is not though the most natural one.

Where the order of words in a reading is particularly challenging it is rearranged in the notes to help translation. Once you have the meaning, look again at the original sentence and read the words as the author meant you to, and so get used to Latin's natural flow.

quarrelled with each other with a similar passion. What we now call Greek literature and art was largely created or at least sponsored by the Athenians. The poet Homer is one of the better known exceptions (the first literary figure in the history of European literature was by legend a native of Ionia in Asia Minor), and there are many architectural remains and things of interest elsewhere in Greece. But much of what we know about these other places, like Thebes, Delphi and Corinth, is derived from what Athenian writers said about them, in mythical tales or historical accounts.

It was the Athenians who in the fifth century set up the world's first known government by democracy (*demos* = people, *kratos* = power). For these citizens, democracy meant more than turning out once in a while to vote. Their lives were abuzz with daily political discussions in the open spaces of the city. It was expected of citizens to participate in public life, otherwise you were an 'idiot' (*idiotes* = someone who keeps to himself). The Greeks loved a good argument. We can see this in their literature, in the poems of Homer, in their histories, dramas and in the dialogues of Plato. This was an extraordinarily creative period, not only for literature but also for architecture and other arts. In Athens the whole community enjoyed this creativity; the whole community breathed life into it. There was a strong sense of shared cultural aspiration, with little sign of the distinct strands we have today of high-brow, populist and 'alternative' artistic outputs.

In some ways Athens was not the perfect model of democracy. Women were not entitled to vote, while the large population of slaves had no rights at all. And it was not long before the ugly side of democratic leadership showed itself, the manipulation of mass opinions for dubious ends.

---

1 A group of words within a larger sentence with its own verb and subject, introduced by a word like 'and', 'but', 'who', 'because', 'if', etc.

The fifth-century thinker Socrates, made famous by Plato's dialogues, challenged contemporary politicians over their preoccupation with the techniques of persuasion at the expense of substance and the evaluation of the right thing for a government to do. Modern democracies may have not improved much in this respect, but at least they have Socrates' voice in their ears (we hope).

During these decades of democracy, Athens was at her most powerful abroad, controlling many of the smaller states in and around the Aegean Sea. Of the city-states in Greece only Sparta seriously challenged the growing power of Athens. Their long, drawn-out war in the last few decades of the fifth century weakened each other enough for Philip of Macedon to subdue all the Greek cities in the following century.

The distant conquests of his son, Alexander the Great, created a new Greek-inspired culture throughout the Near East, in Egypt, and all around the eastern Mediterranean. This is known as the 'Hellenistic' culture. Works of art and literature were deliberately imitative of the classical period, and it was this Hellenistic culture that the Romans inherited. Visitors to Greece liked what they saw and read, and with no similar culture at home in Italy, eagerly made the Hellenistic criteria of good taste their own.

Thus Virgil's story of Aeneas quite deliberately invited association with the *Odyssey* and the *Iliad*, the epic poems of Homer. Virgil's contemporary, the poet Horace, could think of no better achievement than his creation of Greek verse-forms in the Latin language. Our concept of originality would have meant little to these Latin writers. They had a strong sense of form and a liking for Greek models, and the success of their work depended upon the use they made of what they annexed. The *Aeneid* has echoes of Greece on every page, but is a triumph of Italian creativity and the Latin language.

1. The defeat of Carthage gave Rome control over the western Mediterranean. Those ambitious for more power now looked east, tempted particularly by Greece, which at this time was under the control of the kingdom of Macedonia.

    ## pācem Pūnicam bellum Macedonicum excēpit.

    Livy, History of Rome 31.1

    pācem [acc.]   *peace*
    Pūnicus,-a,-um   *Carthaginian*
    Macedonicus,-a,-um   *Macedonian*
    excēpit   *(s/he, it) took the place of*

2. Some decades before the conflict with Hannibal, Rome had fought against Pyrrhus, who was king of Epirus in north-west Greece (roughly modern Albania). Pyrrhus had invaded Italy to support the Greek-colonized city of Tarentum against Rome's advances into southern Italy.

    ## Pyrrhus, Ēpīrōtārum rēx, ut auxilium Tarentīnīs ferret, in Ītaliam vēnit.

    Livy, History of Rome 12 (Summary)

    Ēpīrōtae,-ārum   *the Epirotes, the people of Epirus*
    rēx [nom.]   *king*
    ut   *so that*

auxilium,-ī [n.]   *help, assistance*
Tarentīnīs [dat.pl./abl.pl.]   *the people of Tarentum*
ferret   *(s/he, it) might bring*
vēnit   *(s/he) came*

3.   That was a defensive campaign in so far as it was fought in Italy. Rome now took
the fight to the Macedonians in Greece. The Greeks themselves hoped Rome would
free them from Macedonian rule, even if it meant one master replacing another.
A Roman victory over the Macedonians was announced at the Isthmian Games
in 196 BC:

audītā vōce praecōnis gaudium fuit.

Livy, *History of Rome* 33.32

audītā vōce   *with the voice having been heard,* or *after the voice had been heard*
praecōnis [gen.]   *herald*
gaudium,-ī [n.]   *joy*
fuit   *(s/he/it/there) was*

4.   Greece was regarded by most Romans as the cultural and artistic font of the
world. Pliny reports that some people believed Greece to be behind all sorts of
discoveries.

in Graeciā prīmum hūmānitās, litterae, etiam frūgēs
inventae sunt.

Pliny, *Letters* 8.24

prīmum   *first of all*
hūmānitās [nom.]   *civilization*
litterae,-ārum [f.]   *letters, literature*
etiam   *and even, and also*
frūgēs [nom.pl./acc.pl.]   *crops*
inventae sunt   *were discovered, invented*

5.   Roman presence in Greece was motivated not only by their taste for the arts. There
were political concerns too. Rome wanted to counter the threat from Syria, where
Hannibal had taken refuge (and lived for some twenty years).

Hannibal patriā profugus pervēnerat ad Antiochum.

Livy, *History of Rome* 34.60

patria,-ae [f.]   *one's own country*
profugus,-ī [m.]   *fugitive*
pervēnerat   *(s/he) had come, reached*
Antiochus,-ī [m.]   *Antiochus* (king of Syria)

6. Romans never lost their sense of cultural debt:

Graecia capta ferum victōrem cēpit et artīs / intulit agrestī Latiō.

Horace, *Epistles* 2.1.156–7

Graecia,-ae [f.]   Greece
captus,-a,-um   *captured*
ferus,-a,-um   *wild*
victōrem [acc.]   *conqueror*
cēpit   *(s/he, it) captured, captivated*
artīs [acc.pl.]   *arts*
intulit   *(s/he, it) brought*
agrestī [dat./abl.]   *rustic, uncultivated*
Latium,-ī [n.]   *Latium* (region around Rome)

7. Not all Romans shared this view. In the second century BC Cato argued that the growing enthusiasm for Greek art and literature was a threat to traditional values of a simple and uncluttered lifestyle:

iam nimis multōs audiō Corinthī et Athēnārum ōrnāmenta laudantēs mīrantēsque.

Livy, *History of Rome* 34.4

Word order for translation: 'iam audiō nimis multōs laudantēs mīrantēsque ōrnāmenta Corinthī et Athēnārum'
iam   *now*
nimis   *too* (take with 'multos')
multus,-a,-um   *much, many* (if there is no corresponding noun then 'multōs' is acting as a noun: *many people*)
audiō   *I* (i.e. Cato) *hear*
Corinthus,-ī [m.]   *Corinth*
Athēnae,-ārum [f.]   *Athens*
ōrnāmentum,-ī [n.]   *ornament, accoutrement*
laudantēs [the people doing this are in the nominative or accusative plural]   *praising*
mīrantēs [as above]   *admiring*

8. A century later the historian Sallust saw no shame in Rome's relative scarcity of writers. His people were achievers, not talkers:

populō Rōmānō numquam scrīptōrum cōpia fuit.

Sallust, *Conspiracy of Catiline* 8.5

populus,-ī [m.]   *people* (for the use of the dative see 'fuit' below)
Rōmānus,-a,-um   *Roman*
scrīptōrum [gen. pl.]   *writers*
cōpia,-ae [f.]   *abundance*
fuit [+ dat. to show possession]   *there was to 'x' ('x' had . . .)*

9. Virgil recognized the artistic talent of the Greeks:

vīvōs dūcent dē marmore vultūs.

Virgil, *Aeneid* 6.848

vīvus,-a,-um   *living*
dūcent   *they* (i.e. the Greeks) *will bring, shape, fashion*
dē [+ abl.]   *from*
marmore [abl.]   *marble*
vultūs [acc.pl.]   *faces*

10. And he reminded Romans to concentrate on their own talents – good leadership – and to remember to . . .

. . . pācīque impōnere mōrem, / parcere subiectīs et dēbellāre superbōs.

Virgil, *Aeneid* 6.852–3

pācī [dat.]   *peace*
impōnere   *to impose*
mōrem [acc.]   *way of life*
pācīque impōnere mōrem   *impose your way of life upon peace* (or *add your way of life to peace*
        to account for the dative of 'pācī'), i.e. create peace first, then add the lifestyle
parcere [with its object in the dative]   *to spare*
subiectus,-a,-um   *conquered*
dēbellāre   *to subdue*
superbus,-a,-um   *proud*

11. Cicero was not the only Roman to admire Greek cultural achievements and yet have a lingering distrust of the Greeks of his day:

sed sunt in illō numerō multī bonī, doctī, pudentēs et etiam impudentēs, illiterātī, levēs.

Cicero, *In Defence of Flaccus* 4.9

sed   *but*
illō [abl.]   *that*
numerus,-ī [m.]   *number*
multus,-a,-um   *much, many*
doctus,-a-,um   *learned*
pudentēs [nom.pl./acc.pl.]   *scrupulous*
impudentēs [nom.pl./acc.pl.]   *shameless*
illiterātus,-a,-um   *uneducated*
levēs [nom.pl./acc.pl.]   *superficial, frivolous*
multī . . . etiam: if no corresponding noun say *many (men who are) . . . and also (those
        who are). . .*

12. Classical Greek theatre was held in high esteem, but not so the sham acting of Greeks of Juvenal's day:

> flet, sī lacrimās cōnspexit amīcī, / nec dolet.
> sī dīxeris 'aestuo', sūdat.

Juvenal, Satires 3.101–102,103

flet   *(s/he) weeps* (i.e. a Greek)
lacrima,-ae [f.]   *tear*
cōnspexit   *(s/he) has seen*
nec   *and . . . not, but . . . not*
dolet   *(s/he) grieves*
dīxeris   *you say*
aestuo   *I am hot*
sūdat   *(s/he) sweats*

13. Virgil's story of Laocoön urging the Trojans not to trust the Wooden Horse which the Greeks had left by way of an ambush will have struck a contemporary note:

> Lāocoōn ārdēns summā dēcurrit ab arce,
> et procul 'ō miserī, quae tanta īnsānia, cīvēs?
> quidquid id est, timeō Danaōs et dōna ferentīs.'

Virgil, Aeneid 2.41–2,49

Lāocoōn [nom.]   *Laocoön*
ārdēns [take with a noun in the nominative]   *raging, in a rush of feeling*
summus,-a,-um   *topmost, uppermost*
dēcurrit   *(s/he) runs down*
arce [abl.]   *citadel*
procul   *from afar*
Add a verb to your English version to introduce his words, e.g. *he shouts, cries*
ō miserī cīvēs [voc.]   *o wretched citizens*
quae   *what, why*
tantus,-a,-um   *so much*
īnsānia,-ae [f.]   *madness*
quidquid [take with a noun in the nominative or accusative]   *whatever*
id [nom./acc.]   *that* (i.e. the Wooden Horse)
timeō   *I fear*
Danaī,-ōrum [m.]   *Greeks*
et   *even*
dōnum,-ī [n.]   *gift*
ferentīs [the people doing this are in the accusative plural; alt. form of 'ferentēs']   *bearing*

Exercises 4b

1. Identify the case and number of each underlined word:
(a) Hannibal **patriā** profugus pervēnerat ad Antiochum.
(b) Lucrētia semper flet sī lacrimās **amīcārum** cōnspexit.
(c) miserō **agricolae** nōn est cōpia taurōrum.

2. Translate:
(a) quidquid id est, dōnum novum ā magistrō timeō.
(b) cūr servus miser in vīllā sūdat?
(c) sunt in illō numerō multī optimī, sed etiam miserī īnsānī.
(d) iam nimis multōs poētās audiō dominam meam laudantēs mīrantēsque.
(e) ī, pete rosās aliēnī poētae!
(f) sunt in vīllā multae bonae, doctae, et etiam superbae, saevae, īnsānae.

3. Fill each gap with one word:
(a) servī . . . . {*many*} in agrīs sunt.
(b) Pyrrhus librōs . . . . {*new*} accipit.
(c) numquam agricola est servō miserō . . . . {*kind*}.
(d) puer librum. . . . . {*large*} ā magistrō accipit.

4. Translate into Latin:
(a) The tribune's wine is new.
(b) Catullus does not like the new (male) friends of his arrogant mistress.

5.
(a) What two words in this chapter are represented by the abbreviation 'i.e.'?
(b) Find Latin ancestors in this chapter of *doctor, expat, invention, moral* and *vivid*.

6. English words from Latin are generally less 'Latin-looking' the earlier they arrived. 'Mile' and 'millennium' for instance, from **mīlle** (*thousand*), or 'mister' and 'magistrate' from **magister**. Many French words settled in English during the first half of the second millennium and most of these had Latin roots. Some were later refashioned closer to their Latin parents by scholars and wordsmiths eager to Latinize our vocabulary: e.g. 'secure', modelled on Latin **sēcūrus**, was used along side 'sure' (French *sûr*); and 'placate' (**placet**) with 'please' (*plaît*). Such pairs have since taken on slightly different meanings.
(a) The word 'fragile' was modelled on **fragilis** (*easily broken*). Can you identify the English word which arrived from the same Latin root but via French?
(b) The word 'compute' was modelled on **computō,-āre**. What older English word arrived from the same Latin root, via French?

— 5 —

New factions and old families

Genitive and dative expressing ownership

Both the genitive and dative cases are used to show possession:

> Ascanius lacrimās **amīcī** videt   [genitive]
> *Ascanius sees the tears of a friend*

> **populō Rōmānō** numquam scrīptōrum cōpia fuit   [dative]
> *there never was an abundance of writers for the Roman people (the Roman people never had . . .)* [4.8][1]

The genitive is normally tagged on another noun, the thing(s) owned (**lacrimās amīcī**). The dative is commonly used with a verb (especially 'to be'), in an unemphatic referential way:

> tribūnus **mihi** est dominus
> *the tribune to me is the master/I have the tribune as master*

mihi [dat.]	*to/for me*	
tibi [dat.]	*to/for you* (s.)	

The dative with a verb to show possession or reference
or similar connection is very common, e.g. for characteristics or personal qualities (e.g. 'he has a sad face' = 'there is a sad face to him').[2]

More emphatically *mine* or *yours* are the possessive adjectives **meus,-a,-um** (*my*) and **tuus,-a,-um** (*your*), and plurals **noster,-tra,-trum** (*our*) and **vester,-tra,-trum** (*your* pl.):

> **tua** est Lāvīnia coniūnx
> *Lavinia is your wife* [1.5]

---

1 I.e. chapter 4, text number 8.
2 The verb **habet** (*s/he has, owns*) typically means ownership of things under your control. A slave described as '**servus tribūnum dominum habet**' might appear slightly above himself.

Practice 5a

Translate:

(a) praemium mihi magnum est.

(b) puellīs sunt multa dōna.

(c) praeda tibi in Italiā est.

(d) tuus fīlius, ō amīce, cum dominā triumvirī sedet īnsānī.

Past participles

Past participles are adjectives and have endings like **bonus,-a,-um**. It is worth revisiting these endings until you have them secure. They appear all the time, as adjectives, participles or 1st/2nd declension nouns.

Despite their grammatical role as adjectives, participles are considered to be a part of the verb from which they come. They also have functions over and above those of adjectives. Below are three past participles already seen, with the verb from which each is taken on the right:

captus,-a,-um	*(having been) captured*	**capit**	*s/he captures*
dēligātus,-a,-um	*(having been) bound, tied*	**dēligat**	*s/he binds ties*
trucīdātus,-a,-um	*(having been) slaughtered*	**trucīdat**	*s/he slaughters*

The past participle is passive, i.e. the noun with which the past participle agrees is the one who has been captured, tied or slaughtered, not the one who has done it. Below, it is Greece (**Graecia**) which has been captured (**capta**):

Graecia **capta** ferum victōrem cēpit

captured Greece has (in turn) captured her wild conqueror [4.6]

Past participles can often be translated simply as '. . .-ed' (as 'captured' above). Below a similar phrasing is clear enough though your final translation may need rewording:

dominae Servium **trucīdātum** ostendit

he shows the slaughtered Servius to his mistress [2.2]

It may be that there are other words which depend on the past participle much as they do on a verb. Below, **ad pālum** depends on the past participle **dēligātī**:

stābant **dēligātī ad pālum** cōnsulis līberī

the children of the consul stood tied to the post [2.9]

Practice 5b

1. Give the case, gender and number of (a) 'capta', (b) 'trucīdātum' and (c) 'dēligātī' in the above three examples, and identify the noun with which each agrees.
2. Fill the gaps below with these past participles:

    datus,-a,-um; necātus,-a,-um; dictus,-a,-um; doctus,-a,-um; ductus,-a,-um; occīsus,-a,-um; vīsus,-a,-um; factus,-a,-um; amātus,-a,-um.

Verb	Past participle	
amat (s/he loves)	....	....
audit (s/he hears)	**audītus,-a,-um**	(having been) heard
capit (s/he captures)	**captus,-a,-um**	(having been) captured
creat (s/he appoints)	**creātus,-a,-um**	(having been) appointed
dat (s/he gives)	....	....
dīcit (s/he says)	....	....
docet (s/he teaches)	....	....
dūcit (s/he leads)	....	....
facit (s/he makes, does)	....	....
necat (s/he kills)	....	....
occīdit (s/he kills)	....	....
trucīdat (s/he slaughters)	**trucīdātus,-a,-um**	(having been) slaughtered
videt (s/he sees)	....	....

Past participles with est or sunt

Adjectives are used with **est** or **sunt**:

opulentus est Crassus
Crassus is wealthy

When a past participle is used with the verb *to be*, together they form a verb in the past passive: *was/were . . .* or *has/have been . . .*:

dōna sāncta in forō **vīsa sunt**
the sacred gifts were/have been seen in the forum

Note that past participles when used with **est** or **sunt** are not translated as *is* or *are* but *was/has been* or *were/have been*:

duo cōnsulēs inde creātī **sunt**
two consuls were then appointed [2.5]

Graecia capta **est**
Greece was/has been captured

Practice 5c
Fill each gap with *two* Latin words:
(a) tribūnus ā populō . . . . *{was seen}*
(b) Boudicca nōn . . . . *{was captured}*
(c) captīvī nōn . . . . *{were heard}*
(d) fēminae numquam cōnsulēs . . . .
   {were appointed}

Translating past participles

If a past participle appears with **est** or **sunt**, then it is translated as *was/were* . . . (and sometimes *has/have been* . . .):

praemium servō **prōmissum est**
a gift was promised to the slave

If the participle appears without the verb *to be*, the English words *having been* . . . should be the first into your head, as in *having been woken, having been asked*, etc. Once you have the sense there may be a number of ways you can rephrase this, e.g.:

triumvir pecūniam **vīsam** capit
the triumvir takes the (having been) seen money
the triumvir takes the money which he has seen
after the triumvir sees the money he takes it
the triumvir sees the money and takes it

There are times when an English noun can represent a Latin participle:

Graecia **capta** ferum victōrem cēpit
Greece having-been-captured captured her wild conqueror
after the capture of Greece she (in turn) captured her wild conqueror [4.6]

Practice 5d
Put **dominae Servium trucīdātum ostendit** into English which does not read like an awkward translation.

sum, esse

Here are other forms of *to be*. You have already met **sum**:

esse	to be
sum	I am
es	you are (sing.)
est	(s/he, it, there) is
sumus	we are
estis	you are (pl.)
sunt	(they, there) are

Sextus Tarquinius **sum**
I am Sextus Tarquinius [2.3]

The forms **sum** (*I am*) and **es** (*you are*) will appear in Latin texts but not as often as **est**. If we had more access to conversational Latin than we find scattered through poems and stories and in the surviving handful of Latin plays, then we'd come across **sum** and **es** a good deal more. Here is a summary of what we already know about **sum, esse**:

- the verb *to be* does not take an object in the accusative but a complementary noun or adjective in the same case as the subject

  Clōdius **tribūnus** est
  Clodius is a <u>tribune</u>

- the English for **est** is *he is, she is, it is, there is* or plain *is*; and for **sunt** *they are, there are* or just *are*

  in forō **sunt** multī servī
  <u>there are</u> many slaves in the forum

- sometimes **est** and **sunt** are used with the dative to show a possessive or similar referential connection

  rosae **mihi** sunt novae
  the roses <u>for me</u> are new/my roses are new/I have new roses

- the present of *to be* with a past participle means *was/has been* or *were/have been*

  ego tribūnus **creātus sum**
  I <u>was/have been appointed</u> tribune

Practice 5e

Fill each gap with one word, and translate:

(a)   ō sāncta dea, ... {*are*} tibi multae rosae in mēnsā.

(b)   . . . . {*great*} praemia servīs bonīs sunt.

(c)   ō amīcī, tribūnī . . . . {*appointed*} estis?

(d)   nōn īnsānī . . . . {*we are*}!

(e)   ō magister, ... {*I am*} ēbrius. es tū mihi dominus?

Vocabulary 5

You have now met three words for *killed*: **necātus, trucīdātus** and **occīsus**. Perhaps we should expect that of the Romans, much as the Arabs have many words for *sand* and the Inuit for *snow*. But English has its share too (e.g. murder, kill, slaughter, massacre, cull, hit, take out, knife, bump off). English is a language particularly rich in verbs: think of the many different words for *eat* (e.g. taste, chew, swallow, gulp down, nibble, devour, etc) or *go* (walk, march, stride, pace, hop, limp, crawl, saunter, sprint, stumble, tiptoe, make one's way, etc).

Make sure the genitive endings are added to all nouns in your notebook. Then add these 1st and 2nd declension nouns below to the correct declensions.

animus,-ī [m.]   *mind, intention, courage*
avāritia,-ae [f.]   *greed*
causa,-ae [f.]   *case, cause*
cēna,-ae [f.]   *dinner*
cūra,-ae [f.]   *care, anxiety*
fātum,-ī   *fate*
flagellum,-ī [n.]   *whip*
lībertus,-ī [m.]   *freedman, former slave*

pecūnia,-ae [f.]   *money*
poena,-ae [f.]   *punishment, penalty*
studium,-ī [n.]   *pursuit, eagerness*
triumphus,-ī [m.]   *triumph, i.e. triumphal procession*
vir,-ī [m.]   *man, husband*
vīta,-ae [f.] *life*

Exercises 5a

1. Add the correct ending to each participle:
(a) creāt. . . . . sumus {*we* (females) *were appointed*}.
(b) duct. . . . . sum {*I* (male) *was led*}.
(c) capt. . . . . sunt {*they* (males) *have been captured*}.
(d) fact. . . . . sunt {*things were made*}.
(e) dat. . . . . sunt {*things have been given*}.
(f) audīt. . . . . est {*she was heard*}.

2. Translate:
(a) servī captī in forum ductī sunt.
(b) quis es tū? – ego captus ā Rōmānīs sum.
(c) praeda mihi est nova.
(d) dea sāncta rosās rēgīnae datas videt.
(e) miserī in agrō ad pālum dēligātī sunt.
(f) quis prīmus est creātus tribūnus?
(g) multī ā Sullā occīsī sunt.
(h) gladius tribūnī necātī in vīllā est.
(i) rēgīna sāncta numquam capta est.

3. Who was captured?
(a) tribūnus fīlium rēgīnae captae audit.
(b) tribūnus fīlium rēgīnae captum audit.

New factions and old families

Under the Republic political power was shared between a relatively small elite. There was change, old families short of money, others who found wealth, and some talented or successful individuals broke through into the top echelon. But the Republic was broadly conservative and those with power kept a grip on it. In the latter part of the second century BC the Gracchi brothers each attempted to meet the grievances of the wider population, but both were murdered by those with a vested interest in the status quo. In 91 BC a war broke out between Rome and the Italian towns under her control, who felt unrewarded for the contributions they made to Rome's armies and taxes. Rome won the 'Social War' against these allies (*socii*) and afterwards made concessions. The town of Arpinum, 70 miles south-east of Rome, stayed loyal. One of its citizens had risen to the top in Roman politics: a hugely successful general and many-times consul, Gaius Marius. At the start of his career he was treated as an outsider, a '*novus homo*': the first member of his family to be consul. He was born 50 years before another even more famous

Reading notes

As with other adjectives, you will come across participles without a corresponding noun or pronoun. The missing noun or pronoun is taken as understood. For instance, the Latin for 'things' below is inferred from the neuter plural of **dictus,-a,-um**:

> neque tē teneō, neque **dicta** refellō
> *neither do I keep you nor do I challenge the having-been-said (things)*
> (i.e. *the things you have said*) [3.12]

The neuter **dicta** guides us to '*things*' in our translation. If the participle is masculine, then the missing noun is likely to be '*men*':

> sunt in illō numerō **doctī**
> *there are in that number learned (men)* [4.11]

native of Arpinum and another to become a *novus homo* – Marcus Tullius Cicero. The strength of Arpinum's loyalty during the Social War is not known, although we know that the townspeople had already received some rights of citizenship. No doubt the successes and influence of Marius protected the interests and ties of his townsfolk. Cicero was a teenager when this war was fought, and in slightly different circumstances he might easily have fought in an army against Rome.

The senatorial body was made up of those who had served as magistrates. The typical career path of a highborn young male would be: serve in the army, stand for election as quaestor (public finance), then aedile (water-supply, public games, management of public buildings), praetor (presiding over the courts), and finally consul. There were many more junior positions than senior ones and the ladder of progress grew narrower and more competitive the higher it went. There were also the offices of censor (who kept formal lists of the population), tribune, and from time to time dictator.

An elected magistrate would then become a member of the senate for life. Thus the senate was a consultative body of elders, all with at least some experience of political office. There were also the popular assemblies which would elect the magistrates and ratify the proposals or will of the senate. These assemblies were not without power, and all male citizens were eligible to vote. But voters were not on an equal footing or entirely free to make up their own minds. The *Comitia Centuriata* (Assembly of the Centuries) elected the more senior magistrates. Each 'century' was a voting block, and these blocks were weighted in favour of richer citizens. The *Comitia Tributa* (Assembly of the Tribes) elected other magistrates. Many of these votes were tied by the system of patronage.

Tribunes were traditionally the magistrates who protected the popular interests. They too came from wealthy families, but had to be plebeian, according to ancient law. They were elected by the *Concilium Plebis* (Council of Plebeians) and what was once a power of veto on behalf of the popular interest evolved into a much sought-after position.

1. Tiberius Gracchus, grandson of Scipio Africanus, was tribune in 133 BC. His initiative for land redistribution made him deeply unpopular with some powerful people. Against standard practice he stood for re-election, and was murdered by a gang of senators.

Gracchus in Capitōliō ab optimātibus occīsus est et, inter aliōs quī in eādem sēditiōne occīsī erant, īnsepultus in flūmen prōiectus est.

Livy, History of Rome 58 (Summary)

Capitōlium,-ī [n.]   *the Capitol* (a temple on the summit of the Capitoline Hill)
optimātibus [dat.pl./abl.pl.]   *aristocrats*
occīsus,-a,-um   *killed*
inter [+ acc.]   *among, between*
aliōs [acc.pl.]   *others*
quī   *who*
eādem [abl.]   *the same*
sēditiōne [abl.]   *rebellion*
occīsī erant   *(they) had been killed*
īnsepultus,-a,-um   *unburied*
flūmen [nom./acc.]   *river*
prōiectus,-a,-um   *thrown*

2. Tiberius' younger brother, Gaius Gracchus, was tribune in 121 and continued work on his brother's reforms. Not even the precaution of armed protection protected him from coming to a similar end. He was attacked and killed by men under the command of the consul Lucius Opimius.

Gaius Gracchus ā Lūciō Opimiō cōnsule pulsus et occīsus est.

Livy, History of Rome 61 (Summary)

cōnsule [abl.]   *consul*
pulsus,-a,-um [take 'est' with both past participles 'pulsus' and 'occīsus']   *beaten, put to flight*

3. At the start of the first century BC there were broadly two political groups: the *populares* and *optimates*. The *populares* looked to further their interests through the popular assemblies (e.g. as tribunes), while the *optimates* protected the power base of the elite in

the senate. Marius, a plebeian, was tribune, consul several times, and a successful general. Always a *popularis*, he was conscious of his uneducated ways.

neque litterās Graecās didicī: parum placēbat eās discere.

Sallust, *Jugurthine War 85*

neque   *and . . . not*
litterae,-ārum [f.]   *letters, literature*
Graecus,-a,-um   *Greek*
didicī   *I (have) learned*
parum   *too little, not enough*
placēbat   *it pleased (me), it seemed proper (to me)*
eās [acc.]   *them* (i.e. Greek letters or literature)
discere   *to learn, to study*

4.   Marius did not care for the old established families:

contemnunt novitātem meam, ego illōrum ignāviam.

Sallust, *Jugurthine War 85*

contemnunt   *(they) despise, scorn*
novitātem [acc.]   *novelty, newness,* i.e. his status as a newcomer to high office
meus,-a,-um   *my*
ego [nom.]   *I* (repeat the verb, this time '*I despise . . .*')
illōrum [gen.pl.]   *those people*
ignāvia,-ae [f.]   *idleness, worthlessness*

5.   Marius says the aristocrats sneer at his lack of refinement.

sordidum mē et incultīs mōribus aiunt, quia parum scītē convīvium exōrnō.

Sallust, *Jugurthine War 85*

sordidus,-a,-um   *vulgar*
incultus,-a,-um   *uncultivated, unrefined*
mōribus [dat.pl./abl.pl.]   *way, manner*
aiunt   *(they) say, call*
quia   *because*
parum   *too little, not 'scītē' enough*
scītē   *elegantly, tastefully*
convīvium,-ī   *dinner-party*
exōrnō   *I equip, adorn*

6.   Aristocrats may inherit money and family portraits from their ancestors, says Marius, but they do not inherit their virtues. 'I am treated with contempt . . .

'. . . quia imāginēs nōn habeō et quia mihi nova nōbilitās est.'

Sallust, *Jugurthine War 85*

quia   *because*
imāginēs [nom.pl./acc.pl.]   *portrait*
mihi [dat.]   *me* (dative of possession – see p. 48: translate as *my*)
nōbilitās [nom.f.]   *nobility, high rank*

7.   Marius led the successful campaign against the African king, Jugurtha. He was awarded a 'triumph', a procession through Rome of winners and losers in honour of the successful general.

in triumphō Mariī ductus ante currum eius Iugurtha cum duōbus fīliīs et in carcere necātus est.

Livy, *History of Rome 67* (Summary)

triumphus,-ī [m.]   *triumph*
ductus,-a,-um   *led* (take 'est' with 'ductus' as well as 'necātus': 'ductus est' = *(he) was led*)
ante [+ acc.]   *before, in front of*
currum [acc.]   *chariot*
ēius   *his*
Iugurtha,-ae [m.]   *Jugurtha*

cum [+ abl.]   *with*
duōbus [dat.pl./abl.pl.]   *two*
carcere [abl.]   *prison*
necātus,-a,-um   *killed*

8.   By the start of the first century BC Rome controlled most of Italy. Other towns were regarded as *socii* (allies), who in the early days of this federation enjoyed Rome's protection. Now threats of attack had receded, and these *socii* found themselves contributing money and soldiers to campaigns abroad without receiving enough in return. Some took arms against against Rome.

Ītalicī populī dēfēcērunt: Pīcentēs, Vestīni, Marsī, Paelignī, Marrūcīnī, Samnītēs, Lucānī.

Livy, *History of Rome* 72 (Summary)

Ītalicus,-a,-um   *Italian*
dēfēcērunt   *(they) revolted*

9.   The war against their *socii* (the Social War) started badly for Rome. Sulla, an optimate who had served under Marius in Africa, had more success.

Sulla lēgātus Samnītēs proeliō vīcit.

Livy, *History of Rome* 75 (Summary)

Sulla,-ae [m.]   *Sulla*
lēgātus,-ī [m.]   *commander*
Samnītēs [nom.pl./acc.pl.]   *Samnites*
proelium,-ī [n.]   *battle*
vīcit   *(s/he) conquered, defeated*

10.   Sulla overcame the resistance of towns like Pompeii, and he won much prestige from the final victory. The rights and privileges of the *socii* were improved, who in turn conceded much of their political independence.

  The theatre of war was moving further afield as Rome's boundaries grew. In the east Mithridates of Pontus was a threat to Rome's interests. Marius and Sulla were the two candidates to lead an expedition against him. Sulla belonged to the aristocracy which Marius so despised, and their rivalry escalated. Sulpicius, tribune and ally of Marius, pushed through a decree to appoint Marius commander. So Sulla took the law into his own hands and led his army against the city. Marius escaped to Africa, but not Sulpicius. He hid in a villa where he was betrayed by his own slave, who was later denied the reward he hoped for.

Sulpicius indiciō servī suī ē vīllā retractus et occīsus est. servus, ut praemium prōmissum indicī habēret, manūmissus et ob scelus dē Saxō dēiectus est.

Livy, *History of Rome* 77 (Summary)

indicium,-ī [n.]   *information, evidence*
suus,-a,-um   *his own, her own, their own*
retractus,-a,-um   *dragged back, brought back* (take 'est' with 'retractus' as well as 'occīsus')
Word order for the second sentence: 'servus (est) manūmissus, ut habēret praemium
     prōmissum indicī, et ob scelus dēiectus est dē Saxō'
ut   *so that*
prōmissus,-a,-um   *promised*
indicī [dat.]   *informer*
habēret   *(s/he) might have*
manūmissus,-a,-um   *freed* (take 'est' with 'manūmissus' as well as 'dēiectus')
ob [+ acc.]   *because of*
scelus [nom./acc.]   *crime*
dē [+ abl.]   *from*
Saxum,-ī [n.]   *Tarpeian rock* (traditional place of execution for treachery)
dēiectus est   *he was thrown down*

Exercises 5b

1.   Translate:
(a)   captīvī in Tiberim prōiectī sunt.
(b)   duo servī ad pālum dēligatī sunt.
(c)   contemnunt taurōs meōs, ego illōrum servōs.
(d)   Cleopātra in triumphō triumvirī nōn ducta est.
(e)   cūr est servus manūmissus?
(f)   taurus ē vīllā retractus et in agrōs ductus est.

2.   Fill each gap, and translate your answer:
(a)   ubī est nostra . . . . {*dinner*}?
(b)   Lūcius in vīllā ā . . . . {*by a slave*} occīsus est.
(c)   tribūnus . . . . {*to the wretched*} servīs captīvōs trucīdātōs ostendit.
(d)   dominus imāginēs . . . . {*of his friends*} semper laudat.
(e)   quis ā . . . . {*by Sulla*} amātus est?

3.   Translate:
(a)   miser in vīllā sūdat quia flagellum dominī timet.
(b)   quis praemium servī necātī habet?
(c)   dominusne praemium prōmissum puellae accipit?
(d)   Marius nōn arma bellī sed poētae verba timet.
(e)   dōna dominae in flūmen prōiecta sunt.

4.   Translate into Latin:
     'Friends, your money was given to the wretched sons of the murdered tribune.'

5.   Find Latin ancestors in this chapter of *car, convivial, dejected, project* and *repulsive*.

— 6 —

The Republic under strain

Verbs

Verbs state the action, what happens or is done. They generally appear at the end of a sentence or group of words, though not always. Like nouns and adjectives, verbs are inflected. Inflexion is the modification of a word's ending to express a particular grammatical meaning. The many functional twists of verb-endings may at first seem a handful, but there are clear patterns which will make the learning easier. The functions of verb-endings fall broadly into these categories:

- a personal ending: to show who the subject is (*I.* . ., *you.* . ., *he.* . ., *she.* . ., *it.* . ., *we.* . ., *they.* . . or an external noun)
- the tense, in other words the timing of the action (*he loves, he loved, he will love*)
- the 'mood': statements of fact or of potential (*he loves* or *he may/might/would/should love*)
- the 'voice', i.e. active or passive (*he loves* or *he is loved*).

Personal verb-endings

The '1st person' is the person speaking (in other words 'I', or if more than one person 'we'), the '2nd person' is the person(s) you are talking to i.e. 'you', and the '3rd person' is someone else, a third party – the person(s) being talked about, i.e. 'he', 'she', 'it', 'they'.

The ending of a verb changes depending on the person. In English there is only one change – to the 3rd person singular, e.g. *I live, you live, we live, they live*, but *he lives*. Latin verbs have different endings for all persons.

The present tense

amō (= *I love*), **amāre** (= *to love*)

The endings show the six persons of the verb:

am**ō**	*I love*
am**ās**	*you* [s.] *love*
am**at**	*s/he, it* [or a noun] *loves*
am**āmus**	*we love*
am**ātis**	*you* [pl.] *love*
am**ant**	*they* [or a plural noun] *love*

The present tense in English can be expressed in the present simple or present continuous (see p. 3). The Latin present tense corresponds to both these. So, as feels right in English, you can translate

> Cornēlia fīliōs **laudat**
> as Cornelia *praises* her sons or Cornelia *is praising* her sons

> Cornēlia fīliōs nōn **laudat**
> as Cornelia *does* not *praise* her sons or Cornelia *is* not *praising* her sons

Where no subject appears, i.e. no noun or pronoun in the nominative, then you add an English pronoun to your translation (*I, you, s/he, it, we, they* . . .) according to the verb-ending.

Practice 6a

1. Translate:
   (a) cūr taurum fugāmus?
   (b) Horātiumne laudātis?
   (c) victōriam triumvirī laudāmus.
   (d) dominamne tuam laudās? tē nōn amat.
   (e) semper praedam amīcīs damus.
2. Fill each gap with one word:
   (a) poētam nōn . . . . {*she praises*}.
   (b) Sullam nōn . . . . {*we love*}.
   (c) o amīcī, vestrōs fīliōs . . . . {*you love*}.
   (d) taurōs semper . . . . {*they chase*}.

like **amō**	
dō	*I give*
fugō	*I chase*
laudō	*I praise*

Separate pronouns appearing as subjects

The ending of the verb tells you whether the subject is *I, you, he*, etc.

> patrēs voc**ās**
> *you summon the senators*

A subject pronoun may also appear, for emphasis:

> quā **tū** audāciā patrēs vocās?
> *with what presumption do* you *summon the senators?* [2.1]

tū nunc Karthāginis fundāmenta locās?
you *are now laying the foundations of Carthage?* [3.8]

Or for clarification. The subject pronoun **ego** below implies a repetition of the verb **contemnunt** (but in the 1st person):

ego	*I*
tū	*you* [s.]
nōs	*we*
vōs	*you* [pl.]

contemnunt novitātem meam, **ego** illōrum ignāviam
they despise my new status, I (despise) their worthlessness [5.4]

The 1st and 2nd person pronouns above are in the nominative, as they are subjects. You will see these pronouns frequently in the other cases, especially **mē** (accusative or ablative) and **mihi** (dative) of **ego**; and **tē** (accusative or ablative) and **tibi** (dative) of **tū**:

dēsine **mē**que tuīs incendere **tē**que querēlīs [both accusative]
stop distressing both me and you with your complaints [3.11]

These pronouns are introduced in full on p. 170. Also to come later are 3rd person pronouns (*he, she, it* and *they*). You have already met **id** (*it* or *that*):

quidquid **id** est, timeō Danaōs et dōna ferentīs
whatever that is, I fear Greeks even when bearing gifts [4.13]

The infinitive

The infinitive of an English verb is expressed with *to* . . .

she wants to sing
he is able to walk

The infinitive of **amō** is **amāre** and of **laudō** is **laudāre**.

The perfect tense

The past tenses of English verbs can be dressed in many different ways: *he loved, he has loved, he will have loved, he had loved, he was loving, he used to love, he did love, he would love, he has been loving, he had been loving,* and that is without all the potential or hypothetical *might-have-been*s and *would-have-been*s.

The perfect tense in Latin is the equivalent of the simple past (*he loved*) or the past with *have* (*he has loved*). The stem is **amāv**-ī, **amāv**-istī, etc.

amāv**ī**	*I loved, I have loved (did not love, have not loved)*
amāv**istī**	*you* [s.] *loved, have loved*
amāv**it**	*s/he, it* [or a noun] *loved, has loved*
amāv**imus**	*we loved, have loved*
amāv**istis**	*you* [pl.] *loved, have loved*
amāv**ērunt**	*they* [or a plural noun] *loved, have loved*

Practice 6b

1. Translate each into one Latin word:
   (a) they loved
   (b) they love
   (c) we have chased
   (d) we are chasing
   (e) you [s.] have praised
   (f) you [s.] are praising
   (g) you [pl.] chased
   (h) you [pl.] chase

2. Translate:
   (a) dominam amāvī sed nunc nōn amō.
   (b) cūr tribūnum nōn laudāvistī sed nunc laudās?
   (c) Clōdia poētam amat sed etiam Caelium amāvit.
   (d) puellae taurōs numquam fugāvērunt, sed nunc fugant.
   (e) ego semper elephantōs numquam taurōs fugō.

like **amāvī**
fugāvī *I (have) chased*
laudāvī *I (have) praised*

Perfect stems

The perfect tenses **amāvī, fugāvī** and **laudāvī** share the same forms and these verbs all belong to a regular group of verbs called the 1st conjugation. Here are other examples of this conjugation in the perfect tense, with the present tense in brackets:

Cloelia Tiberim **trānāvit** (trānat)
Cloelia swam across the Tiber (swims) [2.8]

Tarquinius Superbus **rēgnāvit** annōs quīnque et vīgintī (rēgnat)
Tarquinius Superbus ruled for twenty-five years (rules) [2.5]

There are other conjugations and irregular verbs, coming soon, which have a variety of perfect forms. Here are a few already seen:

gaudium **fuit** (est)
there was joy (is) [4.3]

Graecia ferum victōrem **cēpit** (capit)
Greece captured her wild conqueror (captures) [4.6]

urbem Rōmam **condidērunt** Trōiānī (condunt)
the Trojans founded the city of Rome (are founding) [1.2]

Some verbs in the perfect tense change more than their endings. With verbs like **capit/cēpit** and **est/fuit** the whole word changes. This means you will need to know the perfect form as well as the present to know the verb.

Practice 6c
1. Put the underlined verb into the perfect and translate the answer:
    (a) deōs Trōiānī **laudant**.
    (b) ego lībertum nōn **amō**.
    (c) servusne Sulpicium **amat**?
    (d) tūne taurum **fugās**?
    (e) taurōs **fugāmus**.

Principal parts

There are four parts of a verb you need to know:
1. the 1st person of the *present tense*: **amō, capiō**
2. the *infinitive*: **amāre, capere**
3. the 1st person of the *perfect tense*: **amāvī, cēpī**
4. the *past participle*, which you met in the previous chapter: **amātus,-a,-um, captus,-a, -um**)

These are called the four *principal parts* of a verb.

> **amō, amāre, amāvī, amātum** *
> **capiō, capere, cēpī, captum** *

* neuter singular (**-um**) is shown as the principal part

Principal parts: 1st conjugation

	present	infinitive	perfect	past part.
love	amō	amāre	amāvī	amātum
give	dō	dare	dedī #	datum
chase	fugō	fugāre	fugāvī	fugātum
praise	laudō	laudāre	laudāvī	laudātum
prepare	parō	parāre	parāvī	parātum

one of very few eccentric forms in the perfect tense of the 1st conjugation

---

Practice 6d

1.   Fill each gap with one Latin word:
    (a)   Clōdiane tribūnum . . . . {*praised*}?
          — sīc (*yes*), tribūnus ā Clōdiā est laudātus.
    (b)   tūne Sullam amāvistī?
          — numquam ā mē . . . . {*was loved*} est Sulla.
    (c)   ō amīcī, cēnam . . . . {*did you prepare*}?
          — cēna ā servīs nostrīs est . . . . {*was prepared*}.

Missing words or words 'understood'

It's challenging enough to translate the Latin words that appear before you. Sometimes you need to do a bit of detective work to spot words which are *not* there, or ones which appear once but need to be understood elsewhere too. A similar thing happens in English:

> there were two marriages: Octavian married Livia, Antony Octavia

It is not necessary to repeat 'married' after 'Antony'; we say it is 'understood'. Consider this example

> contemnunt novitātem meam, ego illōrum ignāviam
> *they despise my new status, I (despise) their worthlessness* [5.4]

where the verb **contemnunt** (*they despise*) is understood in the second part of the sentence, but in the 1st person: **contemnō** (*I despise*).

The usual suspects for missing words are either a word which has already appeared/about to appear (as with **contemnunt/contemnō** above) or the verb *to be*:

> sī quis adhūc precibus locus
> *if there is still any place for entreaties* [3.10]

Below, **est** is taken with both **pulsus** and **occīsus** (similarly to the English version where *was* is taken with *put to flight* and *killed*):

> Gracchus ā Opimiō pulsus et occīsus est
> *Gracchus was put to flight and killed by Opimius* [5.2]

So every now and then you will need not only to translate a word but guess that it should be there in the first place. The more you read the more obvious such missing words will become.

> **Practice 6e**
> 1. What English word(s) will you add to your translation of the sentence below (which does not appear in the Latin version)?
>
>   et procul 'ō miserī, quae tanta īnsānia, cīvēs?' [4.13]

More adjectives acting as nouns

We have seen adjectives acting as nouns:

> sunt in illō numerō multī **bonī**
> *there are in that number many good (men)*

In some cases this happens frequently enough for the noun version to exist alongside the adjective as a recognized noun-form:

Rōmānus,-a,-um *Roman*	**Rōmānus,-ī** [m.] *a Roman*
Graecus,-a,-um *Greek*	**Graecus,-ī** [m.] *a Greek*
amīcus,-a,-um *friendly*	**amīcus,-ī** [m.], **amīca,-ae** [f.] *a friend*
dīvus,-a,-um *divine*	**dīvus,-ī** [m.], **dīva,-ae** [f.] *god, goddess*
inimīcus,-a,-um *hostile*	**inimīcus,-ī** [m.], **inimica,-ae** [f.] *an enemy*

The context as ever will guide you to the right meaning. Sometimes there is hardly any difference between the two:

> Clōdius **inimīcus** nōbīs est
> *Clodius is hostile (is an enemy) to us* [7.5]

Vocabulary 6

Add some verbs to your notebook. Allow a page for each conjugation (five in all) and then a sixth for a few irregular verbs which do not belong to any of the conjugations.

1st conjugation verbs are very regular and conform to a consistent pattern. One of the very few exceptions is the perfect of **dō, dare** (*give*), which is **dedī, dedistī**, etc:

amō,-āre,-āvī,-ātum *love*	**ōrō,-āre,-āvī,-ātum** *beg, plead*
creō,-āre,-āvī,-ātum *choose, elect*	**parō,-āre,-āvī,-ātum** *prepare*
dēligō,-āre,-āvī,-ātum *tie, bind*	**pugnō,-āre,-āvī,-ātum** *fight*
dō, dare, dedī, datum *give*	**sūdō,-āre,-āvī,-ātum** *sweat*
errō,-āre,-āvī,-ātum *wander, make a mistake*	**trucīdō,-āre,-āvī,-ātum** *slaughter, murder*
fugō,-āre,-āvī,-ātum *chase, put to flight*	
laudō,-āre,-āvī,-ātum *praise*	**vocō,-āre,-āvī,-ātum** *call, summon*
necō,-āre,-āvī,-ātum *kill*	

Look online for more 1st conjugation verbs which appear in the course (see p. 393).

Add these prepositions to your notebook:

ā (ab) [+ abl.] *by, from*	**in** [+ abl.] *in, on*
ad [+ acc.] *to, towards*	**inter** [+ acc.] *among, between*
ante [+ acc.] *before, in front of*	**per** [+ acc.] *through, across, by means of*
contrā [+ acc.] *against*	**post** [+ acc.] *after, behind*
cum [+ abl.] *with, together with*	**sine** [+ abl.] *without*
dē [+ abl.] *from, down from, concerning*	**sub** [+ acc.] *under, up to*
ē (ex) [+ abl.] *from, out of*	**sub** [+ abl.] *beneath, under, at the foot of*
in [+ acc.] *into, on to*	**trāns** [+ acc.] *across*

Exercises 6a

1. Fill each gap with a single word and translate your answer:
(a) cūr tū superbōs . . . . *{you love}*?
(b) ego sum taurus, sed numquam agricolam . . . . *{I have (never) chased}*.
(c) poēta ā Rōmānīs est . . . . *{praised}*.
(d) Graecōs nōn . . . . *{we do (not) love}*.
(e) ō Rōmānī, cūr semper litterās Graecōrum . . . . *{you praise}*?
(f) quis cēnam . . . . *{has prepared}*?
(g) Sullam . . . . *{we have praised}* sed nōn . . . . *{we do (not) love}*.

2. Translate:
(a) quid tū lībertō dedistī? — nihil lībertō datum est.
(b) ego magister cēnam nōn parāvī. — cēna ā servīs parāta est.
(c) vōs, ō Rōmānī, mē tribūnum creāvistis. — tē, ō tribūne, amāmus!
(d) fīliōs Brūtus sine lacrimīs necāvit. — cūr ā Brūtō necātī sunt?
(e) cūr miser servus sūdat? — dominus per agrōs cum flagellō errat.

3. Change the verbs into the equivalent *perfect* tense ending, and translate your answer:
(a) Sulla inimīcōs **necat**.
(b) servī in vīllā **sūdant**.
(c) quis lībertum in forō **ōrat**?
(d) cūr dominam Caeliī **amās**?

4. How do you account for the original Latin endings of *data* and *et cetera*?

The Republic under strain

Sulla made himself dictator and then had the senate publish a list of all his political and personal enemies who were to be put to death ('proscriptions'). These were principally friends and supporters of Marius, who himself had previously bumped off opponents if not in quite such a formalized way. There were rewards for those who aided this brutal policy and death for those who obstructed it. This brought peace of a sort.

By the 60s and 50s BC the political infighting was once again making for uncertain and dangerous times, not only for those in or near positions of power, but their supporters too, whose lives depended on the wellbeing of their *patronus*. The Roman system of patronage – *clientes* seeking help from a *patronus* and supporting him in return – ensured a good return in elections for aristocrats at the apex of this structure. Our word 'patron' is an adequate equivalent. Closer is Italian *padrone* (godfather). Latin temperament, rival families, frequent murders are a familiar picture. But the proscriptions were not the lawless killings of feuding gangs. The murders were carried out with almost constitutional formality, murder justified in law, by people operating levers of a government that headed a vast and still-growing empire. This political violence is the background to the beginning of the period we know as Classical Rome.

The character of Rome had changed from dominant city-state to the capital of the known world. The empire now included Spain, Gaul, Greece, Asia Minor and a tract of north Africa. With the power came an enormous revenue of wealth and resources. Imports flowed into the capital, some essential like corn, others lavish and luxurious, which critics thought decadent and enfeebling.

The business community was thriving on the back of this expanding empire. The *equestres* ('equestrians' or 'knights') were another class of people formally listed by the censors. Sometimes described as Rome's 'middle class', they were in fact among the very richest of the plebeians. Qualification in earlier days had been a horse for military service; it now depended on capital assets. An *equester* might seek office, or live largely at leisure guiding his business interests. And now was a good time for making money. *Equestres* were growing richer and thus politically more powerful, which the traditional channels did not always accommodate.

The concept of 'Rome' was broadening across the globe. The people who performed skilled services or made things – accountants, doctors, builders, architects, artists – for a hundred years or more had been imported from Greece and the east. When Caesar crossed the Rubicon with an army in north central Italy, that was taken as an invasion of the city itself. 'Roman' writers like Catullus, Livy and Virgil were all born on the northern side of the Rubicon. Others including Cicero, Horace and Ovid came from Italian towns, not Rome itself.

The day-to-day business of managing such a large state grew ever more challenging. The early city's relatively small community of patricians mucking along with the plebeians,

---

Reading notes

The genitive case can be 'subjective' or 'objective'. E.g.

> amor **Antōniī**
> *the love of Antony*

may be either subjective (Antony's love for something) or objective (the love others have for Antony). The objective genitive is sometimes better translated as 'for . . .':

> **imperiī** cupīdō crēvit
> *a desire for power grew* (or we might say: *a love of power . . .*) [6.2]

senators with the rest of the citizenry, was long gone. By the first century BC the shape of influence had changed. Now there were citizens at more than a day's journey from the city, powerful generals, vassal monarchs, provincial governors, and all around the empire local big cheeses to be flattered, bribed and where necessary coerced.

Government by annual magistrates topped by a pair of consuls was under some strain. Consuls would compete with each another for military success, which worked well enough for the growth of empire but less so for its management. Victories in battle turned heads in the forum; a competent administrator did not have the same appeal. The one-year term of office, which had been imposed as a check on power, passed too quickly to see the fruits of good planning; and even if prestige-hungry officials could cope with the kudos going to a successor, there were no guarantees the successor wouldn't cast the plans aside and start again. So the cohesion of the new empire began to creak as provinces suffered from inconsistent and short-lived directives.

To make matters worse for the senate, it started to lose control over the military. Armies were posted on the fringes of the empire at great distances from the capital and led by powerful and ambitious generals. Throughout the first century BC there were a number of civil conflicts: Sulla against Marius, Pompey against Caesar, Caesar's heirs against his assassins, and finally Antony against Octavian. Power struggles between aristocrats did not always impact on the lives of ordinary people, but these conflicts made for anxious, difficult and nasty times for almost everyone.

1.   Sallust reflects the pessimism and nostalgia of the first century BC:

primō magis ambitiō quam avāritia animōs hominum exercēbat.

Sallust, Conspiracy of Catiline 11

primō   at first
magis   rather
ambitiō [nom.]   ambition
quam   than
avāritia,-ae [f.]   greed
animus,-ī [m.]   mind
hominum [gen.pl.]   men, people
exercēbat   (s/he) exercised (the '-bat' ending signals another past tense, usually indicating
        a period of some duration; more on this to come later)

2.   Lavish imports and slave labour from the new territories fed growing appetites for luxury and ease. Some blamed the good times for undermining traditional virtues of austerity and simplicity.

primō pecūniae, deinde imperiī, cupīdō crēvit. avāritia fidem, probitātem, cēterāsque artēs bonās subvertit.

Sallust, Conspiracy of Catiline 10

Word order: 'cupīdō crēvit, primō pecūniae, deinde imperiī'
deinde   then, next

cupīdō [nom.; + gen.]   *desire (for)*
crēvit [perfect]   *(s/he, it) grew*
fidem [acc.]   *trust*
probitātem [acc.]   *honesty*
cēterus,-a-um   *the other*
artēs [f.; nom.pl./acc.pl.]   *arts, skills, practices*
subvertit [perfect]   *(s/he, it) ruined*

3.   The historian Livy was similarly gloomy.

nec vitia nostra nec remedia patī possumus.

Livy, *History of Rome* Preface

vitium,-ī [n.]   *vice*
remedium,-ī [n.]   *cure*
patī   *to suffer, endure*
possumus   *we are able*

4.   The classical period is remembered through its many writers, and in particular the prolific Cicero, a lawyer and statesman, whose speeches and personal letters contribute much to the inside story of the fall of the Republic. In 65 BC he stood for the consulship as a *novus homo*, having earned the respect of his peers through his oratory. A candidate for the other consulship was Catiline, who at that point faced charges of corruption from his time as governor in Africa. Cicero thought he should help him:

hōc tempore Catilīnam, competitōrem nostrum, dēfendere cōgitāmus. iūdicēs habēmus quōs voluimus, summā accūsātōris voluntāte.

Cicero, *Letters to Atticus* 1.2

hōc tempore   *at this time*
Catilīna,-ae [m.]   *Catiline*
competitōrem [m.; acc.]   *rival, fellow candidate*
dēfendere   *to defend*
cōgitō,-āre,-āvī,-ātum[1]   *consider, contemplate*
iūdicēs [nom.pl./acc.pl.]   *judges*
habēmus   *we have*
quōs [acc.pl.]   *whom*
voluimus [perfect]   *we wanted*
summus,-a,-um   *utmost*
accūsātōris [gen.]   *prosecutor*
voluntāte [f.; abl.]   *will, wish, good will*

---

1 Verbs whose forms have been explained will be given in their principal parts, e.g. 'cōgitō,-āre,-āvī,-ātum' is like 'amō,-āre,-āvī,-ātum'.

5. Cicero decided against taking the brief. Catiline managed to get himself acquitted but failed to become consul. He then sought power by more violent means. He had many supporters, particularly those in debt. Resentments had surfaced between the new wealthy and others who had bought into the new lavish lifestyles beyond their means. Catiline's promise to cancel debts was well received.

cūncta plēbs, novārum rērum studiō, Catilīnae incepta probābat.

Sallust, *Conspiracy of Catiline* 37

cūnctus,-a,-um   *all, whole, entire*
plēbs [f.; nom.]   *people*
rērum [gen.pl.]   *things* (with 'novus,-a,-um' = *revolution, political change*)
studium,-ī [n.; + gen.]   *desire (for), eagerness (for)*
inceptum,-ī [n.]   *initiative*
probābat   *(s/he, it) commended*

6. Catiline's initiatives gained some momentum. In 63 BC Cicero was consul and stood in his way.

neque intereā quiētus erat, sed omnibus modīs īnsidiās parābat Cicerōnī.

Sallust, *Conspiracy of Catiline* 26

intereā   *meanwhile*
quiētus,-a,-um   *inactive, quiet*
erat   *(s/he, it) was*
omnibus [take with a noun in the dative or ablative plural]   *all*
modīs [dat.pl./abl.pl.]   *ways*
īnsidiae,-ārum [f.; appears only in the plural]   *ambush*
parābat   *(s/he, it) was preparing, prepared*
Cicerōnī [dat.]   *Cicero*

7. Catiline enjoyed good relations with a number of leading men. He and his supporters were confident enough to attend meetings of the senate, which provoked the consul to confront him at such a meeting:

ō tempora, ō mōrēs! senātus haec intellegit, cōnsul videt: hic tamen vīvit. vīvit? immō vērō etiam in senātum venit. hīc, hīc sunt in nostrō numerō, patrēs cōnscrīptī. quotiēns mē cōnsulem interficere cōnātus es!

Cicero, *Against Catiline* 1.2,9,15

ō tempora   *what times!*
ō mōrēs   *what moral standards!*
senātus [nom.]   *senate*
haec [nom.pl./acc.pl.]   *these things*
intellegit   *(s/he) understands*

cōnsul: Cicero means himself
videt   *(s/he) sees*
hic   *this man*
tamen   *yet, still*
vīvit   *(s/he) lives*
immō vērō   *why!*
hīc   *here* (different from 'hic' above)
sunt: *'they'* are Catiline's supporters
patrēs cōnscrīptī [voc.]   *senators* ('patrēs' can mean *senators* as well as *fathers*, 'cōnscrīptī'
     = *enrolled, enlisted*)
quotiēns   *how many times*
cōnsulem [acc.]   *consul*
interficere   *to kill*
cōnātus es   *you (have) tried* (addressing Catiline)

8.   Catiline withdrew from Rome to gather support elsewhere. Cicero imprisoned five
      conspirators still in Rome and ordered their execution, without a trial. The rebellion
      was finally crushed in Italy and Catiline killed. Cicero considered his own actions little
      short of heroic:

rem pūblicam līberāvī. ego vītam omnium cīvium, quīnque
hominum āmentium ac perditōrum poenā, redēmī.

Cicero, In Defence of Sulla 33[1]

rem [acc.]   *thing, matter, issue*
pūblicus,-a,-um   *public* ('rēs pūblica' = *the Republic*)
līberō,-āre,-āvī,-ātum   *free, liberate*
omnium [take with a noun in the genitive plural]   *all, every*
cīvium [gen.pl.]   *citizens*
vītam omnium cīvium: we would say *the <u>lives</u> of all the citizens* or *the life of <u>every citizen</u>*
quīnque   *five*
hominum [gen.pl.]   *men*
āmentium [take with a noun in the genitive plural]   *crazed, demented*
perditōrum [take with a genitive plural as above]   *desperate*
poena,-ae [f.]   *punishment*
redēmī [perfect]   *I (have) saved*

9.   Cicero's consulship was the high point of his political career. In later life he seldom tired
      of talking about his success:

nōbīs rem pūblicam gubernantibus, nōnne togae arma
cessērunt?

Cicero, On Duties 1.77

nōbīs . . . gubernantibus   *with us* (i.e. *me*) *at the helm of* . . .
nōnne   *surely . . ., did not* . . . (expecting the answer 'yes')

1 Not the dictator but his nephew, who was accused of being one of Catiline's conspirators.

toga,-ae [f.]   *toga* (i.e. symbol of peaceful authority)
cessērunt [perfect]   *(they) yielded, submitted*

10. Cicero in fact was no general. He was an orator and intellectual, who believed that
     government should be in the hands of the senate, where policy was debated, consensus
     reached, and by virtue of its prestige, acted upon. But circumstances were changing. The
     protocol of restricted magistracies and power shared within the senate was repeatedly
     punctured by ambitious individuals. Pompey, a man with great prestige for his military
     leadership, was such an individual, but one Cicero believed had the best intentions for
     the Republic and whose good will should be cultivated. Not all the senators shared that
     view. In 60 BC the emerging Caesar took advantage of some bad feeling between Pompey
     and aristocrats in the senate to create an alliance with him. They formed an informal
     coalition along with the exceptionally wealthy Crassus and agreed to do nothing that
     would injure each other's interests. This 'triumvirate' was Caesar's initiative and showed
     his diplomatic skills, for Pompey and Crassus had fallen out after the slave rebellion of
     Spartacus in 71, when Pompey, on his return from a campaign in Spain, had finished off
     the slaves' army and stolen the credit for victory from Crassus, who had conducted most
     of the campaign. In 70 Pompey and Crassus had been consuls together.

Caesar Pompēiō Mārcum Crassum reconciliāvit, veterem
inimīcum ex cōnsulātū, quem summā discordiā simul
gesserant; ac societātem cum utrōque iniit.

Suetonius, Life of Julius Caesar 19

Caesar: nominative
reconciliō,-āre,-āvī,-ātum   *reconcile, appease* (*reconcile* object-noun in the accusative *to*
     another noun in the dative)
veterem [describes a noun in the accusative]   *former, previous, longstanding*
inimīcum: i.e. 'Mārcum Crassum'
ex [+ abl.]   *from*, or here *since*
cōnsulātū [abl.]   *consulship*
quem [acc.]   *which* (i.e. the consulship)
summus,-a,-um   *utmost, extreme*
discordia,-ae [f.]   *disagreement, strife*
simul   *together*
gesserant   *(they) had conducted, managed*
ac   *and*
societātem [acc.]   *political alliance, pact*
utrōque [abl.]   *each, both*
iniit [perfect]   *(s/he) entered*

11. Cicero, despite Caesar's efforts to win his support, was disappointed by this coalition,
     and especially Pompey's role in it. When Pompey was lukewarm about Cicero's success
     with Catiline – probably because he did not want to upset new friends – Cicero did not
     hide his resentment.

aliquam in tuīs litterīs grātulātiōnem exspectāvī.

Cicero, Letters to Friends and Family 5.7

aliquam [acc.]   *some*
litterae,-ārum [f.]   *letters, literature,* (epistolary) *letter*
grātulātiōnem [acc.]   *thanks*
exspectō,-āre,-āvī,-ātum   *expect*

Exercises 6b

1.   Translate:
(a)   prīmō vīnī, deinde cēnae, cupīdō crēvit.
(b)   cūr, ō amīce, Catilīnam dēfendere cōgitās?
(c)   ego ante equum tribūnī ductus sum.
(d)   servus cēnam parat Cicerōnī.

2.   Fill each gap with the correct Latin word, and translate:
(a)   magister semper puerīs īnsidiās . . . . {*prepares*}.
(b)   cūr captīvī in forō . . . . {*are sweating*}?
(c)   neque tē ego amō neque tū mē . . . . {*you love*}.
(d)   quid . . . . {*have you* [s.] *prepared*}?

3.   Translate:
(a)   quis tribūnum necāvit?
(b)   poēta nōn Rōmānōs sed Graecōs laudāvit.
(c)   Fulviane inimīcīs saeva est?
(d)   vīnum tuum amīcīs nostrīs dedimus.
(e)   praemium mihi datum est, sed errāvī!

4.   Change the verbs into the equivalent *present* tense ending, and translate your answer:
(a)   ō domina, cūr tū Sullam **laudāvistī**?
(b)   in vīllā cēnam sine servīs **parāvimus**.

5.   Translate into Latin:
      'Catullus, why did you love Clodia?'

6.   Find Latin ancestors in this chapter of *congratulations, impecunious, insidious, judicious, temporary* and *vital*.

— 7 —

Friends and enemies

Verbs: 2nd conjugation

The second group of verbs is very similar to the first except for the prevalent **e**:

habeō (= *I have, hold*), **habēre** (= *to have, hold*), **habuī** (= *I (have) had, (have) held*)

Present tense:

hab**eō**	*I have*
hab**ēs**	*you have* [s.]
hab**et**	*s/he, it* [or a nominative noun] *has*
hab**ēmus**	*we have*
hab**ētis**	*you have* [pl.]
hab**ent**	*they* [or a plural nominative noun] *have*

Perfect tense:

habu**ī**	*I (have) had*
habu**istī**	*you* [s.] *had*
habu**it**	*s/he, it* [or a nominative noun] *had*
habu**imus**	*we had*
habu**istis**	*you* [pl.] *had*
habu**ērunt**	*they* [or a plural nominative noun] *had*

The four principal parts of **habeō** are: **habeō, habēre, habuī, habitum**

Practice 7a
Change the verbs into the equivalent *perfect* tense ending, and translate your answer:
(a)   multōs servōs **habēmus**.
(b)   quis praemium **habet**?
(c)   taurum **habeō**.
(d)   pecūniamne **habēs**?
(e)   equōs taurōsque **habent**.

3rd declension nouns

Before you look closely at the 3rd declension nouns, review the 1st and 2nd declensions in the grammar tables on p. 356.

Remember that nouns are listed in dictionaries in two cases, the nominative and genitive. Knowing the genitive form is even more important with 3rd declension nouns. With **pater** (*father*) you can see how the stem changes in cases other than the nominative and vocative singular from **pater** to **patr-**. All the other cases share the stem of the genitive singular.

	singular	plural
N.	pater [m.]	patrēs
V.	pater	patrēs
A.	patrem	patrēs
G.	patris	patrum
D.	patrī	patribus
Ab.	patre	patribus

As before there are one or two overlaps: **patrēs** could be nominative, vocative or accusative plural; **patribus** could be dative or ablative plural.

The 3rd declension has many different nominative forms. Many of these nouns have an additional syllable in cases other than the nominative and vocative singular (e.g. **imāgō, imāginis**). As with **pater** above, many have minor changes to the stem (e.g. **dux, ducis**). So, to know a 3rd declension noun is to know both the nominative and the genitive forms. The genitive gives you the shape of the word in all cases outside the nominative and vocative singular.

Practice 7b

Translate each underlined word into one Latin word:
(a) with the <u>fathers</u>
(b) his mother loved his <u>father</u>
(c) I leave a gift for my <u>father</u>
(d) a meeting of the <u>fathers</u>
(e) a letter from my <u>father</u>
(f) the name of my <u>father</u>
(g) <u>fathers/elders/senators</u>, we respect you

singular						
	leader	citizen	consul	portrait, bust	city	wife
N.	dux (m.)	cīvis (m./f.)	cōnsul (m.)	imāgō (f.)	urbs (f.)	uxor (f)
V.	dux	cīvis	cōnsul	imāgō	urbs	uxor
A.	ducem	cīvem	cōnsulem	imāginem	urbem	uxōrem
G.	ducis	cīvis	cōnsulis	imāginis	urbis	uxōris
D.	ducī	cīvī	cōnsulī	imāginī	urbī	uxōrī
Ab.	duce	cīve (-ī)	cōnsule	imāgine	urbe	uxōre

plural

N.	duc**ēs**	cīv**ēs**	cōnsul**ēs**	imāgin**ēs**	urb**ēs**	uxōr**ēs**
V.	duc**ēs**	cīv**ēs**	cōnsul**ēs**	imāgin**ēs**	urb**ēs**	uxōr**ēs**
A.	duc**ēs**	cīv**ēs** (-**īs**)*	cōnsul**ēs**	imāgin**ēs**	urb**ēs** (-**īs**)*	uxōr**ēs**
G.	duc**um**	cīv**ium**	cōnsul**um**	imāgin**um**	urb**ium**	uxōr**um**
D.	duc**ibus**	cīv**ibus**	cōnsul**ibus**	imāgin**ibus**	urb**ibus**	uxōr**ibus**
Ab.	duc**ibus**	cīv**ibus**	cōnsul**ibus**	imāgin**ibus**	urb**ibus**	uxōr**ibus**

* Some 3rd declension nouns in the accusative plural may end either **-īs** or **-ēs** (**-īs** is the older form), e.g. **cīvīs** (*citizens*) for **cīvēs**, **artīs** for **artēs** [4.6]. These same nouns include an **i** in the genitive plural: **cīvi̱um**.

Practice 7c

1. Identify the ablative singular and the accusative plural of
   - (a) mīles, mīlitis [m.] *soldier*
   - (b) nox, noctis [f.] *night*
   - (c) senātor, senātōris [m.] *senator*
2. Fill the gaps:
   - (a) servus .... {*a portrait*} dominī facit.
   - (b) multōsne .... {*senators*} creāvit triumvir?
   - (c) tribūnus cum .... {*with the consul*} in forō errāvit.
   - (d) praemia .... {*to the citizens*} data sunt.
3. Review the Latin readings in Chapters 1–6 and identify ten nouns from the 3rd declension, and give their case and number.

Him, her and *them*

Our English personal pronouns change form according to their function. They are survivors of the case system of Old English:

subjects: *I, he, she, we, they*
objects: *me, him, her, us, them*

The Latin equivalent of the English *she* or *he* as subject is wrapped up in the verb's ending (**amat** = *s/he loves*). Sometimes separate Latin words for *he*, *she* or *they* appear in the nominative for clarification or emphasis. These will be explained on p. 170. You are more likely to meet them in other cases, especially as objects, e.g.:

eum	*him*
eam	*her*
eōs [m.], **eās** [f.]	*them*

If the pronoun refers to a person, then the gender will match the person's sex. If a thing or object, then the pronoun replicates the gender of the noun it stands for:

neque **litterās** Graecās didicī: parum placēbat **eās** discere
and I did not learn Greek letters: it did not appeal (to me) to study them [5.3]

(if we translate **litterās Graecās** as *Greek literature*, then the corresponding English pronoun will be *it*)

His and *her*

The genitive singular of **eum** and **eam** is **eius** (same for all genders). This is used to show possession (*his, her, its*). **Eius** can refer to anyone except the subject of the sentence:

> in triumphō Mariī ductus ante currum **eius** Iugurtha cum duōbus fīliīs et in carcere necātus est
> *in the triumph of Marius, Jugurtha was led before his chariot with his two sons and killed in prison* [5.7]

Eius tells us that the chariot belongs to Marius (the subject of the sentence is **Iugurtha**).

If the *his* or *her* (or *their*) refers to the subject of the sentence (and needs clarification or emphasis), then **suus,-a,-um** is used:

> Sulpicius indiciō servī **suī** ē vīllā retractus est
> *on the information of his own slave, Sulpicius was dragged back from the villa* [5.10]

As we have seen before, it is sometimes necessary to add *his* or *her* to our English version where Latin leaves it out (**māter fīlium amat** = *the mother loves her son*). If we read **māter fīlium eius amat** then it would not be her son, but someone else's. If **māter fīlium suum amat** then she loves her own son, perhaps to distinguish from someone else's, or to add emphasis, as in **Brūtus fīlium suum necat** (*Brutus kills his own son*).

Thus **suus** or **eius** is only used where the ownership needs clarification or emphasis. In the sentence about Marius' triumph above, there is no Latin word for *his* with **fīliīs**. It is obvious they are Jugurtha's.

Practice 7d

1. Whose chariot?
    in triumphō Mariī ductus ante currum suum Iugurtha cum duōbus fīliīs et in carcere necātus est.

2. Whose slave?
    (a) Iūlia nōn poētam sed servum eius amāvit.
    (b) Iūlia nōn poētam sed servum suum amāvit.

Vocabulary 7

Create a page in your notebook for these 2nd conjugation verbs:

dēbeō,-ēre,-uī,-itum   *owe, ought*
doceō,-ēre,-uī, doctum   *teach, show*
doleō,-ēre,-uī,-itum   *grieve*
exerceō,-ēre,-uī,-itum   *keep busy, occupy, work at*
faveō,-ēre, fāvī, fautum [+ dat.*]   *favour*
fleō,-ēre, flēvī, flētum   *weep*
habeō,-ēre, habuī, habitum   *have, hold*
iaceō,-ēre, iacuī, iacitum   *lie*
iubeō,-ēre, iussī, iussum   *order*
timeō,-ēre,-uī,-itum   *fear*
maneō,-ēre, mānsī, mānsum   *remain*

moneō,-ēre, monuī, monitum   *advise, warn*
pāreō,-ēre,-uī,-itum [+ dat.*]   *obey*
placeō,-ēre,-uī, placitum [2; + dat.*]   *please, satisfy*
rīdeō,-ēre, rīsī, rīsum   *laugh (at)*
sedeō,-ēre, sēdī, sessum   *sit*
taceō,-ēre, tacuī, tacitum   *be silent*
teneō,-ēre,-uī,-itum   *hold, keep, occupy*
videō,-ēre, vīdī, vīsum   *see*

* A few verbs take an object not in the accusative but in the dative (and even fewer in the ablative).

In Practice 7(c) you reviewed the 3rd declension nouns to appear so far. Here they are grouped in sub-patterns. Choose some for your notebook.

arx, arcis [f.]   *citadel*
coniūnx, coniugis [m./f.]   *husband, wife*
dux, ducis [m.]   *commander, leader,*
iūdex, iūdicis [m.]   *judge, juror*
nox, noctis [f.]   *night*
pāx, pācis [f.]   *peace, treaty*
rēx, rēgis [m.]   *king*
vōx, vōcis [f.]   *voice, speech, sound*

frāter, frātris [m.]   *brother*
māter, mātris [f.]   *mother*
pater, patris [m.]   *father, patrician, senator*

amor, amōris [m.]   *love, passion*
clāmor, clāmōris [m.]   *shout, cry*
senātor, senātōris [m.]   *senator*
uxor, uxōris [f.]   *wife*
victor, victōris [m.]   *conqueror, winner*

amāns, amantis [m./f.]   *a lover*
mōns, montis [m.]   *mountain*

ambitiō, ambitiōnis [f.]   *ambition*
obsidiō, obsidiōnis [f.]   *siege, blockade*

eques, equitis [m.]   *horseman, equestrian*
mīles, mīlitis [m.]   *soldier, army*

hūmānitās, hūmānitātis [f.]   *civilization*
lībertās, lībertātis [f.]   *freedom, liberty*
nōbilitās, nōbilitātis [f.]   *high rank, nobility*
voluntās, voluntātis [f.]   *wish, choice, inclination*

ars, artis [f.]   *art, skill, practice*
mors, mortis [f.]   *death*
pars, partis [f.]   *part*

mōs, mōris [f.]   *custom, habit, conduct, moral*

plēbs, plēbis [f.]   *people, masses*
urbs, urbis [f.]   *city*

homō, hominis [m.]   *man, person*
imāgō, imāginis [f.]   *portrait*

cīvis, cīvis [m.f.]   *citizen*

cōnsul, cōnsulis [m.]   *consul*
mulier, mulieris [f.]   *woman*

Caesar, Caesaris   *Caesar*
Cicerō, Cicerōnis   *Cicero*
Hannibal, Hannibalis   *Hannibal*

Look online for more 2nd conjugation verbs and 3rd declension nouns (see p. 393).

There are a number of Latin words for 'woman' or 'wife' as there are for 'man' or 'husband': **fēmina** is *woman* or *female*; and **mulier** is *woman*, similar to **fēmina**, but sometimes used in a patronizing, dismissive way (e.g. 8.1).

The standard word for *wife* is **uxor**, while **coniūnx** can be either *wife* or *husband*, i.e. *spouse*. There are two other words for husband: **vir** (*man, male, husband*) and **marītus**.

Homō (*man, person*) can represent both sexes, and in the plural *mankind*.

Exercises 7a
1.   Translate:
(a)   cūr tū flēs? tē rīdēre iubeō.
(b)   tuus marītus numquam tacuit!
(c)   Clōdiusne semper suae uxōrī pāret?
(d)   tribūnus clāmōrēs senātōrum nōn timet.
(e)   Fortūna mihi nōn favet.
(f)   nōbilitās mihi nova est et nunc sum cōnsul!
(g)   cōnsulī pārēre dēbēmus.

2.   Fill each gap with one word:
(a)   in terrā .... {*we lie*}.
(b)   Clōdius .... {*to the senators*} inimīcus est.
(c)   hominēsne .... {*the shouts*} Catilīnae timent?
(d)   cūr uxor .... {*of Caesar*} dolet?
(e)   servīsne .... {*s/he favours*} Fortūna?
(f)   cūr senātōrēs .... {*did they laugh*}? nōbilitās mihi nōn est nova.
(g)   tūne semper .... {*your father*} .... {*and mother*} pārēs?
(h)   cūr Catilīna cum .... {*with the senators*} .... {*and with the soldiers*} sedet?
(i)   Metellusne ab .... {*by his own wife* – use 'uxor'} suā occīsus est?

3.   In whose villa is the portrait?
(a)   poēta imāginem dominae in vīllā eius tenet.
(b)   poēta imāginem dominae in vīllā suā tenet.

4.   How does the original meaning of *decimate* differ from its popular use today?

Friends and enemies

Caesar was born a few years after Cicero, in or close to 100 BC. In early adulthood he survived some dangerous moments. He only just escaped Sulla's proscriptions, for his aunt had married Marius, Sulla's bitter rival, and in his teens he himself married Cornelia, daughter of Cinna, a close ally of Marius. During the 60s Caesar was elected quaestor, aedile, then praetor, and served as a governor in Spain in 61.

Caesar was clever, ambitious, and likeable. An engaging speaker, he charmed his way through his own circle and won wider affection by his public speeches and appearances. His

---

Reading notes

Where a noun (or pronoun) is followed by another noun which explains or describes it, the second noun will be in the same case as the first:

urbem Rōmam condidērunt Trōiānī
the Trojans founded the <u>city</u> (of) <u>Rome</u> [1.2]

hōc tempore **Catilīnam**, **competitōrem nostrum**, dēfendere cōgitāmus
at this time we are considering defending <u>Catiline, our fellow-candidate</u> [6.4]

Caesar Pompēiō **Mārcum Crassum** reconciliāvit **veterem inimīcum** ex cōnsulātū
Caesar reconciled <u>Marcus Crassus</u> to Pompey, a <u>longstanding enemy</u> since the consulship [6.10]

Caesar **Pompēiam** dūxit Quīntī Pompēī **fīliam**
Caesar took <u>Pompeia</u> (as wife), the <u>daughter</u> of Quintus Pompeius [7.1]

The second noun is said to be 'in apposition' to the first.

---

writing was praised by contemporaries, including Cicero. Although very little of his correspondence survives, we have his detailed account of the campaigns in Gaul (*De Bello Gallico*), and a few other works, including studies on literary style and the pronunciation of Latin, some of which he dictated on military campaign.

1.   In 68 BC Cornelia died in childbirth, and Caesar, mindful of the right connections, married Pompeia, granddaughter of Sulla.

Caesar in Cornēliae autem locum Pompēiam dūxit Quīntī Pompēī fīliam, Sullae neptem.

Suetonius, *Life of Julius Caesar* 6

autem   *however, and now*
dūxit   *(s/he) took, led, married*
neptis,-is* [f.]   *granddaughter*

2.   Caesar's early years were troubled by debt, and he was rescued by Crassus. He had a scare when his name was included in a list of Catiline's fellow conspirators by Quintus Curius, who had been voted a reward for being the first to give the plot away. Caesar was quick to make a defence and called on Cicero to testify that Caesar had himself informed Cicero of the plot. Caesar even managed to stop Curius receiving the reward.

Caesar, implōrātō Cicerōnis testimōniō, nē Curiō praemia darentur, effēcit.

Suetonius, *Life of Julius Caesar* 17

Caesar,-is [m.]   *Caesar*
implōrō,-āre,-āvī,-ātum   *invoke, call upon for one's assistance*
Cicerō,-ōnis [m.]   *Cicero*
testimōnium,-ī [n.]   *evidence*
implōrātō . . . testimōniō   *with the evidence of Cicero called upon (i.e. after he had appealed for
    Cicero's evidence)*
nē   *that . . . not*
darentur   *(they) should be given*
effēcit   *(s/he) brought about*

3.   Publius Clodius was a young supporter of Caesar, and a live wire and prankster. He also
    had a liking for Pompeia, Caesar's wife, who in 62 BC was hosting the women-only
    festival of *Bona Dea*. Clodius decided to dress up as a woman and gatecrash the festival.
    He was caught.

Clōdius cum veste muliebrī dēprehēnsus est domī Caesaris.

Cicero, *Letters to Atticus* 1.12

vestis,-is [f.]   *clothes*
muliebrī [describes a noun in the dative or ablative]   *womanly, of a woman*

dēprehēnsus est   *(he) was discovered, caught*
domī   *at home, at the house* (this is the seldom used 'locative' case: see Ch.10)
Caesar,-aris [m.]   *Caesar*

4. Clodius was accused of sacrilege. At his trial in 61 Caesar offered no evidence against him; but he divorced Pompeia.

Caesar, interrogātus cūr repudiāsset uxōrem, 'quoniam,' inquit, 'meī tam suspīciōne quam crīmine carēre dēbent.'

Suetonius, *Life of Julius Caesar* 74

interrogō,-āre,-āvī,-ātum   *ask, question*
cūr   *why*
repudiāsset   *(s/he) had rejected, divorced*
uxor,-ōris [f.]   *wife*
quoniam   *since*
inquit   *(s/he) said*
meus,-a,-um   *my* (meī,-ōrum = *my people*)
tam . . . quam   *as much . . . as*
suspīciō,-ōnis [f.]   *suspicion*
crīmine [abl.]   *crime, charge*
carēre [+ abl.]   *be without, lack* (one of a very few verbs that take an object in the ablative)
dēbeō,-ēre,-uī,-itum   *owe, ought*

5. Cicero did give evidence. Clodius told the court he had been out of town at the time of the *Bona Dea*. He had in fact visited Cicero's house in Rome during this time, and Cicero said so before the jury. The story was that Terentia, Cicero's wife, disliked the Clodii because she thought Clodia, the sister of Clodius, was after her husband. In humiliating Clodius, Cicero may have placated his wife but he made a dangerous enemy. Although Clodius was acquitted, by bribery most likely, the damage was done. Cicero expected trouble.

Clōdius inimīcus nōbīs. Pompēius cōnfirmat Clōdium nihil esse factūrum contrā mē. mihi perīculōsum est crēdere; ad resistendum mē parō.

Cicero, *Letters to Atticus* 2.21

nōbīs [dat.]   *us*
Clōdius . . . nōbīs: the verb is understood ('est')
cōnfirmō,-āre,-āvī,-ātum   *assure, reassure*
Clōdium esse factūrum   *that Clodius will do*
perīculōsus,-a-um   *dangerous*
crēdere   *to believe*
ad resistendum   *for resistance*
parō,-āre,-āvī,-ātum   *prepare*

6. Cicero hoped for support from Pompey, who failed to convince him that Clodius was
    not a threat.

    ## Pompēius dē Clōdiō iubet nōs esse sine cūrā.

    Cicero, *Letters to Atticus* 2.24

    nōs [nom./acc.]   *we, us*
    esse   *to be*
    sine [+ abl.]   *without*
    cūra,-ae [f.]   *care, anxiety*

7. In 59 Caesar was consul. The other consul was Bibulus, the candidate pushed forward
    by the aristocrats in the senate. Caesar – now in cahoots with Crassus and Pompey –
    ignored his partner to the point where it became a joke. Documents appeared with
    spoof signatories . . .

    ## . . . nōn Caesare et Bibulō, sed Iūliō et Caesare cōnsulibus.

    Suetonius, *Life of Julius Caesar* 20

    cōnsul,-is [m.]   *consul*
    A et B cōnsulibus   *with A and B as consuls (in the consulship of A and B)*

8. Clodius[1] stood for a tribuneship. He could then bring to law his initiative to punish
    magistrates for putting citizens to death without a trial: his target was Cicero. But
    Clodius faced an obstacle to his candidature. He came from a patrician family, and so
    was blocked from standing as *tribunus plebis*. The solution – adoption into a plebeian
    family – came with Caesar's help.

    ## Clōdium, frūstrā iam prīdem ā patribus ad plēbem
    ## trānsīre nītentem, Caesar trānsdūxit.

    Suetonius, *Life of Julius Caesar* 20

    Word order: 'Caesar trānsdūxit Clōdium nītentem frūstrā iam prīdem trānsīre ā patribus
        ad plēbem'
    frūstrā   *in vain*
    iam prīdem   *for a long time now*
    patribus: could mean *fathers, senators* or *patricians*
    plēbs,-is [f.]   *the plebs, the plebeians*
    trānsīre   *to cross*
    nītentem [the noun doing this is in the accusative singular]   *striving*
    trānsdūxit   *(s/he) transferred, brought across*

---

1 Clōdius/Claudius: the spelling of 'Clodius' instead of 'Claudius' probably derives from this switch. The 'o' for 'au'
    spelling was evident in other parts of Italy and on the streets in Rome. Plautus the playwright, born in central Italy
    in the mid-third century BC, changed his name from Plotus on arrival in Rome – possibly a comic hypercorrection.

9.   In 59 Caesar married Calpurnia, daughter of Lucius Piso, who was elected to succeed
      him in the consulship (58). And he betrothed his own daughter, Julia, to Pompey, who
      was six years older than Caesar himself.

Caesar Calpurniam Pīsōnis fīliam dūxit uxōrem, suamque Iūliam Gnaeō Pompeiō collocāvit.

Suetonius, Life of Julius Caesar 21

Pīsō,-ōnis [m.]   *Piso*
suus,-a,-um: understand a repetition of 'fīliam' with 'suam'
collocō,-āre,-āvī,-ātum   *place, settle* (a woman) *in marriage to* (look for a husband in the
     dative)

10.   Once his affairs in Rome seemed secure, Caesar started on a military campaign in Gaul,
      which lasted for much of the 50s. Success would bring even more wealth and power to
      his countrymen, not least to himself. Pompey and Piso supported his taking the
      command.

socerō igitur generōque suffrāgantibus, ex omnī prōvinciārum cōpiā Galliās ēlēgit.

Suetonius, Life of Julius Caesar 22

socer, socerī [m.]   *father-in-law*
gener, generī [m.]   *son-in-law* ('socer' and 'gener' decline[1] like 'puer')
igitur   *therefore, accordingly*
suffrāgantibus [the persons doing this will be in the dative or ablative]   *supporting*
omnī [dat./abl.]   *all, whole*
cōpia,-ae [f.]   *abundance, supply*
prōvincia,-ae [f.]   *province, provincial command*
Gallia,-ae [f.]   *Gaul* (the plural 'Galliās' is used because there were two Gauls: 'Gallia
     Cisalpīna', i.e. this side of the Alps, what is now northern Italy, and 'Gallia
     Trānsalpīna', the other side of the Alps, i.e. modern France)
ēlēgit   *(s/he) chose*

11.   Caesar was a very successful general. He reduced Gaul – broadly modern France and
      Belgium – to the status of a province. Additionally he made incursions into Germany,
      and two trips to Britain in 55 and 54 BC.

Germānōs, quī trāns Rhēnum incolunt, Caesar prīmus Rōmānōrum ponte fabricātō aggressus maximīs affēcit clādibus; aggressus est et Britannōs īgnōtōs.

Suetonius, Life of Julius Caesar 25

Germānī,-ōrum [m.]   *Germans*
quī [nom.]   *who*

---

1 To 'decline' a noun is to list the case-endings.

Rhēnus,-ī [m.]   *Rhine*
incolunt   *(they) live*
pōns, pontis [m.]   *bridge*
fabricātus,-a,-um   *built, constructed*
aggressus,-a,-um   *having attacked* (i.e. *he attacked and . . .*)
maximus,-a,-um   *very great*
affēcit   *(s/he) oppressed, afflicted*
clādēs,-is [f.]   *disaster*
aggressus est   *he attacked* (looks like it should mean *was attacked* but doesn't)
et   *and, even, also*
Britannī,-ōrum [m.]   *Britons*
īgnōtus,-a,-um   *unknown*

12.   Meanwhile in 58 BC Clodius was tribune. Cicero knew what was coming, and he sought help from Pompey but none came. Under pressure from Clodius he withdrew into exile across the Adriatic to Greece, from where he reveals his despair to his friend Atticus:

utinam illum diem videam, cum tibi agam grātiās quod mē vīvere coēgistī!

Cicero, Letters to Atticus 3.3

utinam   *if only*
illum [take with a noun in the accusative]   *that*
diem [acc.]   *day*
videam   *I may see*
cum   *when*
agam grātiās [+ dat.]   *I may give thanks*
quod   *because*
vīvere   *to live*
coēgistī   *you compelled*

13.   To his wife Terentia he was more upbeat. The tribunes-elect for 57 and a consul-elect, Lentulus, were supportive, he hoped.

sed tamen, sī omnēs tribūnōs plēbis habēmus, sī Lentulum tam studiōsum quam vidētur, sī vērō etiam Pompēium et Caesarem, nōn est dēspērandum.

Cicero, Letters to Friends and Family 14.1

sed tamen   *but still*
omnēs [nom.pl./acc.pl.]   *all, every*
tribūnōs, Lentulum, Pompēium, Caesarem: all are objects of 'habēmus'
studiōsus,-a,-um   *devoted, supportive*
tam . . . quam   *as . . . as*
vidētur   *(s/he, it) seems*
vērō   *indeed*
est dēspērandum   *it is to be despaired*, i.e. *all hope has gone*

Exercises 7b

1. Identify the case and number of each underlined word:
(a) **clāmōre** incendunt caelum.
(b) centum creat **senātōrēs**.
(c) Porsenna ingentī urbem **obsidiōne** premēbat.
(d) Hannibal **mīlitibus** Ītaliam ostendit.
(e) populō Rōmānō numquam **scrīptōrum** cōpia fuit.
(f) ō miserī, quae tanta īnsānia, **cīvēs**?

2. Translate:
(a) nunc magis pecūnia quam lībertās animōs senātōrum exercet.
(b) pōns ab Hannibale fabricātus est.
(c) agricola servōs iussit dē taurō esse sine cūrā.
(d) Sulla praemium servō prōmissum tenuit.
(e) pecūniam amīcōs etiam mīlitēs habuimus.
(f) cūr uxōrēs semper suīs marītīs pārent?

3. Put the underlined verbs into the equivalent *perfect* tense ending, and translate your answer:
(a) ego neque pecūniam neque imāginēs **habeō**.
(b) senātōrēs **flent** sed nōn **dolent**.
(c) Fortūna nōn **dolet** sed **rīdet**.
(d) cūr cum Catilīnā **sedēs**?
(e) ego cōnsul Catilīnam in urbe **videō**.

4. Put the underlined verbs into the equivalent *present* tense ending, and translate your answer:
(a) quid animum Clōdiī **exercuit**?
(b) mīlitēs Hannibalis in monte **vīdimus**.
(c) cūr **doluistī**? – nōn **doluī**, ego **rīsī**.

5. Whose wife is 'uxor'?
(a) Clōdius et Caesarem et uxōrem suam amāvit.
(b) Clōdius et Caesarem et uxōrem eius amāvit.

Civil war

3rd declension nouns (neuter)

There are neuter nouns belonging to the 3rd declension which, as other neuter nouns, have the same endings in the nominative and accusative cases, and the ending **-a** in the nominative and accusative plural. Like other 3rd declension nouns the stems of these nouns change:

	body	*name*	*head*
singular			
N.	corpus	nōmen	caput
V.	corpus	nōmen	caput
A.	corpus	nōmen	caput
G.	corpor**is**	nōmin**is**	capit**is**
D.	corpor**ī**	nōmin**ī**	capit**ī**
Ab.	corpor**e**	nōmin**e**	capit**e**
plural			
N.	corpor**a**	nōmin**a**	capit**a**
V.	corpor**a**	nōmin**a**	capit**a**
A.	corpor**a**	nōmin**a**	capit**a**
G.	corpor**um**	nōmin**um**	capit**um**
D.	corpor**ibus**	nōmin**ibus**	capit**ibus**
Ab.	corpor**ibus**	nōmin**ibus**	capit**ibus**

Up to this point the ending **-us** has belonged to nouns or adjectives like **servus** or **bonus**. However, the **-us** ending of nouns like **corpus** represents both the nominative *and* accusative. So after all your hard work with **taurus** and his friends, a word ending **-us** might in fact be the object. You have met one already, **scelus,-eris** (*crime*):

> servus ob **scelus** dē Saxō dēiectus est
> [accusative after **ob**]
> *because of the crime the slave was thrown down from the Rock* [5.10]

Practice 8a

Translate each underlined word into one Latin word:

(a) I saw the bodies
(b) a list of names
(c) they lifted the body
(d) I counted the heads
(e) in the name of Iulius
(f) I heard the name
(g) on the bodies

Nouns in dictionaries

Nouns are listed in dictionaries in two cases, the nominative and genitive. You need both forms to be sure of the declension. The genitive shows you the stem of the word in cases other than the nominative and vocative. This is particularly important for 3rd declension nouns, but also nouns like **magister, magistrī**. And remember to note the gender; 3rd declension genders are less obvious than the first two declensions.

The genitive singular **-is** ending is exclusive to the 3rd declension, and *all* 3rd declension nouns have it.

'3rd declension' adjectives

Adjectives like **bonus** share endings with 1st and 2nd declension nouns (**servus, puella, vīnum**). There are a number of adjectives which have endings similar to the 3rd declension, with no difference between the masculine and feminine endings:

Practice 8b

Fill the gaps:

(a) multa sunt .... {*crimes*} Catilīnae.

(b) fugit .... {*time*}.

(c) .... {*the body*} .... {*of the consul*} vīdistī?

Practice 8c

Give (i) the declension of each noun (ii) the ablative singular (iii) the accusative plural of:

(a) tempus,-oris

(b) equus,-ī

(c) urbs, urbis

(d) scelus,-eris

(e) flūmen,-inis

(f) nox, noctis

---

	all, every		*fortunate*		*huge, immense*		*old, longstanding*	
sing.	m. & f.	neuter	m. & f.	neuter	m. & f.	neuter	m. & f.	neuter
N./V.	omnis	omne	fēlīx	fēlīx	ingēns	ingēns	vetus	vetus
A.	omnem	omne	fēlīcem	fēlīx	ingentem	ingēns	veterem	vetus
G.	omnis		fēlīcis		ingentis		veteris	
D.	omnī		fēlīcī		ingentī		veterī	
Ab.	omnī		fēlīcī		ingentī		vetere	
pl.								
N./V.	omnēs	omnia	fēlīcēs	fēlīcia	ingentēs	ingentia	veterēs	vetera
A.	omnēs/-īs	omnia	fēlīcēs	fēlīcia	ingentēs/-īs	ingentia	veterēs	vetera
G.	omnium		fēlīcium		ingentium		veterum	
D.	omnibus		fēlīcibus		ingentibus		veteribus	
Ab.	omnibus		fēlīcibus		ingentibus		veteribus	

They are all similar: **omnis** and **ingēns** have an alternative accusative plural **-īs**; the ablative singular of **vetus** is **-e**, not **-ī** as for the others; and note the neuter singular **omne**, which looks temptingly like an ablative singular e.g. **urbe**:

vigilāre **leve** est, pervigilāre **grave** est
it is trifling to lie awake, but to lie awake all night is serious [19.6]

Adjectives are listed in the different genders of their nominative forms, e.g. **bonus,-a,-um**. For adjectives like **omnis** that means only two forms (**omnis, omne**), and **fēlīx** only one.

omnis,-e	*every, all*	**īnfēlīx**	*unfortunate*
dulcis,-e	*sweet*	**ingēns**	*huge, immense*
gravis,-e	*serious*	**pudēns**	*modest, bashful*
levis,-e	*light, trifling*	**impudēns**	*shameless*
trīstis,-e	*sad*	**vetus**	*old, longstanding*
fēlīx	*fortunate, happy*		

Practice 8d

1. Fill the gaps:
    (a) Clōdia .... {*the name*}
    .... {*of the sad poet*} nōn audit,
    sed cum tribūnīs .... {*shameless*} errat.
    (b) dominus .... {*to the fortunate*} agricolae taurum
    .... {*huge*}, inimīcum ....
    {*longstanding*}, reconciliāvit.

2. Identify the case and number of each underlined word:
    (a) cum **ingentī** terrōre populus in forum fugit.
    (b) Cloelia **omnēs** ad propinquōs restituit.
    (c) Caesar ex **omnī** prōvinciārum cōpiā Galliās ēlēgit.
    (d) sunt in illō numerō doctī, **pudentēs** et etiam **impudentēs**, **levēs**.

The endings of **ingēns** are used for adjectives made from verbs, called the present participle (more on this to come later on p. 261), both **-ēns** and **-āns**:

timeō Danaōs et dōna **ferentīs**   [accusative plural, agreeing with 'Danaōs']
I fear Greeks even bearing gifts [4.13]

Possessive adjectives

You have already met the possessive adjectives in ones and twos:

Suus,-a,-um means *his* or *her* or *their* depending on the subject (see p. 78). If *his* or *her* or *their* refers to someone other than the subject, the genitive of a pronoun is used, typically **eius**, *of him, of her, of it* (i.e. *his, her, its*), and the plural **eōrum** [m./n.] and **eārum** [f.] (*of them*) for *their*.

meus,-a,-um	*my* (voc.masc.sing.: **mī**)
tuus,-a,-um	*your* [s.]
suus,-a,-um	*his, her, their*
noster, nostra, nostrum	*our*
vester, vestra, vestrum	*your* [pl.]

As in Spanish, French and other ex-Latin languages, the gender is established by the gender of the noun which the possessive adjective agrees with (and not by the gender of the person referred to):

> **suam** fīliam Iūliam Gnaeō Pompeiō collocāvit
> *he betrothed his own daughter Julia to Gnaeus Pompēius* [7.9]

Practice 8e

1. Whose dinner is it?
   (a) servus Cicerōnis suam cēnam nōn parāvit.
   (b) servus Cicerōnis cēnam eius nōn parāvit.

2. Fill each gap with one word:
   (a) Clōdia marītum .... {*her*} nōn amat.
   (b) Sulla .... {*his*} imāginēs laudat.
   (c) Marius neque Sullam neque.................... {*his*, i.e. Sulla's} imāginēs laudat.

Vocabulary 8
Start a list for 3rd declension neuter nouns:

corpus, corporis *body*		**nōmen, nōminis** *name*	
facinus, facinoris *crime*		**agmen, agminis** *crowd, throng, troop*	
frīgus, frīgoris *cold, chill*		**carmen, carminis** *poem, song*	
fūnus, fūneris *death, funeral*		**crīmen, crīminis** *crime, charge, offence*	
lītus, lītoris *shore*		**flūmen, flūminis** *river*	
opus, operis *work*		**līmen, līminis** *threshold, doorway*	
scelus, sceleris *crime, wickedness*		**lūmen, lūminis** *light*	
tempus, temporis *time*			

Start a list for 3rd declension adjectives. Include the ones which are listed earlier in the chapter and add these:

brevis,-e *brief, short*	**turpis,-e** *disgraceful*
cīvīlis,-e *civil*	**ūtilis,-e** *useful, suitable*
facilis,-e *easy*	
familiāris,-e *domestic, family, private*	**atrōx (atrōc-)** *fierce, repulsive*
fortis,-e *brave, strong*	**ferōx (ferōc-)** *bold, spirited, headstrong*
humilis,-e *humble, insignificant*	**ultrīx (ultrīc-)** *avenging*
mīrābilis,-e *wonderful, extraordinary*	**dēmēns** *crazy, foolish*
mollis,-e *soft*	**prūdēns** *knowing, experienced, wise*
mortālis,-e *mortal*	**imprūdēns** *without knowing, unwitting*
nōbilis,-e *noble*	**sapiēns** *wise*
terribilis,-e *terrible*	

Look online for more of these adjectives or more 3rd declension neuter nouns (see p. 393).

All these words share the meaning of offence or misdemeanour:

crīmen,-inis [n.]   *accusation, charge, crime, offence*
culpa,-ae [f.]   *error, fault, failure, blame, guilt*
dēlictum,-ī [n.]   *fault, offence, wrong*
facinus,-oris [n.]   *deed, act, misdeed, crime, outrage*
flāgitium,-ī [n.]   *shameful act, disgrace*
peccātum,-ī [n.]   *fault, mistake, transgression, sin*
scelus,-eris [n.]   *evil deed, wicked act, crime*

One word seems to cap them all for its sense of outrage: **nefās** is a neuter noun with a single unchanging ending and means *a deep wrong, a sacrilege, a monstrous thing*. The positive form also appears, often translated as an adjective: **fās** (*right, proper, acceptable to the gods*).

Exercises 8a

1.   Translate:
(a)   mortālibusne dī favent? ['dī' = 'deī']
(b)   agricola fortis est ingentī corpore.
(c)   Pompēius tua contemnit et mea carmina laudat.
(d)   cūr poētae semper veterēs mōrēs laudant?
(e)   cūr dēmēns in forō errat cum muliere turpī?
(f)   suntne Sabīnae fēlīcēs?
(g)   Marius et Sulla inimīcī sunt veterēs.

2.   Fill each gap and translate:
(a)   .... {facilis,-e} est opus.
(b)   cūr cum captīvīs .... {trīstis,-e} sedēmus?
(c)   .... {terribilis,-e} est Catilīnae facinus.
(d)   carmina .... {mīrābilis,-e} in forō audīta sunt.
(e)   carmina nōn .... {ūtilis,-e} sed .... {dulcis,-e} sunt.
(f)   domina nostra ūnō .... {carmen,-inis} nōn contenta est.

3. Translate:
(a) ego amīcōs atrōcēs Clodiī nōn amō.
(b) mīrābilia vīdimus.
(c) in illō numerō sunt multī dēmentēs, turpēs, terribilēs.
(d) dulcis domina tua, mea est gravis et trīstis.
(e) agmen mulierum in forō vīsum est.
(f) Britannīne atrōcēs dēmentēsque sunt?
(g) sapientēs numquam taurōs fugāvērunt.

4. Fill the gap with the right form of **irreparābilis,-e**, and translate (with help from the vocabularies at the end of the book when you need it):

    fugit .... tempus.

Civil war

Rome was a dangerous place to be at this time. Organized gangs roamed the streets under the direction of Clodius and others. While Cicero was in exile, Pompey himself became a target for Clodius's intimidating politics. So in 57 BC Pompey pressed for Cicero's recall, but Clodius, who had already burned down Cicero's houses, refused. Then there was a change in popular feeling. Plutarch, who wrote biographies of many of the leading men of these times (in Greek), tells us that the senate ground to a halt and refused any business until Cicero returned. It went to the popular assembly who voted overwhelmingly for his repatriation.

> **Reading notes**
>
> As you progress through the course you will meet more extended pieces of Latin, including lines of verse where the word order is pulled around by the rhythm, sequence of ideas and other nuances at the play of the poet. The word order of more challenging quotations is rearranged in the notes to help you translate them. Once you have the meaning, it is imperative to read the original lines again, in their right order!

In 54 BC the triumvirate was weakened by the death in childbirth of Julia, Pompey's wife and Caesar's daughter. In the following year it all but collapsed with the death of Crassus and the annihilation of his army at Carrhae in the east, at the hands of the Parthians. Caesar continued to flourish. His successes in Gaul added greatly to his prestige and wealth. He was generous with gifts to build good will, but his peers remained nervous of his popularity at home and of his soldiers abroad, who were flushed with victory and devoted to their general.

1. On his return from exile Cicero renewed his battles with the Clodii. In 56 BC he defended a client by humiliating Clodia, the source of the accusations, a woman labelled by Cicero as a seductress, reveller and drunk:

    rēs est omnis in hāc causā nōbīs, iūdicēs, cum Clōdiā,
    muliere nōn sōlum nōbilī sed etiam nōtā. dē quā ego nihil
    dīcam nisi dēpellendī crīminis causā.

    Cicero, *In Defence of Caelius* 31

rēs [nom.]   *thing, matter, issue*
hāc [abl.fem.]   *this*
causa,-ae [f.]   *cause, case*
nōbīs [dative of possession after 'est']   *us*
iūdex,-icis [m.]   *judge, juror*
mulier,-is [f.]   *woman*
sōlum   *only*
nōbilis,-e   *noble, well-born*
nōtus,-a,-um   *well-known, notorious*
dē [+ abl.]   *concerning*
quā [abl.fem.]   *which, who*
dīcam   *I shall say*
nisi   *unless, except*
dēpellendī crīminis causā   *for the sake of throwing out the charge*

2. The promise to limit his defence to the particular case is a rhetorical sleight of hand. A sentence or two later Cicero mentions his own bad relationship . . .

. . . cum istīus mulieris virō – frātre voluī dīcere; semper hīc errō.

Cicero, In Defence of Caelius 32

istīus [genitive singular]   *that*
frāter,-tris [m.]   *brother*
voluī [perfect]   *I wanted* (here: *I meant*)
dīcere   *to say*
hīc   *here, at this point*

3. And claims he does not want to pick a quarrel with a woman, especially . . .

. . . cum eā quam omnēs semper amīcam omnium potius quam cuiusquam inimīcam putāvērunt.

Cicero, In Defence of Caelius 32

eā [abl.]   *her*
quam [f.acc.]   *who(m)* (can also mean *than* – as later in the sentence)
omnēs: if there is no noun for the adjective to agree with, translate 'omnēs' as *all people, everyone*
amīca,-ae [f.]   *friend, girlfriend*
omnium [gen.pl.]: see 'omnēs' above
potius quam   *rather than*
cuiusquam [gen.]   *anyone*
putō,-āre,-āvī,-ātum   *think, consider*

4. In 52 BC Clodius and his followers clashed with a gang led by Milo just outside Rome. Clodius was injured, taken to an inn, found by Milo's men and beaten to death. Pompey and Cicero had both been supportive of Milo in his quarrels with Clodius, and Cicero now tried (and failed) to convince the judges that Milo had been acting in self-defence:

īnsidiātōrī vērō et latrōnī quae potest īnferrī iniūsta nex?

Cicero, *In Defence of Milo* 10

īnsidiātor,-ōris [m.]   *cut-throat, mugger, bandit*
vērō   *indeed*
latrō,-ōnis [m.]   *robber*
quae [take with a noun in the nominative feminine]   *what . . . ?*
potest   *(s/he, it) is able, can*
īnferrī [+ dat.]   *to be committed against, inflicted upon*
iniūstus,-a,-um   *unjust*
nex, necis [f.]   *(violent) death*

5.   It was a nervous performance by Cicero in front of the two hostile factions and Pompey's soldiers sent to keep order. Clodius' wife, Fulvia, spoke at the trial, a granddaughter of the murdered tribune Gaius Gracchus. She was more active in politics than most women of her time. Cicero argues that when Clodius bumped into Milo he was prepared for a fight, for he didn't have his usual companions and baggage – including his wife. This sideways swipe at Clodius always having Fulvia at his side shows she was not afraid to be seen in public.

Clōdius est expedītus, in equō, nūllā raedā, nūllīs impedimentīs, nūllīs Graecīs comitibus, ut solēbat; sine uxōre, quod numquam ferē.

Cicero, *In Defence of Milo* 10

est expedītus   *(he) was unimpeded, unencumbered*
nūllus,-a,-um   *no, not any*
raeda,-ae [f.]   *carriage*
impedīmenta,-ōrum [n.]   *baggage*
comes,-itis [m./f.]   *companion*
ut   *as*
solēbat   *(s/he) was accustomed*
quod [nom./acc.]   *which* (after 'quod' your translation will need a verb like *happened* or *was*)
ferē   *almost*

6.   In 50 BC the majority of the senate wanted Caesar to give up his command in Gaul. Caesar realized his best prospects lay with his soldiers lined up behind him. At the River Rubicon he paused before crossing it with his army.

Caesar paulum cōnstitit, et conversus ad proximōs, 'etiam nunc,' inquit, 'regredī possumus; quod sī ponticulum trānsierimus, omnia armīs agenda erunt.'

Suetonius, *Life of Julius Caesar* 31

paulum   *briefly*
cōnstitit [perfect]   *(s/he) stopped*
conversus [understand 'est']   *he turned round*

proximī,-ōrum [m.]   *those nearest (to him)*
regredī   *to go back*
possumus   *we are able, we can*
quod sī   *because if, but if, now if*
ponticulus,-ī [m.]   *little bridge*
trānsierimus   *we cross*
omnia [n.pl.]: if no noun with 'omnia', then it means *all things, everything*
agenda erunt   *will have to be resolved, settled*

7.   Caesar kept up diplomatic overtures to those with him and against him, including Cicero:

in prīmīs ā tē petō ut tē videam, ut tuō cōnsiliō, grātiā, dīgnitāte, ope omnium rērum ūtī possim.

Cicero, *Letters to Atticus* 9.6a [Caesar to Cicero]

in prīmīs   *first of all*
petō   *I seek*
ut   *that, so that*
videam   *I may see*
cōnsilium,-ī [n.]   *advice*
grātia,-ae [f.]   *influence*
dīgnitās,-tātis [f.]   *position*
ops, opis [f.]   *support*
rērum [gen.pl.]   *things, kinds*
ūtī [+ abl.]   *to use, to profit by, to benefit from* (look for an object or objects in the ablative)
possim   *I may be able to*

8.   Cicero courteously reminded Caesar he had obligations to Pompey. He distrusted Caesar's populist tactics, but he did not commit himself wholeheartedly to the senate and Pompey. He remained anxious for his beloved Republic: Marius and Sulla had shown what bloodletting would follow a deep schism in power.

rē pūblicā nihil mihi est cārius.

Cicero, *Letters to Friends and Family* 2.15

cārius   *dearer*
rē pūblicā [abl.]   *than the Republic*

9.   Caesar presses for his neutrality at least:

quid virō bonō et bonō cīvī magis convenit quam abesse ā cīvīlibus contrōversiīs?

Cicero, *Letters to Atticus* 10.8b [Caesar to Cicero]

magis   *more*
convenit   *it is suitable, becoming*
quam   *than*

abesse   *to be absent, to be far from*
cīvīlis,-e   *civil, political, public*
contrōversia,-ae [f.]   *quarrel, dispute*

10.   In 49 BC, without much conviction, Cicero joined Pompey in Greece. Caesar crossed
the Adriatic too, with his army. The battle of Pharsalus in 48 was decisive: Pompey fled
to Egypt, where at the prompting of the regent Pothinus, Ptolemy XIII had him
murdered.

Caesar in Macedoniam trānsgressus Pompēium ad extrēmum Pharsālicō proeliō fūdit et fugientem Alexandrēam persecūtus est.

Suetonius, *Life of Julius Caesar* 35

Word order: 'Caesar trānsgressus in Macedoniam fūdit Pompēium ad extrēmum
Pharsālicō proeliō et persecūtus est (Pompēium) fugientem Alexandrēam'
trānsgressus,-a,-um   *having crossed* (as with 'conversus' in no.6 the meaning is
not having been ... but *having* ...; there are a few like this to be seen later, on
p. 188)
ad extrēmum ... fūdit   *(s/he) put ... to flight*
Pharsālicus,-a,-um   *Pharsalian, at Pharsalus*
fugientem [accusative: the person doing this is in the accusative]   *fleeing, escaping*
Alexandrēam   <u>to</u> *Alexandria* (the preposition 'ad' was left out with names of cities:
English also drops prepositions, e.g. 'I am going <u>home</u>')
persecūtus est   *he pursued*

11.   Caesar reached Egypt and after a precarious struggle managed to overthrow Ptolemy
and Pothinus. The king's sister, Cleopatra VII, was already embroiled in a power
struggle with her brother. Royal brothers and sisters of the Ptolemaic line (originally
Greek) often married each other, fought each other, or both. Cleopatra seemed a
dependable ally, and preferable to a rival from Rome taking charge. He put her on the
throne jointly with another younger brother, Ptolemy XIV.

rēgnum Aegyptī victor Cleopātrae frātrīque eius minōrī permīsit.

Suetonius, *Life of Julius Caesar* 35

Aegyptus,-ī [m.]   *Egypt*
victor,-ōris [m.]   *victor* (i.e. Caesar)
Cleopātra,-ae [f.]   *Cleopatra*
ēius   *his, her*
minōrī [take with a noun in the dative]   *younger*
permīsit [perfect]   *(s/he) left, entrusted*

12.   A century later the poet Lucan recalls the conflict between Caesar and Pompey. If Julia
had stayed alive, who knows, perhaps she would have prevented the war:

tū sōla furentem

inde virum poterās atque hinc retinēre parentem.

Lucan, *Civil War* 1.115–6

Word order: 'sōla tū poterās retinēre furentem virum inde atque hinc parentem'

sōlus,-a,-um   *only, alone*

furentem [the person doing this is in the accusative]   *raging*

inde   *from there, from that side*

poterās   *you were able, could*

hinc   *on this side*

retinēre   *to restrain* (both 'virum' and 'parentem' are objects of 'retinēre')

parēns,-entis [m./f.]   *parent* (her 'virum' is Pompey, her 'parentem' is Caesar)

Exercises 8b

1. Identify the case and number of the underlined words:
(a) Catilīna **omnibus** modīs īnsidiās parābat Cicerōnī.
(b) Porsenna **ingentī** obsidiōne urbem premēbat.
(c) ego vītam **omnium** cīvium redēmī.
(d) uxor mea tam suspīciōne quam **crīmine** carēre dēbet.
(e) Caelius sedet cum Clōdiā, muliere nōn sōlum **nōbilī** sed etiam nōtā.
(f) dē Clōdiā ego nihil dīcam nisi dēpellendī **crīminis** causā.
(g) Tiberius Gracchus īnsepultus in **flūmen** prōiectus est.
(h) Caesar Pompēiō Mārcum Crassum reconciliāvit **veterem** inimīcum ex cōnsulātū.

2. Translate:
(a) agricola est expedītus, nūllō taurō, nūllīs servīs, nūllīs līberīs, nūllā uxōre, nūllā dominā, nūllīs amīcīs.
(b) quid dominae dulcī et bonae magis convenit quam abesse ā familiāribus contrōversiīs?
(c) rēs est omnis in hāc causā nōbīs cum servō – magistrō voluī dīcere, semper hīc errō.
(d) estne rēs omnis in hōc librō cum taurō trīstī?

3. Fill each gap, and translate your answer:
(a) bellum est . . . . {*serious*}.
(b) cūr Lūcius uxōrem . . . . {*sweet*} nōn amat?
(c) estne Seneca . . . . {*wise*}?
(d) . . . . {*wonderful*} sunt carmina Tibullī.
(e) dī nōn . . . . {*all*} mortālibus favent.
(f) mīlitēsne . . . . {*all*} sunt . . . . {*brave*}?

4. Our word *bus* is a clipped form of *omnibus*. How do you account for its ending?

— 9 —

The Ides of March

Verbs: revision

You have met the 1st conjugation (verbs like **amō, amāre**) in the present and perfect tenses.

Practice 9a

1. Change the underlined verbs to the perfect ending:
   (a) Romulus centum **creat** senātōrēs.
   (b) quā tū audāciā patrēs **vocās**?
   (c) semper hīc **errō**.

2. Change the underlined verbs to the present ending:
   (a) Caesar Pompēiō Crassum **reconciliāvit**.
   (b) rem pūblicam **līberāvī**.

present	perfect
amō	amāvī
amās	amāvistī
amat	amāvit
amāmus	amāvimus
amātis	amāvistis
amant	amāvērunt

You have also met the 2nd conjugation (verbs like **habeō, habēre**).

Practice 9b

1. Change the underlined verbs to the perfect ending *:
   (a) cōnsul **videt**.
   (b) omnēs tribūnōs **habēmus**.
   (c) servus **flet** sed nōn **dolet**.

2. Change the underlined verbs to the present ending:
   (a) urbem Rōmam ā prīncipiō rēgēs **habuērunt**.
   (b) imāginēs nōn **habuī**.

present	perfect
habeō	habuī
habēs	habuistī
habet	habuit
habēmus	habuimus
habētis	habuistis
habent	habuērunt

* **videō** = *I see*, **vīdī** = *I saw*; **fleō** = *I weep*, **flēvī** = *I wept*; **doleō** = *I grieve*, **doluī** = *I grieved*. Principal parts are listed in full in the Latin-to-English vocabulary towards the end of the book.

These perfect forms are all different from one another, so it is important to know the perfect form of a verb as well as the present in order to fully know the verb. The perfect forms are the third of the four principal parts:

amō, amāre, **amāvī**, amātum
habeō, habēre, **habuī**, habitum
doleō, dolēre, **doluī**, dolitum
fleō, flēre, **flēvī**, flētum
video, vidēre, **vīdī**, vīsum

3rd conjugation verbs

There are three more conjugations of regular verbs. They are all similar.

The 3rd conjugation has an infinitive ending **-ere**, like the 2nd conjugation (**habēre**) but with a short 'e' (**mittĕre**). Here are the principal parts of **mittō**, and the present tense:

mittō, mittere, mīsī, missum *send*

mitt**ō**	*I send*
mitt**is**	*you send* [singular]
mitt**it**	*s/he, it* [or a nominative noun] *sends*
mitt**imus**	*we send*
mitt**itis**	*you send* [plural]
mitt**unt**	*they* [or a plural nominative noun] *send*

The perfect stem of **mittō** is **mīs-ī** *I (have) sent*. The perfect endings are the same for *all* conjugations.

Practice 9c

Put into Latin:
(a) we are sending
(b) they sent
(c) he sends
(d) we have sent
(e) to send
(f) you sent [s.]
(g) she sent
(h) they send
(i) you are sending [pl.]

perfect	
-ī	mīsī
-istī	mīsistī
-it	mīsit
-imus	mīsimus
-istis	mīsistis
-ērunt	mīserunt

The 3rd conjugation has the most verbs. The principal parts of these verbs show that this conjugation is the least uniform in the formation of the perfect (whereas almost all 1st conjugation verbs have the perfect stem **-āvī**).

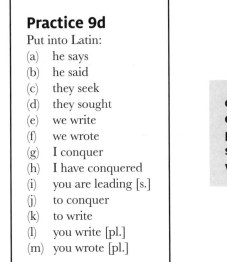

Practice 9d

Put into Latin:
(a) he says
(b) he said
(c) they seek
(d) they sought
(e) we write
(f) we wrote
(g) I conquer
(h) I have conquered
(i) you are leading [s.]
(j) to conquer
(k) to write
(l) you write [pl.]
(m) you wrote [pl.]

dīcō, dīcere, dīxī, dictum	*say*
dūcō, dūcere, dūxī, ductum	*lead*
petō, petere, petīvī (-iī), petītum	*seek*
scrībō, scrībere, scrīpsī, scrīptum	*write*
vincō, vincere, vīcī, victum	*conquer*

4th conjugation verbs

The 4th conjugation is similar to the third but for an 'i' in the stem:

    audiō, audīre, audīvī, audītum *(hear)*

aud**iō**	*I hear*
aud**īs**	*you [s.] hear*
aud**it**	*s/he, it* [or a nominative noun] *hears*
aud**īmus**	*we hear*
aud**ītis**	*you [pl.] hear*
aud**iunt**	*they* [or a plural nominative noun] *hear*

The perfect is **audīvī** *I (have) heard.*

Practice 9e

Put into Latin:
(a) we hear
(b) they heard
(c) he hears
(d) we have heard
(e) I heard
(f) you heard [s.]
(g) she heard
(h) to hear
(i) they hear

	perfect
-ī	audīvī
-istī	audīvistī
-it	audīvit
-imus	audīvimus
-istis	audīvistis
-ērunt	audīvērunt

The 'v' is often omitted from the perfect of the 4th conjugation: **audiī** for **audīvī**.

Practice 9f

Put into Latin:
(a) we know
(b) we knew
(c) they sleep
(d) they slept
(e) we come
(f) we came
(g) I heard
(h) I hear
(i) you sleep [s.]
(j) you slept [s.]
(k) to come
(l) to sleep

More 4th conjugation verbs:

dormiō, dormīre, dormīvī, dormītum   *sleep*
sciō, scīre, scīvī, scītum   *know*
veniō, venīre, vēnī, ventum   *come*

Mixed conjugation verbs

Verbs of the 'mixed conjugation' are traditionally regarded as belonging to the 3rd conjugation; but they are better treated separately. They resemble a mixture of the 3rd and 4th conjugations, which are themselves similar. This conjugation has the 'i' of the 4th in some of its forms, otherwise it is like the 3rd:

capiō, capere, cēpī, captum   (*capture, take*)

cap**iō**	*I capture*
cap**is**	*you* [s.] *capture*
cap**it**	*s/he, it* [or a nominative noun] *captures*
cap**imus**	*we capture*
cap**itis**	*you* [pl.] *capture*
cap**iunt**	*they* [or a plural nominative noun] *capture*

The perfect form is **cēp-ī** *I (have) captured, I have taken, I took*

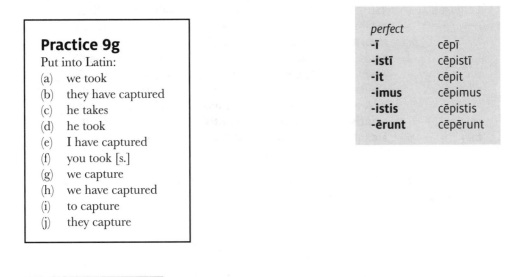

perfect	
-ī	cēpī
-istī	cēpistī
-it	cēpit
-imus	cēpimus
-istis	cēpistis
-ērunt	cēpērunt

Practice 9g

Put into Latin:

(a) we took
(b) they have captured
(c) he takes
(d) he took
(e) I have captured
(f) you took [s.]
(g) we capture
(h) we have captured
(i) to capture
(j) they capture

Practice 9h

Put into Latin:

(a) they received
(b) we made
(c) they flee
(d) they fled
(e) we receive
(f) we received
(g) she made
(h) she makes
(i) you make [s.]
(j) you made [pl.]
(k) to flee
(l) I fled

More verbs from the mixed conjugation:

accipiō, accipere, accēpī, acceptum# *receive, take*
faciō, facere, fēcī, factum *do, make*
fugiō, fugere, fūgī, fugitum *flee, escape*

one of many compounds of **capiō**

Summary: all five conjugations

Now you have seen all the conjugations in the present and perfect tenses. Here again are all five present tenses:

Conjugation	*Present*				
	1st	2nd	3rd	4th	Mixed
	amāre	habēre	mittere	audīre	capere
	to love	*to have*	*to send*	*to hear*	*to capture*
I ...	am**ō**	hab**eō**	mitt**ō**	aud**iō**	cap**iō**
you [s.] ...	am**ās**	hab**ēs**	mitt**is**	aud**īs**	cap**is**
s/he, it ...	am**at**	hab**et**	mitt**it**	aud**it**	cap**it**
we ...	am**āmus**	hab**ēmus**	mitt**īmus**	aud**īmus**	cap**imus**
you [pl.] ...	am**ātis**	hab**ētis**	mitt**itis**	aud**ītis**	cap**itis**
they ...	am**ant**	hab**ent**	mitt**unt**	aud**iunt**	cap**iunt**

The present tense of the 3rd, 4th and mixed conjugations are broadly similar. The perfect endings of all verbs are the same:

Conjugation	*Perfect*				
	1st	2nd	3rd	4th	Mixed
	amāre	habēre	mittere	audīre	capere
	to love	*to have*	*to send*	*to hear*	*to capture*
I ...	amā**vī**	habu**ī**	mīs**ī**	audī**vī**	cēp**ī**
you [s.] ...	amā**vistī**	habu**istī**	mīs**istī**	audī**vistī**	cēp**istī**
s/he, it ...	amā**vit**	habu**it**	mīs**it**	audī**vit**	cēp**it**
we ...	amā**vimus**	habu**imus**	mīs**imus**	audī**vimus**	cēp**imus**
you [pl.] ...	amā**vistis**	habu**istis**	mīs**istis**	audī**vistis**	cēp**istis**
they ...	amā**vērunt**	habu**ērunt**	mīs**ērunt**	audī**vērunt**	cēp**ērunt**

The stems of the perfect are not so uniform. You need to know a verb's principal parts to recognize the perfect and the past participle (e.g. **mittō, mittere, mīsī, missum**).

You can tell a verb's conjugation from the first two principal parts:

1. am**ō**, am**āre**, par**ō**, par**āre**; etc   [-ō, -āre]
2. hab**eō**, hab**ēre**; vid**eō**, vid**ēre**; etc   [-eō, -ēre]
3. mitt**ō**, mitt**ere**; scrīb**ō**, scrīb**ere**; etc   [-ō, -ere]
4. aud**iō**, aud**īre**; ven**iō**, ven**īre**; etc   [-iō, -īre]
M. cap**iō**, cap**ere**; fac**iō**, fac**ere**; etc   [-iō, -ere]

You will find verbs listed in vocabularies with some or all of their principal parts. A number may be added to show the conjugation, e.g. **adoptō,-āre** [1] = *adopt*. [M.] will indicate a verb from the mixed conjugation.

Vocabulary 9

You will probably need two pages for the 3rd conjugation verbs in your notebook. When you meet a verb for the second time, add it to your list. These can be listed now:

cēdō, cēdere, cēssī, cessum *go, give way*	**mittō,-ere, mīsī, missum** *send*
crēdō,-ere, crēdidī, crēditum [+ dat.] *believe, trust*	**occīdō, occīdere, occīdī, occīsum** *kill*
dīcō, dīcere, dīxī, dictum *say*	**petō, petere, petīvī (-iī), petītum** *seek, ask, strive for, attack*
dūcō, dūcere, dūxī, ductum *lead*	**pōnō, pōnere, posuī, positum** *place*
incendō,-ere, incendī, incēnsum *set fire to, inflame, distress*	**scrībō, scrībere, scrīpsī, scrīptum** *write*
	vincō, vincere, vīcī, victum *conquer*

The 4th and mixed conjugations can share a page:

audiō, audīre, audīvī (-iī), audītum *hear*	**capiō, capere, cēpī, captum** *take, capture*
sciō, scīre, scīvī (-iī), scītum *know*	**cupiō,-ere, cupīvī (-iī), cupītum** *desire*
veniō, venīre, vēnī, ventum *come*	**faciō,-ere, fēcī, factum** *make, do*
	fugiō, fugere, fūgī, fugitum *flee, escape*
	iaciō,-ere, iēcī, iactum *throw, hurl*

Look online for the principal parts of other verbs which appear in this course (p. 393).

Exercises 9a

1. Fill each gap with one Latin word, and translate:
(a) mī amīce, quid .... {*are you making*}?
(b) ō domina, quid .... {*are you saying*}?
(c) cūr Caesar est .... {*was killed*}?
(d) quis clāmōrēs Caesaris .... {*hears*}?
(e) ō puerī, carmina trīstia .... {*have you heard*}?
(f) Clōdiumne .... {*feared*} Cicerō?

2. Using the principal parts given in the vocabulary at the end of the book, identify:
   (i)   which conjugation
   (ii) the 3rd person singular (i.e. *s/he . . .*) of the present tense
   (iii) the 3rd person singular of the perfect tense
(a) adveniō,-īre (*arrive*)
(b) appellō,-āre (*call*)
(c) bibō,-ere (*drink*)
(d) cēdō,-ere (*give way, go, submit*)
(e) cōgō,-ere (*compel*)
(f) contemnō,-ere (*despise, scorn*)
(g) dīligō,-ere (*value, love*)
(h) fleō,-ēre (*weep*)
(i) flōreō,-ēre (*blossom, flourish*)
(j) gemō,-ere (*groan*)
(k) incipiō,-ere (*begin, undertake*)
(l) lūdō,-ere (*play, tease*)

(m)   regō,-ere (*rule*)
(n)   vīvō,-ere (*live*)

3. Translate into Latin:
(a)   I came, I saw, I fled.
(b)   My mother came, she wept, I groaned.
(c)   I lived, I drank, I never loved.

The Ides of March

Women's names were simpler than men's. They took the feminine form of the name of the *gens* (the wider family name: the middle of three names for a man). So Fulvia was the daughter of Marcus Fulvius Bambalio, and Tullia the daughter of Marcus Tullius Cicero. If there were sisters they would be distinguished by *maior* and *minor* or *prima*, *secunda* and *tertia*. When women were married they could expect to take their husband's *nomen* in the genitive, e.g. Clodia Metelli, the wife of Quintus Metellus Celer.

Male citizens from wealthy backgrounds usually had three names: a *praenomen*, the first name used by close friends and family; a *nomen*, the name of the *gens*; and thirdly the *cognomen*, the particular family name. Thus: Gaius Iulius Caesar, Marcus Licinius Crassus, and so on. Some people had a further honorific title or nickname or adoptive name added, an *agnomen*: Publius Cornelius Scipio *Africanus* for the general who defeated Hannibal, and *Cunctator* (Delayer) for Quintus Fabius Maximus who kept him at bay. First names were often abbreviated (e.g. C. for Gaius[1], Cn. for Gnaeus, L. for Lucius, M. for Marcus, P. for Publius, etc).

> ## Reading notes
> A few verbs have the same 3rd person singular form in the present and perfect tenses, e.g. **incendit** (*s/he inflames* or *inflamed*), **metuit** (*s/he fears* or *feared*), **ostendit** (*s/he shows* or *showed*). Some have a lengthened vowel in the perfect but are otherwise identical (entirely so in texts without macrons), e.g. **venit** and **vēnit** (*comes/came*).
>
> Vowel contraction: the genitive singular of 2nd declension nouns with an 'i' in the stem (like **Antōnius**) is sometimes reduced to a single **i**, from **Antōnii** to **Antōnī**. You will meet other vowel combinations which are sometimes contracted, e.g. **dī** for **deī** (*gods*).

Not everyone had three or more names. Men from less wealthy backgrounds would be content with two, and slaves would have only one, sometimes taking their master's name. The more important and prestigious you were, the more names you would have. Emperors' titles were inevitably the most fulsome, particularly in formal documents. A loan agreement from the second century AD was dated by the name of the emperor we know as Marcus Aurelius: 'The ninth year of the Emperor Caesar Marcus Aurelius Antoninus Augustus Armeniacus Medicus Parthicus Maximus ...' The text breaks off, and it is not clear whether the list of names is complete.[2]

---

1 Traditional orthography: the Latin 'g' did not appear in written form until the third century BC.
2 *Select Papyri*, Vol. 1 (Loeb), Agreement No.62 (translated from Greek by A.S. Hunt and C.C. Edgar).

1. Caesar was in control of the state for four years. He was away from Rome for much of that time, forcing the remnants of Pompey's faction to come to terms. He showed many qualities: he was generous, shrewd, articulate, persuasive, and forgiving to a fault.

moderātiōnem vērō clēmentiamque cum in administrātiōne tum in victōriā bellī cīvīlis admīrābilem exhibuit.

Suetonius, *Life of Julius Caesar* 75

moderātiō,-ōnis [f.]   *moderation*
vērō   *indeed*
clēmentia,-ae [f.]   *kindness*
cum . . . tum   *both . . . and*
administrātiō,-ōnis [f.]   *government, administration*
admīrābilis,-e   *admirable, unusual*
exhibeō,-ēre,-uī,-itum [2]   *show*

2. Suetonius tells us Caesar had many mistresses. He particularly loved Servilia, so the rumours went, the mother of Brutus, a future assassin. Brutus had sided with Pompey at Pharsalus but was pardoned.

dīlēxit Mārcī Brūtī mātrem Servīliam.

Suetonius, *Life of Julius Caesar* 50

dīligō,-ere,-lēxī,-lēctum [3]   *love*

3. Caesar had a liking for queens, says the biographer, and he acknowledged his son by Cleopatra.

dīlēxit et rēgīnās, sed maximē Cleopātram, quam fīlium nātum appellāre nōmine suō passus est.

Suetonius, *Life of Julius Caesar* 52

et   *and also*
maximē   *especially*
quam [f.acc.]   *who(m)*
nātus,-a,-um   *born*
fīlium nātum   *a son born (to them)*, i.e. Caesarion
appellō,-āre,-āvī,-ātum [1]   *call*
nōmen,-inis [n.]   *name*
passus est   *he allowed*

4. Caesar secured election to various time-limited offices – consul, tribune and dictator – to formalize his authority. In 44 BC he made himself dictator for life, which provoked his enemies to bring it to an end. A few weeks later he was murdered at a meeting of the senate.

ita tribus et vīgintī plāgīs cōnfossus est, ūnō modo ad
prīmum ictum gemitū, sine vōce ēditō, etsī trādidērunt
quīdam Mārcō Brūtō irruentī dīxisse:
'kai su teknon?'

Suetonius, Life of Julius Caesar 82

ita   *thus, so*
tribus et vīgintī [take with a noun in the dative or ablative plural]   *twenty-three*
plāga,-ae [f.]   *blow, wound*
cōnfossus est   *he was stabbed*
ūnō [take with a noun in the ablative singular]   *one*
modo   *only*
ad [+ acc.]   *to, towards, at*
ictum [acc.]   *blow, thrust*
gemitū [abl.]   *groan*
vōx, vōcis [f.]   *voice, sound*
ēdō,-ere, ēdidī, ēditum [3]   *give out, utter*
etsī   *although, albeit*
trādō,-ere, trādidī, trāditum [3]   *hand over, record*
quīdam [nom.]   *some people*
irruentī [the person doing this is in the dative singular]   *rushing in*
dīxisse   *(him) to have said, that he said*
kai su teknon [Greek]   *and you my child*

5.   The assassins, led by Cassius and Brutus, still had to contend with Caesar's lieutenants:
Mark Antony, his co-consul that year, and Lepidus, *Magister Equitum* (Master of the
Horse), the dictator's deputy.

fuerat animus coniūrātīs corpus occīsī in Tiberim trahere,
bona pūblicāre, ācta rescindere, sed metū Mārcī Antōnī
cōnsulis et magistrī equitum Lepidī dēstitērunt.

Suetonius, Life of Julius Caesar 82

fuerat   *(s/he, it) had been*
animus,-ī [m.]   *mind, purpose, intention*
coniūrātus,-ī [m.]   *conspirator*
fuerat animus coniūrātīs: dative with 'to be' shows possession (*the conspirators had had the
intention*)
occīsī: genitive of 'occīsus,-a,-um', i.e. *the* 'corpus' *of the* 'occīsī'
trahō,-ere, traxī, tractum [3]   *drag*
bona,-ōrum [n.]   *goods, property*
pūblicō,-āre [1]   *confiscate*
ācta,-ōrum [n.]   *actions, public acts, decrees*
rescindō,-ere [3]   *repeal, cancel*
metū [abl.]   *fear*
dēsistō,-ere, dēstitī [3]   *cease, stop*

6. There was much public grief at Caesar's funeral, and anger. It is easy enough for us to muddle Romans with similar names. It was a problem for a few Romans as well, not least for poor Helvius Cinna who shared a name with Cornelius Cinna, one of Caesar's assassins.

plēbs statim ā fūnere ad domum Brūtī et Cassiī cum facibus tetendit atque, aegrē repulsa, Helvium Cinnam per errōrem nōminis occīdit caputque eius praefixum hastae circumtulit.

Suetonius, Life of Julius Caesar 85

statim   *immediately*
ad   *towards, in the direction of*
domum [acc.]   *house, home* (say houses as Brutus and Cassius did not live together)
fax, facis [f.]   *torch*
tendō,-ere, tetendī, tentum [3]   *stretch, reach, march*
aegrē   *with difficulty*
repellō,-ere, reppulī, repulsum [3]   *drive back* (take 'repulsa' with 'plēbs')
error,-ōris [m.]   *mistake*
eius   *his, her*
praefixus,-a,-um   *stuck, impaled*
hasta,-ae [f.]   *spear*
circumtulit   *(s/he) carried around* ('plēbs' is a singular subject even though it stands for many people)

7. Mark Antony opened Caesar's will. If he expected to be the principal heir he was disappointed.

Caesar in īmā cērā Gāium Octāvium etiam in familiam nōmenque adoptāvit.

Suetonius, Life of Julius Caesar 83

īmus,-a,-um   *last, at the bottom of*
cēra,-ae [f.]   *writing tablet*
familia,-ae [f.]   *household, family*
adoptō,-āre [1]   *adopt*

8. During the dictatorship Cicero had withdrawn from public life to concentrate on his studies and writing. In the political uncertainty after Caesar's murder he joined the scramble for control of government, hopeful of a return to the Republic. He feared Antony would take over where Caesar left off:

ō mī Attice, vereor nē nōbīs Īdūs Mārtiae nihil dederint praeter laetitiam.

Cicero, Letters to Atticus 14.12

vereor   *I fear*
nē   *lest, that*
Īdūs Mārtiae [nom.pl.]   *Ides of March (15th March)*
dederint   *(they) have given*
praeter [+ acc.]   *except*
laetitia,-ae [f.]   *(a moment of) joy, cheer, hurrah*

9. In June 44 Cicero attended an informal meeting of people who were behind the assassination. He listed three women present, whose political influence he evidently respected: Servilia (the very same mistress described above), her daughter Tertia (called 'Tertulla': Brutus' half-sister and Cassius' wife), and her daughter-in-law Porcia (Brutus' wife).

deinde Brūtus, multīs audientibus, Servīliā, Tertullā, Porciā, quaerere quid placēret.

Cicero, Letters to Atticus 15.11

deinde   *then, next*
multīs audientibus   *with many people listening*
quaerere: infinitive of 'quaerō,-ere' meaning *(he) asked, sought* (a 'historic infinitive' is sometimes used in place of a past tense to make a narrative more vivid)
quid placēret   *what pleased (me)*, i.e. *what I recommended*

10. Cassius felt insulted by Antony's proposal that he should be given the unprestigious duty of securing the corn supply. Servilia said she would have that changed.

'frūmentāriam rem ex senātūs cōnsultō tollam.'

Cicero, Letters to Atticus 15.12

frūmentārius,-a,-um   *relating to the corn supply, of the corn supply*
rem [acc.]   *thing, matter, business*
senātūs [gen.]   *senate*
cōnsultum,-ī [n.]   *decree, resolution*
tollam   *I will remove*

11. Cicero and Antony were old foes. Antony's stepfather was one of Catiline's rebels whom Cicero had executed. In this letter to his secretary Tiro, Cicero reveals he was anxious, for a while at least, to keep on good terms with Antony:

ego tamen Antōnī amīcitiam retinēre sānē volō, scrībamque ad eum.

Cicero, Letters to Friends and Family 16.23

amīcitia,-ae [f.]   *friendship*
retineō,-ēre [2]   *keep*
sānē   *certainly*
volō   *I want*
scrībam   *I shall write*
eum [acc.]   *him*

12. Any good will between them soon evaporated. To make the animosity sharper, Antony was now married to Fulvia, Clodius' widow. In 44 and 43 Cicero delivered a series of speeches attacking Antony. These were called the 'Philippics' after the speeches of the Athenian, Demosthenes, against Philip of Macedon.

dēfendī rem pūblicam adulēscēns, nōn dēseram senex;
contempsī Catilīnae gladiōs, nōn pertimēscam tuōs.

Cicero, Philippics 2.46

dēfendō,-ere,-fendī,-fēnsum [3]   *defend, protect*
adulēscēns,-entis [m.]   *a young man*
dēseram   *I shall abandon*
senex, senis [m.]   *old man*
contemnō,-ere, contempsī, contemptum [3]   *scorn*
gladius,-ī [m.]   *sword*
pertimēscam   *I shall fear*

Exercises 9b

1.   Translate:
(a)   servus Cicerōnis ē forō fūgit metū Antōniī.
(b)   dēfendī populum tribūnus, nōn dēseram cōnsul.
(c)   est animus agricolīs taurum in Tiberim trahere.
(d)   Pompēius Caesaris fīliam Iūliam dūxit uxōrem.
(e)   Fortūna semper mē lūdit. cūr mē vīvere coēgistī?
(f)   ō patrēs, quis nostrum ducem trucīdāvit? fīliusne Servīliae Caesarem occīdit?
       nōnne Caesarem dīlēxit Servīlia?

2.   Put the underlined verbs into the equivalent *perfect* tense ending, and translate your answer:
(a)   quis Clōdiam uxōrem **dūcit**?
(b)   mīlitēs Caesaris **veniunt**, **vident**, **vincunt**.
(c)   tūne **venīs**? tū **vidēs**? tū **gemis**? — sīc, **venīmus**, **vidēmus**, **gemimus**.
(d)   servus **advenit**, vīnum **bibit**, **fugit**. (*Be sure to add the macrons for this one . . .*)

3.   Put the underlined verbs into the equivalent *present* tense ending, and translate your answer:
(a)   Fulviane marītum **iussit** captīvōs occīdere?
(b)   Caesar Gāium Octāvium in familiam **adoptāvit**.
(c)   Cleopātra lacrimās frātris **vīdit**, sed nōn **doluit**.
(d)   dominus mē **contempsit** sed ego **flōruī**.

4.   Translate into Latin:
       'O poet, your mistress came, she heard, she fled.'

5.   (a) Find Latin ancestors in this chapter of *audience, scribble* and *senile*; (b) identify one Latin word from this chapter which is an ancestor of all these words: *cattle, cap, chapter, chattel, capital* and *decapitate*.

— 10 —

A woman in politics

Nouns: 4th declension

This is an old declension of Latin nouns. There are not many of them, but they appear frequently enough to need attention. The **-us** ending occurs in several different cases.

	chariot	
---	*singular*	*plural*
N.	curr**us**	curr**ūs**
V.	curr**us**	curr**ūs**
A.	curr**um**	curr**ūs**
G.	curr**ūs**	curr**uum**
D.	curr**uī**	curr**ibus**
Ab.	curr**ū**	curr**ibus**

In a dictionary a 4th declension noun is recognizable by its genitive singular ending **-ūs**. No other declension has this ending in the genitive.

Catilīna etiam in **senātum** venit   [acc. s.]
Catiline even comes into the senate   [6.7]

ferrum in **manū** est   [abl. s.]
there is a knife in my hand   [2.3]

vīvōs dūcent dē marmore **vultūs**   [acc. pl.]
they will fashion living faces from marble   [4.9]

4th declension nouns
currus,-ūs [m.]   *chariot*
exercitus,-ūs [m.]   *army*
gemitus,-ūs [m.]   *groan*
manus,-ūs [f.]   *hand*
metus,-ūs [m.]   *fear*
senātus,-ūs [m.]   *senate*
spīritus,-ūs [m.]   *spirit*
vultus,-ūs [m.]   *face*

Most 4th declension nouns are masculine, with one or two feminine exceptions like **manus, -ūs** (*hand*). There is a neuter form which you will seldom meet, ending **-ū** in all cases of the singular except the genitive **-ūs**. The only example of a neuter 4th declension in this book is **cornibus**, the ablative plural of **cornū,-ūs** (*horn*). The only other neuter form you are likely to come across is **genū** (*knee*), with the plural **genua**.

Practice 10a

Put the underlined word into Latin in the correct case:

(a)   he spoke with a sad <u>face</u>
(b)   he led <u>an army</u> of slaves
(c)   through <u>fear</u> of the consul we ran away
(d)   Boudicca stood on the <u>chariot</u>
(e)   a decree of the <u>senate</u>
(f)   he spoke with a <u>groan</u>
(g)   he raised his <u>hands</u>

-us **endings**

Currus is yet another noun which ends **-us** in the nominative singular. It also ends **-ūs** in the genitive singular and nominative and accusative plurals, so the **-us** ending can indicate a number of cases. The first guess (if you don't know the word) should be the nominative singular (e.g. **servus, corpus, currus**). If that fails try the accusative singular (3rd declension neuter like **corpus, opus**, etc) or the genitive singular of the 4th declension like **currūs**. And then you have the nominative and accusative plurals of the 4th declension nouns (**currūs**).

So it pays to know the noun and its declension – or to be able to find it out.

	2nd decl.	3rd decl. [n.]	4th decl.
singular			
N.	serv**us**	corp**us**	cur**rus**
V.	serve	corp**us**	cur**rus**
A.	servum	corp**us**	currum
G.	servī	corporis	cur**rūs**
D.	servō	corporī	curruī
Ab.	servō	corpore	currū
plural			
N.	servī	corpora	cur**rūs**
V.	servī	corpora	cur**rūs**
A.	servōs	corpora	cur**rūs**
G.	servōrum	corporum	curruum
D.	servīs	corporibus	curribus
Ab.	servīs	corporibus	curribus

Practice 10b

Identify the declension of each noun (2nd, 3rd or 4th), and give the accusative plural:

(a) **exercitus,-ūs** [m.]   *army*
(b) **genus,-eris** [n.]   *race*
(c) **gemitus,-ūs** [m.]   *groan*
(d) **tempus,-oris** [n.]   *time*
(e) **lībertus,-ī** [m.]   *freedman*
(f) **ictus,-ūs** [m.]   *blow, thrust*

domus: **a declension hybrid**

The 4th declension noun **domus** (*house, home, family*) was much used, and at some point adopted one or two 2nd declension endings. The genitive could be **domūs** or **domī**, the dative **domuī** or **domō** and the ablative always appeared as **domō**. The accusative plural is either **domūs** or **domōs**, and the no longer listed 'locative' case is **domī** (*at home*).[1]

Irregular verbs: sum, possum, volō, eō, ferō

In addition to the regular verb forms of the five conjugations there are some irregular verbs, which, as in many languages, are used more than enough to need careful study:

sum, esse, fuī, —   *be*
possum, posse, potuī, —   *be able*
volō, velle, voluī, —   *wish, be willing*
eō, īre, iī, itum   *go*
ferō, ferre, tulī, lātum   *bear, carry*

I	sum	possum	volō	eō	ferō
you . . . [s.]	es	potes	vīs	īs	fers
s/he, it . . .	est	potest	vult	it	fert
we . . .	sumus	possumus	volumus	īmus	ferimus
you . . . [pl.]	estis	potestis	vultis	ītis	fertis
they . . .	sunt	possunt	volunt	eunt	ferunt

nec vitia nostra nec remedia patī **possumus**
we can endure neither our vices nor the remedies   [6.3]

---

1 The 'locative' case is **-ae** [s.] and **-īs** [pl.] for 1st declension nouns; **-ī** [s.] and **-īs** [pl.] for 2nd declension nouns (**Rōmae**, *at Rome*; **Athēnīs**, *in Athens*).

īnsidiātōrī et latrōnī quae **potest** īnferrī iniūsta nex?
what unjust death <u>can</u> be committed against a cut-throat and a robber?   [8.4]

Antōnī amīcitiam retinēre **volō**
<u>I want</u> to keep the friendship of Antony   [9.11]

relātum est caput ad Antōnium
the head was <u>brought back</u> to Antony   [10.6]

The verbs **eō** and **ferō** are more commonly seen in compound forms (e.g. **adeō, referō**, etc), which appear on p. 116.

The perfect endings are regular although the stems are less so. From the principal parts above you will see how radically different the perfect and past participle (**tulī** and **lātum**) are from the present of **ferre**. The English verb *go* has something of the same with its different forms *go, went, gone* and *been*. *To go* in Latin has a double 'i' in the ending of the perfect (**iit** = *s/he went*), which is very common in the compound forms (e.g. **iniit** = *s/he entered*, **abiit** = *s/he went away*).

Practice 10c

Translate each into one Latin word:
(a)   they are
(b)   we can
(c)   she is willing
(d)   they carry
(e)   we are going
(f)   there is
(g)   they are able
(h)   you [s.] wish
(i)   she bears
(j)   they wish
(k)   he goes
(l)   to bear
(m)   to go

Practice 10d

Put each verb into the perfect, in the same person:
(a)   sunt
(b)   eunt
(c)   vult
(d)   fert
(e)   possum
(f)   it
(g)   possunt
(h)   vīs
(i)   est

Verbs followed by an infinitive

As in English, there are verbs which are normally followed by the infinitive of another verb:

possum, posse: tēcum **venīre** nōn **possum**
be able   *I am unable to come with you*

volō, velle:
want, be willing

patriam **dēfendere volō**
I am willing to defend our country

iubeō, iubēre:
order, tell

domina mē cēnam **parāre iubet**
the mistress orders me to prepare the dinner

dēbeō, dēbēre:
ought, owe

Caesarī grātiās **agere dēbēmus**
we ought to give thanks to Caesar

Practice 10e

Translate into two Latin words:
(a)   she wants to write
(b)   we can see
(c)   I ought to read

Vocabulary 10

List the 4th declension nouns which appeared earlier in this chapter in your notebook. Add these below:

cāsus,-ūs [m.]   *accident, misfortune*
domus, domūs (domī) [f.]   *house, home, family* (see p. 114)
flētus,-ūs [m.]   *weeping, tears*
gemitus,-ūs [m.]   *groan, sigh*
gradus,-ūs [m.]   *step*
lūctus,-ūs [m.]   *grief*

cōnsulātus,-ūs [m.]   *consulship*
manus,-ūs [f.]   *hand*
metus,-ūs [m.]   *fear*
socrus,-ūs [f.]   *mother-in-law*
spīritus,-ūs [m.]   *spirit*
tumultus,-ūs [m.]   *uproar, insurrection*
vultus,-ūs [m.]   *face*

iussū   *on the order, by command* appears only in the ablative singular

Irregular verbs need their own page in your notebook. They have a number of compound forms:

sum, esse, fuī   *be*
absum, abesse, āfuī   *be absent*
adsum, adesse, adfuī   *be present, at hand*

eō, īre, iī, itum   *go*
exeō,-īre, exiī, exitum   *go out*
pereō,-īre, periī, peritum   *perish, die*
trānseō,-īre, trānsiī, trānsitum   *go across, pass through*

ferō, ferre, tulī, lātum   *bear, carry*
afferō, afferre, attulī, allātum   *bring*
auferō, auferre, abstulī, ablātum   *take away, steal*
circumferō, circumferre, circumtulī, circumlātum   *carry around*
perferō, perferre, pertulī, perlātum   *endure, suffer*
referō, referre, rettulī, relātum   *bring back, report*

Look online for more 4th declension nouns and compounds of irregular verbs (see p. 393).

Exercises 10a

1. Translate:
(a) neque rīdēre neque dolēre possum.
(b) nunc adesse in urbe dēbēmus.
(c) quis flūmen trānsīre vult?
(d) taurusne in vīllā adest?
(e) servus gemitū ē vīllā fūgit.
(f) gemitūs miserōs audīre possumus.
(g) semper mea uxor mē flētū vincit.
(h) cūr Cicerō Catilīnam dēfendere parat?
(i) cūr dominus flagellum petit? nōnne omnēs servī fūgērunt et nunc absunt?

2. Identify the infinitive in each sentence, and translate:
(a) Caesar mīlitēs in forō adesse iubet.
(b) neque virum neque parentem Iūlia retinēre potest.
(c) inimīcī Antōniī etiam līberōs eius necāre parant.
(d) Pūblius Clōdius ā patribus ad plēbem trānsīre voluit.

3. Translate:
(a) dēsine socrum tuam lūdere.
(b) dēsine taurum fugāre.
(c) dēsine meam dominam laudāre.
(d) dēsine captīvōs trucīdāre.
(e) dēsine servōs contemnere.
(f) dēsine scelera Catilīnae dēfendere.

4. Fill each gap with the word which does not appear (or reappear) but is taken as understood:

   e.g. Caesar Calpurniam Pīsōnis fīliam dūxit uxōrem, suamque [**fīliam**] Iūliam Pompeiō collocāvit.   [7.9]

(a) Clōdius [....................] inimīcus nōbīs.   [7.5]
(b) contempsī Catilīnae gladiōs, nōn pertimēscam [....................] tuōs.   [9.12]
(c) sī omnēs tribūnōs plēbis habēmus, sī Lentulum [....................], sī vērō etiam Pompēium et Caesarem [....................], nōn est dēspērandum.   [7.13]

A woman in politics

1. When Antony opened Caesar's will he found that young Gaius Octavius had not only been adopted but also inherited the major part of his estate. Octavius immediately took Caesar's name, adding an agnomen created from his own: Gaius Iulius Caesar Octavianus. Contemporaries referred to him as 'Caesar', while we now call him Octavian to distinguish him from his adoptive father. Octavian was the major beneficiary of Caesar's will: his name, property, wealth, contacts, clients and loyalty of the legions.

All of a sudden this youngster (he was still in his teens) had enormous resources at his fingertips, and was quick to take advantage of them. He even found unlikely support from a few of the senators who had welcomed the end of his father, especially from Cicero, who realized that Caesar's heir was the one person who could compete with Antony for the loyalty of the dead dictator's armies.

puer ēgregius est Caesar.

Cicero, *Letters to Friends and Family* 10.28

ēgregius,-a,-um   *outstanding*

2.   Brutus did not share Cicero's confidence in Octavian:

patrem appellet Octāvius Cicerōnem, referat omnia, laudet, grātiās agat; tamen verba rēbus erunt contrāria.

Cicero, *Letters to Brutus* 1.17 [Brutus to Atticus]

appellet   *(s/he) may call, let him/her call*
referat   *(s/he) may refer, let him/her refer*
laudet   *(s/he) may praise, let him/her praise*
grātiās agat   *(s/he) may give thanks, let him/her give thanks*
rēbus [dat.pl./abl.pl.]   *actions*
erunt   *(they) will be*
contrārius,-a,-um   *opposite*

3.   Cicero meanwhile missed no opportunity to attack Antony or Fulvia. He tells the story of a few of Antony's centurions suspected of loyalty to the Republic (Antony's enemies):

Antōnius ad sē venīre centuriōnēs eōsque ante pedēs suōs uxōrisque suae, quam sēcum gravis imperātor ad exercitum dūxerat, iugulārī coēgit.

Cicero, *Philippics* 5.22

Word order: 'Antōnius coēgit centuriōnēs venīre ad sē -que ante pedēs suōs uxōrisque suae, quam gravis imperātor dūxerat sēcum ad exercitum, (coēgit) eōs iugulārī'
sē [acc./abl.]   *him* (i.e. Antony)
centuriō,-ōnis [m.]   *centurion*
eōs [acc.pl.]   *them* ('centuriōnēs')
pēs, pedis [m.]   *foot*
quam [f.,acc.]   *who(m)*
sēcum: i.e. cum sē
gravis,-e   *serious, important, eminent* (sarcastic, because his wife is in the battlecamp)
imperātor,-ōris [m.]   *general*
exercitus,-ūs [m.]   *army*
dūxerat   *(s/he) had brought*
iugulārī   *to have one's throat cut* (like 'venīre', dependent on 'coēgit')
cōgō,-ere, coēgī, coāctum [3]   *compel, force*

4. Antony was defeated at Mutina in the spring of 43 BC by the combined forces of the two consuls, Hirtius and Pansa, and of Octavian. Atticus, though a good friend to Cicero, helped Antony's family in their moment of hardship[1]:

inimīcī Antōniī Fulviam omnibus rēbus spoliāre cupiēbant, līberōs etiam exstinguere parābant. Atticus familiārēs Antōniī ex urbe profugientēs adiūvit.

Cornelius Nepos, *Life of Atticus* 9.2–3

rēbus [dat.pl./abl.pl.]   *things, property*
spoliō,-āre,-āvī,-ātum [1]   *rob, deprive* (victim in accusative, property in ablative)
cupiēbant   *(they) were wanting, desiring*
exstinguō,-ere [3]   *kill*
parābant   *(they) were preparing*
familiāris,-e   *belonging to family, household* ('familiārēs' here is used as a noun)
profugientēs [the persons doing this are in the nominative or accusative plural]   *fleeing away*
adiuvō,-āre, adiūvī, adiūtum [1]   *help, support*

5. Meanwhile Lepidus rallied to Antony's cause, and it wasn't long before Octavian joined him too. Octavian had been ignored by the senate after the victory at Mutina, and he began to feel he had been little more than a pawn in the old senator's conflict with Antony. Cicero's avuncular good will now seemed patronizing. In the summer of 43 BC Octavian formed a new triumvirate together with Antony and Lepidus, which was bad news for Cicero. Unstoppable forces were now gathering against the Republic, and yet this was what dictators and triumvirs and, later, emperors themselves claimed to be protecting, in name at least.

populus mē triumvirum reī pūblicae cōnstituendae creāvit.

Augustus, *My Political Achievements* 1.4

reī pūblicae cōnstituendae   *to manage the Republic*

6. Worse was to follow for Cicero. With Sulla's proscriptions as precedent, the triumvirs agreed on a list of more than two thousand names for immediate execution. There was no escape for Antony's longstanding antagonist. He was caught by soldiers half-heartedly trying to leave for Greece, and beheaded. Antony ordered a gruesome exhibition at the point where Cicero delivered his speeches.

---

1 Cicero's old friend Titus Pomponius Atticus had many friendships, some with people who were themselves bitterly opposed. Antony and Fulvia liked him and so did Octavian. His daughter married Agrippa and his granddaughter was the first wife of Tiberius. Earlier both Sulla and Marius had sought his friendship, then Pompey and Caesar. An impressive list of contacts. Atticus was hugely rich and generous with it, likeable, not politically ambitious – a quality for survival – and no doubt careful how he managed these ties. But when proscriptions were in the air he will have been nervous: a dangerous time for people with a lot of money and property.

ita relātum est caput ad Antōnium iussūque eius inter duās
manūs in rōstrīs positum est. vix hominēs sine lacrimīs
intuērī trucīdātī membra cīvis poterant.

(Elder) Seneca, *Declamations* 6.17 [quoting Livy]

ita   *thus, so*
relātum: from 'referō, referre'
iussus,-ūs [m.]   *command, order* (this noun was only used in the ablative: 'iussū' = *on/at the order*)
eius   *his* (Antony's)
inter [+ acc.]   *between*
rōstra,-ōrum [n.]   *speaker's platform*
pōnō,-ere, posuī, positum [3]   *place, put*
vix   *scarcely, barely*
intuērī   *to gaze at*
trucīdō,-āre-āvī,-ātum [1]   *slaughter, cut down* ('trucīdātī' is genitive, with 'cīvis')
membrum,-ī [n.]   *limb, body-part*
cīvis,-is [m.]   *citizen*
poterant   *(they) could, were able*

7. Fulvia is said to have stuck a hairpin through the dead Cicero's tongue, one of the few surviving anecdotes about her which cannot be said to have come from Cicero's mouth. Fulvia was a powerful and influential personality in Rome at this time. She looked after Antony's interests while he was away on campaign, and still received considerable support from her previous husband's contacts and clients. Her importance was not missed by Octavian, who in the same year (43) married her daughter, Claudia, stepdaughter of Antony and daughter of Clodius. The marriage did not last, for Octavian's rapport with his mother-in-law quickly deteriorated.

Caesar prīvīgnam Antōniī, Claudiam, Fulviae ex Clōdiō fīliam, dūxit uxōrem vixdum nūbilem ac, simultāte cum Fulviā socrū ortā, dīmīsit intāctam adhūc et virginem.

Suetonius, *Life of Augustus* 62

prīvīgna,-ae   *stepdaughter*
vixdum   *scarcely yet, barely yet*
nūbilis,-e   *marriageable*
simultās,-tātis [f.]   *quarrel, animosity*
socrus,-ūs [f.]   *mother-in-law*
ortus,-a,-um   *having arisen, begun*
simultāte ortā   *with animosity having arisen*
dīmittō,-ere, dīmīsī, dīmissum [3]   *dismiss*
intāctus,-a,-um   *untouched, chaste*
adhūc   *still*
virgō,-inis [f.]   *girl, virgin*

8. Brutus had old ties with Antony, and his sister Junia was married to Antony's ally, Lepidus. But Brutus was to die along with Cassius at Philippi in 42 BC against the combined armies of Antony and Octavian. After the battle Caesar's young heir could not contain his rage. He sent Brutus' head to Rome to be displayed beneath the statue of Caesar, and treated other prisoners with contempt. It was Antony who masterminded the victory, but Octavian was more hated by the defeated Republicans.

cēterī, cum catēnātī prōdūcerentur, imperātōre Antōniō honōrificē salūtātō, hunc foedissimō convītiō cōram prōscidērunt.

Suetonius, *Life of Augustus* 13

cēterus,-a,-um   *the other* (here 'cēterī' = *the rest of the prisoners*)
cum   *when*
catēnātus,-a,-um   *chained, in chains*
prōdūcerentur   *(they) were brought forward*
imperātor,-ōris [m.]   *general*
honōrificē   *respectfully*
salūtō,-āre,-āvī,-ātum [1]   *greet, salute*
imperātōre salūtātō   *with the general having been greeted* (or say *after they had greeted the general*)

hunc [acc.]   *him, this man* (Octavian)
foedissimus,-a,-um   *most repulsive, most foul*
convītium,-ī [n.]   *abuse*
cōram   *openly, in public*
prōscindō,-ere,-scidī,-scissum [3]   *revile*

9. The triumvirs divided responsibilities: Antony was to look after the east, Lepidus to take charge of Africa, and Octavian to lead the veterans back to Italy where he would find them land. This land had to be taken from those already farming it. Octavian managed to upset both sides, the displaced inhabitants and veterans who felt they had not been given sufficient reward.

neque veterānōrum neque possessōrum grātiam tenuit.

Suetonius, *Life of Augustus* 13

veterānus,-ī [m.]   *veteran*
possessor,-ōris [m.]   *owner*
grātia,-ae [f.]   *gratitude, good will*
teneō,-ēre, tenuī, tentum [2]   *hold, keep*

10. Lucius Antonius, brother of Mark Antony and consul in 41 BC, drew on this disaffection to pick a fight with Octavian, for which he had the support of his sister-in-law, Fulvia. Octavian managed to force Lucius to take refuge in Perusia (Perugia) where he surrendered and was released. The citizens of Perusia were not so lucky.

ūsus Caesar virtūte et fortūnā suā Perūsiam expugnāvit. Antōnium inviolātum dīmīsit, in Perusīnōs magis īrā mīlitum quam voluntāte saevītum ducis.

Velleius Paterculus, *Compendium of Roman History* 2.74

ūsus,-a,-um [+ abl.]   *having taken advantage of*
virtūs,-tūtis [f.]   *courage*
fortūna,-ae [f.]   *fortune, luck*
expugnō,-āre,-āvī,-ātum [1]   *storm, capture*
Antōnium: Lucius, Antony's brother
inviolātus,-a,-um   *unhurt, unharmed*
Word order within second sentence: 'saevītum (est) in Perusīnōs magis īrā mīlitum quam
     voluntāte ducis'
in: 'in' with the accusative sometimes has an aggressive meaning: i.e. *against*
Perusīnī,-ōrum   *the people of Perusia*
magis   *more, rather*
īra,-ae [f.]   *anger*
mīlitum: gen.pl. of 'mīles,-itis'
quam   *than*
voluntās,-tātis [f.]   *wish*
saevītum (est)   *it was raged*, i.e. *brutal treatment was inflicted*
dux,-cis [m.]   *leader, general*

11. Velleius wrote his account when Octavian was emperor and when criticism or adverse publicity would have been unwise. A century later Suetonius reports that others told a different story:

trecentī ad āram Dīvō Iūliō extructam Īdibus Mārtiīs hostiārum mōre mactātī sunt.

Suetonius, *Life of Augustus* 15

trecentī,-ōrum   *three hundred men*
ad: usually *to* or *towards*, here *before, at*
āra,-ae [f.]   *altar*
Dīvō Iūliō: dative (*to . . .*, or *in honour of . . .*)
extructus,-a,-um   *constructed*
Īdibus Mārtiīs   *on the Ides of March*
hostia,-ae [f.]   *sacrificial victim*
mōs, mōris [m.]   *fashion, custom*
mactō,-āre,-āvī,-ātum [1]   *sacrifice*

12. After the fall of Perusia, Fulvia left for Greece to meet Antony. Before she could see him she died. Antony returned to Italy, but there was no fight with Octavian, not yet, because neither army wanted to fight the other. Their generals were encouraged to come to terms: Antony to return to the east, Octavian to stay in Italy.

adventus deinde in Ītaliam Antōniī apparātusque contrā eum Caesaris habuit bellī metum, sed pāx circā Brundusium composita est.

Velleius Paterculus, *Compendium of Roman History* 2.76

adventus,-ūs [m.]   *arrival*
apparātus,-ūs [m.]   *preparation*
eum [acc.]   *him*
metus,-ūs [m.]   *fear*
pāx,-cis [f.]   *peace*
circā [+ acc.]   *near*
Brundusium,-ī: modern town of Brindisi
compōnō,-ere,-posuī,-positum [3]   *compose, settle*

13. A marriage sealed the new pact.

Octāviam, sorōrem Caesaris, Antōnius dūxit uxōrem.

Velleius Paterculus, *Compendium of Roman History* 2.78

Exercises 10b

1.   Identify the case and number of each underlined 4th declension noun:
(a)   frūmentāriam rem ex **senātūs** cōnsultō tollam.
(b)   senātōrēs **metū** Antōnī ad **domum** Brūtī et Cassiī fūgērunt.
(c)   Antōniī **iussū** caput Cicerōnis inter duās **manūs** in rōstrīs positum est.
(d)   ita cōnfossus est, ūnō modo ad prīmum **ictum gemitū**.

2.   Translate:
(a)   Fulviane mīlitēs dūcere vult?
(b)   cūr cōnsul Caesaris imāginem circumfert?
(c)   Antōnius triumvir esse vult? ego cōnsulātū contentus sum.
(d)   relātum est caput ad triumvirum, manūs ad uxōrem eius.
(e)   dēsine familiārēs Antōniī adiuvāre.
(f)   cūr mīlitēs flūmen trānseunt?
(g)   ego verba Christiānōrum audīvī: 'in nōmine patris et fīliī et spīritūs sānctī'.

3.   Fill each gap with one Latin word, and translate:
(a)   .... {*of the senate*} cōnsultum nōn laudāvit Caesar.
(b)   Antōnius etiam uxōrem suam ad .... {*the army*} dūxit.
(c)   cūr rēgīna .... {*my groans*} meōs rīdet? nōnne nostrō flētū dolet?
(d)   librōsne omnēs Cicerō suā .... {*in his own hand*} scrīpsit?
(e)   captīvīne in .... {*in the chariot*} cum Caesare sedent?

4.   Give the first two principal parts of the irregular verbs of which the underlined verbs are compounds [e. g. relātum [10.6] . . . . . **ferrō, ferre**]:
(a)   Graecia artīs **intulit** agrestī Latiō.   [4.6]
(b)   ego Clōdius ā patribus ad plēbem **trānsīre** volō.   [7.8]
(c)   quid bonō cīvī magis convenit quam **abesse** ā cīvīlibus contrōversiīs?   [8.9]
(d)   plēbs caput Cinnae praefixum hastae **circumtulit**.   [9.6]
(e)   Caesar societātem cum Pompēiō Crassōque **iniit**.   [6.10]

5.   Identify a single English word which has roots in both 'occīdō' (*I kill*) and 'homō' (*man, person*).

— 11 —

Politics and marriage

Verbs: the imperfect tense

The 'imperfect' tense does not describe an action executed poorly or deficiently in any way. It simply means 'unfinished'. This tense is used to describe an unfinished or repeated or on-going action in the past:

> **iacēbant** tot Rōmānōrum mīlia, peditēs passim equitēsque
> *so many thousands of Romans were lying (on the ground), infantry and cavalry everywhere*   [3.6]

The imperfect is sometimes used to describe something that was started or intended, but not completed. So *began to . . .* or *tried to . . .* may help bring out the meaning:

> ingentīque urbem obsidiōne **premēbat**
> *and he began to press the city with an huge blockade*   [2.6]

The imperfect tense is used to set a scene in a narrative to describe what someone was doing (imperfect) when something happened (perfect):

> Dīdō **errābat** silvā in magnā . . .
> *Dido was wandering in a large wood . . .*   [3.13]

Imperfect: stem and endings
The endings are common to almost all verbs:

I was loving/used to love/would love/loved . . .	amā**bam**
you [s.] . . .	amā**bās**
s/he, it . . .	amā**bat**
we . . .	amā**bāmus**
you [pl.] . . .	amā**bātis**
they . . .	amā**bant**

The stems vary slightly according to the conjugation. The 1st conjugation is **-ābam**, etc, while the rest are **-ēbam**. The 4th and mixed conjugations end **-iēbam**, etc.

1st conjugation:	**amābam**	*I was loving/used to love/loved*
2nd conjugation:	**habēbam**	*I was having/used to have/had*
3rd conjugation:	**mittēbam**	*I was sending/used to send/sent*
4th conjugation:	**audiēbam**	*I was hearing/used to hear/heard*
Mixed conjugation:	**capiēbam**	*I was capturing/used to capture/captured*

Practice 11a

Fill the gaps:

(a) in forō .... {*they were wandering*}.
(b) taurum .... {*I used to fear*}.
(c) cūr servī .... {*were weeping*}?
(d) quis .... {*was laughing*}?
(e) vīnumne, ō servī, ... {*were you drinking*}?
(f) lībertōs .... {*I was praising*}.
(g) quid .... {*were we hearing*}?
(h) Fulviane mīlitēs .... {*was leading*}?

Translating the imperfect

A standard way of translating the imperfect tense is *was . . .* or *were . . . .* But the simple past (which also represents the Latin perfect) can be used too:

prīmō magis ambitiō quam avāritia animōs hominum **exercēbat**
at first ambition rather than greed <u>exercised</u> the minds of men   [6.1]

Here are different ways to translate **senātor bibēbat**: *the senator . . . drank, used to drink, was/were drinking, continued to drink, would drink[1], began to drink* or *tried to drink.* Try *was/were . . .* first, and if that seems clumsy then a simple past ('*-ed*') or one of these other expressions.

Imperfect tense of irregular verbs

The imperfect tense of **sum** (and compounds **absum** and **adsum**) and **possum** share eccentric forms in the imperfect. You have seen one or two already:

nōndum mātūrus imperiō Ascanius **erat**
Ascanius <u>was</u> not yet ready for power   [1.6]

eram	*I was*
erās	*you [s.] were*
erat	*s/he, it, there was*
erāmus	*we were*
erātis	*you [pl.] were*
erant	*they were*

1 Not to be confused with the conditional *would*: *Every day the general <u>would ask</u> my opinion* is the equivalent of the imperfect. *If I were important the general <u>would ask</u> my opinion* is a different (conditional) use of *would*.

vix hominēs sine lacrimīs intuērī membra cīvis **poterant**

scarcely could men look without tears at the body-parts of the citizen [10.6]

poteram	*I was able*
poterās	*you [s.] were able*
poterat	*s/he, it was able*
poterāmus	*we were able*
poterātis	*you [pl.] were able*
poterant	*they were able*

The imperfect of **possum** can be translated as *I was able* or *I could*. The imperfect of **absum** (*I am absent*) follows the pattern of **sum**, i.e. **aberam, aberās**, etc, and the same for **adsum** (*I am present*): **aderam, aderās**, etc. Other irregular verbs have the usual imperfect endings:

> eō, īre (*go*): **ībam, ībās**, etc
> volō, velle (*wish*): **volēbam, volēbās**, etc
> ferō, ferre (*bear*): **ferēbam, ferēbās**, etc

The pluperfect tense

This tense is translated into English with the auxiliary *had*. It represents a further step back in the past:

> *I had cleaned the doorway but shortly afterwards it was dirty again*

The pluperfect endings are common to all verbs. The tense is formed with the perfect stem (e.g. **amav**-ī) with these endings (identical to the imperfect of **sum** above):

+ -eram, -erās, -erat, -erāmus, -erātis, -erant:

I had loved...	amāv**eram**
you [s.] had loved	amāv**erās**
s/he, it [or noun] had loved	amāv**erat**
we had loved	amāv**erāmus**
you [pl.] had loved	amāv**erātis**
they [or plural noun] had loved	amāv**erant**

The perfect stem of a verb is shown in the principal parts of a verb:

I had loved = **amāv**-eram	[amō, amāre, **amāvī**, amātum]
I had sent = **mīs**-eram	[mittō, mittere, **mīsī**, missum]
I had captured = **cēp**-eram	[capiō, capere, **cēpī**, captum]
I had been = **fu**-eram	[sum, ess, **fuī**, —]
I had wanted = **volu**-eram	[volō, velle, **voluī**, —]

Practice 11b

Translate into Latin:
(a) he was
(b) she was wishing
(c) they were present
(d) I could
(e) you [pl.] were able
(f) I was absent
(g) there were
(h) you [s.] were
(i) they were going

Hannibal patriā profugus **pervēnerat** ad Antiochum

Hannibal, a fugitive from his own country, <u>had come</u> to Antiochus   [4.5]

fuerat animus coniūrātīs corpus occīsī in Tiberim trahere

*the intention for the conspirators <u>had</u>
<u>been</u> to drag the body of the killed man
into the Tiber*   [9.5]

The difference between the pluperfect
amāverant and the perfect
amāvērunt is one letter. In spoken
Latin, however, it is likely that the
stressing of the two words – and less
so their endings – kept them distinct:
the long 'e' of **amāvērunt** is stressed
but the short 'e' of **amāverant** is
not. See p. 354 for more on stress.

Practice 11c

Put these verbs (now in the present tense) into
the pluperfect tense (in the same person):

(a) amās
(b) dūcō
(c) dīcit
(d) rīdet
(e) sunt
(f) iubeō
(g) accipit
(h) veniunt
(i) laudāmus

Numbers

The numbers *one, two* and *three* have variable endings.

	Cardinals	Ordinals
1	**ūnus,-a,-um** *	**prīmus,-a,-um** *1st*
2	**duo** *	**secundus,-a,-um** *2nd*
3	**trēs, tria** *	**tertius,-a,-um** *3rd*
4	**quattuor**	**quārtus,-a,-um** *4th*
5	**quīnque**	**quīntus,-a,-um** *5th*
6	**sex**	**sextus,-a,-um** *6th*
7	**septem**	**septimus,-a,-um** *7th*
8	**octō**	**octāvus,-a,-um** *8th*
9	**novem**	**nōnus,-a,-um** *9th*
10	**decem**	**decimus,-a,-um** *10th*
100	**centum**	
1000	**mīlle** (pl. **mīlia** *)	

* variable endings

	Masculine	Feminine	Neuter
N.	ūnus	ūna	ūnum
A.	ūnum	ūnam	ūnum
G.	ūnīus	ūnīus	ūnīus
D.	ūnī	ūnī	ūnī
Ab.	ūnō	ūnā	ūnō
N.	duo	duae	duo
A.	duōs	duās	duo
G.	duōrum	duārum	duōrum
D.	duōbus	duābus	duōbus
Ab.	duōbus	duābus	duōbus
N.	trēs	trēs	tria
A.	trēs	trēs	tria
G.	trium	trium	trium
D.	tribus	tribus	tribus
Ab.	tribus	tribus	tribus

Look online for more numbers (see p. 393).

Practice 11d

Identify the case of each underlined word, and translate:

(a) **duo** cōnsulēs inde creātī sunt.

(b) in triumphō Mariī ante currum eius Iugurtha cum **duōbus** fīliīs ductus est.

(c) **tribus** et vīgintī plāgīs cōnfossus est, **ūnō** modo ad **prīmum** ictum gemitū.

(d) Cicerōnis caput inter **duās** manūs in rōstrīs positum est.

(e) iacēbant tot Rōmānōrum **mīlia**.

Vocabulary 11

Here are similar-looking words which are easy to confuse. Some are the same words used differently, and others will look identical in a text without macrons, e.g. **occīdō** and **occidō** (which have very different meanings . . .)

put to flight, chase **fugō, fugāre**	.....	**fugiō, fugīre** *flee, escape*
this, he **hic**	.....	**hīc** *here*
free **līber,-era,-erum**	.....	**liber, librī** *book*
knock down, kill **occīdō, occīdere**	.....	**occidō, occidere** *fall, die*
prepare **parō, parāre**	.....	**pāreō, pārēre** [+ dat.] *obey*
which, whom [f.] **quam**	.....	**quam** *than, as, how*
indeed, even **quidem**	.....	**quīdam** *a certain (one), somebody*
who, which **quis**	.....	**quis** *any(one), some(one)*
which, that which **quod**	.....	**quod** *because*
keep, protect **servō, servāre**	.....	**serviō, servīre** [+ dat.] *serve*

Keep a space in your notebook for words which look alike or have more than one meaning. There are other ways to help your memory, for instance by listing opposite or paired meanings (e.g. **bonus** – **malus**, **rēx** – **rēgīna**, etc).

Add more words with fixed endings to your notebook:

deinde (sometimes shortened to **dein**) *then, next, afterwards*	**nōnne** *surely . . .?* (expecting the answer 'yes')
ēheu, heu *alas, oh no*	**num** *surely . . .not?* (expecting the answer 'no')
inde *then, after that, from that place*	
intereā *meanwhile*	**sīc** *so, thus, in this way, just so, yes*
igitur *therefore, then, accordingly*	**tamen** *nevertheless, yet, still, for all that, however*
ita *so, in such a way, thus*	
minimē *not at all*	**umquam** *ever*
modo *only, recently*	**vērō** *indeed, yes*

Latin can express a liking or preference with **placet** (**placeō, placēre**), used impersonally, meaning *it is pleasing, acceptable, agreeable*, with its object in the dative, e.g.:

> **litterās discere Latīnās mihi <u>placet</u>**
> <u>*it is pleasing*</u> *to me to learn Latin literature* (*I like . . .*)

Exercises 11a

1. Put each verb into the equivalent imperfect and then pluperfect forms:
(a) mittunt
(b) scrībō
(c) sum
(d) accipis
(e) iubet
(f) parāmus
(g) fugit
(h) audīmus

2. Translate:
(a) ō mulier, quid nunc tibi placet?
(b) quis Cleopātrae venēnum parāverat?
(c) Iūlius sōlus et Pompēium et Crassum retinēre poterat.
(d) nōs omnēs flētūm mulieris dēmentis audīverāmus.
(e) servus Caesarī corpus Antōniī ostenderat.
(f) Clōdia marītō erat contenta ūnō.

3. Translate:
(a) quis aderat?
 — iussū Caesaris aderāmus.
(b) Brūtus Caesarem occīdere parābat.
 — nōnne māter Brūtī Caesarem dīlēxit?
(c) tū Caesarem trucīdātum vidistī?
 — vērō, ego etiam ictūs gladiōrum audīvī.
(d) ego lībertus meam dominam amō.
 — sed tuam dominam dūcere uxōrem nōn potes.
(e) corpora mīlitum in flūmen tracta sunt.
 — minimē, in viā relicta sunt.
(f) cūr semper tibi servus pārēre vult?
 — in meā manū est flagellum.
(g) vīsne verba audīre Cicerōnis?
 — minimē, ego carmina Catullī.
(h) ēheu, in vīllā erant vestīgia meī taurī.
 — minimē, erant tuae socrūs.

4. Translate into Latin:
(a) Clodia, why were you laughing? Surely you were sad?
(b) I used to love Clodia but now I love Tullia.

Politics and marriage

Marriage for the Roman elite at this time was very much motivated by political match-making. Divorce was a regular fact of life. A few women are recorded as divorcing even while pregnant. That may seem shocking to us, but barely raises an eyebrow of writers reporting it. Women kept control over the dowry they brought to the relationship, so any divorce would make a husband poorer. The marriage of Cicero and Terentia lasted some thirty years, unusually long, before they too divorced; and Cicero found himself short of funds after she left him. Some of these partnerships were built on loyalty and love: the match of Pompey with Caesar's daughter Julia was said to be a loving relationship, despite the age difference; and Fulvia's energetic loyalty to Clodius and then Antony deserves a mention in the face of an overwhelmingly hostile press (Cicero). After Fulvia's death Antony married Octavian's sister Octavia – wife number four – when he was already linked with Cleopatra, queen of Egypt. Throughout their marriage, which was spent almost entirely apart, Octavia brought up Fulvia's children by Antony together with her own.

Clodia was known for many amorous relationships, even seducing slaves if her enemies are to be believed. The poet Catullus most probably was one of her lovers. But only one husband is recorded for her, Quintus Metellus Celer, whom in 59 BC she was rumoured to have poisoned. As with Fulvia, her character is known through the unflattering words of Cicero. She disappears from view in the late 50s.

In the past few years there has been a good deal of research into the role of women in the ancient world. Much of this is interpreting scraps of evidence and reading between the lines, weighing inferences from texts all written by men. Women tend to be the stuff of anecdotes, models of virtue, eye-catching stories of wicked or wild behaviour. But they were bit-part players: Romans created the genre of biography without producing one full portrait of a woman. What we would

Reading notes

From this chapter on there appear not just isolated fragments of poetry but whole lines and verses. For a close look at the metres which appear in the course, see Poetic Metres, available with other online supports (p. 393). However, before you go into the detail, it is worth noting that if you are able to pronounce the words clearly, with attention to both vowel length (macron or not) and natural stress (see p. 354), and if you have a good feel for the meaning and tone of what is written, you will read the verses perfectly well. And the more you read (or hear) the more you will recognize the rhythm patterns.

There is one rule for reading poetry which you do need to know now, and that is elision. Elision takes place where a word which ends in a vowel is followed by a word starting with a vowel: the final vowel (and therefore syllable) of the first word loses its value as a syllable and the sound glides into the following word.[1] E.g.:

moeni(a) et addictōs   [11.12]
Aegyptum vīrīsqu(e) Orientis   [11.5]
aus(a) et iacentem   [11.14]

1 A final syllable ending '-m' also disappears, and an initial 'h' has no value as a consonant.

give for more lengthy treatments of some of the women we glimpse at this time. Fragments of evidence reveal wives or mothers of leading politicians who had considerable influence behind the scenes and no doubt shaped the course of events. We can see at the meeting Cicero attended with Brutus' female relatives a revealing cameo of politics behind closed doors [9.9].

Whatever political influence women had, it was not through open channels. They were not entitled to vote, stand for office, address an assembly or participate in public debate. Even appearing in the forum was frowned upon. Romans were not entirely unfamiliar with the idea of women in public roles of authority, whether through myths and legends (e.g. Dido), or as vassal-rulers in other parts of the world (Cleopatra, Boudicca, Cartimandua), or in worship of their implacable goddesses – Juno, Diana, Fortuna, *inter alia*. But any woman who sought a public role was treated with derision – by her enemies at least – and the view persisted that *reginae* were like *reges*; only worse, they were female.

Octavian's marriage to Claudia, the daughter of Fulvia and Clodius, and stepdaughter of Antony, was according to Velleius demanded by the soldiers of the two generals. For a short while Octavian enjoyed closer relations with Fulvia, who evidently was a powerful presence in Rome and in the public eye, unlike a typical *domina*.

After divorcing Claudia, Octavian married again: Scribonia. She was the niece of the wife of Pompey's son, Sextus, who was the fourth man in the triumvirate as it were. During this period Sextus Pompeius was a constant threat to the triumvirate, controlling much of the western Mediterranean: Spain, Sicily and the other islands, and crucially the sea. He had with him survivors of the Republican cause, including many who had escaped the proscriptions of 43. They pinned their hopes on his pedigree – he was Pompey's actual son (not adopted like Octavian). Sextus was however criticized for not sharing his father's old-fashioned qualities. He put his trust in freedmen and less so in the old nobles. He even had the temerity to use slaves as rowers for his ships. But Sextus was living a precarious life in exile, and managing with some success. He controlled the sea to the extent that corn supplies to Rome were under threat. It was some time before Octavian and his general Agrippa finally brought his resistance to an end (36 BC).

1.   Octavian's marriage to Scribonia did not last long. Suetonius records that he divorced her, unable to put up with her bad character, and immediately took his third wife, Livia, a marriage which lasted until he died some fifty years later.

statim Līviam Drūsillam mātrimōniō Tiberiī Nerōnis et
quidem praegnantem abdūxit, dīlēxitque et probāvit ūnicē
ac perseveranter.

Suetonius, Life of Augustus 62

The subject here is Octavian

statim   *immediately*

mātrimōniō Tiberiī Nerōnis   *from the marriage of Tiberius Nero*   (i.e. her marriage to . . .)

et quidem   *even though*

praegnantem [acc.]   *pregnant* (i.e. with Drusus, the second of her two sons by Tiberius
    Nero; the elder boy was the future emperor Tiberius)

abdūcō,-ere,-ūxī,-uctum [3]   *lead away*

probō,-āre,-āvī,-ātum [1]   *cherish*

ūnicē   *especially, above all*

perseverānter   *perseveringly, steadfastly*

2.   Octavian recorded his campaign against Sextus Pompeius in his own account of his achievements written at the end of his life (*Res Gestae*). Sextus was described as a pirate.

> mare pācāvī ā praedōnibus. eō bellō servōrum, quī
> fūgerant ā dominīs suīs et arma contrā rem pūblicam
> cēperant, trīgintā ferē mīlia capta dominīs ad supplicium
> sūmendum trādidī.

Augustus, My Political Achievements 25

mare, maris [n.]   *sea*
pācō,-āre [1]   *pacify*
praedō,-ōnis [m.]   *robber, pirate*
Word order: 'eō bellō ferē trīgintā mīlia servōrum capta, quī fūgerant ā dominīs suīs et arma contrā rem pūblicam cēperant, trādidī dominīs ad supplicium sūmendum' (Once you have the meaning, always re-read the actual sentence in the right order)
eō [abl.]   *that*
servōrum: for the genitive see 'mīlia trīgintā' below
fūgerant, cēperant: pluperfect of 'fugiō,-īre' and 'capiō,-ere'
mīlia trīgintā   *thirty thousand* (take as a noun, i.e. *thirty thousands of . . .*)
ferē   *almost, approximately*
supplicium,-ī [n.]   *punishment* (typically, execution in a supplicant's position, i.e. kneeling)
ad supplicium sūmendum   *for punishment to be exacted*
trādidī: perfect of 'trādō,-ere'

3.   Lepidus' part in the triumvirate fizzled out during Octavian's campaign against Sextus. Between 36 and 32 things deteriorated further between Octavian and Antony. In 32 Antony divorced Octavia. He was now openly acknowledging Cleopatra as his wife, and fathered children by her. In 31 BC the conflict between the two leaders reached its climax at Actium.

> Caesar navālī proeliō apud Actium vīcit.

Suetonius, Life of Augustus 17

navālis,-e   *naval*
apud [preposition + acc.]   *in the presence of, near*

4.   The sea battle was regarded as the decisive moment sealing Octavian's singular authority over Rome. Virgil describes it depicted on the shield which the god Vulcan makes for Aeneas. The gods, the highest symbols of state, line up behind Octavian, and with them the precious *Penates*, the spirits of the home.

> hinc Augustus agēns Italōs in proelia Caesar
> cum patribus populōque, penātibus et magnīs dīs.

Virgil, Aeneid 8.678-9

hinc   *on this side (is)*
agēns [the person doing this is in the nominative]   *leading*
Italus,-ī [m.]   *Italian*

proelium,-ī [n.]   *combat, battle*   (in plural 'war')
penātēs,-ium [m.]   *spirits of the household*
dīs = deīs: dat./abl.pl. of 'deus,-ī'

5.   Antony's forces are shown full of foreigners.

**Aegyptum vīrīsque Orientis et ultima sēcum
Bactra vehit, sequiturque (nefās) Aegyptia coniūnx.**

Virgil, *Aeneid* 8.685-8

The subject of 'vehit' is Antony
Aegyptum . . . vīrīs . . . Bactra: all are accusative, objects of 'vehit'
vīrīs: acc. of 'vīrēs,-ium' [f.pl.]   *(military) strength*
Oriēns,-entis   *the east*
ultimus,-a,-um   *farthest, remote*
sēcum = cum sē
Bactra,-ōrum [n.pl.]   *Bactra* (about 200 miles north-west of what is now Kabul in
    Afghanistan).
vehō,-ere, vēxī, vectum [3]   *carry, bring*
sequitur   *(s/he) follows*
nefās   *a monstrous thing, an abomination* (see p. 92)
Aegyptius,-a,-um   *Egyptian*

6.   In fact Antony still had many friends and supporters in Italy, including the two current
consuls. Octavian allowed them to leave Italy and join Antony.

**remīsit tamen Antōniō amīcōs omnēs, atque inter aliōs
Sosium et Domitium tunc adhūc cōnsulēs.**

Suetonius, *Life of Augustus* 17

The subject is Octavian
remittō,-ere,-mīsī,-missum [3]   *send back, allow to return*
aliōs [acc.pl.]   *others*
tunc   *then, at that time*

7.   The actual sea battle was not altogether decisive, but showed the momentum
was now with Octavian. After a limited engagement Cleopatra set sail for Egypt and
Antony followed. He may have been escaping final defeat or simply avoiding a contest.

**prīma occupat fugam Cleopātra. Antōnius fugientis
rēgīnae quam pugnantis mīlitis suī comes esse māluit.**

Velleius Paterculus, *Compendium of Roman History* 2.85

occupō,-āre [1]   *take, seize*
fugientis [gen.]   *escaping, fleeing*
pugnantis [gen.]   *fighting*
mīlitis: here used in the singular (genitive) for *army* or *soldiers*
comes,-itis [m.]   *companion*
māluit   *(s/he) preferred*

8.   Octavian caught up with him the following year.

proximō deinde annō persecūtus rēgīnam Antōniumque
Alexandrēam, ultimam bellīs cīvīlibus imposuit manum.

Velleius Paterculus, Compendium of Roman History 2.87

The subject is Octavian
persecūtus [nom.]   *having followed, chased*
Alexandrēam: *to Alexandria* (Pompey had fled here a few years before, chased by Caesar;
   see 8.10)
ultimam imposuit manum   *he applied the finishing touches to*

9.   Both Antony and Cleopatra committed suicide.

Antōnium, sērās condiciōnēs pācis temptantem, ad
mortem adēgit vīditque mortuum.

Suetonius, Life of Augustus 17

The subject is Octavian
sērus,-a,-um   *late, belated*
condiciō,-ōnis [f.]   *condition, term*
temptantem [the person doing this is in the accusative singular]   *trying, proposing*
mors, mortis [f.]   *death*
adigō,-ere, adēgī, adāctum [3]   *drive to, push to*
mortuus,-a,-um   *dead*
vīditque mortuum   *and he saw him dead*, i.e. he inspected Antony's corpse to confirm his
   death

10. Octavian wanted Cleopatra alive, to show her in Rome.

Cleopātrae, quam servātam triumphō magnopere
cupiēbat, etiam psyllōs admōvit, quī venēnum exsūgerent,
quod perīsse morsū aspidis putābātur.

Suetonius, Life of Augustus 17

Cleopātrae: dative, indirect object of 'admōvit'
quam [f.; acc.]   *who(m)*
servō,-āre ,-āvī,-ātum [1]   *save, keep*
magnopere   *greatly*
psyllī,-ōrum [m.]   *serpent charmers*
admoveō,-ēre,-ōvī,-ōtum [2]   *move to, bring in*
quī [nom.]   *who*
venēnum,-ī [n.]   *poison*
exsūgerent   *(they) might suck out*
quod   *because*
perīsse   *to have perished*
morsus,-ūs [m.]   *bite*
aspis, aspidis [f.]   *viper, asp*
putābātur   *(s/he) was thought*

11.   The son Cleopatra bore to Julius Caesar stood little chance despite a desperate effort to escape. Octavian had no intention of sharing his father with an actual offspring.

Caesariōnem, quem ex Caesare Cleopātra concēpisse praedicābat, retractum ē fugā suppliciō affēcit.

Suetonius, *Life of Augustus* 17

The subject of the main verb 'affēcit' is Octavian
Caesariō,-ōnis   *Caesarion* (see ch.9, no.3)
quem [m.; acc.]   *who*
Caesare: i.e. Julius
concēpisse   *to have conceived*
praedicō,-āre,-āvī,-ātum [1]   *proclaim, say publicly*
retrahō,-ere,-traxī,-tractum [3]   *drag back, bring back*
fuga,-ae [f.]   *flight*
afficiō,-ere, affēcī, affectum [M.]   *afflict*

12.   What the writers do not say once Octavian was in power, was how the old-school Republicans had favoured Brutus and Cassius over him and Antony, how they then supported the 'pirate' Sextus, and throughout the triumvirate pinned more faith in Antony than Octavian himself. Antony's absence in the east allowed Octavian to redress this and build up more support. By the time of Actium, many defections coupled with the eastern composition of Antony's fleet made propaganda against him easy. Antony had threatened to impose on Rome a foreigner, a *regina*, a whore, who . . .

coniugī obscēnī pretium Rōmāna poposcit
moenia et addictōs in sua rēgna patrēs.

Propertius, *Elegies* 3.11.31–2

coniugium,-ī [n.]   *union, marriage*
obscēnus,-a,-um   *obscene, foul*
pretium,-ī [n.]   *price (she demanded <u>as</u> a price . . .)*
poscō,-ere, poposcī [3]   *demand*
moenia,-ōrum [n.pl.]   *walls, city*
addictus,-a,-um   *enslaved to a creditor, made subject to*
patrēs: here *senators*
Word order: 'poposcit pretium obscēni coniugī Rōmāna moenia et patrēs addictōs in sua rēgna'

13.   While Cleopatra was still at large there was no time for partying, says Horace:

antehāc nefās dēprōmere Caecubum
cellīs avītīs, dum Capitōliō

rēgīna dēmentīs ruīnās
fūnus et imperiō parābat.

Horace, *Odes* 1.37.5–8

antehāc [only two syllables: the middle 'e' fades into the following syllable]   *before this,*
  hitherto
nefās   *improper, wrong, a sacrilege* (understand 'erat' with 'nefās')
dēprōmō,-ere [3]   *bring forth*
Caecubum: understand 'vīnum' (*Caecuban wine*, named after the district in Latium where
  it was grown)
cella,-ae [f.]   *cellar*
avītus,-a,-um   *ancestral*
dum   *while*
dēmentīs: accusative plural (alt. spelling of 'dēmentēs')
ruīna,-ae [f.]   *fall, destruction, ruin* (plural because of the multiple destruction)
fūnus,-eris [n.]   *death*
parābat   *(s/he) was preparing*
Word order for 'dum . . . parābat': 'dum rēgīna parābat dēmentīs ruīnās Capitōliō et
  fūnus imperiō.' Note how in verse 'et' can hop out of what appears to us its proper
  position: we take it *before* 'fūnus'.

14. Later in the same poem Horace's patriotism gives way to a more sympathetic view of
    Cleopatra, who refuses to walk through Rome in chains.

ausa et iacentem vīsere rēgiam
vultū serēnō, fortis et asperās
    tractāre serpentēs, ut ātrum
        corpore combiberet venēnum,

dēlīberātā morte ferōcior:
saevīs Liburnīs scīlicet invidēns
    prīvāta dēdūcī superbō,
        nōn humilis mulier, triumphō.

Horace, Odes 1.37.25–32

ausa [understand 'est' and take as the main verb]   *she was emboldened, she dared*
iacentem [acc. singular]   *lying, fallen, powerless*
vīsō,-ere, vīsī [3]   *go to see, gaze on*
rēgia,-ae [f.]   *palace*
serēnus,-a,-um   *calm*
fortis,-e   *brave* (here nominative agreeing with the subject 'she')
asper,-era,-erum [like 'miser']   *harsh, bitter*
tractō,-āre [1]   *touch, handle*
serpēns,-ntis [f.]   *serpent*
ut   *so that*
āter,-tra,-trum [like 'noster, nostra, nostrum']   *black, dismal*
corpus,-oris [n.]   *body* (abl.: *with her body*, i.e. *throughout her body*)
combiberet   *(she) might drink entirely*
dēlīberō,-āre,-āvī,-ātum [1]   *resolve, decide* ('dēlīberātā morte' = *with her death decided,*
  i.e. *having resolved to die*)

ferōcior [nom.]   *more defiant*

Liburnī,-ōrum [m.]   *the Liburni*   (a people from mod. Croatia who supported Octavian
   with ships and, Horace imagines, would have transported the prisoner to Rome)

scīlicet   *no doubt, to be sure*

invidēns [nom.; with its object in the dative]   *cheating* (the person doing this is 'she', i.e.
   Cleopatra)

prīvātus,-a,-um   *private, stripped of one's rank*

dēdūcī   *to be led away*

humilis,-e   *lowly, insignificant, humble*

Word order for the last three lines: 'scīlicet invidēns saevīs Liburnīs dēdūcī prīvāta superbō
   triumphō, nōn humilis mulier.' The adjective 'superbō' may be distant from its noun
   'triumphō' but the two words are brought together not only by their endings and the
   expected sense but also their corresponding positions at the ends of their lines.

Exercises 11b

1.   Identify the tense of each underlined verb:

mare **pācāvī** ā praedōnibus. eō bellō servōrum, quī **fūgerant** ā dominīs suīs et arma
contrā rem pūblicam **cēperant**, trīgintā ferē mīlia capta dominīs ad supplicium
sūmendum **trādidī**.

2.   Why do you think **praedicābat** [11.11] is imperfect and not perfect?

3.   Translate:
(a)   puerīsne placēbat Graecās litterās discere?
(b)   vix sine lacrimīs vōcem Cleopātrae audīre poterāmus.
(c)   Pompēius et Crassus cōnsulātum summā discordiā simul gesserant.
(d)   domina dēmēns mihi fūnus parābat.

4.   Put each underlined verb into the *imperfect* tense and translate your answer:
(a)   arma virumque **canō**. *(canō,-ere)*
(b)   multī cīvēs Corinthī et Athēnārum ōrnāmenta **laudant**. *(laudō,-āre)*
(c)   **contemnunt** novitātem meam senātōrēs. *(contemnō,-ere)*
(d)   nec vitia nostra nec remedia patī **possumus**. *(possum, posse)*
(e)   ego Caesaris amīcitiam retinēre **volō**. *(volō, velle)*

5.   Put each underlined verb into the *present* tense and translate your answer:
(a)   Dīdō silvā in magnā **errābat**. *(errō,-āre)*
(b)   Octāviam, sorōrem Caesaris, Antōnius **dūxit** uxōrem. *(dūcō,-ere)*
(c)   Iūlius Caesar **dīlēxit** Mārcī Brūtī mātrem Servīliam. *(dīligō,-ere)*
(d)   nōnne togae arma **cessērunt**? *(cēdō,-ere)*
(e)   plēbs caput Cinnae praefixum hastae **circumtulit**. *(circumferō, circumferre)*

6.   Find a Latin word from this chapter which is an ancestor of both *mile* and *millennium*.

— 12 —

The sweetness of peace

Nouns: 5th declension

The 5th declension has the fewest nouns, but they appear frequently enough, especially **rēs** (*thing*) and **diēs** (*day*). The endings are similar to the 3rd declension, but watch for the genitive singular (**-eī**), which is the same as the dative. Remember that it is the genitive singular which is listed in dictionaries after the nominative.

rēs, reī [f.] *thing, matter*

	singular	plural
N.	**rēs**	**rēs**
V.	**rēs**	**rēs**
A.	**rem**	**rēs**
G.	**reī**	**rērum**
D.	**reī**	**rēbus**
Ab.	**rē**	**rēbus**

You have met **rēs** a few times already:

ūnus homō nōbīs cūnctandō restituit **rem**
one man recovered the situation for us by delaying [3.7]

rēs est omnis in hāc causā nōbīs, iūdicēs, cum Clōdiā
the whole issue for us in this case is with Clodia [8.1]

cūncta plēbs, novārum **rērum** studiō, Catilīnae incepta probābat
all the ordinary people, with their eagerness for new things (i.e. *political change*), *approved of Catiline's initiatives* [6.5]

verba **rēbus** erunt contrāria
the words will be opposite to the actions [10.2]

With the adjective **pūblica, rēs** means *the Republic*:

dēfendī **rem pūblicam** adulēscēns, nōn dēseram senex
in my youth I defended the Republic, and now, an old man, I'll not abandon it [9.12]

Practice 12a

Put each underlined word into Latin in the correct case:

(a)   in matters of health
(b)   she managed the affairs of the household
(c)   in the matter of your debts
(d)   friends of the Republic
(e)   I gave everything to the Republic

The future tense

The future tense expresses what is to happen in the future, usually translated with *shall* or *will*. The future endings of the first two conjugations are similar and the other three likewise.

The future tense of the 1st and 2nd conjugations:

	1st	2nd
I shall . . .	amā**bō**	habē**bō**
you [s.] will . . .	amā**bis**	habē**bis**
s/he, it will. . .	amā**bit**	habē**bit**
we shall. . .	amā**bimus**	habē**bimus**
you [pl.] will. . .	amā**bitis**	habē**bitis**
they will. . .	amā**bunt**	habē**bunt**

The future tense of the 3rd, 4th and mixed conjugations:

	3rd	4th	Mixed
I shall. . .	mitt**am**	audi**am**	capi**am**
you [s.] will. . .	mitt**ēs**	audi**ēs**	capi**ēs**
s/he, it will. . .	mitt**et**	audi**et**	capi**et**
we shall . . .	mitt**ēmus**	audi**ēmus**	capi**ēmus**
you [pl.] will. . .	mitt**ētis**	audi**ētis**	capi**ētis**
they will . . .	mitt**ent**	audi**ent**	capi**ent**

vīvōs **dūcent** dē marmore vultūs
they will bring living faces from marble [4.9]

cum surgit, **surgēs**; dōnec sedet illa, **sedēbis** (surgō,-ere, sedeō,-ēre)
when she rises, you will rise, for as long as she sits, you will sit [13.7]

Practice 12b

Translate each into one Latin word:
(a) I shall praise
(b) he will grieve
(c) they will see
(d) you [pl.] will read
(e) they will flee
(f) we shall hear
(g) she will come
(h) they will conquer

The future tense of irregular verbs

There are of course some irregular forms. The principal suspect is **sum**, along with its compounds **absum** and **adsum**, and **possum**:

verba rēbus **erunt** contrāria
the words will be opposite to the actions [10.2]

erō	*I shall be*
eris	*you [s.] will be*
erit	*s/he, it will be*
erimus	*we shall be*
eritis	*you [pl.] will be*
erunt	*they will be*

The compound forms take the future endings of **sum**: for **adsum** (*I am present*) that is **aderō, aderis**, etc. For **absum** (*I am absent*) it is **aberō, aberis**, etc; and the future of **possum** (*I am able*) is **poterō, poteris**, etc.

Other irregular verbs have reasonably standard forms in the future tense:

eō, īre (*go*): **ībō, ībis, ībit, ībimus, ībitis, ībunt**
volō, velle (*wish*): **volam, volēs, volet, volēmus, volētis, volent**
ferō, ferre (*bear*): **feram, ferēs, feret, ferēmus, ferētis, ferent**

Practice 12c

Translate into one Latin word:
(a) I shall go
(b) he will be present
(c) I shall wish
(d) I shall be able
(e) they will go
(f) she will bear

(g) they will be absent
(h) you [s.] will be able
(i) it will be
(j) I shall bear
(k) you [pl.] will wish
(l) we shall be absent

Imperatives

If you were at an amphitheatre you might have heard people shouting at someone battling in the arena:

occīde! verberā! ūre!
kill! whip! burn! [21.7]

These are all imperatives, from **occīdō,-ere** [3], **verberō,-āre** [1] and **ūrō,-ere** [3].

The imperative of the verb carries a note of urgency, either as a command or a plea. The singular imperative is said to one person, the plural to more than one:

	singular	plural	
1st conjugation **amō,-are**	amā	am**āte**	*love!*
2nd conjugation **habeō,-ēre**	habē	hab**ēte**	*have!*
3rd conjugation **mittō,-ere**	mitte	mitt**ite**	*send!*
4th conjugation **audiō,-īre**	audī	aud**īte**	*hear!*
Mixed conjugation **capiō,-ere**	cape	cap**ite**	*take!*

tacē, Lucrētia   (taceō,-ēre,2)
be quiet, Lucretia   [2.3]

dēsine mēque tuīs incendere tēque querēlīs   (dēsinō,-ere,3)
stop distressing both me and you with your complaints   [3.11]

The singular imperative of the irregular verb **eō, īre** (*go*) is **ī**, and is probably the longest-sounding single letter in the Latin alphabet: 'eeee!'.

ī, sequere Ītaliam ventīs, pete rēgna per undās   [eō, īre]
go, make for Italy with (the help of) the winds, seek the lands across the waves   [3.12]

In the same example, **pete** (*seek!*) is an imperative, from **petō,-ere**, and so too **sequere** (*follow!*) – but this verb works along different lines, which you will meet on p. 188.

Imperatives are naturally short sharp sounds, and one or two much-used Latin ones were shortened further, their final **-e** clipped: **fac** (*do!, make!*), the imperative of **facio,-ere, dīc** (*say!, tell!*) from **dīcō,-ere,** and **fer** (*bring!, take!*) from **ferō, ferre**:

> aut **dīc** aut **accipe** calcem
> *either tell (me) or take a kicking* [13.15]

Practice 12d

Fill each gap with the correct imperative form:

(a) .... {sedeō,-ēre}. *Sit!* [*said to one person*]
(b) .... {carpō,-ere} diem. *Pluck the day!* [*said to one person*]
(c) vīnum.................... {afferō, afferre}. *Bring the wine!* [*said to one person*]
(d) discipulōs.................... {dīmittō,-ere} tuōs. *Dismiss your students!* [*said to one person*]
(e) .... {reddō,-ere} quae Caesaris sunt Caesarī. *Return (the things) to Caesar which are Caesar's.* [*said to more than one*]

Uses of the accusative

This case is most often used as the direct object of a verb; and it can also follow a preposition (**ad, ante, per**, etc).

The accusative case is also used to express the duration or extent of something:

> Tarquinius rēgnāvit **annōs** quīnque et vīgintī
> *Tarquin ruled for twenty-five years* [2.5]

The accusative sometimes appears with an infinitive after a verb of saying or thinking (called the 'accusative and infinitive', which appears fully on p. 286). Where in English we might say *I think that he is foolish*, Latin says *I think him to be foolish*:

> Pompēius cōnfirmat **Clōdium** nihil **esse** factūrum contrā mē
> *Pompey confirms that Clodius will do nothing against me*
> (lit.:. . . *Pompey confirms Clodius to be about to do nothing against me*) [7.5]

Uses of the ablative

In Chapter 2 the ablative case was said to correspond with English prepositional phrases *in . . ., on . . ., with . . ., by . . ., from . . .* and *out of . . .*, sometimes with a Latin preposition, e.g. **in, cum, ā (ab), ē (ex)**, and sometimes without. Here is a summary of the principal uses of the ablative which have appeared in the texts so far:

- to describe a <u>fixed place or time</u> (*in . . ., on . . ., at . . .*), often with the preposition **in**
- to describe <u>by whom</u> something is done, generally with the preposition **ā (ab)**
- to say <u>from</u> . . ., sometimes with the prepositions **ā (ab)** or **ē (ex)**
- to express <u>accompaniment</u> (i.e. *together with* . . ., often with the preposition **cum**)
- to say <u>how</u> something has happened, sometimes by intention (i.e. the instrument or method) which is translated *with . . ., by . . ., through . . ., by means of . . .*)
- or to say <u>how</u> in a less deliberate sense, as the manner or cause of something
- to express the standard or point of a comparison, as in

> **rē pūblicā** nihil mihi est cārius
> *nothing is dearer to me <u>than the Republic</u>* [8.8]

- with <u>prepositions</u> such as the ones seen above and **dē, prō, sine** and **sub**
- ablative phrases (called the 'ablative absolute', to be explained in detail on p. 260) as in

> Cleopātra **dēlīberātā morte** ferōcior erat
> *Cleopatra was more defiant after resolving to die* (lit. <u>*with death decided upon*</u>) [11.14]

> **nōbīs** rem pūblicam **gubernantibus**, nōnne togae arma cessērunt?
> *while I was steering the Republic, did not weapons of war give way to the toga?*
> (lit. <u>*with us steering the Republic* . . .</u>) [6.9]

Uses of all the cases are reviewed in Chapters 25 and 26.

Vocabulary 12

Add these 5th declension nouns to your notebook:

aciēs, aciēī [f.] *battleline*	**fidēs, fideī** [f.] *faith, loyalty, trust*
diēs, diēī [m./f.] *day*	**rēs, reī** [f.] *thing, matter, business, issue*
faciēs, faciēī [f.] *face, shape*	**spēs, speī** [f.] *hope*

More words with fixed endings:

adhūc *still, yet*	**quidem** *indeed, certainly, no less*
aut *or*	(emphasizes the word before it)
aut . . . aut *either . . . or*	**nē . . . quidem** *not even . . .*
autem *however, but, and now*	**quod** *which, because*
enim *for, you see, the fact is*	**quoque** *also, too*
ergō *therefore, so, accordingly, then*	**statim** *immediately*
itaque *and so, and thus*	**ubīque** *everywhere*
magis . . . quam *rather . . . than*	**vel** *or*
mox *soon*	**vix** *barely, hardly, scarcely*

There were two words for *emperor*: **imperātor,-ōris**, which meant a *general* or *commander*, and was included in an emperor's formal title, thus coming to mean *emperor*; and also **prīnceps,-cipis**, which meant *the first man, chief, principal*, and with Augustus *first citizen* and then *emperor*.

Exercises 12a

1. Fill the gaps, and translate ['dōnec' = *while, for as long as*]:
(a) nunc cane! dōnec tua domina canit, ... {*you will sing*}.
(b) dōnec dominus scrībit, servus .... {*will write*}.
(c) dōnec mē amās, tē .... {*I shall love*}.
(d) dōnec prīnceps rīdit, senātōrēs .... {*will laugh*}.
(e) dōnec dolēs, ... {*I shall grieve*}.
(f) dōnec puellae flent, servī .... {*will weep*}.

2. Give the nominative and genitive singular of each underlined word:
avāritia **fidem**, **probitātem**, cēterāsque **artēs** bonās subvertit

3. Give the nominative and genitive singular of all nouns in the ablative:
(a) Lāocoōn ab arce dēcurrit.
(b) nōnō diē in iugum Alpium vēnit.
(c) iūdicēs habēmus quōs voluimus, summā accūsātōris voluntāte.
(d) hōc tempore Catilīnam dēfendere cōgitāmus.
(e) ferrum in meā manū est.

4. (i) Identify the tense of the underlined verbs; (ii) put these verbs into their equivalent future forms; and (iii) translate your answer:
(a) Romulus centum **creat** senātōrēs.
(b) imperātor rēgīnam vidēre vīvam **cupiēbat**.
(c) quis librōs omnēs poētārum accipere **vult**?
(d) Caesar nōn Fulviam **dūxit** uxōrem.

5. Translate:
(a) ī! vīnum affer!
    — nōnne iam vīnum bibistī multum?
    ēheu, mihi īgnōsce.
    (b) mihi placuit eum suppliciō afficere.
    — sed ille erat tuus marītus?
    heu, semper hīc errō.

The sweetness of peace

Octavian had already proved himself to be determined, astute and ruthless when necessary. He now showed himself to be highly capable in government and administration. At the point of Antony's defeat few would have anticipated the next 44 years of his political supremacy: over ten times the length of Caesar's dictatorship. He had the gift of political timing and made the most of his luck. And he certainly was lucky – in retrospect it is easy to

> ## Reading notes
>
> More word order eccentricity: words like **et, quī, ut** and **sī** sometimes appear out of position, or so it seems to us, especially in verse:
>
> > . . . dum Capitōliō/rēgīna dēmentīs ruīnās/fūnus <u>et</u> imperiō parābat [11.13]
> > *. . . while the queen plotted mad destruction upon the Capitol and death for the empire*
> >
> > . . . fortis <u>et</u> asperās/tractāre serpentēs [11.14]
> > *. . . and brave to handle the bitter serpents*
>
> In each example we understand the conjunction **et** *before* the word in front of it.

overlook the many moments of his rise to power when things hung perilously in the balance. To many ancients, deeply superstitious, he was favoured by the gods. Suetonius tells us that Octavian predicted the outcome of a naval engagement from the behaviour of a small fish. Implausible as it may seem, such sign-reading was an integral part of religious belief. We might say tactics and strategy were more influential than the spasms of a fish, but the Romans were more sensitive than perhaps we are to the role of chance and coincidence. And they liked a good story.

Octavian's political entrenchment as the singular authority in Rome was helped by a sense of his 'coming', the one who rescued the state from decades of civil war, often brutal, which had brought the people of Italy to such a state of fear that they were desperate for a leader with the authority to bring peace. He carefully nurtured this growing optimism. He wanted to be seen as the one returning everything to how it should be, if quietly overlooking how his singular authority had suffocated that Republican ideal of government by a consensus of senators. He made much of old-fashioned ideas and practices: forgotten rituals were restored; stricter discipline returned to the army; temples were repaired and new ones built. He promoted the wellbeing of family life, which had been undermined by all the many divorces, adoptions and deaths in the civil wars. There were incentives for having children, and penalties for divorce; adoption was discouraged: children could not be discarded (at least not before they were three years old). The wild partying days of socialites like Clodia were frowned upon, even if his own daughter Julia did not pick up this message.

Augustus (he took this *agnomen* in 27 BC) laid down the precedent for autocratic government for which Sulla and Caesar had already sown the seeds. He avoided the image of king or dictator, preferring the prestige of being *primus inter pares* (first among equals). But with him the character of government changed decisively from an oligarchy with some electoral input – where ideas were openly challenged and debated – to the control of a single authority against whom dissension was unwise. The offices and functions of the senate and its magistracies remained as before, outwardly at least. From now on 'rhetoric' begins to assume the meaning we are familiar with today, that emptier language of posers and flatterers.

1.   Once he was settled back in Rome Octavian formally handed power back to the state, or so he said in his own record, *Res Gestae* (My Political Achievements). The reality was that he could expect the state to do as he willed. He was voted the agnomen 'Augustus'.

rem pūblicam ex meā potestāte in senātūs populīque
Rōmānī arbitrium trānstulī. quō prō meritō meō senātūs
cōnsultō Augustus appellātus sum.

Augustus, *My Political Achievements* 34

potestās,-tātis [f.]   *power*
arbitrium,-ī [n.]   *authority*
trānsferō, trānsferre, trānstulī, trānslātum   *transfer*
quō [abl.]   *which, this*
prō [+ abl.]   *in return for*
meritum,-ī [n.]   *service*
Augustus,-ī   *Augustus* (i.e. *Hallowed One*)
appellātus <u>sum</u>: *I was* . . .

2.   Tacitus, writing more than a century later, summarizes his emergence as *princeps*:

Lepidī atque Antōniī arma in Augustum cessērunt, quī
cūncta discordiīs cīvīlibus fessa nōmine prīncipis sub
imperium accēpit.

Tacitus, *Annals* 1.1

cūnctōs dulcēdine ōtiī pellexit.

Annals 1.2

arma: i.e. *the armed forces*
cēdō,-ere, cessī, cessum [3]   *submit, give way*
quī [nom.]   *who* (Augustus)
cūnctus,-a,-um   *all* (if with no visible noun = *all men/women/things* depending on the gender)
fessus,-a,-um   *exhausted*
prīnceps,-ipis [m.]   *'princeps', leading citizen, emperor*
sub [+ acc.]   *beneath, under*
dulcēdō,-inis [f.]   *sweetness, pleasantness*
ōtium,-ī [n.]   *peace*
pelliciō,-ere, pellexī, pellectum [3]   *win over, entice*

3.   Velleius, born during Augustus' reign, writes warmly of the new peace:

fīnīta vīcēsimō annō bella cīvīlia, revocāta pāx, restitūta vīs
lēgibus, iūdiciīs auctōritās, senātuī maiestās. rediit cultus
agrīs, sacrīs honōs, sēcūritās hominibus.

Velleius Paterculus, *Compendium of Roman History* 2.89

Understand 'est' or 'sunt' with 'fīnīta', 'revocāta' and 'restitūta'
fīniō,-īre [4]   *finish*
vīcēsimus,-a,-um   *twentieth*
revocō,-āre,-āvī,-ātum [1]   *recall, restore*

restituō,-ere, restituī, restitūtum [3]   *bring back, restore*
vīs [nom.f.; an irregular 3rd decl. noun: acc. 'vim', gen. and dat. are rare; abl. 'vī', nom.pl./
   acc.pl. 'vīrēs', gen.pl. 'vīrium', dat.pl./abl.pl. 'vīribus'] *force, potency* (in the plural = *strength*)
lēx, lēgis [f.]   *law*
iūdicium,-ī [n.]   *court*
auctōritās,-tātis [f.]   *power, authority*
senātus,-ūs [m.]   *senate*
māiestās,-tātis [f.]   *dignity*
restitūta senātuī maiestās: on the surface perhaps, but the authority of the senate was
   reduced
redeō,-īre, rediī, reditum   *return*
cultus,-ūs [m.]   *cultivation*
sacer,-cra,-crum [like 'noster-tra,-trum']   *sacred* ('sacra', n. pl. = *sacred rites, sacrifices*)
honōs,-ōris [m.]   *honour, respect* (the nominative 'honōs' is sometimes written 'honor', as
   with 'labōs/labor')
sēcūritās,-tātis [f.]   *security, safety*

4.   Augustus was quicker to punish his opponents than Julius Caesar had been.

quī parentem meum trucīdāvērunt, eōs in exilium expulī.

Augustus, *My Political Achievements* 2

quī [m.; nom./nom.pl.]   *who*
eōs [acc.pl.]   *those men*
exilium,-ī [n.]   *exile*
expellō,-ere, expulī, expulsum [3]   *banish*

5.   On the surface politics carried on as before the civil wars, although in reality anything
   of significance would be referred to Augustus. He increased the number of senators,
   depleted by civil wars and proscriptions, and filled the gaps with newcomers who would
   be well-disposed to himself. He retained control over those provinces with military
   sensitivity (and more troops), and had *imperium* (consular authority) in Italy and Rome.
   But he was careful to avoid symbols of power which had provoked the assassination of
   his adoptive father.

dictātūram mihi dēlātam et ā populō et ā senātū nōn recēpī.

Augustus, *My Political Achievements* 5

dictātūra,-ae [f.]   *dictatorship*
dēferō, dēferre, dētulī, dēlātum   *offer*
recipiō,-ere,-cēpī,-ceptum [M.]   *accept*

6.   He raised the profile of former traditions, religious, social and moral.

multa exempla maiōrum redūxī et ipse multārum rērum exempla imitanda posterīs trādidī.

Augustus, *My Political Achievements* 8

exemplum,-ī [n.]   *example, precedent*
maiōrēs,-um [m.]   *ancestors*
redūcō,-ere,-dūxī,-ductum [3]   *bring back*
ipse [nom.]   *(I) myself*
imitandus,-a,-um   *to be imitated*
posterī,-ōrum [m.]   *descendants, coming generations*

7.   And he was careful to include the gods in his new plans for old Rome.

aedēs sacrās vetustāte collāpsās aut incendiō absūmptās refēcit, eāsque et cēterās opulentissimīs dōnīs adōrnāvit.

Suetonius, *Life of Augustus* 30

aedēs,-is [f.]   *temple, shrine*
vetustās,-tātis [f.]   *old age*
collāpsus,-a,-um   *fallen, collapsed*
aut   *or*
incendium,-ī [n.]   *fire*
absūmptus,-a,-um   *consumed*
reficiō,-ere,-fēcī,-fectum [M.]   *restore, repair*
eās [f.; acc.pl.]   *these* (i.e. 'aedēs')
cēterus,-a,-um   *the other, the rest*
opulentissimus,-a,-um   *very lavish*
adōrnō,-āre,-āvī,-ātum [1]   *decorate*

8.   Augustus claimed that he had inherited the city built in brick and left it decked in marble.

urbem inundātiōnibus incendiīsque obnoxiam excoluit adeō ut iūre sit glōriātus marmoream sē relinquere quam laterīciam accēpisset.

Suetonius, *Life of Augustus* 28

inundātiō,-ōnis [f.]   *flood*
obnoxius,-a,-um [+ dat.]   *liable to*
excolō,-ere,-coluī,-cultum [3]   *tend, improve* (the subject is Augustus)
adeō   *so much, to such an extent* (take this adverb with 'excoluit')
ut   *that, with the result that*
iūre   *rightly, justifiably*
sit glōriātus   *he boasted, claimed*
marmoreus,-a,-um   *made of marble* ('marmoream' agrees with 'urbem'; so too 'laterīciam')
sē relinquere   *him to be leaving, that he was leaving (it,* i.e. 'urbem')
quam [f.; acc.]   *which*
laterīcius,-a,-um   *made of bricks*
accēpisset   *(s/he) had received*
Word order: 'excoluit urbem obnoxiam inundātiōnibus incendiīsque adeō ut iūre sit glōriātus sē relinquere [urbem] marmoream quam accēpisset laterīciam'

9.   Despite his efforts to cleanse social and sexual mores, Suetonius suggests that Augustus
       was not the perfect model:

adulteria exercuisse nē amīcī quidem negant.

Suetonius, Life of Augustus 69

adulterium,-ī [n.]   *act of adultery*
exercuisse   *(him) to have practised, that he practised*
nē . . . quidem   *not even . . .*
negō,-āre,-āvī,-ātum [1]   *deny, say . . . not*

10.   How else could he know what was going on?

cōnsilia adversāriōrum per cuiusque mulierēs exquīrēbat.

Suetonius, Life of Augustus 69

cōnsilium,-ī [n.]   *intention, plan*
adversārius,-ī [m.]   *opponent*
cuiusque [gen.]   *each one*
exquīrō,-ere, exquīsīvī, exquīsītum [3]   *search out, discover*

11.   Augustus worked hard himself.

ipse iūs dīxit assiduē et in noctem nōnnumquam.

Suetonius, Life of Augustus 33

ipse [nom.]   *(he) himself*
iūs, iūris [n.]   *justice ('iūs dīcere' = to administer justice)*
assiduē   *constantly, unremittingly*
et: can also mean *even*, as here
nōnnumquam   *sometimes*

12.   And he expected similar standards from others.

cohortēs, sī quae locō cessissent, decimātās hordeō pāvit.

Suetonius, Life of Augustus 24

cohors,-ortis [f.]   *troop*
quae [f.; nom.pl.]   *any*
cessissent   *(they) had given way*
decimō,-āre,-āvī,-ātum [1]   *decimate, execute every tenth man*   ('decimātās' agrees with
    'cohortēs')
hordeum,-ī [n.]   *barley* (they had to eat barley bread, less appetizing than wheat bread)
pāscō,-ere, pāvī, pāstum [3]   *feed*

13. The administration of the empire was overhauled.

exiit ēdictum ā Caesare Augustō, ut dēscrīberētur
ūniversus orbis.

Luke, *Gospel* 2.1 (trans. Jerome)

exeō,-īre, exiī   *go out*
ēdictum,-ī [n.]   *decree*
ut   *that*
dēscrīberētur   *(s/he, it) should be registered*
ūniversus,-a,-um   *whole, entire*
orbis,-is [m.]   *circle, world*

14. People outside the senatorial body, and even former slaves, were given roles within the
new administration. But newcomers were discouraged from abusing their powers.

Augustus, quod Thallus prō epistulā prōditā dēnāriōs
quīngentōs accēpisset, crūra eī frēgit.

Suetonius, *Life of Augustus* 67

quod   *because*
Thallus: an employee in the new administration
prō [+ abl.]   *in return for*
epistula,-ae [f.]   *letter*
prōditus,-a,-um   *disclosed*, i.e. *leaked*
dēnārius,-ī [m.]   *denarius*
quīngentī,-ae,-a   *five hundred* (500 denarii was roughly what a semi-skilled hireling might
  be paid in a year)
accēpisset   *(s/he) had received*
crūs, crūris [n.]   *leg*
eī [dat.]   *him* (dative showing possession, i.e. *his*)
frangō,-ere, frēgī, frāctum [3]   *break*

15. The Parthians, who had destroyed Crassus' army in 53 BC, were brought to terms –
though they continued to be a menace to Rome long after Augustus.

Parthōs trium exercituum Rōmānōrum spolia et signa
reddere mihi supplicēsque amīcitiam populī Rōmānī
petere coēgī.

Augustus, *My Political Achievements* 29

spolia,-ōrum [n.]   *plunder, spoils* (i.e. stripped from dead soldiers)
signum,-ī [n.]   *sign, standard*
reddō,-ere, reddidī, redditum [3]   *give back* (both 'reddere' and 'petere' depend on 'coēgī')
supplex,-icis [m.]   *supplicant, humble petitioner* ('Parthōs supplicēs petere coēgī' = *I forced
  the Parthians <u>as</u> supplicants to seek . . .*)

16. The only reversals came in Germany, one particularly bad one in AD 9 where three legions were ambushed and slaughtered along with their commander Quintilius Varus. Suetonius tells us that Augustus would hit his head against a door and shout:

"Quīntilī Vāre, legiōnēs redde!"

Suetonius, Life of Augustus 23

legiō,-ōnis [f.]   legion
redde: an imperative

17. This defeat was exceptional. In general the empire was strengthened and increased during Augustus' principate. Unlike his father he did not trust a vassal ruler to control Egypt, which was rich in corn, but made the country a province and kept it under his close personal control, a move which enhanced his own power and wealth.

Aegyptum imperiō populī Rōmānī adiēcī.

Augustus, My Political Achievements 27

adiciō,-ere, adiēcī, adiectum [M.]   add

18. His political fame reached as far east as India.

ad mē ex Indiā rēgum lēgātiōnēs saepe missae sunt.

Augustus, My Political Achievements 31

rēgum: gen.pl. of 'rēx'
lēgātiō,-ōnis [f.]   embassy
saepe   often

19. Fourty-four years at the top was a remarkable achievement in light of what had gone on before. Augustus set the precedent for 'Imperial' Rome under the emperors.

Augustus prīmum cum Antōniō Lepidōque, deinde tantum cum Antōniō per duodecim ferē annōs, novissimē per quattuor et quadrāgintā sōlus rem pūblicam tenuit.

Suetonius, Life of Augustus 8

prīmum   at first
tantum   only, just
novissimē   most recently, lastly
rem pūblicam: no longer the Republic as ruled by a consensus of senators, but simply 'the state'

20. Towards the end of his life few people were talking about a return to the Republic. It was before their time. No one worried what would come afterwards . . .

. . . dum Augustus aetāte validus sēque et domum et pācem sustentāvit.

Tacitus, Annals 1.4

dum   *while, for as long as*
aetās,-tātis [f.]   *age, life* (ablative: *with respect to . . .*)
validus,-a,-um   *healthy* (understand 'erat' with 'validus')
sustentō,-āre,-āvī,-ātum [1]   *maintain, preserve*

21. Augustus justified his power not as a replacement for the Republic but as a means for keeping it alive. Cicero, a symbol of Republican Rome, had been killed in the triumvirs' proscriptions, but years later Augustus let him be remembered with admiration. The blame for his murder could be laid entirely at Antony's door.

citiusque ē mundō genus hominum quam Cicerō cēdet.

Velleius Paterculus, *Compendium of Roman History* 2.66

citius   *more quickly*
mundus,-ī [m.]   *world*
genus,-eris [n.]   *race*
quam   *than*
cēdō,-ere, cessī, cessum [3]   *give way, fade away*

Exercises 12b

1. Identify the tense of each underlined verb, and translate:
(a) verba Caesaris rēbus **erunt** contrāria.
(b) **dēfendērunt** rem pūblicam adulēscentēs, nōn **dēserent** senēs.
(c) Cicerō **contempsit** Catilīnae gladiōs, nōn **pertimēscet** Antōniī.
(d) frūmentāriam rem ex senātūs cōnsultō **tollēmus**.
(e) ego tamen Antōnī amīcitiam retinēre sānē **volō**, **scrībam**que ad eum.

2. (i) Identify the tense of each underlined verb, and (ii) give the equivalent future form:
(a) Porsenna ingentī urbem obsidiōne **premēbat**. (premō,-ere, 3)
(b) Lāocoōn ārdēns summā **dēcurrit** ab arce. (dēcurrō,-ere, 3)
(c) Aegyptum imperiō populī Rōmānī **adiēcī**. (adiciō,-ere, 5)
(d) ego dictātūram nōn **recēpī**.   (recipiō,-ere, 5)
(e) Catilīna etiam in senātum **venit**.   (veniō,-īre, 4)
(f) aliquam in tuīs litterīs grātulātiōnem **exspectāvī**. (exspectō,-āre, 1)
(g) Augustus aedēs sacrās opulentissimīs dōnīs **adōrnāvit**. (adōrnō,-āre, 1)
(h) nōn mihi **placēbat** litterās Graecās discere. (placeō,-ēre, 2)

3. Fill each gap with a Latin word, and translate:
(a) mox Cleopātra venēnum .... {*will drink*}.
(b) quīntō .... {*day*} mīlitēs montēs vidēre poterant.
(c) captīvōrum vōcēs audīre .... {*we were able*}.
(d) ego cōnsul .... {*the Republic*} semper dēfendī.
(e) ō Fulvia, ... {*the soldiers*} Antōniī dūcēs?
(f) ō puellae, fugere cum Cloeliā .... {*will you be able*}?

4. Find Latin ancestors in this chapter of *collapse, concede, jury, revoke* and *valid*.

— 13 —

Dissenting voices

The future perfect tense

The last of the six Latin tenses for you to meet is the future perfect. As the name implies, it is a mixture of looking forward and then back. It imagines a point in the future when the action of the verb has been completed:

> *tomorrow I shall have finished my exams*

The future perfect takes the perfect stem with the endings in bold:

I shall have loved	amā**verō**
you [s.] will have loved	amā**veris**
s/he will have loved	amā**verit**
we shall have loved	amā**verimus**
you [pl.] will have loved	amā**veritis**
they will have loved	amā**verint**

The future perfect is found in 'if' or 'when' clauses, projecting forward to a point in the future:

> sī ponticulum **trānsierimus**, omnia armīs agenda erunt
> *if we cross the little bridge, everything will have to be resolved by armed conflict* [8.6]
> (trānseō,-īre, **trānsiī**, trānsitum = *cross*)

trānsierō
trānsieris
trānsierit
trānsierimus
trānsieritis
trānsierint

In English we seldom say *if we shall have crossed . . .* and instead use the simple present. But you can see the meaning, pointing forward to a time when the bridge has been crossed, for only once that has happened will everything *have to be resolved by armed conflict*. In Latin the present would mean *if we are crossing the bridge (now) . . . .*

There is another set of endings very similar to these which you will meet on p. 203.

Practice 13a

Fill each gap with the correct verb in the future perfect tense, and translate:

(a) sī taurum . . . . {*we capture*}, quid fugābimus?

(b) Octāviānus, sī Cleopātram vīvam . . . . {*finds*}, in triumphō dūcet.

(c) servus, sī . . . . {*you* [s.] *say*} 'aestuo', sūdābit.

Tenses review

You have now met all six Latin tenses. Perhaps it is fitting to review them with the help of the 1st conjugation verb **sūdō,-āre** (*sweat*):

Present	*I sweat, I am sweating, I do (not) sweat*
Future	*I shall sweat, I am going to sweat, I am sweating, I sweat*
Imperfect	*I was sweating, I sweated, I used to sweat, I began to sweat, I would sweat*
Perfect	*I sweated, I have sweated, I did sweat, I have been sweating*
Fut. perfect	*I shall have sweated, I sweat*
Pluperfect	*I had sweated, I had been sweating*

	Present	Future	Imperfect	Perfect	Fut. Perfect	Pluperfect
I	**sūdō**	**sūdābō**	**sūdābam**	**sūdāvī**	**sūdāverō**	**sūdāveram**
you [s.]	**sūdās**	**sūdābis**	**sūdābās**	**sūdāvistī**	**sūdāveris**	**sūdāverās**
s/he, it	**sūdāt**	**sūdābit**	**sūdābat**	**sūdāvit**	**sūdāverit**	**sūdāverat**
we	**sūdāmus**	**sūdābimus**	**sūdābāmus**	**sūdāvimus**	**sūdāverimus**	**sūdāverāmus**
you [p.]	**sūdātis**	**sūdābitis**	**sūdābātis**	**sūdāvistis**	**sūdāveritis**	**sūdāverātis**
they	**sūdant**	**sūdābunt**	**sūdābant**	**sūdāvērunt**	**sūdāverint**	**sūdāverant**

These six tenses are recognizable to anyone who speaks or has learned sub-Latin languages (Italian, Spanish, French, Portuguese, etc). But one look at the English equivalents will show how ill-matched are the Latin and English systems. You saw above how the future perfect in Latin is often presented in English like a present tense, especially after 'if'. Likewise we sometimes express the simple future in English as if it were present as in *tomorrow I am going home*. And the imperfect *would* is a way of describing a regular past event (*every week she would visit us*), which is not the same as a hypothetical *would* (*what would he do if the factory were to close?*).

Practice 13b

Translate into Latin:

(a) he has sweated (b) we shall sweat (c) they have sweated (d) she had sweated
(e) they will sweat (f) you [s.] are sweating (g) you [pl.] were sweating
(h) they will have sweated.

Principal parts review

The principal parts of a verb are those four forms you need to know to be able to recognize all the different shapes of the verb whatever the tense or if it appears as a participle (e.g. **missus** from **mittō,-ere**). So to know a verb is to know the four principal parts. And then of course you will need to be able to recognize the endings of the different tenses which tell you who is doing it and when.

The principal parts of most 1st conjugation verbs are regular:

> amō,-āre,-āvī,-ātum (*love*)
> laudō,-āre,-āvī,-ātum (*praise*)
> sūdō,-āre,-āvī,-ātum (*sweat*)
> etc

There are one or two mildly eccentric 1st conjugation verbs:

> dō, dare, **dedī**, datum (*give*)

2nd conjugation verbs also conform to a pattern:

> habeō,-ēre,-uī,-itum (*have*)
> exerceō,-ēre,-uī,-itum (*occupy*)

But within this conjugation there are one or two less regular forms:

> doceō,-ēre,-uī, **doctum** (*teach*)
> iubeō,-ēre, **iussī**, **iussum** (*order*)
> rīdeō,-ēre, **rīsī**, **rīsum** (*laugh*)
> videō,-ēre, **vīdī**, **vīsum** (*see*)

The 3rd conjugation is even more varied in the latter two principal parts:

> mittō,-ere, **mīsī**, **missum** (*send*)
> dīcō,-ere, **dīxī**, **dictum** (*say*)
> dūcō,-ere, **dūxī**, **ductum** (*lead*)
> scrībō,-ere, **scrīpsī**, **scrīptum** (*write*)

4th conjugation verbs are more regular, with a few exceptions:

> audiō,-īre, audīvī (-iī), audītum (*hear*)
> sciō,-īre, scīvī (-iī), scītum (*know*)
> veniō,-īre, **vēnī**, **ventum** (*come*)

Mixed conjugation verbs are broadly similar if not identical:

> capiō,-ere, cēpī, captum (*take, capture*)
> accipiō,-ere, accēpī, acceptum (*receive*)
> faciō,-ere, fēcī, factum (*do, make*)
> fugiō,-ere, fūgī, fugitum (*flee, escape*)

Remember that the perfect, future perfect and pluperfect are formed with the perfect stem of a verb, i.e. the third principal part (**amō**, **amāvī**; **mittō**, **mīsī**; **veniō**, **vēnī**; etc).

Practice 13c

Translate each into one Latin word:

(a)	he will love	(e)	you [s.] will capture	(i)	we wrote
(b)	she was ordering	(f)	I was fleeing	(j)	they will laugh
(c)	they said	(g)	they see		
(d)	we hear	(h)	they will send		

Compound verbs

You have already met a few compound verbs. One or two of these compounds appear even more than the simple form: e.g. **accipiō,-ere** (**ad** + **capiō**), which in this course appears more than **capiō,-ere** itself.

> Examples of compound verbs
> **abdūcō,-ere, abdūxī, abductum**   *lead away, take away* [dūcō,-ere]
> **adiciō,-ere, adiēcī, adiectum**   *throw to, add* [iaciō,-ere]
> **recipiō,-ere, recēpī, receptum**   *take, accept, recover* [capiō,-ere]
> **trānseō,-īre, trānsiī (-īvī), trānsitum**   *go across, pass through* [eō, īre]

dictātūram nōn **recēpī**
I did not <u>accept</u> the dictatorship [12.5]

Aegyptum imperiō populī Rōmānī **adiēcī**
I <u>added</u> Egypt to the empire of the Roman people [12.17]

Practice 13d

These prefixes show their assimilated forms in brackets. What do they typically add to a verb's meaning? (I.e. for most, what does the preposition mean?)

(a)   **ā-**, **ab-**, **abs-**, (au-)
(b)   **ad-** (acc-, aff-, agg-, all-, ann-, app-, arr-, att-, āsp-, ass-, att-)
(c)   **ante-**
(d)   **con-** [i.e. **cum**] (co-, coll-, comm-, comb-, comp-, corr-)
(e)   **ē-**, **ex-**, (eff-)
(f)   **in-** (ill-, imb-, imm-, imp-, irr-)
(g)   **per-**
(h)   **post-**
(i)   **re-**, **red-**
(j)   **sub-** (succ-, suff-, sugg-, summ-, supp-, surr-, sus-)
(k)   **trāns-**, **trā-**

The spelling of some prefixes changed to match how they were spoken, e.g. **collocō** for **conlocō**, and **surrīdeō** for **subrīdeō**.

Some prefixes just strengthen or intensify the meaning, the extra syllable giving the speaker more force in expression. This can happen with **ad-, con-, dē-, ē-, per-**. The prefix **sub-**, by contrast, sometimes means the same as the simple form but to a lesser (or lower) extent, e.g. **rīdeō** = *I laugh*, **surrīdeō** = *I smile*.

Some compounds can govern a direct object, even though their simple forms cannot, e.g. **veniō/circumveniō**: you cannot *come* something, but you can *surround* it.

In certain compounds the first vowel of the simple form is weakened:

> capiō: **accipiō**, **recipiō**, etc
> faciō: **dēficiō**, **reficiō**, etc
> teneō: **retineō**, etc

The meaning of certain compounds may be less obvious. For instance, **dēbellō,-āre** means *fight a war to the finish (successfully)*, while **dēspērō,-āre** does not mean to 'have hope successfully' but *despair*. We might contrive an explanation (as an aide-memoire) that **dēspērāre** is 'to be <u>down</u> on hope' – if we didn't already have the derived word *despair* as a big clue.

> ### Practice 13e
> Break these compounds down into their literal meanings:
> (a)   trāns – ferō (trānsferō)
> (b)   in – pōnō (impōnō)
> (c)   re – teneō (retineō)
> (d)   in – veniō

Vocabulary 13

These 'simple' verbs have many compounds. Know them well and you will find their many relatives easier to recognize:

capiō,-ere, cēpī, captum	*take, capture*		**iaciō,-ere, iēcī, iactum**	*throw, hurl*
cēdō,-ere, cessī, cessum	*give way, go*		**mittō,-ere, mīsī, missum**	*send*
dūcō,-ere, dūxī, ductum	*lead, bring*		**moveō,-ēre, mōvī, mōtum**	*move, stir*
eō, īre, īvī (iī)	*go*		**pōnō,-ere, posuī, positum**	*put, place*
faciō,-ere, fēcī, factum	*do, make*		**teneō,-ēre,-uī, tentum**	*hold, control*
ferō, ferre, tulī, lātum	*carry, bear, say*		**veniō,-īre, vēnī, ventum**	*come*

Look online for more compound verbs (see p. 393).

As a preposition with a noun in the ablative **cum** means *with, together with*. **Cum** also appears as a conjunction, still a linking word of sorts, meaning *as, when*, or *since*, or occasionally *although* or *whereas*. There is more on **cum** on p. 204.

Exercises 13a

1.   The verbs below have all appeared in the course so far. Identify the simple verbs of which they are compounds [e. g. refugit [3.14] ..... **fugiō, fugere, fūgī, fugitum**]:

(a) excēpit [4.1]   (b) inventae sunt [4.4]   (c) impōnere [4.10]   (d) subiectīs [4.10]
(e) prōiectus est [5.1]   (f) dēfēcērunt [5.8]   (g) manūmissus [5.10]   (h) dēiectus [5.10]
(i) effēcit [7.2]   (j) trānsdūxit [7.8]   (k) permīsit [8.11]   (l) retinēre [9.11]   (m) revocāta [12.3]   (n) exquīrēbat [12.10]

2.   Identify the ancestral Latin prefix and the simple verb for each word [e.g. suffer . . . . .
    sub + ferō]:
    (a) accept   (b) defer   (c) emissary   (d) exhibit   (e) product   (f) project   (g) recession
    (h) rejection   (i) satisfaction   (j) adjacent

3.   Translate into Latin:
(a) Atticus was a friend to Cicero and to Brutus and to Fulvia and to Antony and to Octavian.
(b) If the senators kill Caesar, who will lead us?

Dissenting voices

Augustus not only established his own singular authority, he laid down the precedent for centuries to come. With him Republican Rome passes into the Imperial era. The senate would remain, along with the various offices of state, but without the same powers. Senators could still debate political topics so long as it did not counter the will of the man in charge. Criticisms and jokes levelled at those in power were heard less frequently, at least in public.

> ## Reading notes
> A verb with two 'i's in the ending, **-iī** (1st person) or **-iit** (3rd person), indicates the perfect tense, contracted from **-īvī** and **-īvit**. The verb **eō** (*go*) and its compounds usually appear in their contracted forms: **iī** (*I went*) for **īvī**; **iit** (*s/he went*) for **īvit**:
>
> **iniit** [6.10], **rediit** [12.3], **exiit** [12.13], **periī** [18.6]

However, a large part of the population fared no worse under the emperors and for many life improved. The loss of political freedoms were felt most by a relatively small group of well-to-do citizenry. Many of the writers of the era belonged to this class and so it is no surprise a sense of nostalgic loss for the Republic should be well flagged in their work. There were large numbers for whom such a change would not have made much difference; and around a third of the population of Rome, the slaves, had no freedom at all. If anything, under the emperors, the opportunities for freed slaves improved.

Dissent towards Augustus faded more quickly than against Caesar, who had spent much of his time as dictator overcoming pockets of resistance. Many newcomers to positions and privileges had Augustus to thank for their advancement. People from Italy and the provinces were employed to support the running of government, and more and more freed slaves took significant backroom roles. Even senators were grateful to participate in debates which he quietly controlled, for he had enrolled a good number of them. And most people were too young to remember peace under the Republic. Their experience had been a state torn apart by civil wars.

1.   During the Republic, those in power would expect a degree of criticism, ridicule and perhaps a few smutty verses like this below by Catullus about Julius Caesar (from the 50s BC):

pulchrē convenit improbīs cinaedīs,
Māmurrae pathicōque Caesarīque.

Catullus, Poems 57.1–2

pulchrē   *well, splendidly*
convenit [+ dat.]   *it is suitable, there is unanimity in respect to* (i.e. the two objects suit each other)
improbus,-a,-um   *shameless, naughty*
cinaedus,-ī [m.]   *sodomite*
Māmurra,-ae [m.]: Mamurra was a friend of Caesar, and known for his extravagant lifestyle
Māmurrae, Caesarī: dative in apposition to 'cinaedīs', i.e. explaining who the 'cinaedīs' are
pathicus,-a,-um   *lustful*

2.   These lines are maybe sharper than you'd find in a satirical show today, but sexuality was more openly talked about, with fewer taboos. Caesar took all this in his stride: being able to take jokes was part of his charm. He quickly forgave Catullus, whose father used to entertain him in the family home at Verona, where Caesar had his winter quarters.

Catullum satisfacientem eādem diē adhibuit cēnae.

Suetonius, Life of Julius Caesar 73

satisfacientem [the person doing this is in the accusative]   *apologizing, making amends*
eādem [abl.]   *same*
adhibeō,-ēre,-uī,-itum [2]   *summon, invite* (the subject is Caesar)

3.   Augustus was nothing like as forgiving. A little joke said to be Cicero's, who had sought the young Octavian's support in the wake of Caesar's murder, did more harm to the Republic than Cicero may have realized. He is said to have commented that the young Octavian should be . . .

. . . laudandus, ōrnandus, tollendus.

Cicero, Letters to Friends and Family 11.20

laudandus,-a,-um   *should be praised*
ōrnandus,-a,-um   *should be honoured*
tollendus,-a,-um   *should be elevated, should be removed* (Cicero is playing with these two meanings)

4.   Octavian abandoned Cicero's faction to join Antony, and did nothing to prevent the old consul's murder a short while later. But he was kinder to poets. Virgil, Horace and others were well looked after by Maecenas, a member of Augustus' inner circle. The poets played their part in sealing his authority.

praesēns dīvus habēbitur
Augustus adiectīs Britannīs
imperiō gravibusque Persīs.

Horace, Odes 3.5.2–4

praesēns   *here and now*
habēbitur [habeō,-ēre]   *(s/he) will be held, regarded as*
adiciō,-ere, adiēcī, adiectum [M.]   *add*
Britannus,-ī [m.]   *a Briton*
gravis,-e   *threatening*
Persēs [Persīs: dat.pl./abl. pl.]   *a Persian*
adiectīs Britannīs gravibusque Persīs   *with the B.s and threatening P.s added to 'imperiō'.*

5.   Augustus and Maecenas knew full well how literature and the arts might help to secure his position. But poets had suffered like many others during the civil wars, and their relief at the peace Augustus brought was genuine enough. Virgil shudders at the agents of war wreaking havoc, shown on the shield of Aeneas:

et scissā gaudēns vādit Discordia pallā,
quam cum sanguineō sequitur Bellōna flagellō.

Virgil, Aeneid 8.702–3

scindō,-ere, scidī, scissum [3]   *tear*
gaudēns [the person doing this is in the nominative]   *delighting, gleeful*
vādō,-ere [3]   *go, walk*
Discordia,-ae [f.]   *Discord* (spirit of strife)
palla,-ae [f.]   *cloak* ('scissā pallā' = *with her cloak torn*)
quam [f.; acc.]   *who(m)*
sanguineus,-a,-um   *bloody, bloodstained*
sequitur   *(s/he) follows*
Bellōna,-ae [f.]   *Bellona* (spirit of war)

6.   One poet earned Augustus' displeasure. After the deaths of Virgil (20 BC) and Horace (8 BC), the most popular poet then alive was Ovid. Then in AD 8, all very suddenly, he was banished for an indiscretion (or two indiscretions, a poem and an undisclosed 'error'), as he tells us himself:

perdiderint cum mē duo crīmina, carmen et error,
   alterius factī culpa silenda mihi.

Ovid, Tristia 2.207–8

perdiderint   *(they) ruined*
cum   *although*
crīmen,-inis [n.]   *crime, charge, indiscretion*
carmen: Ovid's *Ars Amatoria*, which appeared around 2 BC
alterius [gen.]   *one (of two)*
factum,-ī [n.]   *deed, action, thing done*
culpa,-ae [f.]   *blame, error, offence*
alterius factī culpa   *the offence of one action (of the two)*, i.e. *of one of the two actions*
silendus,-a,-um   *had to be kept quiet* (Augustus did not want the 'culpa' mentioned again)
mihi: though dative take as '*by me*'

7.   The 'carmen' was the *Ars Amatoria* (Art of Love) which is a light and humorous take on the didactic tradition within poetry to instruct and give advice: he offers a set of tips for lovers to attract partners, which at face value appears to be a manual of seduction and adultery.

> cum surgit, surgēs; dōnec sedet illa, sedēbis;
>   arbitriō dominae tempora perde tuae.

Ovid, Art of Love 1.503–4

cum   *when*
surgō,-ere [3]   *rise*
dōnec   *while, for as long as*
illa [nom.]   *she*
arbitrium,-ī [n.]   *will, bidding*
tempora: translate in the singular
perdō,-ere [3]   *lose, waste* ('perde' is an imperative)

8.   Ovid was born almost a generation after Virgil. By the time he came to Rome in his early teens from his hometown of Sulmo (mod. Sulmona) Augustus was already in power. The relief of earlier poets at the *Pax Augusta* had for Ovid become a poetic convention to play with, and in his light jaunty way, no doubt inoffensive to his mind, he played with it. In one of his early poems, the *Amores* (Passions of Love), which appeared only a few years after the *Aeneid*, he addresses the love god Cupid as though he were a victor in battle, and Augustus, said to be 'divine' by other poets, was therefore Cupid's relative. Ovid imagines himself in the love god's triumphal procession:

> ergō cum possim sacrī pars esse triumphī,
>   parce tuās in mē perdere, victor, opēs!
> aspice cognātī fēlīcia Caesaris arma:
>   quā vīcit, victōs prōtegit ille manū.

Ovid, Amores 1.2.49–52

ergō   *so, accordingly*
cum   *since*
possim   *I can*
pars, partis [f.]   *part*
parcō,-ere [3]   *spare, refrain from* ('parce' is an imperative)
in mē   *against me, upon me*
ops, opis [f.]   (in the plural) *power, resources*
aspiciō,-ere [M.]   *look upon, consider* ('aspice' is an imperative)
cognātus,-ī [m.]   *kinsman* (Cupid was one of the few gods Augustus might not want to be identified with)
fēlīx   *fortunate, successful*
arma: i.e. *military campaigns*
quā [f.; abl.]   *which*
victōs: past participle of 'vincō,-ere'
Word order for the 4th line: 'ille prōtegit victōs manū quā vīcit'

9.   It was not the kind of divine profile that Augustus aspired to. Ovid's fresh, inventive humour was widely liked, no doubt adding to the emperor's growing irritation, which was further provoked by the culpable 'carmen', the *Ars Amatoria*, a decade or so later. Ovid's sudden banishment happened a few years after this poem first appeared, so it was probably the 'error' which tipped Augustus over the edge. The emperor's grip on public affairs prevented it from ever being disclosed, and even the rich vein of political gossip which surfaces in later (and safer) written records failed to pick it up.

Ovid's error may have had some connection with Augustus's daughter Julia, who herself had been banished in 2 BC: it is conceivable that the emperor was reminded of something he did not want to remember. Augustus had long had a difficult relationship with his daughter, arguably since the day of her birth, on which he divorced her mother Scribonia.

Julia was married first to Augustus' general, Agrippa, and then, after he died, to Tiberius, her stepbrother and future *princeps*. This marriage failed, not least because of Julia's indiscretions elsewhere. In the wake of his public commitment to family values Augustus felt undone by her rejection of Tiberius. Nor did he like her lovers, least of all Iullus Antonius, the son of Antony and Fulvia. The couple were accused of concocting plots against the emperor's plans for succession (Tiberius), and Julia was banished and Iullus was forced to take his own life. When Ovid caused his offence, some years later, there was no forgiveness. His poem *Tristia* (Sadness) is a plaintive and unsuccessful attempt to win a recall from Tomis on the Black Sea, in which his pleading apologetic tone contrasts with Catullus' irreverent fun at Caesar's expense. Here he recalls the moment of his banishment:

iam prope lūx aderat, quā mē discēdere Caesar
    fīnibus extrēmae iusserat Ausoniae.

Ovid, *Tristia* 1.3.5–6

prope   *almost*
lūx, lūcis [f.]   *light, daylight, day*
quā [abl.]   *which*
discēdō,-ere [3]   *depart*
fīnis,-is [m.]   *boundary, limit, border, frontier*
extrēmus,-a,-um   *final, furthest*
Ausonia,-ae [f.]   *Ausonia* (i.e. Italy)

10.   Writers under the emperors were just as sharp and critical as their predecessors, but their targets were no longer their rulers. At least not ones alive at the time. Rumours that Octavian had gained his adoption by giving himself to his great-uncle were written down long after his death:

M. Antōnius adoptiōnem avunculī stuprō meritum esse
rettulit.

Suetonius, *Life of Augustus* 68

adoptiōnem meritum esse   *the adoption to have been obtained*, i.e. *that the adoption (of Octavian)
    was obtained*
avunculus,-ī [m.]   *uncle, great-uncle* (i.e. Julius Caesar)
stuprum,-ī [n.]   *lust, defilement*
rettulit: from 'referō, referre, rettulī, relātum' (here: *reported*)

11. Tacitus, master of invective, pulled no punches in his *Annals*. He himself witnessed the tyranny of the emperor Domitian, and he was largely responsible for the dark and chilling portraits of the earlier emperors, Tiberius and Nero. Along with the more gossipy Suetonius he remains an important source for the first century AD. Here, Tacitus admires the histories written before the rule of emperors:

veteris populī Rōmānī prospera vel adversa clārīs scrīptōribus memorāta sunt.

Tacitus, Annals 1.1

veteris [genitive singular]   *old, ancient*
prosperus,-a,-um   *favourable* (n.pl. 'prospera' = *successes*)
vel   *or*
adversum,-ī [n.]   *calamity, misfortune*
clārus,-a,-um   *famous, distinguished*
scrīptor,-ōris [m.]   *writer*
clārīs scrīptōribus: Tacitus here adopts the poetic habit of leaving out the preposition (**ā**)
memorō,-āre,-āvī,-ātum [1]   *relate, tell*

12. Tacitus writes that it was in Augustus' time when flattery and fawning began to undermine the value of literature. He says he will start his *Annals* with a few words about Augustus and then move on to the succeeding emperors when literary distortions were rife. He himself, he argues, is free from such inaccuracies:

Tiberiī Gāīque et Claudiī ac Nerōnis rēs flōrentibus ipsīs ob metum falsae, postquam occiderant, recentibus ōdiīs compositae sunt. inde cōnsilium mihi est pauca dē Augustō trādere, mox Tiberiī prīncipātum et cētera, sine īrā et studiō, quōrum causās procul habeō.

Tacitus, Annals 1.1

Tiberiī ... Nerōnis: the emperors Tiberius, Gaius (Caligula), Claudius and Nero
    followed Augustus
rēs [nom. pl. of 'rēs, reī']   *affairs, deeds*
flōrentibus ipsīs   *with them flourishing, in their prime*
postquam   *after*
occidō,-ere, occidī, occāsum [3]   *fall, die* ('occidō' is easily confused with 'occīdō,-ere' = *kill*)
recēns   *fresh, recent*
ōdium,-ī [n.]   *hatred, animosity, ill-feeling*
compōnō,-ere, composuī, compositum [3]   *write, record* (take this verb twice, with the first line too)
inde   *after that, because of that*
paucus,-a,-um   *few*
mox   *soon, afterwards, presently*
prīncipātus,-ūs [m.]   *principate, reign*

īra,-ae [f.]   *anger*
studium,-ī [n.]   *favour*
quōrum [gen.pl.]   *which*
causās: i.e. 'metum' and 'ōdiīs'
procul   *far off, distant*
procul habeō   *I hold at a distance, am removed from*, i.e. *I do not have*

13. Tacitus' forthright claim – *sine ira et studio* – is tested a few lines later. Agrippa Postumus
     was the son of Julia and Agrippa, born after his father died. He was evidently a potential
     rival to Augustus' heir, Tiberius, and Tacitus had no doubt who was behind his murder.

prīmum facinus novī prīncipātūs fuit Postumī Agrippae caedēs.

Tacitus, Annals 1.6

caedēs,-is [f.]   *killing, murder*

14. Martial, active in the second half of the first century AD, wrote hundreds of short
     poems. These epigrams were always teasing and some sharply critical or satirical. His
     targets were people known to him, his patrons and people with influence, but not the
     emperor. In this poem the emperor Domitian is thanked for his edict of AD 92 which
     prevented shops and stalls from spilling into the streets. This is about as polite as Martial
     gets. The satirist's rub is not a wrestle with the world of ideas, but with dangerously
     crowded streets, street vendors, and carts and horses.

iussistī tenuīs, Germānice, crēscere vīcōs,
et modo quae fuerat sēmita, facta via est.
tōnsor, cōpo, cocus, lanius sua līmina servant.
nunc Rōma est, nūper magna taberna fuit.

Martial, Epigrams 7.61.3–4,9–10

tenuīs [accusative plural of 'tenuis,-e']   *narrow*
Germānicus: the emperor Domitian
crēscō,-ere [3]   *grow, widen*
vīcus,-ī [m.]   *village, street*
modo   *only, lately*
quae [f.; nom.]   *which, what*
sēmita,-ae [f.]   *narrow path, narrow track*
via,-ae [f.]   *road*
tōnsor,-ōris [m.]   *barber*
cōpo,-ōnis [m.]   *barman* (alt. spelling of 'caupō')
cocus,-ī [m.]   *cook* (alt. spelling of 'coquus')
lanius,-ī [m.]   *butcher*
servō,-āre,-āvī,-ātum [1]   *save, keep*, here: *keep to*
nūper   *recently, not long ago*
taberna,-ae [f.]   *shop*

15. Juvenal was another satirist whose targets were the more immediate irritations of life. His surviving poems, sixteen satires, were written in the early part of the second century AD. They are longer than Martial's and tackled themes such as the folly of human ambition, the pretentiousness of wealth, the poverty of writers, and meanness to clients. Martial touched similar sores but picked on particular instances. Juvenal offered a more structured perspective if just as irreverent and even more tongue-in-cheek. As with Martial, Juvenal's verse is flecked with everyday detail, with the bustle and clatter of busy street life. Below, a nocturnal robber avoids rich travellers who are lit up by their torches and attendants and instead sets upon a man protected only by the light of the moon and his candle.

stat contrā stārīque iubet. pārēre necesse est;
nam quid agās, cum tē furiōsus cōgat et īdem
fortior? 'unde venīs? aut dīc aut accipe calcem.'

Juvenal, Satires 3.290–1 and 292/5

stō,-āre [1]   *stand* (the subject is *he*, i.e. the robber)
contrā   *opposite*
stārī [from 'stō,-āre']: lit. *to be stood still*, i.e. *a halt*
pāreō,-ēre [2]   *obey*
necesse   *necessary, unavoidable*
nam   *for*
agās   *you do*
cum   *when*
furiōsus,-a,-um   *mad*
cōgat   *(s/he) compels, forces*
īdem   *at the same time, as well*
fortior [nom.]   *stronger* (understand 'est' with 'fortior')
unde   *from where*
dīc   *say!, tell!*
calx, calcis [f.]   *heel* (i.e. *a kicking*)

Exercises 13b

1.   Identify the case and number of each underlined word, and translate:
(a)   **prīmum** facinus fuit tribūnī caedēs.
(b)   **pallā** scissā in vīllam iniit Clōdia?
(c)   **arbitriō** dominae tempora perde tuae.
(d)   cōnsilium mihi est **pauca** dē taurō trādere.
(e)   placetne **fīliō** Cicerōnis Graecās litterās discere?
(f)   plēbs **caput** senātōris praefīxum **hastae** circumtulit.

2.   Put the underlined verbs into the tense as directed, and translate your answer:
(a)   laniīne sua līmina **servant**? (*future*)
(b)   **stābant** dēligātī ad pālum cōnsulis līberī. (*present*)
(c)   Augustus aedēs sacrās **refēcit** et dōnīs **adōrnāvit**. (*both future*)
(d)   Hannibal in montibus **manet**. (*imperfect*)

(e) iūdicēs **habēmus** quōs **voluimus**. (*imperfect, pluperfect*)

(f) **contemnunt** novitātem meam, ego illōrum ignāviam. (*imperfect*)

(g) **errat** mediō in forō Fulvia. (*future*)

(h) amīcī Catilīnae in senātum **veniunt**. (*future*)

(i) Graecia capta victōrem **cēpit**. (*future*)

(j) vestīgia fēminae aliēnae, ō Catulle, in lectō **sunt** tuō. (*imperfect*)

(k) nimis multōs **audiō** Corinthī et Athēnārum ōrnāmenta laudantēs. (*perfect*)

3. Find Latin ancestors in this chapter of *avuncular, contrast, scissors, tavern* and *trade*.

— 14 —

Songs and suppers

The passive voice

In the last chapter there was an exercise where you turned the words around but expressed much the same meaning:

> **senātōrēsne Caesarem occīdērunt?**
> **— vērō, Caesar ā senātōribus occīsus est.**

The difference between the two sentences is that the verb in the first sentence (**occīdērunt**) is <u>active</u> (*they killed*) whereas in the second (**occīsus est**) it is <u>passive</u> (*he was killed*). When the verb is passive, the subject is no longer the 'doer', but the 'done to'.

See how the object of the active verb **occīdērunt** (**Caesarem**) becomes the subject of the passive **occīsus est**. And the subject of **occīdērunt** (**senātōrēs**) is put into the ablative (**ā senātōribus**) when the verb is passive. This ablative is called the ablative of agent, the one who 'does it' when the verb is passive.

Present, future and imperfect passive
Passive endings of the 3rd person in the present, future and imperfect tenses are the same as the active with the addition of **-ur**:

dīvus **habēbitur** / Augustus
Augustus <u>will be</u> considered a god [13.4]

	active	passive
sing.	-t	-tur
plur.	-nt	-ntur

Practice 14a
Put each sentence into the passive, and translate your answer:
e.g. cōnsul Clōdiam amat > **Clōdia ā cōnsule amātur**
(a) tribūnus servum fugat.
(b) Romulus centum creat senātōrēs.
(c) Porsenna urbem premēbat.
(d) Camilla habēnās linquēbat.

The active or passive is called the 'voice' of a verb. There are the same tenses in the passive as there are active, all of which are shown on p. 357ff. Note the 1st person ending **-or** in the present ('*I am being . . .*'). The good news is you have already met nearly half of these forms. The perfect and pluperfect passive have appeared before.

Perfect and pluperfect passive

The perfect and pluperfect passive are created with the past participle + verb *to be*. The perfect passive can mean *was . . . -ed* or *has been . . . -ed*:

> duo cōnsulēs **creātī sunt**
> *two consuls were/have been appointed* [2.5]

The pluperfect passive (i.e. *had been* . . .) is a combination of the past participle with the imperfect of *to be* (**eram, erās, erat**, etc):

> in eādem sēditiōne **occīsī erant**
> *(they) had been killed in the same rebellion* [5.1]

The past participle is thus used with *to be* to create the past tenses of the passive. As such it is always nominative, agreeing with its subject noun or pronoun (above: **creātī** and **occīsī**). The past participle without *to be* may appear in any of the cases, like any other adjective:

> dictātūram mihi **dēlātam** et ā populō et ā senātū nōn recēpī
> *I did not accept the dictatorship (which was) offered to me by both the people and by the senate* [12.5]

Practice 14b

Fill each gap with the past participle with its correct ending, and translate:
(a) Clōdius numquam cōnsul .... {creō,-āre,-āvī,-ātum} est.
(b) clāmōrēs captīvōrum in forō .... {audiō,-īre,-īvī,-ītum} erant.
(c) frāter Cicerōnis ā triumvirīs nōn erat .... {occīdō,-ere,-īdī,-īsum}.
(d) fīliī cōnsulis ē carcere sunt .... {dūcō,-ere,-ūxī,-uctum}.
(e) cohortēs ā duce .... {decimō,-āre,-āvī,-ātum} sunt.
(f) equus dictātūram ā Caligulā .... {dēferō, dēferre, dētulī, dēlātum} nōn recēpit.

Personal pronouns: 1st and 2nd persons

1st and 2nd person pronouns (*I, we, you*) were introduced on p. 61.

> **mē** vīvere coēgistī
> *you compelled/have compelled me to live* [7.12]

neque **tē** teneō, neque dicta refellō
I neither keep you nor challenge what you say [3.12]

	I/me	you (s.)
N.	ego	tū
A.	**mē**	**tē**
G.	meī	tuī
D.	mihi	tibi
Ab.	mē	tē

There is no vocative. Talking to oneself is not given a distinctive grammatical form, and it is arguable that the nominative **tū** and **vōs** are in fact vocative as they are inevitably used as forms of address.

The dative is frequently used to show possession:

mihi nova nōbilitās est
for me (i.e. my) high rank is new [5.6]

The 1st and 2nd persons plural are **nōs** (*we/us*) and **vōs** (*you* pl.):

Pompēius dē Clōdiō iubet **nōs** esse sine cūrā
Pompey tells us[1] not to worry about Clodius [7.6]

	we/us	you (pl.)
N.	nōs	vōs
A.	nōs	vōs
G.	nostrum/trī[2]	vestrum/trī
D.	**nōbīs**	**vōbīs**
Ab.	nōbīs	vōbīs

dīcō **vōbīs**
I say to you [26.4]

Practice 14c

Fill each gap with the correct pronoun:
(a) Sulla inimīcus .... {*we/us*} est.
(b) omnēs .... {*you*} amō!
(c) et .... {*you*}, ō amīce?

Personal pronouns: 3rd person

Subject pronouns are conveyed by the verb's ending, so separate pronouns in the nominative are only used to lend emphasis, clarification or more pointing (*this* person, *that* person). They more frequently appear in other cases, as objects etc.

---

1 Cicero and others sometimes use **nōs**, i.e. plural, for *me*, i.e. singular, what in Britain is called 'the royal we'. Latin does not seem to have an equivalent for **vōs**, which one might have expected, given the use of the plural in Romance languages for a singular *you* in polite or formal circumstances.
2 The genitive of 1st or 2nd person pronouns is seldom used to show possession. The personal adjective **meus, tuus, noster** or **vester** is used instead. The genitive of these pronouns occurs either in a partitive sense (**magna pars nostrum**, *a great part of us*) or as the objective genitive (**amor vestrī**, *a love of (for) you*). The genitive forms of **nōs** and **vōs** tend to be **nostrum** and **vestrum** when used partitively, and **nostrī** and **vestrī** when used objectively.

hic, haec, hoc

hic can be a pronoun or an adjective (a 'pronominal' adjective):

> **hic**:   *he, this man, this* (masculine)
> **haec**:   *she, this woman, this* (feminine)
> **hoc**:   *this* (neuter)

<u>**hic**</u> tamen vīvit
yet <u>this man</u> lives [6.7]

rēs est omnis in <u>**hāc**</u> causā nōbīs, iūdicēs, cum
   Clōdiā
the whole issue for us in <u>this</u> case, judges, is with Clodia
   [8.1]

<u>**hōc**</u> tempore
at <u>this</u> time [6.4]

senatus **haec** intellegit
the senate understands <u>these things</u> [6.7]

<u>**hīs**</u> dictīs
with <u>these things/words</u> spoken [14.12]

singular

	M	F	N
N.	**hic**	haec	hoc
A.	hunc	hanc	hoc
G.	huius	huius	huius
D.	huic	huic	huic
Ab.	hōc	**hāc**	**hōc**

plural

	M	F	N
N.	hī	hae	haec
A.	hōs	hās	**haec**
G.	hōrum	hārum	hōrum
D.	hīs	hīs	hīs
Ab.	hīs	hīs	**hīs**

Practice 14d

Replace each underlined noun with the right form of the pronoun **hic**, and translate
your answer:
(a)   <u>Catilīnam</u> dēfendere cōgitāmus.
(b)   <u>Antōnī</u> amīcitiam retinēre sānē volō.
(c)   Caesar <u>captīvōs</u> Antōniō remīsit.

---

ille, illa, illud

ille is similar to **hic** except that if **hic** is *this one here*, **ille** is *that one there*:

> **ille**:   *he, that man, that* (masculine)
> **illa**:   *she, that woman, that* (feminine)
> **illud**:   *that* (neuter)

Pronouns tell you the subject's gender, which the verb ending alone does not:

dōnec sedet **illa**, sedēbis
as long as that woman/she is sitting, you will sit [13.7]

ille mī pār esse deō vidētur
that fellow/he seems to me to be equal to a god [15.7]

The genitive of 3rd person pronouns is used to show possession:

contemnunt novitātem meam, ego **illōrum** ignāviam
they despise my new status, I (despise) their worthlessness [5.4]

As with **hic, ille** can be an adjective instead of a pronoun:

sunt in **illō** numerō
there are in that number [4.11]

singular			
	M	F	N
N.	**ille**	**illa**	illud
A.	illum	illam	illud
G.	illīus	illīus	illīus
D.	illī	illī	illī
Ab.	**illō**	illā	illō

plural			
	M	F	N
N.	illī	illae	illa
A.	illōs	illās	illa
G.	**illōrum**	illārum	illōrum
D.	illīs	illīs	illīs
Ab.	illīs	illīs	illīs

Practice 14e

Replace each underlined noun with the right form of the pronoun **ille**, and translate your answer:
(a) **bellum** maximē omnium memorābile erat.
(b) Sulla **Samnītēs** proeliō vīcit.
(c) **Dīdō** silvā in magnā errābat.

---

is, ea, id

The pronoun **is, ea, id** is similar again, but not as forceful or emphatic as **hic** or **ille**. It is probably the one you will see the most, referring to someone or something already mentioned:

quidquid **id** est timeō Danaōs et dōna ferentīs
whatever that is I fear Greeks even when bearing gifts [4.13]

scrībamque ad **eum**
and I shall write to him [9.11]

singular			
	M	F	N
N.	is	ea	**id**
A.	**eum**	eam	id
G.	**eius**	eius	eius
D.	**eī**	eī	eī
Ab.	eō	eā	**eō**

The genitive singular **eius** (same in all genders) is used to show possession:

in triumphō Mariī ductus est ante currum **eius** Iugurtha
in the triumph of Marius, Jugurtha was led before his chariot [5.7]

The dative is sometimes used to show possession, particularly if the person concerned is coming off well or badly (called the dative of 'advantage' or 'disadvantage': see p. 338).

> Augustus, quod Thallus prō epistulā prōditā dēnāriōs quīngentōs accēpisset, crūra **eī** frēgit
>
> *Augustus, because Thallus had received five hundred denarii in return for a disclosed letter, broke his legs* [12.14]

As with **ille** and **hic**, the gender of **is, ea, id** corresponds with the gender of the person it represents:

> quī parentem meum trucīdāvērunt, **eōs** in exilium expulī
>
> *those men who murdered my father I drove into exile* [12.4]

plural			
	M	F	N
N.	eī	eae	ea
A.	**eōs**	**eās**	ea
G.	eōrum	eārum	eōrum
D.	eīs	eīs	eīs
Ab.	eīs	eīs	eīs

The masculine and feminine forms of pronouns also represent inanimate nouns, according to their gender, which we translate in a neutral way:

> aedēs sacrās vetustāte collāpsās refēcit, **eās**que et cēterās opulentissimīs dōnīs adōrnāvit
>
> *he restored sacred shrines which had collapsed with age; and these and the other temples he decorated with the most lavish gifts* [12.7]

As with the others, this pronoun is also used as an adjective. While **hic** and **ille** are forcefully *this* one or *that* one, **is** is less emphatic or directional (*this* or *that* . . .):

> **eō** bellō
>
> *in that war* [11.2]

To sum up, a 3rd person pronoun (**hic, ille, is**) can appear as a <u>pronoun</u> representing a noun (*he, she, it, they, this, that,* etc); or as an <u>adjective</u> in agreement with a noun (*this friend, that day,* etc).

Practice 14f

Replace each underlined noun with the right form of the pronoun **is**, and translate your answer:

(a) **Līviam** dūxit uxōrem.

(b) mīlitēs corpus **Caesaris** vidērunt.

(c) 'Quīntilī Vare, **legiōnēs** redde!'

Reflexive pronoun: sē

The reflexive pronoun refers to the subject; in fact it *is* the subject in another case. We use it in English: *he washed himself, they hid themselves.*

The Latin reflexive pronoun is **sē**. It is the same for *himself, herself, themselves* or *itself*. Which of these you choose for your translation depends on the subject:

> Catullus Lesbiam plūs quam **sē** amāvit
> *Catullus loved Lesbia more than he loved himself* [15.9]

N.	—
A.	**sē**
G.	suī
D.	sibi
Ab.	sē

There is no nominative for the reflexive pronoun because it is never the subject of a sentence. From the subject you pick up whether the reflexive pronoun is masculine or feminine, singular or plural:

> omnēs Britannī **sē** vitrō īnficiunt
> *all Britons colour themselves with woad* [23.1]

Practice 14g

Translate:
(a) Narcissus sē amat?
(b) mīlitēs uxōrēs sēcum in Britanniam nōn dūcunt.
(c) Augustus dictātūram sibi dēlātam nōn recēpit.

---

ipse, ipsa, ipsum

Like **sē, ipse** can be translated as *himself*. But the meaning is quite different: **ipse** is not a reflexive but an intensifying or emphasizing pronoun. **Ipse** can be used with any person (**ego ipse** = *I myself*, **tū ipse** = *you yourself*, **Clōdia ipsa** = *Clodia herself*, etc):

> **ipse** iūs dīxit
> *he himself administered justice* [12.11]

> nēmō tē **ipsum** sequitur
> *no one attends you yourself* [14.5]

singular

	M	F	N
N.	**ipse**	ipsa	ipsum
A.	**ipsum**	ipsam	ipsum
G.	ipsīus	ipsīus	ipsīus
D.	ipsī	ipsī	ipsī
Ab.	ipsō	ipsā	ipsō

Ipse works like an adjective. In the example **ipse iūs dīxit** above, **ipse** agrees with the subject implied in the verb-ending (*he*). In the second example, **ipsum** agrees with **tē**. And like other adjectives it can stand alone:

> Tiberiī Gāīque et Claudiī ac Nerōnis rēs flōrentibus **ipsīs** ob metum falsae compositae sunt
> *the deeds of Tiberius, of Gaius, of Claudius and of Nero were falsely recorded, when (they) themselves were in their prime, because of fear* [13.12]
> (lit. *with (they) themselves being in their prime*)

plural

	M	F	N
N.	ipsī	ipsae	ipsa
A.	ipsōs	ipsās	ipsa
G.	ipsōrum	ipsārum	ipsōrum
D.	ipsīs	ipsīs	ipsīs
Ab.	**ipsīs**	ipsīs	ipsīs

Practice 14h

Choose the better word for each gap, and translate:

(a)   tū etiam Clōdiam amās? illam ego .... {ipse/sē} amō!
(b)   mēne domina amat? scīlicet illa .... {ipsam/sē} plūs quam mē amat!
(c)   īnfēlīx Narcissus .... {sē/ipsum} cupit.
(d)   miser vēnātor deam .... {sē/ipsam} vīdit.

Vocabulary 14

Pronouns/pronominal adjectives:

hic, haec, hoc   *this (man, woman, thing), he, she*
ille, illa, illud   *that (man, woman, thing), he, she*
is, ea, id   *this, that, he, she, it*
sē   *himself, herself, itself, themselves* (reflexive)
ipse, ipsa, ipsum   *(my/your/him/her/it)self, (our/your/them)selves* (emphatic)

Some words similar to the pronouns above:

hīc (not **hic** as above)   *here*
illīc   *in that place, over there*
hūc   *to here, hither*
illūc   *to that place, thither*
hinc   *from here, on this side*
īdem: a combination of **is, ea, id** with unchanging suffix **-dem**, and means *(the) same*:
   īdem, eadem, idem (is-dem, ea-dem, id-dem)
   eundem, eandem, idem (eum-dem, eam-dem, id-dem)
   eiusdem, etc (eius-dem, etc)
iste, ista, istud: another pronoun very like **ille, illa, illud** is **iste**, which has the same endings and means much the same, except that the **-te** gives it the sense of *that . . . near you, that . . . of yours.*

Exercises 14a

1.   Make each sentence passive, keeping the meaning [e.g. tribūnus dominam amāvit > **domina ā tribūnō amāta est**]:
(a)   servus cēnam parāvit.
(b)   magister puerōs docuit.

(c)   Augustus epistulam scrībit.

(d)   Caesar legiōnēs dūcet.

2.   Now make each sentence active [e.g. dōna ā dominā sunt accepta > **domina dōna accēpit**]:

(a)   Antōnius ab Octāviānō victus est.

(b)   cēna ab omnibus servīs parāta erat.

(c)   mīlitēs Cicerōnem occīdere ab Antōniō iussī sunt.

3.   Choose the replacement for each underlined word, and translate your answer:

(a)   **Antōnium** .... {is, ea, id} ad mortem adēgit.

(b)   imperātor **Cleopātram** .... {hic, haec, hoc} dūcere in triumphō cupiēbat.

(c)   rēs est omnis in hāc causā cum **Clōdiā** .... {ille, illa, illud}.

4.   Identify the right word to agree with each underlined noun, and translate your answer:

(a)   .... {ille, illa, illud} **fēminam** nōn amō.

(b)   .... {hic, haec, hoc} **rem** ex senātūs cōnsultō tollam.

(c)   imperātor .... {hic, haec, hoc} **cohortēs** hordeō pāvit.

5.   Identify:

(a)   Whose chariot?

   (i)   captīvus in triumphō Caesaris ante currum eius ductus est.

   (ii)   captīvus in triumphō Caesaris ante currum suum ductus est.

(b)   Whose mother?

   (i)   Catullus dominam plūs quam mātrem suam amāvit.

   (ii)   Catullus dominam plūs quam mātrem eius amāvit.

(c)   Who is not to be trusted?

   (i)   dominam appellet Catullus Lesbiam, tamen verba eius rēbus erunt contrāria.

   (ii)   dominam appellet Catullus Lesbiam, tamen verba sua rēbus erunt contrāria.

Songs and suppers

1.   By the first century BC the culture of patronage and deference in Rome was well established. A patron provided his clients with support and protection, for instance through the courts, while a client would be expected to help with business activities, rally support when needed, vote for his patron at elections and generally show deference. In the following century the rise of the class of *libertini*[1] (freed slaves) created many more clients,

Reading notes

In this chapter you will meet a number of vocatives. Most have the same ending as the nominative, with the principal exception of 2nd declension nouns like **servus** (vocative: **serve**).

In poetry, prepositions are sometimes left out:

   vestibulīs abeunt

   they depart from porches

---

1 *Libertini* was the generic name for freedmen. They were called *liberti* in relation to their former owners (the freedman of . . .).

who were increasingly regarded as flatterers and parasites. Some *libertini* became rich enough to have their own clients. Freeborn clients like Juvenal and Martial saw themselves as hard-done-by retainers, who might if they were lucky get a dinner or two from their patron. Even that might be hard to come by.

vestibulīs abeunt veterēs lassīque clientēs
vōtaque dēpōnunt, quamquam longissima cēnae
spēs hominī; caulis miserīs atque ignis emendus.

Juvenal, Satires 1.132–4

vestibulum,-ī   *hallway, porch*
abeunt: from 'abeō,-īre'
lassus,-a,-um   *tired, exhausted*
vōtum,-ī [n.]   *promise, wish, desire*
dēpōnō,-ere, dēposuī, dēpositum [3]   *put aside*
quamquam   *although*
longissimus,-a,-um   *very long, very longlasting*
spēs,-eī [f.]   *hope*
quamquam . . . hominī   *although* ('longissima' *is the* 'spēs' *of a* 'cēnae' *for a* 'hominī')
caulis,-is [m.]   *cabbage stalk*
miserīs: dative of agent (*by the wretched fellows*)
ignis,-is [m.]   *fire, firewood*
emendus,-a,-um   *must be bought*

2.   In the first century AD, some *libertini* were competing with freeborn clients for their patrons' favours. A client could be made to feel inferior at his patron's dinner, even by a slave:

quando rogātus adest calidae gelidaeque minister?
quippe indīgnātur veterī pārēre clientī
quodque aliquid poscās et quod sē stante recumbās.

Juvenal, Satires 5.63–5

quandō   *when*   (by Juvenal's time the final '-ō' had shortened)
rogātus,-a,-um: from 'rogō,-āre' (*having been asked for, summoned*)
calidus,-a,-um   *hot, warm* (understand 'aquae', *water*, with 'calidae' and 'gelidae')
gelidus,-a,-um   *ice-cool*
minister,-trī [m.]   *servant, attendant*
quippe   *indeed, to be sure*
indīgnātur   (*the attendant*) *thinks it demeaning, resents, is offended* (looks passive but see p. 188)
quod(que)   (*and*) *because*
aliquid (n.; nom./acc.)   *something*
poscās   *you may demand, ask for*
sē stante   *with him standing*
recumbās   *you may recline*

3.   Juvenal describes the bread given to clients as hard and mouldy. The bread served to the patron is more appetizing:

sed tener et niveus mollīque silīgine fictus
servātur dominō.

Juvenal, Satires 5.70–71

tener,-era,-erum   *tender, soft* (agrees with the implied 'panis' [m.; nom.]: *bread*)
niveus,-a,-um   *snowy-white*
silīgō,-inis [f.]   *white flour*
fingō,-ere, finxī, fictum [3]   *make, fashion*
servō,-āre,-āvī,-ātum [1]   *keep*

4.   A client would call on his *patronus* in the morning, for a *salutatio* (greeting). It is possible the patron might not receive him, either because he himself would be visiting his own patron, or because he was too busy, tired or bored to give his client the time. Here Martial grumbles about a steep climb up to his patron's house past mules pulling blocks of marble only to find it has been a waste of time:

illud adhūc gravius quod tē post mīlle labōrēs,
    Paule, negat lassō iānitor esse domī.

Martial, Epigrams 5.22.9–10

illud [n.; nom./acc.]   *that (is* – understand 'est')
gravius [n.; nom./acc.]   *more serious*
quod [n.; nom./acc.]   *in that*
post [+ acc.]   *after*
labor,-ōris [m.]   *toil, exertion*
Paule: Paulus is the man Martial is calling upon
negō,-āre,-āvī,-ātum [1]   *deny, say that . . . not* ('tē negat esse': *says you not to be*, i.e. *that you are not*)
lassō: understand 'mihi'
iānitor,-ōris [m.]   *doorkeeper*
domī   *at home*

5.   But clients could be fickle:

nēmō tē ipsum sequitur, sed aliquid ex tē. amīcitia ōlim
petēbātur, nunc praeda; mūtābunt testāmenta dēstitūtī
senēs, migrābit ad aliud līmen salūtātor.

Seneca, Moral Epistles 2.19

nēmō [nom.]   *no one*
tē ipsum [acc.]   *you yourself*
sequitur   *follows, attends* (looks passive but see p. 188)
ōlim   *once, previously*
petēbātur: imperfect passive of 'petō,-ere' (*seek*)
mūtō,-āre,-āvī,-ātum [1]   *change*
testāmentum,-ī [n.]   *will*
dēstitūtus,-a,-um   *lonely*
migrō,-āre,-āvī,-ātum [1]   *move*

aliud [n.; nom./acc.]   *other*
salūtātor,-ōris [m.]   *visitor, caller*

6. Caecilianus wants Martial, his client, to call him *domine*:

māne salūtāvī vērō tē nōmine cāsū
   nec dīxī dominum, Caeciliāne, meum.
quantī lībertās cōnstet mihi tanta, requīris?
   centum quadrantēs abstulit illa mihi.

Martial, Epigrams 6.88

māne   *this morning*
salūtō,-āre,-āvī,-ātum [1]   *greet*
vērus,-a,-um   *actual, real*
cāsus,-ūs [m.]   *chance*
quantī [genitive of value]   *(at) how much*
lībertās,-tātis [f.]   *liberty, licence*
cōnstet   *(s/he, it) costs*
requīrō,-ere [3]   *seek to know*
quadrāns,-ntis [m.]   *coin*
auferō, auferre, abstulī, ablātum   *take away, steal*
illa [f.; nom.]   *that* (i.e. 'lībertās')
mihi [dative of disadvantage, see p. 338]   *from me*

7. A century earlier Horace wrote about his patrons too, in a somewhat different vein, although it has to be said that Augustus and Maecenas were rather special patrons. It was Virgil who introduced him to Maecenas, and Horace's gratitude and warmth to all three is sprinkled through his Odes:

tua, Caesar, aetās
frūgēs et agrīs rettulit ūberēs,
et signa nostrō restituit Iovī
   dērepta Parthōrum superbīs
     postibus.

Horace, Odes 4.15.4–8

aetās,-tātis [f.]   *age, era*
et . . . et   *both . . . and*
rettulit: referre can mean *bring back* (as here) or *report*
ūberēs [acc.pl.]   *rich, plentiful*
signum,-ī [n.]   *standard* (these standards were lost by Crassus at Carrhae in 53 BC)
nostrō Iovī: i.e. *to our (temple of) Jove*   (Jove is another name for Jupiter: 'Iuppiter' [nom.], 'Iovem' [acc.], 'Iovis' [gen.], 'Iovī' [dat.], 'Iove' [abl.])
dēripiō,-ere, dēripuī, dēreptum [M.]   *tear down*
postis,-is [m.]   *doorpost*

8.   The note of fawning adulation is impossible to miss; but it was not contrived. Horace had fought on the wrong side with Brutus and Cassius at Philippi, and this had been forgiven. His personal circumstances hadn't been easy – his father was once a slave. And now here he was lapping up a comfortable life with all expenses paid. He had much to thank his muse for.

In our time patronage of the arts is largely commercial, while in the past it was more likely to come from a wealthy individual. In 1755 Samuel Johnson famously wrote to his patron, Lord Chesterfield, who Johnson felt had exaggerated his support after warm reviews greeted the publication of his Dictionary: 'Is not a patron, my lord, one who looks with unconcern on a man struggling for life in the water, and, when he has reached ground, encumbers him with help?' You might say little has changed. Few enterprises will risk their brand by sponsoring an outfit that is yet to become a success.

All but the richest artists need a patron. The question is whether the patronage compromises the integrity of the work. Organizations which use the arts for publicity or propaganda make us wary, from TV adverts to Goebbels, and artists are well advised to choose their patrons with care. A performer as celebrated and successful as Frank Sinatra was once hauled over the coals for singing at a few mafia suppers. But even some of our own worthier funding-bodies can be clumsy if well-intentioned patrons, their in-vogue orthodoxies snuffing out creative sparks.

It's hard to escape a slightly sinister sense of manipulation behind the poets of Maecenas' circle, and yet we should also remember that without the patronage there may have been no Virgil, no Horace. Few doubt that the poets shared a deep sense of relief at the end of hostilities, and the warmth of Horace to his benefactor I suspect was every bit as sincere as today's applicant ticking boxes for an Arts Council grant:

> ego nec tumultum
> nec morī per vim metuam tenente
> Caesare terrās.

Horace, *Odes* 3.14.14–16

tumultus,-ūs [m.]   *insurrection, civil war*
per vim   *through violence*
metuam   *I shall fear* ('metuō,-ere')
tenente Caesare   *with Augustus occupying*

9.   Virgil and Horace dealt with their obligations to Maecenas and Augustus in different ways. There was an expectation of something largescale. Greek literature provided the models in the epic poems the *Iliad* and *Odyssey*. Could Virgil or Horace refashion these well-known stories into something Roman and Augustan? Horace sidestepped such an undertaking, preferring less grandscale themes. Virgil did accept the challenge, and the result was the *Aeneid*, written over ten years and unrevised when the poet died in 19 BC.

> arma virumque canō, Trōiae quī prīmus ab ōrīs
> Ītaliam fātō profugus Lāvīnaque vēnit
> lītora.

Virgil, *Aeneid* 1.1–3

ōra,-ae [f.]   *shore, land*
fātum,-ī [n.]   *fate*
Lāvīnus,-a,-um   *Lavinian* (Lavinium was a town by the coast of Latium)
Ītaliam: in prose a preposition would be used with this
lītus,-oris [n.]   *shore, coast*
Word order for 'quī . . . lītora': 'quī prīmus ab ōrīs Trōiae fātō profugus vēnit Ītaliam
     Lāvīnaque lītora'

10. Virgil had grown up in northern Italy, where the family farmstead was vulnerable to the
     mayhem of the civil wars. The settling of veterans on lands already occupied brought
     more hardship. If Virgil's own farm escaped – and that is uncertain – he will have
     known others less lucky. Peace was tangible, a relief shared by all, scarcely imaginable to
     those who have not lived through the horrors of civil war.
         The *Aeneid* has a certain agony about it: Aeneas wrestling with uncertainties within a
     very certain destiny; the jilting of Carthage and harsh fate of the African queen Dido;
     the grim wars as Aeneas seizes the lands he is destined to inherit. Twice in the poem he
     leaves behind the woman he loves, their dead bodies lost in distant plumes of smoke.
     There is of course an implicit Aeneas–Augustus parallel. But even that is not always so
     rosy. Aeneas is an invader. Not unlike Augustus, he swoops on lands in Italy and
     slaughters those who stand in his way.

tum caput ōrantis nēquīquam et multa parantis
dīcere dēturbat terrae, truncumque tepentem
prōvolvēns super haec inimīcō pectore fātur:
'istīc nunc, metuende, iace.'

Virgil, Aeneid 10.554–7

Aeneas is the subject of the verb 'dēturbat'
tum   *then, at that moment*
ōrāns   *begging* ('ōrantis' = *of the man begging*: the man under attack from Aeneas is
     Tarquitus)
nēquīquam   *in vain, fruitlessly*
multa: neuter plural, i.e. *many things, much*
parāns   *preparing*
dēturbō,-āre,-āvī,-ātum [1]   *beat down, cut off, dash*
terrae: poets sometimes use the dative where in prose we might expect 'in terram'
truncus,-ī [m.]   *trunk*
tepēns   *warm*
prōvolvēns [nom.: the person doing this is the subject of 'dēturbat' and 'fātur']   *rolling
     forward*
super   *from above*
haec [n.; nom.pl./acc.pl.]   *these (words)*
inimīcō pectore: ablative (*from*); the 'pectore' belongs to Aeneas
fātur   *(s/he) speaks, utters* (looks passive but see p. 188)
istīc   *there*
metuendus,-a,-um   *fearsome*
iace: imperative from 'iaceō,-ēre'

11. There are explicit mentions of Augustus in the poem. He appears in the description of the shield made for Aeneas by Vulcan, and during Aeneas' visit to the underworld where the spirit of his father Anchises shows him Romans yet to be born:

hic vir, hic est, tibi quem prōmittī saepius audīs,
Augustus Caesar, dīvī genus, aurea condet
saecula quī rūrsus Latiō rēgnāta per arva
Sāturnō quondam.

Virgil, Aeneid 6.791–4

hic [m.; nom.]   *this*
quem [m.; acc.]   *who*
prōmittī [passive infinitive]   *to be promised, being promised*
saepius   *not infrequently, quite often*
genus,-eris [n.]   *race, stock, offspring*
aureus,-a,-um   *golden*
condō,-ere, condidī, conditum [3]   *found, establish*
saeculum,-ī [n.]   *generation, lifetime* (in the plural: *age, times*)
quī [m.; nom.]   *who*
rūrsus   *again*
arvum,-ī [n.]   *ploughed field, plain*
Sāturnus,-ī [m.]   *Saturn* (Italian god of the countryside, farming and harvests, who came to be identified with Greek Kronos, father of Zeus)
quondam   *formerly*
Word order for 'aurea . . . quondam': 'quī condet aurea saecula rūrsus Latiō per arva quondam rēgnāta Sāturnō'

12. Virgil tells us there are two gates from the underworld to the world above: the gate of horn through which true dreams pass above, and the gate of ivory for false dreams and vain fancies. Aeneas and the Sibyl leave by the gate of ivory, not as we might expect by the gate for true dreams:

hīs ibi tum nātum Anchīsēs ūnāque Sibyllam
prōsequitur dictīs portāque ēmittit eburnā.
ille viam secat ad nāvīs sociōsque revīsit.

Virgil, Aeneid 6.897–9

hīs [dat.pl./abl.pl.]   *these* (take with 'dictīs' = *with these things said*)
ibi   *there*
tum   *at that time*
nātus,-ī [m.]   *son*
Anchīsēs: nominative
ūnā   *together*
Sibyllam: the Sibyl is Aeneas' guide on the visit to the underworld
prōsequitur   *(s/he) escorts, accompanies* (looks passive but see p. 188)
porta,-ae [f.]   *gate*
ēmittō,-ere, ēmīsī, ēmissum [3]   *send out*

eburnus,-a,-um   *of ivory*
ille   *he* (Aeneas)
secō,-āre,-uī, sectum [1]   *cut*   (with 'viam' = *cut a path, make one's way*)
nāvis,-is [f.]   *ship*   ('nāvīs' = acc.pl. 'nāvēs')
socius,-ī [m.]   *colleague, comrade*
revīsō,-ere, revīsī, — [3]   *revisit, rejoin*

13. No one has ever quite put their finger on why Aeneas leaves by the exit for falsehoods.
     Some suggest a textual problem. Would Virgil have amended it if he'd lived the three
     years he wanted to revise the poem? Or perhaps it was later tinkering, or inaccurate
     copying. Others imagine a poet touching on philosophical and doctrinal observations
     about the futility of mortal awareness. It is true that Virgil was a contemplative soul with
     a taste for philosophical musing – and he was well versed in schools of thinking. But if
     there was anything systematic in his moment of musing, more than a poetic echo of
     current beliefs, it escapes us today.
         On the other hand we can take the falsehood of these gates at face value. It is the
     moment Aeneas is waking up, and with a bit of a jolt, so do we. Of course we expect
     him to use the true gates after such a pageant and tribute to his emperor. But he didn't,
     and Augustus – who insisted on publishing the poem despite Virgil's instructions to have
     it destroyed after his death – would have to live with it. That the thinnest of cracks
     should appear in this cosy panegyric of his friend and emperor should not surprise us.
     The melancholic poet did not share Ovid's impish humour but his deep sense of doubt
     must be allowed to surface from time to time, caught here in a flicker of irony.
         Augustus would have heard Virgil read aloud some of the work, and been deeply
     touched by the lines about his dead son, Marcellus, in the parade of spirits yet to be
     born:

heu, miserande puer, sī quā fāta aspera rumpās,
tū Mārcellus eris.

Virgil, Aeneid 6.882–3

heu   *oh! alas!*
miserandus,-a,-um   *pitiable*
quā   *in any way*
rumpās   *you might break*
eris: future of 'sum'

14. His loss was echoed in the later narrative of Aeneas' ally Evander coming upon the
     corpse of his son Pallas:

at nōn Ēvandrum potis est vīs ūlla tenēre,
sed venit in mediōs. feretrō Pallanta repostō
prōcubuit super atque haeret lacrimānsque gemēnsque.

Virgil, Aeneid 11.148–50

at   *but*
potis,-e   *capable, able*

vīs [f.]   *force, power* (see Ch.12, no.3, for a note on 'vīs')
ūllus,-a,-um   *any*
mediōs: if no noun, then supply one
feretrum,-ī [n.]   *bier, stretcher*
Pallanta: acc. of 'Pallas'
repōnō,-ere, reposuī, repos(i)tum [3]   *put away, put down*
prōcumbō,-ere, prōcubuī, prōcubitum [3]   *sink down*
super [+ acc.]   *on, upon*   (take with 'Pallanta')
haereō,-ēre, haesī, haesum [2]   *cling to*
lacrimāns   *weeping*
gemēns   *groaning*

Exercises 14b

1.   Translate:
(a)   tuumne testāmentum mūtāvistī? sed ego tibi semper amīcus fuī.
(b)   ita tē salūtāvī, ō Iūlia, nec dīxī dominam. quid ergō?
(c)   cūr salūtātōrēs impudentēs semper ad meum vestibulum adeunt?

2.   Identify the case, gender and number of each underlined pronoun:
(a)   cum surgit, surgēs; dōnec sedet **illa**, sedēbis.
(b)   **hōc** tempore Catilīnam, competitōrem nostrum, dēfendere cōgitāmus.
(c)   rēs est omnis in **hāc** causā nōbīs, iūdicēs, cum Clōdiā.
(d)   rēgnum Aegyptī victor Cleopātrae frātrīque **eius** minōrī permīsit.
(e)   Antōnius ad **sē** venīre centuriōnēs **eōs**que ante pedēs suōs uxōrisque suae, quam **sē**cum gravis imperātor ad exercitum dūxerat, iugulārī coēgit.

3.   Fill each gap with the correct pronoun, and translate:
(a)   ad resistendum .... {*us/ourselves*} parāmus.
(b)   cūr tū .... {*me*} vīvere coēgistī!
(c)   Clōdius .... {*to you* [pl.]} est inimīcus.
(d)   ō Lepide, populus .... {*you*} triumvirum creāvit.

4.   Change each sentence into an active one, keeping the meaning:
(a)   servus ā mīlitibus dē Saxō dēiectus est.
(b)   captīvī in triumphō ā centuriōne ductī sunt.

5.   Change each sentence into a passive one, keeping the meaning:
(a)   Caesar Gāium Octāvium in familiam adoptat.
(b)   dux mīlitibus Ītaliam ostendit. (*say* Italy is shown to the soldiers by . . .)
(c)   prīmō magis ambitiō quam avāritia animōs hominum exercēbat.

6.   Find Latin ancestors in this chapter of *coherent, fiction, ignition, prosecution* and *section*.

— 15 —

Tales of love

Introducing the subjunctive

All the tenses you have studied so far are called 'indicative': they describe an actual event, something that happens. It may have already happened (past tenses), or not happened yet (future), or if negative not happen at all, but it still deals with an actual and not a hypothetical event. These uses of **veniō,-īre** are all indicative:

> domum **vēnit**   (perfect indicative)
> *s/he came home*

> domum **veniet**   (future indicative)
> *s/he will come home*

> domum nōn **venit**   (present indicative)
> *s/he is not coming home*

The indicative is called the 'mood' of a verb. The subjunctive is a different mood. It deals with ideas, with potential, with hopes and desires, with intention or speculation, with what might happen or might have happened, with what would happen if:

> domum **veniat**!   (present subjunctive, expressing a wish)
> *may s/he come home!*

> sī captīvus **esset** domum nōn **venīret**   (2 x imperfect subjunctives, expressing a hypothetical and unfulfillable condition)
> *if he were a captive he would not be coming home*

> sī Antōnius domum **vēnisset** eum **vīdissem**   (2 x pluperfect subjunctives, as above but dealing with the past)
> *if Antony had come home I would have seen him*

There are four tenses of the subjunctive: present, imperfect, perfect and pluperfect.

A verb in the subjunctive may be the main or only verb in a sentence; or it may appear in a dependent clause after a conjunction like **ut, nē, cum** and, as above, **sī**. If it appears alone, as the main verb, it is more often than not the present subjunctive.

The present subjunctive

The present subjunctive endings seem like a switch with the indicative ones. All conjugations *except* the first (**amāre**) have an **a** in the ending; while **amāre** adopts an **e**; and **esse** predictably does its own thing:

1 amō,-āre	2 habeō,-ēre	3 mittō,-ere	4 audiō,-īre	M. capiō,-ere	sum, esse
am**em**	hab**eam**	mitt**am**	aud**iam**	cap**iam**	**sim**
am**ēs**	hab**eās**	mitt**ās**	aud**iās**	cap**iās**	**sīs**
am**et**	hab**eat**	mitt**at**	aud**iat**	cap**iat**	**sit**
am**ēmus**	hab**eāmus**	mitt**āmus**	aud**iāmus**	cap**iāmus**	**sīmus**
am**ētis**	hab**eātis**	mitt**ātis**	aud**iātis**	cap**iātis**	**sītis**
am**ent**	hab**eant**	mitt**ant**	aud**iant**	cap**iant**	**sint**

The present subjunctive often expresses a <u>wish or desire</u>. This is often in the 1st person, an enthusiastic hope or prayer, or simply a sigh of frustration. The 'wishing' subjunctive is sometimes preceded by **utinam** (*if only*):

utinam illum diem **videam**
if only <u>I may see</u> that day [7.12]

present subjunctive (indicative in brackets)	
videam	(videō)
videās	(vidēs)
videat	(videt)
videāmus	(vidēmus)
videātis	(vidētis)
videant	(vident)

Practice 15a
Translate:
(a)   utinam ego Lesbiam videam!
(b)   ēheu, utinam ē mundō cēdam!

The present subjunctive is also used to give advice or an instruction (the 'jussive' subjunctive). You have seen how the imperative gives a command:

dīc aut **accipe** calcem
<u>*tell*</u> *(me) or* <u>*get*</u> *a kicking* [13.15]

The present subjunctive is softer at the edges: '*may you hurry!*' instead of '*hurry!*'. In English, orders are sometimes voiced more politely than '*hurry up!*' or '*put your stuff away!*' as in '*would you mind hurrying up?*' and '*do you want to put your stuff away?*', which of course are not really questions at all, at least not in my house. A more polite robber might have said:

dīcās aut **accipiās** calcem
may you tell (me) or may you get a
kicking (i.e. *would you mind telling*
me or do you want to get a kicking)

dīcam (dīcō)	accipiam (accipiō)
dīcās (dīcis)	**accipiās** (accipis)
dīcat (dīcit)	accipiat (accipit)
dīcāmus (dīcimus)	accipiāmus (accipimus)
dīcātis (dīcitis)	accipiātis (accipitis)
dīcant (dīcunt)	accipiant (accipiunt)

Practice 15b

Translate:
(a) ō Auguste, dictātūram recipiās.
(b) ō Caesar, parcās subiectīs et dēbellēs superbōs.

The 1st person plural of the present subjunctive is used as an <u>exhortation</u> (*let us . . .*):

vīvāmus mea Lesbia atque **amēmus**
let us live, my Lesbia, and let us love [15.6]

vīvam (vīvō)	amem (amō)
vīvās (vīvis)	amēs (amās)
vīvat (vīvit)	amet (amat)
vīvāmus (vīvimus)	**amēmus** (amāmus)
vīvātis (vīvitis)	amētis (amātis)
vīvant (vīvunt)	ament (amant)

Practice 15c

Translate:
(a) corpus Caesaris in flūmen trahāmus!
(b) Catilīnam, competitōrem nostrum, dēfendāmus.

The subjunctive is sometimes used to express a <u>rhetorical question</u>, i.e. where the answer is obvious, and the desired response is agreement or sympathy:

quis fallere **possit** amantem?
who <u>can</u> deceive a lover? [3.9]

quid **agās**?
what <u>are you to do</u>? [13.15]

possim (possum)	agam (agō)
possīs (potes)	**agās** (agis)
possit (potest)	agat (agit)
possīmus (possumus)	agāmus (agimus)
possītis (potestis)	agātis (agitis)
possint (possunt)	agant (agunt)

A similar expression is used in the 1st person, called the 'deliberative' subjunctive, which carried a rhetorical flavour similar to the above, but such a question in the 1st person could well receive a response.

quid **faciam**?
what am I to do?

faciam (faciō)
faciās (facis)
faciat (facit)
faciāmus (facimus)
faciātis (facitis)
faciant (faciunt)

In the next example the subjunctive carries a similar sense of exhortation or encouragement but in a somewhat ironical way. The speaker (Brutus) does not like what he sees. This is the 'concessive' use of the subjunctive (*although he may . . .*):

patrem **appellet** Octāvius Cicerōnem, **referat** omnia, **laudet**, grātiās **agat**, tamen verba rēbus erunt contrāria
(although) Octavius may call Cicero his father, refer everything (to him), praise and thank (him), nevertheless his words will be opposite to his actions [10.2]

This subjunctive can have a dismissive tone:

eādem igitur operā **accūsent** Catullum   (pres. subj. 'accūsō,-āre',1)
then by the same token let them accuse (they may as well accuse) Catullus [15.11]

Practice 15d

1.   Identify the corresponding *indicative* forms (same person and tense) of the five underlined verbs in the last two examples.

2.   Translate:
     (a) quid dīcās?
     (b) quid agam?

3.   The 3rd conjugation form **dīcam** (dīcō,-ere), **dūcam** (dūcō,-ere), etc, can be indicative or subjunctive. Which tenses?

Deponent verbs

In the last chapter we saw the passive at work:

(pānis) tener **servātur** dominō
tender bread is kept for the master [14.3]

You have also met a number of verbs which *look* passive but are translated as *active* verbs and which take direct objects in the accusative as active verbs do:

quotiēns mē cōnsulem interficere **cōnātus es**!
how many times have you tried to kill me, the consul! [6.7]

nēmō tē ipsum **sequitur**
no one attends you for yourself [14.5]

haec inimīcō pectore **fātur**
he says these words with a hateful heart [14.10]

These are 'deponent verbs'. They have no active forms, only passive ones, but have active meanings and can take direct objects. One of the most common is **sequor** (*I follow*):

Ītaliam nōn sponte **sequor**
it is not my choice I make for Italy [3.11]

Another common deponent verb is **gradior** (*I step, walk, go*), more often seen in compound forms, such as **aggredior** and **trānsgredior**. Past participles are normally passive (**amātus** = *having been loved*, not *having loved*), but deponent verbs (and *only* deponent verbs) have an active past participle:

    trānsgressus,-a,-um (trānsgredior)   *having crossed over*
    secūtus,-a,-um (sequor)   *having followed* (and not *having been followed*)

Similarly, the past tenses of deponent verbs look passive but have active meanings:

Caesar **aggressus est** Britannōs īgnōtōs
Caesar attacked the unknown Britons [7.11]

Caesar in Macedoniam **trānsgressus** Pompēium ad extrēmum Pharsālicō proeliō fūdit et fugientem Alexandrēam **persecūtus est**
Caesar, having crossed into Macedonia, put Pompey to flight at the battle of Pharsalus and pursued him as he fled to Alexandria [8.10]

Instead of four principal parts deponents have only three (the third and fourth merge, as the perfect includes the past participle):

    sequor *I follow*, **sequī** *to follow*, **secūtus** (sum) (*I*) *followed*
    ūtor *I use*, **ūtī** *to use*, **ūsus** (sum) (*I*) *used*

Vocabulary 15

Here are some of the more common deponent verbs. Note that the present infinitive of all passive and deponent verbs ends **-ī**.

cōnor, cōnārī, cōnātus [1] *try*
fateor, fatērī, fassus [2] *speak*
gradior, gradī, gressus [M.] *step, walk, go*
loquor, loquī, locūtus [3] *speak*
mīror, mīrārī, mīrātus [1] *admire, marvel at, be surprised*
morior, morī, mortuus [M.] *die*

patior, patī, passus [M.] *allow, endure, suffer*
reor, rērī, ratus [3] *think, imagine, suppose*
sequor, sequī, secūtus [3] *follow*
ūtor, ūtī, ūsus [3; + abl.] *use*
vereor, verērī, veritus [3] *fear*

Many have compound forms (e.g. **alloquor, cōnfiteor, persequor, trānsgredior**)

Look online for all the deponent verbs which appear in the course (see p. 393).

Exercises 15a

1. Translate:
(a) utinam tē videam! hūc veniās!
(b) salūtātōrēs discēdant!
(c) veniāmus, videāmus, vincāmus.
(d) utinam vultūs vīvōs dē marmore dūcam!
(e) haec locūtus abiit.
(f) quis illa remedia patī poterit?
(g) cūr tē sequimur?

2. Fill the gaps with each noun in turn:
(a) *of Caesar, of the consuls, of the soldiers, of the teacher*
     cūr tibi placet de vitiīs .... loquī?
(b) *the matron, the poets, the judges, the prostitutes*
     miserōsne in harēnā spectāre .... placuit?
(c) *the gladiators, the bulls, the conspirators, the robbers*
     ille dēmēns semper .... sequitur.
(d) *roads, mountains, rivers, fields, the sea*
     vīsne .... trānsgredī?
(e) *the senate, the army, the emperor, kings, conquerors*
     Fortūna .... favet.
(f) *on the bed, on a mountain, on a horse, on the waves, on the shore, in the sea, in prison*
     mea domina in .... sedet.
(g) *with the laws, with the flowers, with the poem, with the silver*
     illa mātrōna .... nōn contenta erat.
(h) *by love, by ambition, by the shouts, by grief, by courage, by the story*
     meus amīcus .... mōtus est.

3. What Latin verb is an ancestor to the English word 'jussive'?

Tales of love

The first love stories to have survived are those of the comic writers, Plautus and Terence, where lovesick fellows denied their ladies are regular figures of fun. Love stories appear in narrative epic, such as Dido and Aeneas in Virgil's *Aeneid*, and many more in Ovid's *Metamorphoses*. In Catullus' short poems we read of his highs and lows with Lesbia, while the elegiac poetry of Propertius, Tibullus and Ovid seldom strays far from the theme of how to keep a loved one sweet. A Latin or Greek 'elegy' is so called because of its metre: pairs of lines (the elegiac couplet), starting with a hexameter (this line is used exclusively throughout the *Aeneid* and *Metamorphoses*) followed by the pentameter, which is shorter and usually brings the unit of sense to a close. See the online supports (p. 393) for more on reading verse.

> **Reading notes**
> When **video,-ēre, vīdī, vīsum** (*see*) appears in the passive it can be translated as *be seen* or *seem*:
>
> ille mī pār esse deō **vidētur**
> *that man seems to me to be equal to a god* [15.7]
>
> nōn illa mihi fōrmōsior umquam / **vīsa** (est)
> *she never seemed more beautiful to me* [15.12]

1. The theme of love and devotion was more appealing to some poets than war and conquest. Sometimes they mixed the two, as here, where Ovid compares a lover barred from the house of his mistress with the hardship of a soldier:

    quis nisi vel mīles vel amāns et frīgora noctis
        et dēnsō mixtās perferet imbre nivēs?

    Ovid, Amores 1.9.15–16

    nisi   *except*
    vel . . . vel   *either . . . or*
    amāns, amantis [m./f.]   *one who loves, a lover*
    frīgus,-oris [n.]   *cold, chill*
    dēnsus,-a,-um   *thick, heavy*
    misceō,-ēre, miscuī, mixtum [2]   *mix, mingle*
    perferō, perferre, pertulī, perlātum   *endure, suffer* (for the ending see p. 360)
    imber, imbris [m.]   *pouring rain*
    nix, nivis [f.]   *snow*

2. Myth furnished imagery to tickle all appetites, in paintings and literature. The gods are cheerfully depicted as randy, jealous and dangerous. They gave metaphoric value to all parts of life, especially tales of sauce. This nymph, Io, was trying to escape the advances of Jupiter when . . .

    deus inductā lātās cālīgine terrās
    occuluit tenuitque fugam rapuitque pudōrem.

    Ovid, Metamorphoses 1.599–600

indūcō,-ere,-dūxī,-ductum   *draw upon, spread over*
lātus,-a,-um   *broad, wide*
cālīgō,-inis [f.]   *darkness, mist*
occulō,-ere,-uī, occultum [3]   *hide, cover*
fuga,-ae [f.]   *(her) flight, escape*
rapiō,-ere,-uī, raptum [M.]   *seize, take*
pudor,-ōris [m.]   *(her) modesty,* i.e. *chastity, 'honour'*

3.   Virtually all surviving Latin literature is credited to male authorship and if we read of a woman expressing a wish or opinion, it is always a man telling us about it. Women seldom appear in historical 'factual' writing. In mythical stories they have a more prominent role, but the perspective remains resolutely male, such as the comedy of Jupiter's lustful wanderings, which make his wife Juno so resentful.

   The story of Echo and Narcissus, a beautiful episode in Ovid's *Metamorphoses*, allows the poet to play with the cinematic toys of sound and picture. Echo is punished by Juno for distracting her with chat while nymphs bedded by Jupiter make their escape. Echo loses her voice, at least the ability to say anything of her own. Then she falls in love with the handsome Narcissus.

forte puer comitum sēductus ab agmine fīdō
dīxerat: 'ecquis adest?' et 'adest' responderat Ēcho.

Ovid, *Metamorphoses* 3.379–80

forte   *by chance*
comes,-itis [m.]   *companion*
sēdūcō,-ere, sēdūxī, sēductum   *lead apart, separate*
agmen,-inis [n.]   *crowd, band*
fīdus,-a,-um   *faithful, loyal*
ecquis: like 'quis', with 'ec-' adding more voice to the question
respondeō,-ēre, respondī, respōnsum [2]   *answer, reply*

4.   He spurns her and all other young men and women who desire him. One of these prays that Narcissus too be denied what he loves (these stories are driven by recurring themes of desire, rejection, jealousy and revenge), and after the prayer is granted Narcissus falls in love with his reflection in a pool.

cūnctaque mīrātur, quibus est mīrābilis ipse:
sē cupit imprūdēns et, quī probat, ipse probātur,
dumque petit, petitur, pariterque accendit et ārdet.

Ovid, *Metamorphoses* 3.424–6

mīror,-ārī, mīrātus [1; deponent]   *admire*
quibus [dat.pl.]   *for which*
mīrābilis,-e   *admirable, worthy of admiration*
imprūdēns   *unaware, without realizing*
probō,-āre,-āvī,-ātum [1]   *cherish*
accendō,-ere, accendī, accēnsum [3]   *kindle, set on fire*
ārdeō,-ēre, ārsī, ārsum [2]   *be on fire*

5. Women did not compose poetry, or at least were not credited with it, but they were certainly appreciative. Virgil's sympathy for the hapless Dido, who is manipulated by the gods and let down by Aeneas, will not have escaped his female audience. Here Dido faces Aeneas on the point of his departure from Carthage:

nam quid dissimulō aut quae mē ad maiōra reservō?
num flētū ingemuit nostrō? num lūmina flexit?

Virgil, Aeneid 4.368–9

nam *for*
quid *why*
dissimulō,-āre [1] *make a pretence*
quae [n.; nom.pl./acc.pl.] *which, what*
mē: the 1st person pronoun is here used reflexively
maiōra [n.pl.] *greater things (in the future)*
reservō,-āre,-āvī,-ātum [1] *keep back*
num: expects a negative answer, and can tip a question into a disparaging remark
flētus,-ūs [m.] *weeping*
ingemō,-ere, ingemuī, ingemitum [3] *groan*
nostrō: treat as singular
lūmen,-inis [n.] *light, eye*
flectō,-ere, flexī, flexum [3] *bend, turn*

6. Catullus' love poems are addressed to 'Lesbia', who has long been recognized as Clodia, the sister of Clodius. We know of her husband, Metellus, who died in 59 BC, and a relationship with Caelius, which turned sour in the mid-50s. If we believe the gossip that Cicero uses in his defence of Caelius against Clodia in court, then add her brother Clodius and numerous slaves to her list of paramours. There were rumours that Cicero himself may have been closer to Clodia at the time of his consulship (p. 83). It might explain his later bitterness. But such things, if true, never came to light. Catullus' feelings by contrast are preserved in his poems.

vīvāmus mea Lesbia atque amēmus
rūmōrēsque senum sevēriōrum
omnēs ūnius aestimēmus assis.

Catullus, Poems 5.1–3

vīvāmus: see p. 187
mea Lesbia: vocative
rūmor,-ōris [m.] *rumour, gossip*
senex,-is [m.] *old man*
sevēriōrum [gen.pl.] *rather/too strict*
ūnius: genitive of value (*at one penny*); here 'ūnius', not 'ūnius'
aestimō,-āre,-āvī,-ātum [1] *value* ('aestimēmus' is pres. subjunctive: *let us . . .*)
as, assis [m.] *as* (an as was a coin worth little, say *a penny, a cent*)

7.   Many of his poems were closely modelled on previous Greek ones, *de rigueur* for all
      Roman poets. Greek stories, themes and even their rhythms were the material poets
      worked with. Some of his lines have an almost plagiaristic look about them, but they still
      feel feel fresh, spontaneous and Catullus' own. This poem is reworked from a poem by
      Sappho, and it opens with Catullus jealously regarding a rival:

ille mī pār esse deō vidētur,
ille, sī fās est, superāre dīvōs.

Catullus, *Poems* 51.1–2

pār, paris [m./f.; + dat.]   *equal*
vidētur [passive of 'videō,-ēre']   *(s/he, it) seems*
fās [like 'nefās', does not decline]   *proper, permitted, possible*
superō,-āre,-āvī,-ātum [1]   *overcome, surpass*

8.   Catullus will lose faith in this promise:

nūllī sē dīcit mulier mea nūbere mālle
    quam mihi, nōn sī sē Iuppiter ipse petat.

Catullus, *Poems* 70,1–2

nūllī [dat.]   *not any(one)*
sē mālle [after 'dīcit']   *(says) herself to prefer*, i.e. *that she prefers*
nūbō,-ere, nūpsī, nūptum [3; + dat.]   *marry*
quam   *than*
petat: present subjunctive of 'petō,-ere' after 'sī' (*if . . . were to ask*)

9.   There is a view that Lesbia did not exist at all but was an imaginative creation, a
      hypothetical fancy dreamt up with the help of the poet's schooling in rhetoric, where
      unreal speculations were used for practice. Here is a poet, young (he died within a few
      months of his 30th birthday), with an easy-come brilliance with the poetic tradition. But
      it is hard to imagine he was playing rhetorical games with no identifiable person in mind
      or that he lacked genuine emotions. The rhetorical games were more likely a front for
      flirting. We cannot pin down all the feelings or experience that a poet draws upon, but if
      Catullus was writing in a vacuum of personal emotion, if Lesbia is a purely rhetorical
      creation out of thin air, then he has fooled a good many of us. And the case for Lesbia
      being someone very particular, Clodia, remains persuasive. This poem addressed to
      Caelius is one of the clues:

Caelī, Lesbia nostra, Lesbia illa,
illa Lesbia, quam Catullus ūnam
plūs quam sē atque suōs amāvit omnēs,
nunc in quadriviīs et angiportīs
glūbit magnanimī Remī nepōtēs.

Catullus, *Poems* 58

Caelī: see no.6 above
quam: line 2 = [f., acc.] *who(m)*; line 3 = *than*
ūnam [f., acc. from 'ūnus,-a,-um'] *alone*
plūs *more*
quadrivium,-ī [n.] *crossroads*
angiportum,-ī [n.] *alley*
glūbō,-ere [3] *pick off, peel off, rob* (perhaps an obscene meaning, or simple robbery, or both)
magnanimus,-a,-um *highminded* (ironic)
Remus,-ī: Remus was the brother of Romulus
nepōs, nepōtis [m./f.] *descendant*

10. No doubt many literate and lovesick men put their training to use and poured out their
woes in verse. Not all were as successful as Catullus, or Martial:

cūr nōn mittō meōs tibi, Pontiliāne, libellōs?
nē mihi tū mittās, Pontiliāne, tuōs.

Martial, Epigrams 7.3

Pontiliāne: Pontilianus creates poetry which Martial doesn't want to read
libellus,-ī [m.] *(short) book, writing*
nē . . . mittās *lest you send*

11. The use of a pseudonym with the same metrical value as a lover's name (e.g. Lesbia for
Clodia) was common practice. Apuleius, a writer of the second century, defended his
use of substitute names, listing Catullus with other poets who had disguised their
mistresses' identities:

eādem igitur operā accūsent Catullum, quod Lesbiam
prō Clōdiā nōminārit.

Apuleius, Apology 10.2

eādem operā *by the same token, in the same manner*
igitur *therefore, then*
accūsent *they* (i.e. his critics) *may as well accuse*
prō [+ abl.] *in place of*
nōminārit [contraction of 'nōmināverit', perfect subjunctive after 'quod': see pp. 203
and 289] *(s/he) named, used the name of*

12. The poet Propertius was younger than Virgil and just a few years older than Ovid. He
was one of those encouraged by Maecenas. His tales of rough and tumble with 'Cynthia'
(real name: Hostia) were very popular.

māne erat, et voluī, sī sōla quiēsceret illa,
    vīsere: at in lectō Cynthia sōla fuit.
obstipuī: nōn illa mihi fōrmōsior umquam
    vīsa, neque ostrīnā cum fuit in tunicā.

Propertius, Elegies 2.29B.1–4

māne   *early in the morning*
sōlus,-a,-um   *alone*
quiēsceret   *(she) was resting*
vīsō,-ere, vīsī [3]   *go to see*
at   *and indeed*
obstipēscō,-ere, obstipuī [3]   *be amazed*
fōrmōsior [m./f., nom.]   *more beautiful*
umquam   *ever*
vīsa (est)   *she seemed*
neque   *not even*
ostrīnus,-a,-um   *purple*
cum   *when*
tunica,-ae [f.]   *under-garment, tunic*

13.   Tibullus, a contemporary of Propertius, sees himself as a prisoner of his girl, thereby losing his ancestral freedoms:

> hīc mihi servitium videō dominamque parātam:
>   iam mihi lībertās illa paterna valē.

Tibullus, Poems 2.4.1–2

hīc   *here*
mihi: take 'mihi' in line 1 after 'parātam' (i.e. *ready for me*); in line 2, *as for me, for my part*
servitium,-ī [n.]   *slavery*
parātam: from 'parō,-āre,-āvī,-ātum'
paternus,-a,-um   *belonging to my fathers, of my fathers*
valē   *farewell*

14.   Poets took from comedy and from Greek poetry the figure of the lovesick male shut outside the doors of the girl he is after. Here Ovid addresses the doorkeeper:

> quid faciēs hostī, quī sīc exclūdis amantem?
>   tempora noctis eunt; excute poste seram!

Ovid, Amores 1.6.31–2

faciēs: future of 'faciō,-ere'
hostis,-is [m.]   *foe, enemy*
sīc   *thus*
exclūdō,-ere [3]   *shut out*
tempora: translate in the singular
eunt: from 'eō, īre', here *pass, disappear*
excutiō,-ere [M.]   *take off, remove* ('excute' is an imperative or plea)
postis,-is [m.]   *doorpost*
sera,-ae [f.]   *bar*

15.   The trappings of soldiery were extended to girls. Camilla, athletic and warlike, stabs one of Aeneas' Etruscan allies and then mocks him for assuming she and her troops would be as easy to kill as game in the woods:

'silvīs tē, Tyrrhēne, ferās agitāre putāstī?'

Virgil, *Aeneid* 11.686

Tyrrhēnus,-a,-um   *Etruscan*
fera,-ae [f.]   *wild animal*
agitō,-āre [1]   *rouse, stir up* (as a hunter driving animals into a net)
tē agitāre   *yourself to be stirring up, that you were stirring up*
putāstī: for 'putāvistī'

16. Shortly afterwards Camilla herself is fatally wounded:

'hāctenus, Acca soror, potuī: nunc vulnus acerbum
cōnficit, et tenebrīs nigrēscunt omnia circum.'

Virgil, *Aeneid* 11.823–4

hāctenus   *thus far*
Acca: her comrade
possum, posse, potuī   *be able, have power, be in control*
vulnus,-eris [n.]   *wound*
acerbus,-a,-um   *bitter*
cōnficiō,-ere [M.]   *finish (me)*
tenebrae,-ārum [f.pl.]   *darkness, shadows*
nigrēscō,-ere   *grow dark, become black*
circum   *around* (sometimes a preposition, but here an adverb taken with the verb)

Exercises 15b
1.   Translate:
(a) utinam ille poēta nostrum līmen relinquat!
(b) Caesar superbam rēgīnam dēdūcat in triumphō.
(c) Cicerōnī īnsidiās parēmus!
(d) utinam ego amīcitiam Augustī retineam!
(e) ō miser puer, utinam fāta aspera rumpās!
(f) cēdant omnia arma in Augustum!
(g) ō Hannibal, in montibus maneāmus.

2.   Fill the gaps, and translate:
(a) carmen .... {*let us praise*}, mea Lesbia.
(b) cēnam mihi domina .... {*may she prepare*}.
(c) quid faciēs servō, quī sīc senātōrem exclūdere .... {*you have tried*}?
(d) omnēs amīcōs nostrōs ad .... {*dinner*} invitēmus!

3.   Imagine you are writing the lines below not about a male but a female. Without adding or removing any words change the endings accordingly (four changes in all):

ille mī pār esse deō vidētur,
ille, sī fās est, superāre dīvōs.

4.   Fill the gaps, and translate:

(a)   sed nōnne es novus homō?

        — quid ergō? mē .... {*let them despise*} senātōrēs! plēbs mē semper .... {*have admired*}.

(b)   ubī est ille servus?

        — hīc ego .... {*I am present*}.

— 16 —

Women: warriors, drunks and literary critics

The imperfect subjunctive

The imperfect subjunctive is easy enough to recognize, provided you know the verb's infinitive. The imperfect subjunctive is in effect the infinitive with these endings added:

-m	e.g.	amāre + m = **amārem**
-s		audīre + m = **audīrem**
-t		
-mus		esse + m = **essem**
-tis		ferre + m = **ferrem**
-nt		

If you cannot see the infinitive in the word then it is not the imperfect subjunctive. See p. 359 for all the endings.

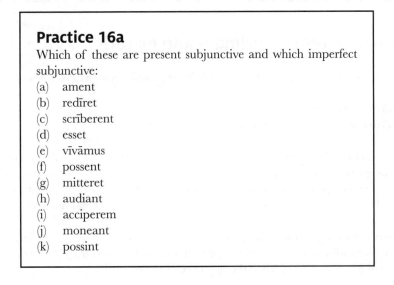

Practice 16a
Which of these are present subjunctive and which imperfect subjunctive:
(a) ament
(b) redīret
(c) scrīberent
(d) esset
(e) vīvāmus
(f) possent
(g) mitteret
(h) audiant
(i) acciperem
(j) moneant
(k) possint

Subjunctive in subordinate clauses

The imperfect subjunctive is frequently used in subordinate clauses, in groups of words with their own separate verb which are dependent on the main body of the sentence, typically after one of the conjunctions **ut, nē, cum** or **sī**.

ut **or** nē **to express purpose**

The conjunction **ut** (*that, so that*) or **nē** (*so that . . . not, lest*) can introduce a subordinate clause expressing intention or purpose. The verb in the subordinate clause is in the subjunctive:

> Pyrrhus, **ut** auxilium Tarentīnīs **ferret**, in Ītaliam vēnit
> *Pyrrhus came into Italy <u>so that he might bring</u> help (to bring help) to the people of*
> *Tarentum* [4,2]
>
> (ferō, ferre = *bear, carry, bring*)

| ferrem |
| ferrēs |
| **ferret** |
| ferrēmus |
| ferrētis |
| ferrent |

The subordinate clause is **ut . . . ferret**, while **vēnit** is the main verb, i.e. the principal verb in the sentence.

Practice 16b

(i)   Identify the main verb;
(ii)   identify the verb in the subordinate clause (in the subjunctive);
(iii)   translate:
(a)   **servus, ut praemium prōmissum indicī habēret, manūmissus est.** [5.10]
(b)   **cūr nōn mittō meōs tibi libellōs? nē mihi tū mittās tuōs.** [15.10]

Sequence of tenses: primary and historic

The perfect tense can be represented in English in two ways, with *have* or without *have*:

> **amāvī**   *I have loved*   or   *I loved* (active)
> **amātus sum**   *I have been loved*   or   *I was loved* (passive)

The version in English with *have* is sometimes called the 'present perfect', as the action described may still be going on, whereas the past tense without *have* suggests an episode now completed. For instance a tennis player who says 'we have played for three hours' may still have some of the match to play, whereas a player who says 'we played for three hours' has finished.

In a sentence with a purpose clause, the main verb, if perfect, is translated *with have* if the verb in the subordinate clause is in the present subjunctive, and *without have* if it is in the imperfect subjunctive. This is called the sequence of tenses:

Primary sequence:

> Pyrrhus, ut auxilium **ferat** [*present subjunctive*], in Ītaliam **vēnit**
> *Pyrrhus <u>has come</u> into Italy so that <u>he may bring</u> help (to bring help)*

Historic sequence:

> Pyrrhus, ut auxilium **ferret** [*imperfect subjunctive*], in Ītaliam **vēnit**
> *Pyrrhus <u>came</u> into Italy so that <u>he might bring</u> help (to bring help)*

A verb in the imperfect subjunctive in a purpose clause is put into English as *might . . .* while a verb in the present subjunctive in primary sequence is *may . . . .*

If the main verb is present, future or future perfect the sequence is always primary. If imperfect or pluperfect it is historic. The perfect, as we see above, can be either.

Practice 16c

Identify the sequence of tenses for each sentence (i.e. primary or historic), and translate:
(a) Sabīnī cum līberīs ac coniugibus vēnērunt ut urbem novam vidērent.
(b) Cicerō ad Antōnium scrībet ut eius amīcitiam retineat.
(c) Caesar in Macedoniam trānsgressus est ut Pompēium persequerētur.
(d) Caesar effēcit nē Clōdius pūnīrētur.
(e) captīvī ad pālum dēligātī sunt ut suppliciō afficiantur.

---

ut **or** nē **with an indirect command**

A direct instruction is expressed in Latin with an imperative or a subjunctive:

> cēnam **parā**!
> *prepare the dinner!*

> cēnam **paret**!
> *may s/he prepare the dinner*

Instructions are also described or reported by a third party (called an 'indirect command'). The subordinate clause, i.e. what had been the direct instruction, is introduced by **ut** or **nē** with the verb in the subjunctive:

> Mārcus servō imperāvit **ut** cēnam **parāret**   (imperō,-āre [+ dat.] = *order, command*)
> *Marcus ordered the slave <u>that he prepare</u> the dinner (i.e. Marcus ordered the slave to prepare the dinner)*

An indirect command can be introduced by a number of different verbs to indicate the kind of instruction given. It may not be a blunt order but a recommendation or piece of advice. A common expression of saying goodbye in Latin is an indirect command. In fact this expression contains a direct command as well:

cūrā ut valeās　(valeō,-ēre [2] = *be well*)[1]
take care that you keep well

Although Latin uses **ut** followed by a verb in the subjunctive for an indirect command, in English a simple infinitive will provide a perfectly good translation (above: *to prepare the dinner*). One Latin verb, **iubeō,-ēre** (*order, tell*), is an exception to the **ut** construction and is followed by an infinitive, as in English:

Pompēius **iubet** nōs **esse** sine cūrā.
Pompey orders/tells us to be without anxiety [7.6]

The sequence of tenses also applies to indirect commands. If the main verb is perfect, then translate it with *have* if the subordinate verb is present subjunctive and without *have* if imperfect subjunctive.

Practice 16d
1. Choose the right translation of 'imperāvit':
   (a) domina nōbīs <u>imperāvit</u> {*ordered/has ordered*} ut cēnam parēmus.
   (b) domina nōbīs <u>imperāvit</u> {*ordered/has ordered*} ut cēnam parārēmus.

2. Translate:
   (a) Lāocoōn nōs ōrāvit nē equum acciperēmus.
   (b) magister monuit ut omnēs historiās legāmus.

3. Choose the correct verb, and translate:
   (a) Turnus mē .... {iussit/imperāvit} Lāvīniam dūcere uxōrem.
   (b) Lāvīnia .... {iussit/imperāvit} ut vīllam relinquerem.

---

ut **to express a consequence or result**

As well as a purpose or intention, and an indirect command, an **ut** clause can express the result of something. Below, pity (ironical) is expressed for the spectator at the games who has to sit through all the bloodshed:

tū quid meruistī, miser, ut hoc **spectēs**?　(pres. subj. 'spectō,-āre')
what have you deserved, wretch, that you <u>should watch</u> this (i.e. with the consequence that . . .) [21.7]

There is often a word in the main clause which signals that a result clause will complete the sense, such as 'so', 'such', 'so many', etc.

<u>tanta</u> Augustī erat auctōritās <u>ut omnēs eum timērent</u>
<u>*so great*</u> *was the authority of Augustus* <u>*that all feared him*</u>

---

1 The briefer form is the simple imperative **valē**.

adeō	*to such an extent*
ita	*in such a way*
tālis,-e	*such, of such a kind*
tam	*so*
tantus,-a,-um	*such, so great, so many*
tot	*so many*

Practice 16e

Translate:
(a) es tam saevus ut semper servī tē timeant?
(b) poēta dominam adeō laudāvit ut illa sē plūs quam eum mīrārētur.
(c) tam acerbum est hoc vulnus ut nigrēscant omnia circum.

---

ut **with the indicative**

To sum up, **ut** followed by a verb in the subjunctive generally means *that*. It may be *so that*, *in order that*, *with the result that* or plain *that*, introducing a clause describing an intention, reported command or a consequence.

But if **ut** is followed by an indicative, or in a short phrase with no verb, it usually means *as* or *when*:

> nūllīs Graecīs comitibus, **ut solēbat**   (impf. indicative 'soleō,-ēre')
> *with no Greek companions, as he was accustomed* [8.5]

The perfect subjunctive

The perfect subjunctive is created with the perfect stem + these endings:

-erim	e.g.	amāv(ī) + erim = **amāverim** *
-erīs		habu(ī) + erim = **habuerim**
-erit		audīv(ī) + erim = **audīverim**
-erīmus		fēc(ī) + erim = **fēcerim**
-erītis		fu(ī) + erim = **fuerim**, etc
-erint		

> * 1st conjugation verbs are sometimes reduced to **amārim, amārīs, amārit**, etc.

As a main verb the perfect subjunctive appears mostly in the 2nd person as a prohibition (a negative command) after **nē**:

tū nē **quaesierīs**, scīre nefās
do not ask, to know is wrong . . . [25.6]

(quaerō, -ere, **quaesiī**, quaesītum = *seek*)

The perfect subjunctive also appears in a variety of subordinate clauses (causal, conditional, consequential, temporal and others).

The perfect subjunctive has very similar endings to the future perfect (p. 154), varying in the 1st person (**quaesierim** not **quaesierō**), and in the long 'ī' in both 2nd persons and 1st person plural (**quaesierīs, quaesierīmus, quaesierītis**).

| quaesierim |
| **quaesierīs** |
| quaesierit |
| quaesierīmus |
| quaesierītis |
| quaesierint |

The perfect passive subjunctive is like the indicative except that the participle is used with the subjunctive of *to be*: **amātus est** = indicative, **amātus sit** = subjunctive.

> ## Practice 16f
> Translate:
> (a) nē trānsierīs flūmen.
> (b) nē mortem timuerīs.
> (c) o mīlitēs, nē rēgīnam occīderītis.

The pluperfect subjunctive

The imperfect subjunctive is recognizable by the presence of the present infinitive in the stem (**amārent**). The pluperfect subjunctive has the same endings with the <u>perfect infinitive</u> in the stem (for more on the perfect infinitive see p. 287):

-m		
-s	e.g.	amāvisse + m = **amāvissem**
-t		vīdisse + m = **vīdissem**
-mus		vēnisse + m = **vēnissem**
-tis		fuisse + m = **fuissem**, etc
-nt		

The pluperfect passive is created with the past participle in tandem with the imperfect subjunctive of *to be*: **amātus essem, amātus essēs**, etc.

The subjunctive after cum

You have already seen the many functions of **cum**. It can be a preposition meaning *with* (with a noun in the ablative) or a conjunction meaning *when, since* or occasionally *although*.

Cum is usually used with a subjunctive, although there are times when the indicative is used (almost always when **cum** means *when*). For now the distinction does not matter. Translate a subjunctive with **cum** much as you would an indicative:

| vēnissem |
| vēnissēs |
| **vēnisset** |
| vēnissēmus |
| vēnissētis |
| vēnissent |

Maria, cum **vēnisset**, cecidit ad pedēs eius
Maria, when she had come, fell at his feet [26.5]

(veniō,-īre, **vēnī**, ventum = *come*)

The subjunctive after a verb expressing fear

If someone expresses in Latin a fear that something will happen or has
happened, the equivalent of English *that* or *lest* is **nē**, and the verb which
follows is subjunctive:

vereor **nē** nōbīs Īdūs Mārtiae nihil **dederint** praeter laetitiam
I fear that the Ides of March have given us nothing but a hurrah [9.8]

(dō, dare, **dedī**, datum = *give*)

dederim
dederīs
dederit
dederīmus
dederītis
dederint

The use of **nē** as *that* (and not **ut** as elsewhere) lies in the original thought. For example, 'I
fear that he may do it' is founded on the wish 'May he not do it!'. We may also translate **nē**
as *lest*, not only for fearing clauses but also negative purpose clauses. There is an underlying
similarity between the two:

pauperēs, **nē contemnantur**, suprā vīrēs sē extendunt   (Purpose clause)
the poor, lest they be despised, push themselves beyond their means [16,7]

pauperēs **nē contemnantur** timent   (Fearing clause)
the poor fear lest they be despised

Practice 16g
Translate:
(a) rēgīna verētur nē Trōiānī discēdant.
(b) Cicerō nōn timēbat nē militēs Antoniī advēnissent.
(c) metuō nē senātōrēs novitātem meam contemnant.
(d) Cicerō timet nē Clōdius sibi inimīcus sit.
(e) rēgīna metuēbat nē in triumphō dūcerētur.

Typical verbs of fearing
timeō,-ēre [2]   *fear*
metuō,-ere [3]   *fear, be apprehensive*
vereor, verērī [2; deponent]   *fear, respect*

The subjunctive in an indirect question

An indirect question is a subordinate clause governed by a verb of asking, telling or thinking:

> *he asked <u>why they were leaving</u>*
> *she told us <u>what he was doing</u>*
> *he does not know <u>who she is</u>*

In some examples the 'question' is not obvious for no answer is needed:

> *she told us <u>what he was doing</u>*

There is though an implicit question which she has answered (*What is he doing?*). The verb in an indirect question is in the subjunctive:

> discite, quae faciem **commendet** cūra, puellae   (pres. subj. 'commendō,-āre')
> *learn, girls, what (how) care <u>improves</u> the face* [16.9]

Practice 16h

Translate:
(a) Caesar rogāvit quis adesset.
(b) voluī scīre num Romulus Rōmam condidisset.
(c) prīnceps ē fīliā quaesiit quid poēta dīxisset.
(d) volō scīre quis patrēs vocāverit.
(e) īnsidiātor quaesiit unde vēnissem.

num	*surely . . . not, whether* (in an indirect question)
quid	*what*
quis	*who*
quōmodo	*how*
unde	*from where*

Summary: ut and nē

The subjunctive has a number of functions, and a good number have been spread before you in this chapter. Before you reach for the smelling salts, let us review what we have covered so far, and in particular **ut** and **nē**.

Put broadly, **ut** followed by a verb in the subjunctive is a conjunction that introduces something which someone wants to happen or is the result of something that has happened. More often than not, *that* will serve as a translation. But if **ut** appears with the indicative or in a phrase with no verb, take it as *as* or *when*.

The negative **nē** introduces a clause that describes something which someone does not want to happen. It could be a prohibition (negative command), or a fear or act of prevention.

There are four tenses of the subjunctive: present, imperfect, perfect and pluperfect. Subjunctives of regular and irregular verbs are listed in the tables on p. 359ff.

Vocabulary 16

ut [+ subjunctive]   *that, so that, in order that, with the result that*
ut [+ indicative]   *as, when*
nē [introducing a subordinate clause]   *that . . . not*
nē [after a verb of fearing]   *lest, that*
nē [+ perfect subjunctive]   *do not . . .*
cum [preposition + ablative]   *(together) with*
cum [conjunction]   *when, since, although*

Some verbs which introduce indirect commands:

cūrō,-āre,-āvī,-ātum [1]   *take care, see (that)*
imperō,-āre,-āvī,-ātum [1; + dat.]   *order*
iubeō,-ēre, iussī, iussum [2] *   *order, tell*
moneō,-ēre, monuī, monitum [2]   *advise*
ōrō,-āre,-āvī,-ātum [1]   *plead, entreat*
petō,-ere, petīvī (-iī), petītum [3]   *seek*
poscō, poscere, poposcī, — [3]   *demand, desire, beg*
postulō,-āre,-āvī,-ātum [1]   *demand*
rogō,-āre,-āvī,-ātum [1]   *ask*
* followed not by **ut** + subjunctive as the others but by an infinitive

Verbs of fearing:

metuō,-ere, metuī [3]   *fear, be apprehensive*
timeō,-ēre, timuī [2]   *fear, be afraid of*
vereor, verērī, veritus [2; deponent]   *fear, respect*

Some verbs which introduce indirect questions:

interrogō,-āre,-āvī,-ātum [1]   *ask, question, interrogate*
quaerō, quaerere, quaesīvī (quaesiī), quaesītum [3]   *ask, inquire, seek*
rogō,-āre,-āvī,-ātum [1]   *ask, question*
sciō,-īre, scīvī, scītum [4]   *know*

Exercises 16a

1.   Identify the verb in the subjunctive (and its tense), and translate:
(a)   Lesbia mihi imperat ut arbitriō suō tempora perdam.
(b)   amīcī ā mē petēbant ut dictātūram reciperem.
(c)   rēgīna cum Trōiānī urbem relīquissent vītam fīnīvit.
(d)   volō scīre num Sabīnī cum līberīs ac coniugibus vēnerint.

(e)   poēta rogāvit quis nisi amāns frīgora noctis perferret.
(f)   Camilla ē Tyrrhēnīs quaesiit num ferās in silvā agitārent.

2.   Identify whether the subordinate clause(s) in each sentence is one of purpose, result, indirect command, indirect question or after a verb of fearing; and translate:
(a)   ego metuō nē toga armīs cēdat.
(b)   Cicerō rogāvit quid rē pūblicā nōbīs esset cārius.
(c)   tē amō adeō ut Lesbiam relinquam.
(d)   Cleopātra amīcīs imperāvit ut venēnum afferrent.
(e)   rēgīna sē necāvit nē in triumphō dūcerētur.
(f)   patrōnus verētur nē impudēns salūtātor sē 'mī amīce' appellet.

3.   Use **nē** + perfect subjunctive to put into Latin:
(a)   Marcus, do not praise the slaves.
(b)   Farmer, do not chase the bulls.
(c)   Friend, do not weep.

4.   Identify the wife mentioned in each sentence:
(a)   ō Terentia, vir tuus cum Clōdiī sorōre sedet.
(b)   ō Tullia, mea soror cum marītō Semprōniae sedet.

5.   Identify the husband mentioned in each sentence:
(a)   ō Caesar, tuam sorōrem Antōnius uxōrem dūxit.
(b)   Līvia, uxor Tiberiī Claudiī Nerōnis, nunc Caesarem amat.

Women: warriors, drunks and literary critics

Reading notes
Word order

Here are more examples of words appearing where you might not expect them:

> arma virumque canō, Trōiae **quī** prīmus ab ōrīs . . .
> *I sing of arms and a man, <u>who</u> first from the lands of Troy* . . . [14.9]

> quotiēns mōnstrāvī tibi virō **ut** mōrem gerās
> *how many times have I pointed out to you <u>that</u> you should humour your husband* [16.5]

Vowel reduction

By the end of the first century AD some long vowels were treated as short. This is noticeable in Juvenal: the verb ending **-ō** (*I* . . .) was often shortened, e.g. **putŏ** [16.4] and **volŏ** [18.2]. Similarly, **ergŏ** for **ergō** in 18.2.

---

1.   The elegists' picture of devoted lovers was not of course the full story. Almost as an antidote comes Juvenal's sixth satire, a structured attack on women sustained for over six

hundred lines. The satire is addressed to a male who intends to get married. Why, Juvenal asks, when so many opportunities for suicide are available?

ferre potēs dominam salvīs tot restibus ūllam,
cum pateant altae cālīgantēsque fenestrae,
cum tibi vīcīnum sē praebeat Aemilius pōns?

Juvenal, Satires 6.30–2

ferre potēs: from 'fero' and 'possum'
salvus,-a,-um   safe, in tact
tot   so many
restis,-is [f.]   rope
ūllam: emphatic at the end of the line
cum   when
pateō,-ēre, patuī [2]   stand open, lie open
altus,-a,-um   high
cālīgāns [from 'cālīgō,-āre']   dizzy
fenestra,-ae [f.]   window
vīcīnus,-a,-um   neigbouring, in the neighbourhood
praebeō,-ēre, praebuī, praebitum [2]   offer
Aemilius pōns: a bridge in Rome

2.   There is enough in the first few lines of the poem to give it away as a tease, but there are more shocks to come. Juvenal depicts women on their way home after a drunken party, stopping by the statue of Chastity:

noctibus hīc pōnunt lectīcās, micturiunt hīc
effigiemque deae longīs sīphōnibus implent
inque vicēs equitant ac nūllō teste moventur
inde domōs abeunt: tū calcās lūce reversā
coniugis ūrīnam magnōs vīsūrus amīcōs.

Juvenal, Satires 6.309–13

noctibus: 'nocte' is the usual word for at night; the plural suggests a regular event
lectīca,-ae [f.]   litter
micturiō,-īre [4]   urinate
effigiēs,-ēī [f.]   image
deae: Pudicitia (Chastity)
longīs sīphōnibus   with jets of spray ('sīphō,-ōnis' = siphon)
impleō,-ēre,-ēvī,-ētum [2]   fill
in vicēs   in turns (they take it in turns to . . .)
equitō,-āre,-āvī,-ātum [1]   ride
testis,-is [m.]   witness (also means testicle – suggesting a pun)
moventur [present passive of 'moveō,-ēre']   they are moved, are excited, gyrate
abeunt: from 'abeō,-īre'
calcō,-āre,-āvī,-ātum [1]   tread on, in

lūce reversā   *with daylight ('lūx, lūcis') having returned*
ūrīna,-ae [f.]   *urine*
magnōs amīcōs: i.e. patrons
vīsūrus,-a,-um   *about to see, on one's way to see*

3.   Women are devious, adulterous, bully their husbands, fritter away resources, treat slaves cruelly, sleep with freshly castrated youths to avoid pregnancy, and – as bad as it gets – offer opinions on the subject of literature:

illa tamen gravior, quae cum discumbere coepit
laudat Vergilium, peritūrae īgnōscit Elissae.
cēdunt grammaticī, vincuntur rhētores, omnis
turba tacet.

Juvenal, Satires 6.434–5, 438–9

gravior [nom.]   *more serious, troublesome*
quae [f.; nom.]   *who*
cum   *when, as soon as*
discumbō,-ere [3]   *recline at table*
coepit   *s/he has begun* ('coepī' does not appear in the present, future or imperfect)
Vergilium: by Juvenal's time Virgil's place in the Roman literary tradition is similar to
     Shakespeare's in our own
peritūrus,-a,-um   *about to die*
īgnōscō,-ere [3; + dat.]   *forgive, excuse*
Elissa: another name for Dido
grammaticus,-ī [m.]   *teacher*
rhētor,-oris [m.]   *professor*
turba,-ae [f.]   *crowd*

4.   The female guest has the affrontery to put in a good word for Dido 'peritūrae'. Not even the queen's death softens the hearts of reactionary Romans, whom Juvenal is teasing almost as much as the dinner guest. Dido, after all, is a Carthaginian, set on abducting Aeneas from Italy's future, and – can it get this low? – a woman with political power.
     Roman women who tried to take an active part in politics were remembered in much less flattering ways than, say, the mythical Camilla [1.4; 15.15,16]. The campaign which Augustus (then Octavian) fought against Fulvia and Antony's brother [10.10] is remembered for some verses scratched on missiles aimed at Fulvia's soldiers. A century later Martial quotes them to justify his own ribald verse. He claims the words are Octavian's.

quod futuit Glaphyran Antōnius, hanc mihi poenam
    Fulvia cōnstituit, sē quoque utī futuam.
Fulviam ego ut futuam? quod sī mē Mānius ōret
    pēdīcem? faciam? nōn puto, sī sapiam.
'aut futue, aut pugnēmus' ait. quid quod mihi vītā
    cārior est ipsā mentula? signa canant!

Martial, Epigrams 11.20.3–8

quod   *because*

futuō, futuere, futuī, futūtum [3]   *make love to, fuck*

Glaphyran: Greek accusative; Glaphyra was the mistress of Antony, Fulvia his wife

cōnstituō,-ere, cōnstituī, cōnstitūtum [3]   *decide*

utī [for 'ut']   *that* (take 'utī' at the beginning of the clause, i.e. before 'sē': see Reading Notes above)

futuam: present subjunctive

quod sī   *what if*

Mānius: these are said to be Octavian's words, but Martial himself writes of a male lover called Manius[1] so this might be his own addition. It would have taken a brave man to reel these lines off in earshot of Augustus.

ōret [present subjunctive of 'ōrō,-āre']   *(s/he) should beg* (in an indirect command 'ut' is sometimes omitted, as here)

pēdīcem [present subjunctive of 'pēdīcō,-āre']   *that I should sodomize (him)*

sī sapiam   *if I were wise*

pugnēmus   *let us fight*

ait   *s/he says*

quid quod   *what about the fact that*

vītā ipsā: abl. of comparison (*than life itself*)

cārior [nom.]   *more dear*

mentula,-ae [f.]   *penis*

signum,-ī [n.]   *standard, signal, sign* (here: *trumpet*)

canant [present subjunctive of 'canō,-ere']   *let (them) sound*

---

5.   Wives kept control of their dowries even after marriage, which gave wealthier women
     some leverage over their husbands. In earlier times a dowry would remain with the
     woman's father, and a man who married into a generous dowry would have to keep his
     father-in-law sweet. Below, a wife appeals to her father for help in a marital quarrel. His
     unexpected response will have tickled at least the men in the audience.

F/D: Father/Daughter

F: quotiēns mōnstrāvī tibi virō ut mōrem gerās,
     quid ille faciat nē id observēs, quō eat, quid rērum gerat.
D: at enim ille hinc amat meretrīcem ex proxumō.
F: sānē sapit
     atque ob istanc industriam etiam faxō amābit amplius.
D: atque ibī pōtat.
F: tuā quidem ille causā pōtābit minus?
     quandō tē aurātam et vestītam bene habet, ancillās, penum
     rēctē praehibet, melius sānam est, mulier, mentem sūmere.

                              Plautus, *The Twin Brothers* 787–92, 801–2

quotiēns   *how many times*
mōnstrō,-āre,-āvī,-ātum [1]   *show*
mōrem gerō,-ere [+ dat.]   *accommodate the will or custom of, humour*
gerās: present subjunctive of 'gerō,-ere'
observēs: present subjunctive of 'observō,-āre' (*watch*)
quid ille faciat, quō eat, quid rērum gerat: all depend on 'nē observēs'
quō   *to where*
eat: pres. subj. of 'eō, īre'
quid rērum gerat   *what he gets up to*
at enim   *but I tell you*
hinc   *from here*, i.e. *from our house* (the stage setting would be a street with two or three
     house-fronts)
meretrīx,-īcis [f.]   *prostitute*
ex proxumō   *from next-door* ('proxumus,-a,-um' is an archaic form of 'proximus')
sānē   *clearly*
sapiō,-ere [M.]   *have sense, be wise, have good taste*
ob [+ acc.]   *because of*
istanc [f.; acc.]   *that, that . . . of yours*
industria,-ae [f.]   *diligence*
faxō   *I'll warrant* (stands alone as an extra comment to reinforce his point)
amplius   *more so*
ibī   *there*
pōtō,-āre,-āvī,-ātum [1]   *drink*

tuā causā   *on your account, for your sake*
minus   *less*
quandō   *since*
aurātus,-a,-um   *in gold, jewellery*
vestītus,-a,-um   *dressed*
ancilla,-ae [f.]   *servant*
penus,-ī [m.]   *provisions*
rēctē   *properly*
praehibeō,-ēre [2; uncontracted form of 'praebeō,-ēre']   *provide, furnish*
melius   *better*
sānus,-a,-um   *healthy, sound*
mēns, mentis [f.]   *mind*
sūmō,-ere, sūmpsī, sūmptum [3]   *take*

6.   About the same time Plautus was writing his plays Rome was at war with Hannibal. Amid a public sense of crisis and austerity, women were forbidden to wear gold, coloured clothing, or ride in carriages except during festivals. When peace and prosperity returned, women asked for the law to be relaxed. Stern old Cato warned against concessions, without success:

volō tamen audīre propter quod mātrōnae cōnsternātae prōcucurrerint in pūblicum ac vix forō sē et contiōne abstineant. extemplō, simul parēs esse coeperint, superiōrēs erunt.

Livy, *History of Rome* 34.3

propter quod   *on account of what, why*
mātrōna,-ae [f.]   *lady, matron*
cōnsternātus,-a,-um   *agitated*
prōcucurrerint: perfect subjunctive of 'prōcurrō,-ere' (*rush forth*)
vix   *scarcely*
contiō,-ōnis [f.]   *assembly*
abstineō,-ēre, abstinuī, abstentum [2]   *hold back*
extemplō   *immediately*
simul   *as soon as*
pār, paris   *equal*
coeperint: future perfect; translate into the present tense in English (*they begin*)
superiōrēs [nom.pl./acc.pl.]   *betters*

7.   Equality for women was desirable argued Cato, but with each other, not with men.

vultis hoc certāmen uxōribus vestrīs īnicere, Quirītēs, ut dīvitēs id habēre velint quod nūlla alia possit, et pauperēs, nē ob hoc ipsum contemnantur, suprā vīrēs sē extendant?

Livy, *History of Rome* 34.4

vultis: 2nd person plural, present indicative of 'volō, velle'

certāmen,-inis [n.]   *competition*

īniciō,-ere, īniēcī, īniēctum [M.]   *throw on, impose*

Quirītēs[1]   *Romans*

dīvitēs [nom.pl./acc.pl.]   *rich, the rich* (here feminine)

velint: present subj. of 'volō, velle' after 'ut' expressing consequence (*with the result that they want . . .*)

quod [nom./acc.]   *which*

alia [nom.f. sing.]   *other*

possit: subjunctive tells us this is the thinking of the character(s), i.e. the women, rather than the writer (see p. 289)

pauperēs [nom.pl./acc.pl.]   *poor*

ob hoc ipsum   *because of this very thing*

contemnantur: present subjunctive passive, expressing purpose after 'nē' ('contemnō,-ere' [3] = *despise*)

suprā vīrēs   *beyond their strength*

extendant: present subj. of 'extendō,-ere' (*overreach*); subjunctive after 'ut', like 'velint' above

8.   Lucius Valerius took a different view:

mātrem familiae tuam purpureum amiculum habēre nōn sinēs, et equus tuus speciōsius īnstrātus erit quam uxor vestīta.

Livy, History of Rome 34.7

amiculum,-ī [n.]   *cloak*

sinō,-ere, sīvī, situm [3]   *allow*

speciōsius   *more showily, handsomely*

īnstrātus,-a,-um   *covered*

quam   *than*

9.   By the first century BC women such as Clodia and Fulvia seem to enjoy more independence. But in general their role remained behind closed doors, and it was not theirs to imitate the lives of the men. One or two men, on the other hand, by Ovid's time, had picked up a few habits of their women:

discite, quae faciem commendet cūra, puellae:
    et quō sit vōbīs fōrma tuenda modō.
nec tamen indīgnum: sit vōbīs cūra placendī,
    cum comptōs habeant saecula nostra virōs.

Ovid, Face Make-up 1–2, 23–4

---

1 This ancient title probably derives from the ancient Sabine town, Cures, after the Romans and Sabines merged as one people [p. 9].

discite: imperative of 'discō,-ere' (*learn*)

quae [agrees with 'cūra']   *what* (translate here as *how*)

faciēs,-ēī [f.]   *face*

commendō,-āre,-āvī,-ātum [1]   *enhance*

cūra,-ae [f.]   *care, attention*

quō . . . modō   *in what way, how*

sit: the present subjunctive is used in line 2 in an indirect question; and in line 3, exhortative (*let there be a* 'cūra placendī' *to you, i.e. you should have . . .*)

vōbīs [line 2]: dative of agent (*by you*)

fōrma,-ae [f.]   *beauty*

tuendus,-a,-um   *to be preserved, protected*

indīgnus,-a,-um   *unworthy, demeaning*

placendī   *of pleasing, to please*

cum   *since*

cōmptus,-a,-um   *adorned* ('cōmō,-ere, cōmpsī, cōmptum' = *adorn, embellish*)

Exercises 16b

1. State whether these verbs are subjunctive because they are part of an indirect question, purpose clause, indirect command, result clause, fearing clause, or after 'cum':
(a) pateant [16.1]
(b) futuam [16.4, line 2]
(c) gerās [16.5]
(d) eat [16.5]
(e) prōcucurrerint [16.6]
(f) contemnantur [16.7]
(g) commendet [16.9]
(h) habeant [16.9]
(i) cōnstet [14.6]
(j) dēscrīberētur [12.13]

2. Translate:
(a) ō magister, tibi pecūniam dare volō ut taceās.
(b) es tam inimīca ut gemitūs meōs rīdeās?
(c) dux Trōiānōrum rēgīnam ōrāvit nē cīvēs querēlīs incenderet.
(d) in silvās vēnistī, Tyrrhēne, ut ferās agitēs?
(e) Cassius aliōs coniūrātōs rogāvit ut corpus Caesaris in Tiberim traherent.
(f) quotiēns tibi mōnstrāvī quid ego faciam nē id observēs, quō eam, quid rērum geram.

3. Identify verbs in the subjunctive (and tense), and translate:
(a) Cloelia Tiberim trānāvit ut sospitēs omnēs ad propinquōs restitueret.
(b) Caesar pontem fabricāvit ut Germānōs aggrederētur.
(c) utinam sim tuus amīcus!
(d) Lāocoōn cum ab arce advēnisset nōs monuit nē equum reciperēmus.

4. Find Latin ancestors in this chapter of *abstention, ancillary, disturb, parity* and *vicinity*.

Family ties

Interrogative: *who, what* or *which* asking a question

The interrogative pronoun and adjective **quis** has appeared a few times already:

quis fallere possit amantem?
who can deceive a lover? [3.9]

quā tū **audāciā** patrēs vocās?
<u>*with what presumption*</u> *do you summon*
the senators? [2.1]

	Interrogative pronoun/adjective		
	masculine	*feminine*	*neuter*
N.	**quis**/quī	quis/quae	quid/quod
A.	quem	quam	quid/quod
G.	cuius	cuius	cuius
D.	cui	cui	cui
Ab.	quō	**quā**	quō

This interrogative word can appear by itself (i.e. a <u>pronoun</u>), as in the first example above (**quis**), or as an <u>adjective</u> in agreement with a noun, as in the second example (**quā audāciā**). This is true of many pronouns: they can be pronouns by themselves, or adjectives, in agreement with a noun:

quae mē ad **maiōra** reservō?
for <u>*what greater things*</u> *do I keep myself?*
[15.5]

plural			
N.	quī	quae	quae
A.	quōs	quās	**quae**
G.	quōrum	quārum	quōrum
D.	quibus	quibus	quibus
Ab.	quibus	quibus	quibus

This interrogative can be used for asking questions which are not really questions at all but expressions of wonder, surprise or dismay:

ō miserī, **quae** tanta īnsānia, cīvēs?
wretched citizens, who such madness (is this)? i.e. why such madness? [4.13]

N.	quis/quī	quis/**quae**	quid/quod
A.	quem	quam	**quid**/quod
G.	cuius	cuius	cuius
D.	cui	cui	cui
Ab.	quō	quā	quō

Quid? means *what?*; but it can also mean *why?* when it appears early in the sentence. This is the accusative of respect: *in respect of what?*, hence *why?*

quid dissimulō?
why do I make a pretence? [15.5]

Practice 17a

Give the case and number of the underlined word, and translate:

(a) **cuius** taurus est?
(b) **quibus** pecūniam dedistī?
(c) **quid** tuīs līberīs trādēs?

Relative: *who, which* giving information

The relative does not ask a question but introduces a subordinate clause relating to someone or something already mentioned (or about to be mentioned), called the antecedent:

Octavian decided to marry Livia, who at the time was married to someone else

The antecedent to *who* is *Livia*.

In Latin, we identify the antecedent by its gender and number. Below, **quam** is feminine singular, pointing us to the antecedent **Discordia**.

The case, however, is dictated by what 'who' or 'which' is doing in its own subordinate clause – subject, object, etc. Here, it is accusative, object of **sequitur**:

N.	quī	quae	quod
A.	quem	**quam**	quod
G.	cuius	cuius	cuius
D.	cui	cui	cui
Ab.	quō	quā	quō

et vādit Discordia, **quam** sequitur Bellōna
and there goes Discord, whom Bellona follows [13.5]

Below, **quōs** and **quī** are masculine plural: **quōs** has its antecedent **iūdicēs**, and **quī** has **aliōs**. But **quōs** is accusative because it is the object of **voluimus**, whereas **quī** is nominative as the subject of **occīsī erant**:

iūdicēs habēmus **quōs** voluimus
we have the judges whom we wanted [6.4]

inter aliōs, **quī** in eādem sēditiōne occīsī erant, īnsepultus in flūmen prōiectus est
among the others, who had been killed in the same rebellion, he was thrown unburied into the river [5.1]

plural			
N.	**quī**	quae	quae
A.	**quōs**	quās	quae
G.	quōrum	quārum	quōrum
D.	quibus	quibus	quibus
Ab.	quibus	quibus	quibus

To repeat the rule: a relative pronoun takes its case from its role within its own subordinate clause, and the gender and number from the thing(s) it refers to, the antecedent.

Practice 17b
Choose the correct form of the pronoun, and translate:
(a)   ego sum rēgīna . . . . {*whom*} Caesar amāvit.
(b)   Germānōs, ... {*who*} trāns Rhēnum incolunt, Caesar aggressus est.
(c)   Caesar Cleopātram dīlēxit, ... {*to whom*} rēgnum Aegyptī permīsit.

Correlative pronouns
The relative pronoun is often paired with another pronoun, typically **is, ea, id**, and so balances two parts of a sentence:

dīvitēs **id** habēre volunt **quod** nūlla alia possit
the rich want to have that which no other can (have) [16.7]

N.	quī	quae	quod
A.	quem	quam	**quod**
G.	cuius	cuius	cuius
D.	cui	cui	cui
Ab.	quō	quā	quō

The pronoun **is, ea, id** is the antecedent. It sometimes appears *after* the relative pronoun:

quī parentem meum trucīdāvērunt, **eōs**
in exilium expulī
*who murdered my father those I drove into exile (I
drove into exile those who murdered . . .)* [12.4]

plural			
N.	**quī**	quae	quae
A.	quōs	quās	quae
G.	quōrum	quārum	quōrum
D.	quibus	quibus	quibus
Ab.	quibus	quibus	quibus

Missing antecedent
Sometimes the antecedent is missing and taken as understood:

reddite ergō **quae** Caesaris sunt Caesarī
therefore return (those things) which are Caesar's to Caesar [26.2]

Here we understand a pronoun in the neuter plural like **ea** or **illa** (*those things*) as an antecedent
to **quae**. Below, no antecedent appears for **quī** or for **cui**. We understand a pronoun such as
ille and then **illa**:

dīxerat, et lacrimīs vultum lavēre profūsīs,
tam **quī** mandābat, quam **cui** mandāta dabantur
*he had spoken, and they bathed their face(s) with streaming tears, as much (he) who was giving the
instructions as (she) to whom the instructions were being given* [17.5]

In the line 'tam quī . . .', **quam** is not the relative pronoun in the accusative feminine singular
but a conjunction meaning *as* or *than*.

Practice 17c
Translate:
(a) quāe in silvā errat inimīca est.
(b) quī ā dominīs fūgerant ad supplicium sūmendum trāditī sunt.
(c) quae mē querēlīs incendit īnsāna est.
(d) Clōdia quam Catullus plūs quam sē amāvit nunc Caelium amat.

Relatives as adjectives
The relative can be used as an adjective, in harness with a noun. Here **quō** is ablative
agreeing with **meritō**, after the preposition **prō** which takes the ablative:

rem pūblicam ex meā potestāte in senātūs populīque Rōmānī arbitrium trānstulī. **quō** prō **meritō** meō senātūs cōnsultō Augustus appellātus sum.

I transferred the Republic from my power to the authority of the senate and the people of Rome. In return for <u>which/this service</u> of mine I was named Augustus by decree of the senate [12.1]

N.	quī	quae	quod
A.	quem	quam	quod
G.	cuius	cuius	cuius
D.	cui	cui	cui
Ab.	quō	quā	**quō**

Note that **quō meritō** above introduces a complete sentence, not unusual in Latin, but something the English relative does not do: thus **quō** is translated as *this*, not *which*.

Indefinite: *any, anyone, anything*

So far we have seen that **quis/quī** can be used to ask questions (interrogative) or to introduce a relative clause. A third use is the indefinite pronoun or adjective:

ōrō, sī **quis** adhūc precibus locus – exue mentem
I beg (you), if there is still <u>any</u> place for entreaties, change your mind [3.10]

N.	**quis**/quī	quae/qua	quid/quod
A.	quem	quam	quid/quod
G.	cuius	cuius	cuius
D.	cui	cui	cui
Ab.	quō	quā	quō

As with the interrogative and the relative, the indefinite can be an adjective or pronoun, i.e. it can appear in agreement with a noun or by itself. Above, **quis** agrees with **locus**.

This indefinite is never the first word in a sentence, and is often preceded by **sī** (*if*), **nisi** (*unless*), **nē** (*lest*) or **num** (*whether*).

cohortēs, sī **quae** locō cessissent, decimātās hordeō pāvit
he decimated the troops if <u>any</u> had given way from their position, and fed them with barley [12.12]

plural			
N.	quī	**quae**	quae/qua
A.	quōs	quās	quae/qua
G.	quōrum	quārum	quōrum
D.	quibus	quibus	quibus
Ab.	quibus	quibus	quibus

> ### Practice 17d
> Translate:
> (a) sī quis adest, nunc abeat!
> (b) tē ōrō, sī quis adhūc lacrimīs locus,
>   nē mē relinquās.

Summary: quis/quī

With minor variations (e.g. masculine: **quis/quī**, feminine: **quis/quae/qua**, neuter: **quid/quod**) the pronoun can be:

* interrogative *who?*, *which?* asking questions
* relative *who . . .*, *which . . .*, explanatory
* indefinite, meaning *any*
* an adjective instead of a pronoun for any of the above (i.e. with a noun)

If interrogative or indefinite, **quī** and **quod** tend to appear as adjectives and **quis** and **quid** as pronouns; but this is not altogether consistent so treat as much the same.

Quis? can be masculine or feminine (if you don't know *who* it is, you may not know the gender). The feminine **quae?** is used where the gender is clear, typically as an adjective with a feminine noun (**quae uxor?** *which wife?*).

The relative pronoun or pronominal adjective is always **quī** or **quae** or **quod** in the nominative, never **quis** or **quid**.

The indefinite in the nominative feminine singular or neuter plural can be **quae** or **qua**.

More adjectives: alius, tōtus, nūllus, ūllus **and** sōlus

The adjectives **tōtus,-a,-um** (*whole*), **nūllus,-a,-um** (*none, no*), **ūllus,-a,-um** (*any*) and **sōlus,-a-um** (*only, alone*) are very like **bonus,-a,-um**, but not identical. In the singular they have a different genitive (**-īus**) and dative (**-ī**), like **ūnus** on p. 128.

Alius (*other, another*) is the same but for the neuter form **aliud** (like **ille, illa, illud**).

All plural forms are the same as **bonī, bonae, bona**.

Ascanius urbem novam ipse **aliam** condidit
Ascanius himself founded another new city [1.7]

N.	alius	alia	aliud
A.	alium	**aliam**	aliud
G.	alīus	alīus	alīus
D.	alī	alī	alī
Ab.	aliō	aliā	aliō

Augustus per quattuor et quadrāgintā annōs
sōlus rem pūblicam tenuit
*Augustus alone/by himself had control over the
Republic for forty-four years (A. had sole control of
. . .)* [12.19]

N.	**sōlus**	sōla	sōlum
A.	sōlum	sōlam	sōlum
G.	sōlīus	sōlīus	sōlīus
D.	sōlī	sōlī	sōlī
Ab.	sōlō	sōlā	sōlō

haec fuit in **tōtō** notissima fābula caelō
this story was best known in all heaven [24.5]

N.	tōtus	tōta	tōtum
A.	tōtum	tōtam	tōtum
G.	tōtīus	tōtīus	tōtīus
D.	tōtī	tōtī	tōtī
Ab.	tōtō	tōtā	**tōtō**

Clōdius est expedītus, in equō, **nūllā** raedā
*Clodius was unencumbered, on horseback, with no
carriage* [8.5]

N.	nūllus	**nūlla**	nūllum
A.	nūllum	nūllam	nūllum
G.	nūllīus	nūllīus	nūllīus
D.	nūllī	nūllī	nūllī
Ab.	nūllō	**nūllā**	nūllō

dīvitēs id habēre volunt quod **nūlla** alia possit
the rich want to have what no other can (have) [16.7]

nōn argentī scrīpulum est **ūllum** in illā īnsulā
there is not any scrap of silver in that island [23.2]

N.	ūllus	ūlla	**ūllum**
A.	ūllum	ūllam	ūllum
G.	ūllīus	ūllīus	ūllīus
D.	ūllī	ūllī	ūllī
Ab.	ūllō	ūllā	ūllō

The difference between the indefinite pronoun/adjective **quis** and the adjective **ūllus** is that
the first is indefinite (*anyone here?*), whereas **ūllus** is emphatic and often used to emphasize a
negative (*there is not any food left*).

Vocabulary 17

quis/quī (m.), **quis/quae** (f.), **quid/quod** (n.)   *who?, which?, what?* (interrogative)
  who, which (relative)
  any (indefinite)
quam   *as, than,* or acc.fem.sing. of **quis/quī** above (*whom, which*)
alius, alia, aliud   *other, another*
nūllus, nūlla, nūllum   *none, no*
sōlus, sōla, sōlum   *only, sole*
tōtus, tōta, tōtum   *whole, entire*
ūllus, ūlla, ūllum   *any*

Exercises 17a

1.   Translate:
(a)   quis aderat? ā quō es tū vīsa?
(b)   cui favēbō?
(c)   ostendite mihi dēnārium: cuius habet imāginem et īnscrīptiōnem?
(d)   quae poētam laudat est mea uxor.
(e)   ego quī numquam ūllās imāginēs habuī nunc cōnsul sum.

2.   Give the case, number and gender of the underlined word, and translate:
(a)   **quā** tū audāciā patrēs vocās?
(b)   Dīdō **quae** in silvā errābat inimīca refūgit.
(c)   **quid** agās?
(d)   **quae** mē ad maiōra reservō?
(e)   ōrō, sī **quis** adhūc precibus locus, exue mentem.
(f)   **quī** novitātem meam contemnunt superbī sunt.

3.   Identify the antecedent of each underlined relative pronoun, and translate:
(a)   iūdicēs habēmus **quōs** voluimus.
(b)   **quī** parentem meum trucīdāvērunt, eōs in exilium expulī.
(c)   illa est Lesbia **quam** Catullus plūs quam sē amāvit.
(d)   Fortūna gemitūs rīdet **quōs** ipsa fēcit.

4.   If this line were addressed to a female, which word should be changed and how?
'quid faciēs hostī, quī sīc exclūdis amantem?'

5.   Translate:

haec est mulier, mea domina sōla, quam dūcere meam uxōrem cupiō!
    — sed nōnne illa etiam domina est Caeliī?

mēne rīdēs?
    — imperatne domina tua, quae nunc Caelium amat, ut tū sibi dōna afferās?

sīc. quid agam?
    — eam dīmitte!

Family ties

The *paterfamilias* (father of the family) was the formal head of the household, while the *matrona* pulled most of the strings in the home. She looked after domestic arrangements and in many cases the children's education. There was an ancient law which gave a father the right to execute a child but as far as we know it was seldom exercised; more likely (though still rare) he might sell them into slavery, perhaps to avoid starvation. A mother had less legal authority over her young, and a widow was dependent on her children for support.

The Roman gods (Jupiter, Juno, Venus, Mars, etc) reflect a view of family life and structure instantly recognisable to the ancients. Jupiter was the paterfamilias, Mercury, Venus and others the dutiful-ish children; Juno was the powerful wife but careful not to cross the line with her husband. The gods were the 'first family' of the ancient world, Jupiter the *capo* of all *capos*. However, the sense of 'family' in Sicily or New York was not a particularly Roman thing. The Romans had no single and striking word for 'family' to focus the sense of loyalty. There was *gens*, which means clan or family in the broader sense, identified by the middle name of a well-to-do male; there was *familia*, which was the whole household including dependants and slaves; and *domus*, similar to *familia*, the home.

Reading notes

A few names of people or places have unusual endings. Some nouns from Greek retained their Greek forms:

Glaphyr<u>an</u> (accusative of 'Glaphyra') [16.4]
Hyl<u>an</u> (accusative of 'Hylas') [20.8]

Some older Latin nouns kept their archaic forms:

Tiber<u>im</u> (accusative of 'Tiber') [2.8 and 22.8]
secūr<u>im</u> (accusative of 'secūris') [25.11]

The civil wars saw family members fight on either side – and in defeat family members plead for mercy for their kinsmen. The triumvir Lepidus was married to the sister of Brutus but they fought each other at Philippi. In the previous century the murder of Tiberius Gracchus had been orchestrated by his cousin, a Scipio. Brothers, cousins and relatives-in-law frequently ended up fighting each other, or opposing each other's policies. The political use of marriage, often short-lived, did nothing to ease dissension and rivalry within a family. Again and again we see people marrying into the families of those they have had conflict with, in an attempt to pull them closer together. Then comes a divorce and remarriage, in many cases after the union has produced a litter of half-siblings. A sustained sense of larger family loyalty became lost in such a confused nexus of interrelationships. The many adoptions did nothing to strengthen the bond. 'Loyalty' is spoken of as *pietas* (a sense of duty) to the gods, to Rome, to one's comrades and to one's parents – not to family as such. There was always a higher calling than your family, and that was the state itself.

1.   Those who put the state above family interests were roundly praised. Brutus, the founder of the Republic, executed his sons [2.9]. He is one of the Romans-to-come revealed to Aeneas in the underworld by the spirit of his father:

vīs et Tarquiniōs rēgēs, animamque superbam
ultōris Brūtī, fascēsque vidēre receptōs?
cōnsulis imperium hic prīmus saevāsque secūrēs

accipiet, nātōsque pater nova bella moventēs
ad poenam pulchrā prō lībertāte vocābit.

Virgil, Aeneid 6.817–21

vīs: 2nd person sing. of 'volō' (Anchises is addressing Aeneas)
anima,-ae [f.]   *spirit*
ultor,-ōris [m.]   *avenger*
fascēs, fascium[1] [m.pl.]   *fasces* (a bundle of rods with an axe)
receptōs [recipiō,-ere, recēpī, receptum]   *(which he) accepted*
saevās: Virgil has in mind the parent putting his children to death
secūris,-is [f.]   *axe* (these axes are symbols of authority)
nova bella: i.e. rebellion
moventēs [the persons doing this are in the nominative or accusative plural]   *moving, stirring*
pulcher,-chra,-chrum [like 'noster']   *beautiful, noble, glorious*

2.   The conflict of loyalty in the case of Coriolanus (fifth century BC) was also between family and state, but here the state was not Rome. Coriolanus had sided with the enemy, and members of his own family were Rome's final defence:

Vetūria, māter Coriolānī, et Volumnia, duōs parvōs ferēns
fīliōs, in castra hostium ībant. ubī ad castra ventum est,
nuntiātumque Coriolānō est adesse ingēns mulierum
agmen, prīmum multō obstinātior adversus lacrimās
muliebrēs erat. dein familiārium quīdam inter cēterās
cognōverat Vetūriam: 'nisi mē frūstrantur,' inquit, 'oculī,
māter tibi coniūnxque et līberī adsunt.'

Livy, History of Rome 2.40

parvus,-a,-um   *small*
ferēns [the person doing this is in the nominative singular]   *carrying*
castra, castrōrum [n.]   *(military) camp* ('castra' usually appears in the plural)
hostēs, hostium [m.]   *enemy* (used in the plural for a collective enemy, i.e. an army)
ībant: imperfect of 'eō, īre'
ubī   *where, when*
ventum est   lit. *it was come*, i.e. *they came*
nuntiō,-āre,-āvī,-ātum [1]   *announce*
agmen,-inis [n.]   *crowd, throng*
prīmum   *at first*
multō obstinātior [nom.]   *much more resistant*
dein   *then*
quīdam   *one, a certain member*
cognōscō,-ere, cognōvī, cognitum [3]   *recognize*
frūstror, frūstrārī, frūstrātus [1; deponent]   *deceive*

---

1 The *fasces* was a symbol of authority: a bundle of rods tied together around an axe. Attendants would carry one each ahead of a magistrate as he went about his business.

3.   Cicero's beloved daughter, Tullia, had already separated from her third husband by the time of her death in her 30s. Cicero was devastated by her loss, which provoked a friend to write to him: family bereavement was one thing, but Caesar's dictatorship was surely more troubling?

> quid tē commovet tuus dolor intestīnus? ea nōbīs ērepta sunt, quae hominibus nōn minus quam līberī cāra esse dēbent, patria, honestās, dīgnitās, honōrēs omnēs. at vērō malum est līberōs āmittere. malum; nisi peius est haec sufferre et perpetī.

> Cicero, *Letters to Friends and Family* 4.5

quid   (here) *why*
commoveō,-ēre, commōvī, commōtum [2]   *excite, disturb*
dolor,-ōris [m.]   *pain, grief*
intestīnus,-a,-um   *private*
ea: neuter pl. of 'is, ea, id'
ēripiō,-ere, ēripuī, ēreptum [M.]   *take from, snatch*
quam: either the acc. fem. of 'quis/quī', or conjunction meaning *than*
cārus,-a,-um   *dear*
honestās, honestātis [f.]   *reputation*
dīgnitās, dīgnitātis [f.]   *prestige, rank*
honor,-ōris [m.]   *public honour*
āmittō,-ere, āmīsī, āmissum [3]   *lose*
peius   *worse*
sufferō, sufferre, sustulī, sublātum   *suffer*
perpetior, perpetī, perpessus [deponent]   *endure*

4.   The sadness of loss touched everyone. Pliny reports the death of two girls, sisters, both in childbirth:

> afficior dolōre nec tamen suprā modum doleō; ita mihi lūctuōsum vidētur, quod puellās honestissimās in flōre prīmō fēcunditās abstulit.

> Pliny, *Letters* 4.21

afficior: passive of 'afficiō'
suprā modum   *beyond measure*
lūctuōsus,-a,-um   *sorrowful*
quod   *because, namely that*
honestissimus,-a,-um   *most honourable*
flōs, flōris [m.]   *flower*
fēcunditās,-tātis [f.]   *fruitfulness*

5.   Some children were discarded in infancy, which happened enough for Augustus and others to discourage it. Many ancient plays draw on stories of abandoned babies who are rescued and then identified. There was nothing other-worldly about this for

audiences of the time. The discarding was a part of their lives. Some parents were too poor to bring up a child; for others children were a burden they could do without. If rudimentary methods of contraception failed (always female), the next step was to induce a miscarriage, sometimes with serious consequences. If that didn't work, final rejection was to discard the infant to an almost certain death. Girls were at greater risk than boys, who had more earning power and would not cost a dowry. Ovid touches this theme in his story of the birth of Iphis, who was born a girl but becomes a boy. Her/his father tells his pregnant wife they must kill the child if it is a girl, so upsetting them both:

dīxerat, et lacrimīs vultum lāvēre profūsīs,
tam quī mandābat, quam cui mandāta dabantur.

Ovid, Metamorphoses 9.680–81

vultum: translate as a plural
lavō,-āre, lāvī, lautum [1]   *wash, bathe* ('lāvēre': poetic form of 'lāvērunt')
profundō,-ere, profūdī, profūsum [3]   *pour forth*
lacrimīs profūsīs   lit. *with tears poured forth*, i.e. *with streaming tears*
tam ... quam   *as much ... as*
quī ... cui: understand subject pronouns in both parts of the line (*as much* <u>he</u> *who ... as*
   <u>she</u> *to whom*)
mandō,-āre,-āvī,-ātum [1]   *instruct, order*

6.   Adoption was a convenient alternative to natural children. Augustus was adopted by his great-uncle, Julius Caesar, and he later adopted Tiberius to secure the succession. After Tiberius came Caligula, then Claudius, who adopted his stepson Nero:

Nerō ūndecimō aetātis annō ā Claudiō adoptātus est.

Suetonius, Nero 7.1

ūndecimus,-a,-um   *eleventh*
aetās,-tātis [f.]   *age, life*

7.   Within the imperial family, love and loyalty gave way to fear, rivalry and suspicion. Nero, once he became emperor, had Claudius' real son, the young Britannicus, poisoned at dinner:

ita venēnum cūnctōs eius artūs pervāsit, ut vōx pariter et
spīritus raperentur. post breve silentium repetīta convīviī
laetitia. facinorī plērīque hominum īgnōscēbant, antīquās
frātrum discordiās et īnsociābile rēgnum aestimantēs.

Tacitus, Annals 13.16;17

ita ... ut   *in such a way ... that*
artus,-ūs [m.]   *limb*
pervādō,-ere, pervāsī, pervāsum [3]   *spread through, reach*
pariter   *at the same time*
spīritus,-ūs [m.]   *breath*
raperentur: subjunctive after 'ut' expressing consequence ('rapiō,-ere' = *seize, take*)
brevis,-e   *short*

silentium,-ī [n.]   *silence*
repetō,-ere, repetīvī, repetītum [3]   *renew*
convīvium,-ī [n.]   *banquet, dinner-party*
plērīque [nom.]   *the majority, a very great part*
īgnōscō,-ere, īgnōvī, īgnōtum [3; + dat.]   *forgive*
antīquus,-a,-um   *ancient, longstanding*
īnsociābilis,-e   *unshareable*
aestimantēs [the persons doing this are the subject of 'īgnōscēbant']   *putting it down to*

8. Divorce and remarriage were commonplace, even in myth. In Virgil's story of Aeneas
    he is linked to not one but three romances. Before Dido in Carthage or Lavinia in Italy,
    his first wife Creusa is left to die in the burning streets of Troy, having fallen behind the
    escaping Trojans. When Aeneas discovers she is missing he rushes back into the city
    where she appears as a ghost:

'quid tantum īnsānō iuvat indulgēre dolōrī,
ō dulcis coniūnx? nōn haec sine nūmine dīvom
ēveniunt; nec tē hinc comitem asportāre Creūsam
fās, aut ille sinit superī rēgnātor Olympī.'

Virgil, Aeneid 2.776–9

tantum   *so much* (take as an adverb with 'indulgēre')
iuvō,-āre, iūvī, iūtum [1]   *help, please*
indulgeō,-ēre, indulsī, indultum [2; + dat.]   *gratify, yield*
nūmen,-inis [n.]   *divine will*
dīvom: for 'dīvōrum'
ēveniō,-īre, ēvēnī, ēventum [4]   *happen*
hinc   *from here*
asportō,-āre,-āvī,-ātum [1]   *carry away, bring away*
comes, comitis [m./f.]   *comrade, companion*
aut: the negative of 'nec' is retained in the second part of the sentence (<u>nor</u> *does Jupiter allow it*)
sinō,-ere [3]   *allow*
superus,-a,-um   *above, on high*
rēgnātor,-ōris [m.]   *ruler*

9. In the same poem is Virgil's image of the virtuous mother. This homely ethic shines in
    contrast to some other impressions of the time, and no doubt appealed to Augustus in
    his effort to strengthen family values.

(māter) . . . cinerem et sōpītōs suscitat ignīs,
noctem addēns operī, famulāsque ad lūmina longō
exercet pēnsō, castum ut servāre cubīle
coniugis et possit parvōs ēdūcere nātōs.

Virgil, Aeneid 8.410–13

cinis, cineris [m.]   *ashes*
sōpītus,-a,-um   *sleeping*
suscitō,-āre,-āvī,-ātum [1]   *arouse*

ignīs: alt. accusative plural ending for 'ignēs'
addēns [the person doing this is in the nominative]   *adding*
operī: dat. of 'opus, operis'
famula,-ae [f.]   *maidservant*
lūmen,-inis [n.]   *light, lamplight*
longus,-a,-um   *long, time-consuming*
exerceō,-ēre, exercuī, exercitum [2]   *put to work*
pēnsum,-ī [n.]   *weight (of wool*: the daily portion for each slavegirl to spin)
castus,-a,-um   *pure, chaste*
ut: introduces a purpose clause (and take it before 'castum')
cubīle, cubīlis [n.]   *bed*
ēdūcō,-ere, ēdūxī, ēductum [3]   *bring up*

10. Mothers would supervise their children's education. Tacitus records that the mother of
     his own father-in-law, Agricola, discouraged her son from reading philosophy:

Agricola prīmā in iuventā studium philosophiae ācrius, ultrā
quam concessum Rōmānō ac senātōrī, hausisset, nī prūdentia
mātris incēnsum ac flagrantem animum coercuisset.

Tacitus, *Life of Agricola* 4

iuventa,-ae [f.]   *youth*
studium,-ī [n.]   *pursuit, study*
philosophia,-ae [f.]   *philosophy*
ācrius   *rather keenly, too keenly*
ultrā quam   *more than, beyond*
concēdō,-ere, concessī, concessum [3]   *concede*
hauriō,-īre, hausī, haustum [4] *drain, drink up*
nī   *if not*
prūdentia,-ae [f.]   *good sense*
incēnsus,-a,-um   *inflamed* (from 'incendō,-ere')
flagrantem [accusative singular]   *burning*
animus,-ī [m]   *mind, intellect*
coerceō,-ēre,-uī, coercitum [2]   *restrain*
hausisset . . . nī . . . coercuisset   *would have drunk . . . had not . . . restrained . . .*

11. Too much study of ethical questions was considered impractical for future rulers. Nero's
     mother, Agrippina, imposed similar restraint:

ā philosophiā eum māter āvertit monēns imperātūrō
contrāriam esse.

Suetonius, *Life of Nero* 52

āvertō,-ere, āvertī, āversum [3]   *turn away, deflect*
monēns [the person doing this is in the nominative singular]   *warning, advising*
imperātūrus,-a,-um   *(one) about to rule*
contrārius,-a,-um   *opposite, counter-productive*

monēns . . . contrāriam esse   *warning it* (philosophy) *to be counter-productive . . . (warning that it was . . .)*

Exercises 17b

1. Choose the correct form of the pronoun, and translate:
(a) Caesar, ... {*who*} Pompēiam dīmīserat, Calpurniam uxōrem dūxit.
(b) haec mea mulier, haec mea domina, ... {*whom*} vestītam bene habeō.
(c) Iugurtha .... {*whom*} Marius in triumphō dūxerat in carcere necātus est.
(d) Volumnia, ... {*who*} duōs parvōs fīliōs ferēbat, in castra hostium vēnit ut coniugem vidēret.

2. Identify the antecedent of each underlined relative pronoun, and translate:
(a) modo **quae** fuerat sēmita, facta via est.
(b) Caesar Pompēiō Mārcum Crassum reconciliāvit veterem inimīcum ex cōnsulātū, **quem** summā discordiā simul gesserant.

3. Give the case, number and gender of the underlined word, and translate:
(a) **quā** vīcit, victōs prōtegit ille manū.
(b) nē quaesierīs **quid** tuus vir faciat.
(c) discite, **quae** faciem commendet cūra, puellae.
(d) cohortēs, sī **quae** locō cessissent, decimātās hordeō pāvit.

4. Translate:
quod ego aliam amāvī, hanc mihi poenam uxor (quae alium ipsa amat!) cōnstituit ut arbitriō mātris suae tempora perdam.

5. Find Latin ancestors in this chapter of *Cinderella, exhaustion, illuminating* and *pension.*

— 18 —

Slavery

quod

You have met **quod,** the neuter singular of **quī**, meaning *what?*, *which* or *any(thing)*. You have also seen it as a conjunction meaning *that, in that* or *because*:

> quippe indīgnātur veterī pārēre clientī
> **quod**-que aliquid poscās et **quod** sē stante recumbās
> *to be sure he thinks it demeaning to obey an old client and (is resentful) <u>because</u> you ask for something and <u>because</u> you recline while he stands* [14.2]

> eādem operā accūsent Catullum, **quod** Lesbiam prō Clodiā nōminārit
> *by the same token they may as well accuse Catullus, <u>because</u> he used the name Lesbia in place of Clodia* [15.11]

This conjunction is at root the neuter of the pronoun **quī** in the accusative, known as the accusative of respect (*in respect of which*):

> **illud** adhūc gravius, **quod** tē post mīlle labōrēs,
>   Paule, negat lassō iānitor esse domī
> *<u>that</u> is still more serious, <u>in respect of which (because/in that)</u> after a thousand toils, Paulus, your doorkeeper says to the exhausted (me) that you are not at home* [14.4]
> i.e. *what is still more serious is that after . . .*

The 'because' **quod** is very similar in meaning to **quia**.

Practice 18a
Translate:
(a)   quod Lesbia Caelium amat Catullus est trīstis.
(b)   illud gravius, quod flūmen Caesar cum exercitū trānsiit.
(c)   volō audīre propter quod mātrōnae cōnsternātae prōcucurrerint in pūblicum.

quam

Here are different meanings for **quam** which you have already seen:

as the accusative feminine singular of **quis/quī** (i.e. *whom*):

Cleopātrae, **quam** servātam triumphō magnopere cupiēbat, etiam psyllōs admōvit
he even brought in serpent charmers to Cleopatra, <u>whom</u> he greatly wanted preserved for a triumphal procession [11.10]

as the conjunction in a comparison, i.e. *than*:

prīmō magis ambitiō **quam** avāritia animōs hominum exercēbat
at first ambition rather <u>than</u> greed exercised the minds of men [6.1]

meaning *as* when coupled with **tam** (*so, as*):

meī **tam** suspīciōne **quam** crīmine carēre dēbent
my (people) ought to be <u>as</u> free from suspicion <u>as</u> from the crime [7.4]

And here are more uses of **quam** which you will come across:

with an adjective or adverb in the superlative form (i.e. *most . . ., very . . .*) to mean *as . . . as possible* (more on this on p. 249):

quam celerrimē
<u>as</u> quickly <u>as possible</u>

meaning *how*, to introduce a question or exclamation:

tū **quam** dulcis es!
<u>how</u> sweet you are!

Practice 18b
Translate:
(a) Lesbia, quam poēta miser amat, in forō cum Caeliō errat.
(b) quam fēlīx est Caelius!
(c) nōnne ego tam fēlīx sum quam Caelius?

---

aliquis, aliqua, aliquid

Aliquis (with the indefinite endings **-quis, -qua, -quid**) is a pronoun meaning *someone, anyone, something, anything*:

quodque **aliquid** poscās
and because you demand <u>something</u> [14.2]

It can also be an adjective (endings like **-quī, -quae, -quod**). The extra two syllables at the front, **ali-**, give this word more presence than the shorter indefinite **quis**:

aliquam in tuīs litterīs grātulātiōnem exspectāvī
in your letter I expected <u>some</u> congratulation [6.11]

Here **aliquam** is emphatic. The rub is Cicero didn't get any congratulation at all. Had he said *I did not receive any . . .* he probably would have used **ūllus,-a,-um**, which is often used with a negative.

alter, altera, alterum

Alter is a pronoun similar in meaning to **alius** but usually deals in pairs, meaning *one (of two)* or *the other (of two)*:

duās bybliothēcās habeō, ūnam Graecam, **alteram** Latīnam
I have two libraries, one Greek, <u>the other</u> Latin [21.1]

duōs flāminēs adiēcit, Martī ūnum, **alterum** Quirīnō
he added two priests, one for Mars, <u>the other</u> for Quirinus [24.11]

singular			
	M	F	N
N.	**alter**	altera	alterum
A.	**alterum**	**alteram**	alterum
G.	alterīus	alterīus	alterīus
D.	alterī	alterī	alterī
Ab.	alterō	alterā	alterō

Alter can also mean more generally *another, the next man*:

plūs in diē nummōrum accipit, quam **alter** patrimōnium habet
he takes more coins in a day than <u>the next man</u> has (as) an inheritance [20.3]

Like other words with a genitive **-īus** (e.g. **ūnus**), the 'i' can be short (**alterius**). The plural is **alterī, alterae, altera** (like **bonus**).

quisquis, quidquid

Where you see the pronoun **quis** 'doubled up', i.e. **quisquis, quidquid**, etc, it means *who<u>ever</u>, which<u>ever</u>, what<u>ever</u>* (and can be a pronoun or adjective):

quidquid id est, timeō Danaōs et dōna ferentīs
<u>whatever</u> that is, I fear Greeks even when bearing gifts [4.13]

quisquam, quidquam

The final syllable of this pronoun (**-quam**) is fixed. The neuter can be **quidquam** or **quicquam**. It means *anyone (anything), anyone (anything) at all*.

Clōdiam omnēs semper amīcam omnium potius quam **cuiusquam** inimīcam putāvērunt
everyone always thought Clodia to be the friend of everyone rather than <u>anyone's</u> enemy [8.3]

quisque, quaeque, quodque

It means *each, every*. The final syllable **-que** is fixed.

cōnsilia adversāriōrum per **cuiusque** mulierēs exquīrēbat.
he discovered the plans of opponents through the wives <u>of each one</u> [12.10]

quīdam

This is another indefinite word, though not quite as vague as **quis** or **aliquis**. The speaker or writer may know who is meant by **quīdam**, but if so does not see any point in saying who. It can be an adjective (*a certain . . .*) or pronoun (*a certain person, some people*).

trādidērunt **quīdam**
<u>*some people*</u> *related*

The front half of the word declines like **quis/quī**; the last syllable **-dam** is fixed.

quō **and** quā

Quō is the ablative of **quis/quī**. It can also mean *to where, whither*, introducing a question or relative clause (e.g. <u>*to where*</u> *are you going?* *I am going* <u>*to where*</u> *my friends have gone*):

quō prīmum virgō quaeque dēducta est
<u>*to where*</u> *(to whose home) each girl was first taken* [23.1]

Quā is the ablative feminine of **quis/quī**. This too has an additional meaning: *by which way, by what way*. At some earlier point the noun in the phrase became redundant (**quā viā**). **Quā** can be an interrogative, relative, or indefinite as below:

sī **quā** fāta aspera rumpās / tū Mārcellus eris
if <u>*by some way*</u> *you break the harsh fates you will be Marcellus* [14.13]

Practice 18c

Translate:

(a) quō it poēta?
(b) familiārium quīdam inter cēterās cognōverat Vetūriam.
(c) nōnne, ō amīce, aliquam pecūniam habēs?
(d) quisquis taurum fugat est dēmēns.
(e) duo cōnsulēs multōs legiōnēs dūcēbant, alter in Africā, alter in Galliā.
(f) nēmō tē ipsum sequitur, sed aliquid ex tē.

Vocabulary 18

quod *which, what, that, namely that, in that, that which, because, any*
quia *because*
quam *whom, which, any* (feminine accusative of **quis/quī**)
  as, than, how . . . ? how . . . !
quam + superlative *as . . . as possible*
quamquam *although*

---

alter, altera, alterum   *one . . . another, the one . . . the other*
aliquis, aliqua, aliquid (aliquī, aliquae, aliquod)   *any, some, anyone, someone,*
   anything, something
quisquis, quidquid   *whoever, whichever, whatever*
quisquam, quidquam   *anyone at all*
quisque, quaeque, quodque   *each, every*
quīdam, quaedam, quiddam/quoddam   *a certain (person, thing)*
quidem   *indeed, certainly, no less*
nē . . . quidem   *not even*
quō   *in/on/by/with/from . . . whom/which/any* (masc./neut.abl. of **quis/quī**)
   to where
quā   *in/on/by/with/from . . . whom/which/any* (fem.abl. of **quis/quī**)
   by which way
   by any way

Exercises 18a

1.   Translate the words which are in bold:
(a)   vultis hoc certāmen uxōribus vestrīs īnicere, Quirītēs, ut dīvitēs id habēre velint **quod** nūlla alia possit, et pauperēs, nē ob hoc ipsum contemnantur, suprā vīrēs sē extendant?
(b)   Augustus, **quod** Thallus prō epistulā prōditā dēnāriōs quīngentōs accēpisset, crūra eī frēgit.
(c)   **quid** virō bonō et quiētō et bonō cīvī magis convenit **quam** abesse ā cīvīlibus contrōversiīs?
(d)   in Perusīnōs magis īrā mīlitum **quam** voluntāte saevītum ducis.
(e)   dīxerat, et lacrimīs vultum lāvēre profūsīs, / tam quī mandābat, **quam** cui mandāta dabantur.
(f)   dīlēxit et rēgīnās, sed maximē Cleopātram, **quam** fīlium nātum appellāre nōmine suō passus est.

2.   Translate:
(a)   quis arma virumque canit?
(b)   quisquis es, hoc carmen audiās Vergiliī.
(c)   ō domine, utinam in patriam redeam!
(d)   omnēs Cloeliam laudāvērunt quod cum aliīs puellīs Tiberim trānāverat.
(e)   cui Tullia corpus suī patris ostendet?
(f)   duo tribūnī occīsī sunt, alter ā senātōribus, alter ā cōnsule.
(g)   poēta dīlēxit quāsdam fēminās, sed maximē Lesbiam.
(h)   ō coniūnx, quō fugis?
(i)   duōs servōs habeō, ūnum Graecum, alterum Britannum.

3.   Translate into Latin:
(a)   Whichever visitor will come, dismiss him.
(b)   Now I will not love Lesbia, who herself has not loved me.
(c)   I saw the body of Caesar, which was lying on the ground.

Reading notes

Singulars and plurals do not always correspond between different languages. A few Latin nouns which appear only or mostly in the plural are translated into a singular noun in English (if in some cases a collective one), e.g. **litterae,-ārum** (*letters, epistolary letter, literature*), **īnsidiae,-ārum** (*ambush*), **castra,-ōrum** (*camp*), **rōstra,-ōrum** (*speaker's platform*: a **rōstrum** was the beak of a ship, and captured beaks were used to adorn the platform).

Some Latin nouns have singular forms, but even in the plural may be put into English in the singular:

> **dolōs** (dolus,-ī)   *deception* [3.9]
> **ruīnās** (ruīna,-ae)   *ruin* [11.13]
> **tempora** (tempus,-oris)   *time* [13.7 and 15.14]
> **saecula** (saeculum,-ī)   *age, era* [14.11, 16.9 and 22.7]
> **nivēs** (nix, nivis)   *snow* [15.1]
> **aurās** (aura,-ae)   *air* [24.12 and 25.9]
> **dolōrēs** (dolor,-ōris)   *suffering, distress* [25.3]
> **noctēsque diēsque**   *both night and day* [25.9]
> **tormenta** (tormentum,-ī)   *torture* [26.7]

There are a few Latin nouns which in the singular may carry a collective or multiple sense (and, where so, translate as a plural):

> ego **vītam** omnium cīvium redēmī
> *I saved the <u>lives</u> of all the citizens (the life of every citizen)* [6.8] See also **vītam** in 20.3.

> plēbs statim ā fūnere ad **domum** Brūtī et Cassiī cum facibus tetendit
> *the people marched immediately from the funeral with torches to the <u>homes</u> of Brutus and Cassius* [9.6]

> Antōnius fugientis rēgīnae quam pugnantis **mīlitis** suī comes esse māluit
> *Antony preferred to be the companion of the fleeing queen rather than of his own fighting <u>army</u>* [11.7] See also **mīlitem** in 23.5.

> dīxerat, et lacrimīs **vultum** lavēre profūsīs
> *he had spoken, and they bathed their <u>faces</u> with streaming tears* [17.5]

Where Latin uses a neuter plural of an adjective or pronoun (with no other noun), a translation will often be singular:

> senātus **haec** intellegit
> *the senate understands <u>this</u>* (lit. *these things*) [6.7]

> **hīs** dictīs
> *with <u>this</u> said* (lit. *these things*) [14.12]

Slavery

To become a slave you were a prisoner of war, a criminal, in deep financial trouble, or the child of a slave. Life was generally grim for the wretched no-hopers who had to labour in mines, quarries, on large estates, in galleys, sewers, building sites, performing all the menial jobs without much rest. Those who stepped out of line were whipped, branded, crucified or fed to wild animals. Life expectancy was cheerlessly short.

Not all suffered so badly. A slave was an investment with a value dependent on condition, a material resource to be looked after, if dehumanized. The lack of evidence from slaves themselves continues to conceal their individual humanity. We think of slaves as one class of person, overworked, demeaned and in captivity. They were in fact all sorts of people from many different backgrounds. Some were trained, skilled and clever, and performed jobs carried out by professionals today: accountants, architects, artists, doctors, librarians, secretaries and teachers were slaves or ex-slaves; artists too. A few slaves were held in high affection by some owners and good service might win freedom. But in return loyalty was expected to continue: a freedman could be very useful to the former owner's business interests, perhaps in his country of origin.

Horace's father was a freedman who struggled to get by, but in later imperial times *libertini* might become wealthy or even politically powerful. By the mid-first century AD two freedmen, Narcissus and Pallas, are entrusted by Nero to look after administrative duties. We read of another freedman, Trimalchio, at his own dinner party lording it over educated freeborn guests. This would have been unimaginable in Caesar's time a hundred years earlier. Not every freedman like Trimalchio became a millionaire, and it has to be said he was a work of fiction (from Petronius' *Satyricon*). But his rise in fortune was believable, if exaggerated for effect. There clearly was some mobility, with people making good, although very few on Trimalchio's scale.

There is evidence of affection felt to a few individual slaves, but hardly anyone believed that slavery *per se* was wrong. Slaves were taken for granted. Take away their contribution to both public and private wellbeing and the state would have been in turmoil. There was discussion of how slaves should be treated, but the central question of right and wrong just didn't come up. Cruelty might provoke disapproval, such as the man who fed his slave to a pondful of lampreys [18.3] or the (fictional) woman who wanted a slave pinned to a cross just because she felt like it [18.2], and there was a rarely seen surge of public sympathy for slaves which engulfed the city in AD 61 [18.7] when a large household of slaves faced execution. But few freeborn citizens took to heart the notion that their slaves were people like themselves.

There was always the threat of organized resistance. In the first century AD slaves counted for around a third of the city's population, and a careful eye had to be kept on possible trouble. In fact there was remarkably little, that we know of. The most serious outbreak happened in 73 BC when Spartacus and his fellow gladiators broke out of their training school in Capua and were joined by thousands of slaves from the Italian peninsula. The rising was only suppressed by a major military effort [6.10].

1.   Martial observes the displeasure of a dinner host:

> esse negās coctum leporem poscisque flagella.
> māvīs, Rūfe, cocum scindere quam leporem.

Martial, Epigrams 3.94

negō,-āre,-āvī,-ātum [1]   *say . . . not*
coquō,-ere, coxī, coctum [3]   *cook*
lepus,-oris [m.]   *hare*
flagella: plural, but translate as a singular
māvīs   *you prefer, you'd rather*
scindō,-ere   *tear, cut up*

2. This imagined conversation between a wife and husband is from Juvenal's satire against
    women. As ever Juvenal doesn't let a realistic representation get in the way of a good
    story. But the vulnerability of the slave is believable.

'pōne crucem servō.' 'meruit quō crīmine servus
supplicium? quis testis adest? quis dētulit? audī;
nūlla umquam dē morte hominis cūnctātiō longa est.'
'ō dēmēns, ita servus homo est? nīl fēcerit, estō:
hoc volo, sīc iubeō, sit prō ratiōne voluntās.'
imperat ergo virō.

Juvenal, *Satires* 6.219–24

pōne: imperative (the wife speaks first)
crux, crucis [f.]   *cross*
servō: probably dative not ablative '*(set up the cross) for the slave*'
mereō,-ēre, meruī, meritum [2]   *deserve, earn*
testis,-is [m./f.]   *witness*
dēferō, dēferre, dētulī, dēlātum   *accuse*
audī [imperative of 'audiō,-īre']   *hear him, give him a hearing*
cūnctātiō,-ōnis [f.]   *delay*
fēcerit [future perfect]   *(if) s/he has done*
estō [3rd person imperative of 'esse']   *let it be, so be it*, i.e. *so what?*
sit: subjunctive to express a command (i.e. *let my* 'voluntās' *be/serve for* 'ratiōne')
ratiō,-ōnis [f.]   *procedure*
voluntās,-tātis [f.]   *will, whim*

3. Vedius Pollio, a friend of Augustus, was especially cruel to slaves.

invēnit in hōc animālī documenta saevitiae Vedius Pollio
eques Rōmānus vīvāriīs eārum immergēns damnāta
mancipia.

Pliny (the Elder), *Natural History* 9.39

animal,-ālis [n.]   *animal* (here, *lamprey*)
documentum,-ī [n.]   *example, demonstration*
saevitia,-ae [f.]   *cruelty*
eques, equitis [m.]   *knight, of the equestrian order*
vīvārium-ī [n.]   *pond, aquarium*
eārum: from 'is, ea, id' referring to the word used for lampreys but not appearing here
    ('mūrēna')

immergēns [the person doing this is in the nominative singular]   *plunging*
damnō,-āre,-āvī,-ātum [1]   *condemn*
mancipium,-ī [n.]   *slave*

4.   Farm slaves had a meaner existence than domestic ones, but they could expect some care and protection. They were after all an investment.

gravia loca ūtilius est mercēnāriīs colere quam servīs.

Varro, On Agriculture 1.17.3

ūtilius [neuter]   *more profitable*
mercēnārius,-ī [m.]   *mercenary, hired hand*
colō,-ere, coluī, cultum [3]   *cultivate*

5.   Slaves were often perceived as clever and conniving.

nam lingua malī pars pessima servī.

Juvenal, Satires 9.121

nam   *for, in fact*
lingua,-ae [f.]   *tongue, speech*
pessimus,-a,-um   *worst*

6.   The crafty slave depicted in ancient comedy has its descendants in the quick wits and wise counsel of characters like Jeeves of P.G. Wodehouse. The ancient servant, however, was generally portrayed as a wily rogue (and more often than not a Greek). In Plautus' *Comedy of Asses*, Argyrippus is desperate for his slave Libanus to hand over some money which will pay for the purchase of his girlfriend from her mother, a procuress. Libanus makes the most of his new power, and insists on riding his master like a horse:

Libanus: vehēs pol hodiē mē, sī quidem hoc argentum
ferre spērēs.
Argyrippus: tēn ego veham?
Libanus: tūn hoc ferās argentum aliter ā mē?
Argyrippus: periī hercle. sī vērum quidem et decōrum erum
vehere servum, īnscende.
Libanus: sīc istī solent superbī subdomārī.

Plautus, Comedy of Asses 699–702

vehēs: 2nd person singular, future, of 'vehō,-ere' (*carry*)
pol   *indeed, truly, by Pollux!* ('pol' is a clipped form of 'Pollux', a deity)
hodiē   *today*
argentum,-ī [n.]   *silver*
sī . . . spērēs [present subjunctive of 'spērō,-āre' = *hope*]   *if you were hoping, assuming you hope*
tēn: tēne

tūn: tūne

ferās: present subjunctive of 'fero, ferre' for a rhetorical question

aliter   *otherwise, by another way*

pereō,-īre,-iī,-itum [compound of 'eō, īre']   *perish, die*

hercle   *indeed, by Hercules!*

vērus,-a,-um   *true, right*

decōrus,-a,-um   *fitting, becoming, proper*

erus,-ī [m.]   *master*

īnscendō,-ere, inscendī, inscēnsum [3]   *climb on, up*

istī [take with a nominative masculine plural]   *those*

soleō,-ēre [2]   *be accustomed*

subdomō,-āre,-āvī,-ātum [1]   *tame, break in* ('subdomārī' is the passive infinitive = *to be tamed*)

7.   Such a spectacle will have caused hilarity all round, except perhaps for the slaves, whose owners once the laughter died down might dish out a few beatings to prevent the same rot happening at home. Actual role reversal took place each year during the festival of Saturnalia in December when amid the festive jollities the server and the served briefly swapped positions. A cautionary party-game for some, no doubt.

In AD 61, Lucius Pedanius Secundus, prefect of the city, was killed by one of his own slaves. An ancient law was invoked which decreed death to all the slaves within the same household. In Pedanius' house there were some four hundred slaves, children, elderly, whole families of slaves. There was a public outcry against this mass execution. It was debated in the senate, where Gaius Cassius argued in favour of the ancient law:

dēcernite hercule impūnitātem: at quem dīgnitās sua dēfendet, cum praefectō urbis nōn prōfuerit? quem numerus servōrum tuēbitur, cum Pedānium Secundum quadringentī nōn prōtexerint?

Tacitus, Annals 14.43

dēcernite: plural imperative of 'dēcernō,-ere' [3] (*decide, make a judgement*)

hercule: for 'hercle'

impūnitās,-tātis [f.]   *impunity*

sua: here refers to the object (normally refers to the subject)

praefectus,-ī [m.]   *commander, prefect*

prōsum, prōdesse, prōfuī [+ dat.]   *be of use to*

numerus,-ī [m.]   *number* (but not many: *a gathering, handful*)

tueor, tuērī [2; deponent]   *protect, watch over*

quadringentī [nom. pl.]   *four hundred*

prōtegō,-ere, prōtexī, prōtectum [3]   *protect*

8.   His view prevailed, but people still protested.

tum Caesar populum ēdictō increpuit atque omne iter quō damnātī ad poenam dūcēbantur mīlitāribus praesidiīs saepsit.

Tacitus, Annals 14.45

Caesar: the emperor Nero
increpō,-ere,-uī,-itum [3]   *rebuke*
iter, itineris [n.]   *route, way*
mīlitāris,-e   *military*
praesidium,-ī [n.]   *protection, guard*
saepiō,-īre, saepsī, saeptum [4]   *fence in, barricade*

9. A visitor to someone's house might find an inscription above the door like this one in Petronius' story:

   ## quisquis servus sine dominicō iussū forās exierit accipiet plāgās centum.

   Petronius, *Satyricon* 28

   quisquis servus   *any slave whatsoever who*
   dominicus,-a,-um   *of a master, belonging to a master*
   forās   *out of doors*
   exierit: future perfect of 'exeō, exīre' (*go out*)
   plāga,-ae [f.]   *blow, lash*

10. Not all slaves were despised and abused. Cicero struggles to accept the death of a young slave:

   ## puer fēstīvus anagnōstēs noster Sositheus dēcesserat, mēque plūs quam servī mors dēbēre vidēbātur commōverat.

   Cicero, *Letters to Atticus* 1.12

   fēstīvus,-a,-um   *agreeable, pleasant*
   anagnōstēs   *reader*
   dēcēdō,-ere, dēcessī, dēcessum [3]   *die*
   plūs quam   *more than*

11. As a reward for good service or act of affection some domestic slaves were given their freedom; or because it freed them up to perform other services. A *libertus* would remain close to the *familia*. Here Pliny shows his concern for the health of his *libertus*, Zosimus.

   ## nihil aequē amōrem incitat et accendit quam carendī metus.

   Pliny, *Letters* 5.19

   aequē   *as much, equally*
   amor,-ōris [m.]   *love*
   incitō,-āre,-āvī,-ātum [1]   *arouse*
   accendō,-ere, accendī, accēnsum [3]   *stimulate*
   carendī   *of losing, of loss*

12. *Libertini* were no doubt sneered at and distrusted on account of their origin, but having escaped slavery they were usually clever enough to prosper. They first fought in Roman armies in the first century BC during the Social War.

lībertīnī tunc prīmum mīlitāre coepērunt.

Livy, History of Rome 74 (Summary)

tunc   *then, at that time*
mīlitō,-āre [1]   *fight, perform military service*
coepērunt   *(they) began*

13. Very poor citizens were in some respects no better off than slaves, but they still felt their difference keenly. In Petronius' *Satyricon*, a hired worker complains about the weight of the luggage he is carrying:

'quid vōs,' inquit, 'iūmentum mē putātis esse aut lapidāriam nāvem? hominis operās locāvī, nōn caballī. nec minus līber sum quam vōs, etiam sī pauperem pater mē relīquit.' nec contentus maledictīs tollēbat subinde altius pedem et strepitū obscēnō simul atque odōre viam implēbat.

Petronius, Satyricon 117

iūmentum,-ī [n.]   *pack animal*
putātis: 2nd person plural, present indicative of 'putō,-āre'
lapidārius,-a,-um   *stone-carrying*
opera,-ae [f.]   *task, service*
locō,-āre,-āvī,-ātum [1]   *contract, sign up to*
caballus,-ī [m.]   *horse*
pauper,-is [m.]   *poor man*
maledictum,-ī [n.]   *abuse*
tollō,-ere, sustulī, sublātum   *lift, raise*
subinde   *then, immediately, thereupon*
altius   *higher* (i.e. one foot higher than the other)
strepitus,-ūs [m.]   *noise*
simul   *at the same time, simultaneously*
odor,-ōris [m.]   *smell*

14. At dinner with friends Pliny tells the story of how he once dined with a man who gave his guests food and wine according to their social status. He explains how he managed his own dinners:

'eadem omnibus pōnō, quōs ad cēnam, nōn ad notam invītō.'
'etiamne lībertīs?'
'etiam; convīctōrēs enim tunc, nōn lībertōs putō.' et ille:
'magnō tibi cōnstat.'
'minimē.'

'quī fierī potest?'
'quia scīlicet lībertī meī nōn idem quod ego bibunt, sed idem
ego quod lībertī.'

Pliny, Letters 2.6

eadem: neuter plural of 'īdem, eadem, idem'
nota,-ae [f.]   *social grading*
invītō,-āre,-āvī,-ātum [1]   *invite*
etiam   *even, also, yes*
convīctor,-ōris [m.]   *table companion, fellow diner*
enim   *for, you see*
magnō: ablative of price (*at a great price, much*)
cōnstō,-āre, cōnstitī [1]   *stand at, cost*
minimē   *not at all*
quī: archaic form of the ablative (all genders) of 'quī, quae, quod' which survives to
    mean *how (by what way)*
fierī   *to be done*
scīlicet   *of course, let me tell you* (often used with irony, but not here)

Exercises 18b

1.   Translate:
(a)   vīnum affer, ō miser.
(b)   quae hercle est cūnctātiō? poscam flagellum? [poscam: from 'poscō,-ere']
(c)   servus ipse coquētur quia leporem nōn coxit.
(d)   es tam obscēnus quam dēmēns.
(e)   illīs servīs aliquis det aquam. [det: from 'do, dare']
(f)   pessima pars meae dominae est vōx.
(g)   quisquis servus fūgerit ad mortem flagellīs in amphitheātrō caedētur.
(h)   rogāsne, ō serve, ut ego tē veham? — sīc, ut equus. [veham: from 'vehō,-ere']
(i)   nihil tam lūctuōsum est quam līberōs āmittere.
(j)   quisquis mīles mēcum flūmen trānsierit hoc argentum accipiet.
(k)   mihi imperās velut servō? [velut(i) = *like, just as*]
(l)   sum tam lībera quam vōs. ego sum Boudicca, Icēnōrum rēgīna, nōn serva Rōmae.
    [serva,-ae = *female slave*].

2.   Translate the words in bold:
(a)   sed tamen, sī omnēs tribūnōs plēbis habēmus, sī Lentulum tam studiōsum **quam**
    vidētur, sī vērō etiam Pompēium et Caesarem, nōn est dēspērandum.
(b)   Cleopātrae, **quam** servātam triumphō magnopere cupiēbat, etiam psyllōs admōvit,
    quī venēnum exsūgerent, **quod** perīsse morsū aspidis putābātur.
(c)   Clōdius erat sine uxōre, **quod** numquam ferē.
(d)   citiusque ē mundō genus hominum **quam** Cicerō cēdet.
(e)   rēs est cum eā **quam** omnēs semper amīcam omnium potius quam **cuiusquam**
    inimīcam putāvērunt.
(f)   **illa** est Lesbia, **quam** Catullus ūnam plūs **quam** sē atque suōs amāvit omnēs.

3.   Find Latin ancestors in this chapter of *crucify, imperious, linguistic, negative, pessimist* and *utility*.

— 19 —

Education

Adjectives

An adjective qualifies a noun or pronoun, adding a descriptive touch or defining quality. A Latin adjective matches the gender, number and case of the noun or pronoun it qualifies. There are adjectives that share the endings of 1st and 2nd declension nouns (**bonus,-a,-um, magnus,-a,-um**, etc), and there are those with endings similar to 3rd declension nouns (**omnis,-e, ingēns, fēlīx**). To the '3rd declension' adjectives we can add **vetus** (genitive **veteris**) *old*, **ācer** (gen. **ācris**) *keen*, **celer** (gen. **celeris**) *quick*, **pār** (gen. **paris**) *equal*.

Participles are also adjectives (e.g. **amātus,-a,-um** = *loved*), for although they are taken from verbs and retain one or two characteristics of verbs they decline and agree with nouns as adjectives do.

Adverbs

Whereas an adjective lends more detail to a noun, an adverb does the same but to a verb:

> *she walked <u>slowly</u> across the room*

Slowly tells us how she walked. The '-ly' ending is a recognizable tag of English adverbs (*quickly, usually, loudly*, etc), but not all English adverbs have it (*also, never, often*).

Adverbs add meaning not only to verbs but also to adjectives and other adverbs:

> *the bridge was <u>dangerously</u> weak*

Some adverbs are prepositions in disguise, or vice versa. If the word is used with a noun then it is a preposition, if by itself it is an adverb:

> *he jumped <u>off the bridge</u>*   (preposition)
> *he jumped <u>off</u>*   (adverb)

The same is true of some Latin adverbs:

servī arma **contrā** rem pūblicam cēperant   (preposition)
the slaves had taken arms against the Republic   [11.2]

stat **contrā** stārīque iubet   (adverb)
he stands in my way and orders (me) to stop   [13.15]

Practice 19a

1.   Identify whether the underlined word is an adjective, adverb, verb or preposition:
    (a)   The <u>fast</u> car raced around the mountain.
    (b)   He drove <u>fast</u> around the mountain.
    (c)   Every year they <u>fast</u> at this time.
    (d)   She spoke <u>angrily</u> about their rights.
    (e)   She has spoken <u>before</u> me.
    (f)   She has spoken <u>before</u>.
    (g)   She performed <u>quite</u> <u>well</u>.

2.   Identify all the adverbs, and translate:
    (a)   plēbs statim ā fūnere ad domum Brūtī et Cassiī tetendit.   (one adverb)
    (b)   Caesar statim Līviam Drūsillam mātrimōniō Tiberiī Nerōnis et quidem praegnantem abdūxit, dīlēxitque et probāvit ūnicē ac persevertanter.   (four adverbs)

Comparison

An adjective describes or qualifies a noun (*a fast horse*). An adjective may also be used to compare two nouns, where one is more or less than the other:

the horse is faster than the donkey

'Fast-er' is one of the few inflexions surviving in English. Many English adjectives have this same ending in the comparative form: *bigger, sharper, richer*, etc. Not all do. Older English adjectives tend to end '-er'; those which have their roots in early, inflexional English. Other comparative adjectives are expressed with 'more':

is a horse is more expensive than a donkey?

Latin comparative adjectives have the syllable **-ior-** in most of the cases:

positive		comparative	('more')
opulentus	*rich*	**opulentior**	*richer*
saevus	*cruel*	**saevior**	*more cruel*
facilis	*easy*	**facilior**	*easier*

The masculine and femine of the comparative are the same in all cases, and the neuter only varies in the nominative and accusative (singular and plural):

nōn illa mihi **fōrmōsior** umquam vīsa est
she never seemed more beautiful to me [15.12]

(fōrmōsus,-a,-um = *beautiful*)
(fōrmōsior = *more beautiful*)

[sing.]	M/F	N
N.	**fōrmōsior**	fōrmōsius
A.	fōrmōsiōrem	fōrmōsius
G.	fōrmōsiōris	fōrmōsiōris
D.	fōrmōsiōrī	fōrmōsiōrī
Ab.	fōrmōsiōre	fōrmōsiōre

simul parēs esse coeperint, **superiōrēs** erunt
once they start to be our equals, in no time they'll be superiors [16.6]

(superus,-a,-um = *above, on high*)
(superior = *higher, superior*)

[pl.]	M/F	N
N.	**superiōrēs**	superiōra
A.	superiōrēs	superiōra
G.	superiōrum	superiōrum
D.	superiōribus	superiōribus
Ab.	superiōribus	superiōribus

Some much-used adjectives have irregular comparative forms:

positive		comparative	('more')
bonus	*good*	**melior**	*better*
malus	*bad*	**peior**	*worse*
multus	*much, many*	**plūs** *	*more*
magnus	*great*	**maior**	*greater*
parvus	*small*	**minor**	*less*

* **plūs** is often used as a neuter noun in the singular, with a noun in the genitive (*more of*...), and as an adjective in the plural (**plūrēs**). **Plūs** is also the adverbial '*more*' as in 'Catullus Lesbiam **plūs** quam sē amāvit.' See comparative adverbs below.

The second noun in the comparison, the standard or point of comparison, either follows **quam** (*than*) and is in the same case as the first noun, or is in the ablative, called the 'ablative of comparison':

rē pūblicā nihil mihi est **cārius**
nothing is dearer to me than the Republic [8.8]

(cārus = *dear*)
(cārior = *dearer*)

	M/F	N
N.	cārior	**cārius**
A.	cāriōrem	cārius
G.	cāriōris	cāriōris
D.	cāriōrī	cāriōrī
Ab.	cāriōre	cāriōre

To qualify the comparative and say how much more (_much_ more . . . . _a little_ more . . .) Latin uses the ablative neuter singular of words like **multus,-a,-um** (_much_) or **paulus,-a,-um** (_a little_), called the 'ablative of measure of difference' (_by_ much more, _by_ a little more):

> prīmum **multō** obstinātior adversus lacrimās muliebrēs erat
> _at first he was_ much _more resistant to the tears of the women_ [17.2]

Practice 19b

Give the case, number and gender of each underlined adjective, and translate:
(a)   quis Crassō erat **opulentior**?
(b)   Graecōs habuimus servōs multō **doctiōrēs** ipsīs amīcīs meīs.
(c)   ego uxōrem **fōrmōsiorem** quam Cleopātram dūxī.
(d)   lībertīne tibi **ūtiliōrēs** quam servī sunt?

Comparative adverbs

Adverbs also have comparative forms. Like the ordinary or 'positive' adverb, the comparative has a single fixed ending. It is the same form as the neuter of the comparative adjective (**-ius**):

> **citius** ē mundō genus hominum **quam** Cicerō cēdet
> _sooner will the human race fade away from the world_ than _will Cicero_   [12.21]

positive		comparative	('more')
bene	well	**melius**	better
facile	easily	**facilius**	more easily
male	badly	**peius**	worse
multum	much	**plūs**	more
trīste	sadly	**trīstius**	more sadly

This replication of the neuter adjective is not a coincidence. The accusative neuter singular of a number of adjectives may be used adverbially, e.g. **multum** (_much_), **prīmum** (_firstly_) and **tantum** (_only, so much_).

Sometimes a comparative adjective or adverb is used without a standard or point of comparison, i.e. the 'than something' is not included. We take these to mean 'more than normal', and translate as _rather_ . . ., or possibly _quite_ or _too_ . . .: similarly in English '_rather_ cold' suggests colder than average.

> hic vir, hic est, tibi quem prōmittī **saepius** audīs
> _this is the man whom you_ quite often _hear being promised to you_   [14.11]

> rūmōrēsque senum **sevēriōrum** / omnēs ūnius aestimēmus assis
> _let us value all the chatter of_ too strict _old men at one as_   [15.6]

The superlative

The superlative is *the most . . .*, or *the . . .-est*; it can also mean *very . . .*:

> the <u>fastest</u> horse (a very fast . . .)
> the <u>most expensive</u> horse (a very expensive . . .)

Most Latin superlatives have the ending **-issimus,-a,-um** (endings like **bonus,-a,-um**). Other endings are **-illimus (facilis, facillimus)** and **-errimus (miser, miserrimus)**:

positive		comparative ('more')		superlative ('most')	
facilis	*easy*	facilior	*easier*	**facillimus**	*easiest*
miser	*wretched*	miserior	*more wretched*	**miserrimus**	*most wretched*
opulentus	*rich*	opulentior	*richer*	**opulentissimus**	*richest, most lavish*
saevus	*cruel*	saevior	*more cruel*	**saevissimus**	*most cruel*

And there are the irregular superlatives:

> quis ex omnibus gladiātōribus est **maximus**?
> *who is the <u>greatest</u> out of all the gladiators?*

positive		comparative (more')		superlative ('most')	
bonus	*good*	melior	*better*	**optimus**	*best, excellent*
magnus	*great*	maior	*greater*	**maximus**	*greatest*
malus	*bad*	peior	*worse*	**pessimus**	*worst*
multus	*much, many*	plūs	*more*	**plūrimus**	*most*
parvus	*small*	minor	*less*	**minimus**	*least*

Practice 19c

Give the case, number and gender of each underlined adjective, and translate:
(a) rē pūblicā nihil mihi est **cārius**.
(b) Caesar aedēs sacrās **opulentissimīs** dōnīs adōrnāvit.
(c) puellās **honestissimās** in flōre prīmō fēcunditās abstulit.
(d) gravia loca **ūtilius** est mercēnāriīs colere quam servīs.

Superlative adverbs

Adverbs are also used in the superlative:

> she danced <u>most/very beautifully</u>

Latin adverbs in the superlative have the fixed ending **-ē**:

positive		comparative ('more')		superlative ('most')	
bene	*well*	melius	*better*	**optimē**	*very well*
facile	*easily*	facilius	*more easily*	**facillimē**	*most/very easily*
magnopere	*greatly*	magis	*more*	**maximē**	*greatest, especially*
male	*badly*	peius	*worse*	**pessimē**	*very badly*
paulum	*little*	minus	*less*	**minimē**	*least, not at all*
saepe	*often*	saepius	*more often*	**saepissimē**	*most/very often*
trīste	*sadly*	trīstius	*more sadly*	**trīstissimē**	*most/very sadly*

The superlative after **quam** means *as . . . as possible*:

> **quam celerrimē** mihi librārius mittātur
> *let a clerk be sent to me as quickly as possible*   [19.13]

A few Latin adjectives do not have comparative or superlative endings, and so are used with a separate word for *more* or *most*:

> bellum **maximē** omnium **memorābile** erat
> *the war was the most memorable of all*   [3.1]

Vocabulary 19

Here are some of the adverbs which appear in this course:

ācrius	*more keenly*	**numquam**	*never*
adhūc	*still, yet*	**nunc**	*now*
bene	*well*	**ōlim**	*once upon a time*
certē	*surely, certainly*	**paene**	*nearly, almost*
diū	*for a long time*	**paulātim**	*little by little, gradually*
etiam	*also, even, yes*	**quoque**	*also, too*
facile	*easily*	**saepe**	*often*
forte	*by chance*	**sānē**	*certainly*
frūstrā	*in vain*	**satis**	*enough*
hīc	*here*	**semper**	*always*
iam	*now, already*	**simul**	*at the same time*
intereā	*meanwhile*	**sponte**	*willingly, of one's own accord*
maximē	*especially, very, most*	**statim**	*immediately*
minimē	*in the smallest degree, not at all, no*	**turpiter**	*disgracefully*
modo	*only, recently*	**umquam**	*ever*
mox	*soon, presently*	**vix**	*hardly, scarcely, with difficulty*

These adverbs help to create comparisons. With the exception of **minus** (*less*), they all share the meaning 'more', but in slightly different if overlapping ways:

minus   *less*
amplius   *more, more fully, more abundantly, more extensively*
magis   *more, rather, in a higher degree, more completely*
plūs   *more* (in general of quantity and measure)
potius   *more, rather, preferably*
ultrā   *more, above, beyond*

This comparative form is regularly used as a noun:

maior   *greater, larger, elder*
maiōrēs,-um [m.pl.]   *ancestors*

Look online for more adverbs which appear in this course (see p. 393).

Exercises 19a

1. Translate:
(a) Cleopātra victōrem plūs quam suum frātrem amāvit.
(b) terror magis quam avāritia animōs servōrum exercēbat.
(c) quis librōs maiōrum legere vult?
(d) eāmus quam celerrimē!
(e) quid peius est quam miserās vōcēs captīvōrum audīre?
(f) plūs vīnī bibāmus!
(g) timeō nē illī salūtātōrēs saepius veniant.
(h) quis mihi cārior est Līviā?
(i) certē ego multō sapientior sum quam vōs!
(j) lībertus convīvia opulentius exōrnābat quam patrōnus suus.
(k) Caesar Clōdiō quam uxōrī benignior erat.

2. Fill each gap with the correct form of the adjective:
(a) quis est .... {*stronger* from 'fortis,-e'} quam tū?
(b) certē Cleopātra Caesarī .... {*very dear* from 'cārus,-a,-um'} erat.
(c) Crassus erat .... {*more lavish* from 'opulentus,-a,-um'} quam Caesar.
(d) meum venēnum nōn .... {*more bitter* from 'acerbus,-a,-um'} est tuō.
(e) dea est .... {*too unfeeling, quite cruel* from 'dūrus,-a,-um'}.
(f) meam uxōrem .... {*most tender* from 'tener,-era,-erum'} dīligō.
(g) ō Britannī, vōs estis .... {*more stubborn* from 'ferōx'} ipsīs Gallis.

3. Who deserves most sympathy?
(a) cōnsul servō quam uxōrī benignior erat.
(b) cōnsul servō quam uxor benignior erat.

Education

Youngsters from all backgrounds would learn skills and trades from their parents and others, but a more formal schooling under the direction of a teacher was restricted to those who could afford it. In the early Republic girls would learn to sew and cook; boys would learn how to fight and farm the land, and if from a wealthy family, to take part in public debates.

Once the world of Greece had become part of the Roman one, the curriculum became more sophisticated. Previous subjects such as husbandry, horseriding, swimming, martial arts, numeracy, literacy, law, and public-speaking took a more literary turn. Boys continued to prepare for duties of government and to speak in public, but now they would learn Greek, to read (and learn from) histories, to become poets and men of letters, to reel off quotations from Greek

> ## Reading notes
> Sometimes it may be better to translate a Latin adjective (or participle) as an adverb:
>
> Cloelia Tiberim trānāvit **sospitēs**que omnēs ad propinquōs restituit
> *Cloelia swam across the Tiber and returned everyone safe (safely) to their relatives* [2.8]
>
> Tiberiī Gāīque et Claudiī ac Nerōnis rēs flōrentibus ipsīs **falsae** compositae sunt
> *the deeds of Tiberius, of Gaius, of Claudius and of Nero were falsely recorded while they themselves were in their prime* [13.12]
>
> vītaque cum gemitū fugit **indīgnāta** sub umbrās
> *and with a groan his life flees resentfully to the shades below* [24.13]

and Latin authors, to join debates and plead a case with rhetorical flourish. There were a few reactionaries like Cato who clung to the previous virtues of old-fashioned no-nonsense toughening up; but he was an exception.

The majority of freeborn children had little more than a basic grounding in numeracy and literacy. Some of these children whose parents could afford it would study with a *litterator* (7–12 years), after which boys and one or two girls might go on to study with a *grammaticus* (12–16 years), and then finally only a handful of boys (no girls) would make it to the third stage with a *rhetor*.

One subject missing from the curriculum was engineering. Engineers and architects did not share the same *dignitas* of generals and speakers, despite some breathtaking feats of construction. Like other applied skills they were left to others. The arts were similarly overlooked, for though richer Romans had lavish appetites for finished works of art, they did not aspire to be artists themselves.

Greek philosophy was read keenly by Roman intellectuals but less so in Roman schools. Boys did get to study philosophy, but only with a *rhetor* in their later education. Greeks loved the to and fro of philosophical discussions and made philosophy almost a national sport. Romans took this up, with a firmer grip on the practical value of such debates. We have already seen how two well-born mothers prevented their sons from studying ethical questions too closely [17.10 and 17.11].

1. Education became more sophisticated after Romans started to immerse themselves in Greek culture. A few resisted these Hellenizing trends, like Cato, who continued to teach his children how to speak in public, ride a horse, swim (in cold rivers), fight and throw a javelin. He preferred to educate his son himself rather than trust the duty to a Greek, a feeling echoed by Tacitus some two hundred and fifty years later:

at nunc nātus īnfāns dēlēgātur Graeculae alicui ancillae,
cui adiungitur ūnus aut alter ex omnibus servīs, plērumque
vīlissimus nec cuiquam sēriō ministeriō adcommodātus.
hōrum fābulīs et errōribus tenerī statim et rudēs animī
imbuuntur; nec quisquam in tōtā domō pēnsī habet quid
cōram īnfante dominō aut dīcat aut faciat.

Tacitus, Dialogue on Oratory 29

īnfāns   *not able to speak, infant*
dēlēgō,-āre,-āvī,-ātum [1]   *commit, entrust*
Graeculus,-a,-um   *little Greek* ('-ulus' is a diminutive or patronizing suffix)
adiungō,-ere, adiūnxī, adiūnctum [3]   *join, attach*
ūnus aut alter   *one or another*
plērumque   *very often*
vīlis,-e   *worthless*
cuiquam: dative of 'quisquam'
sērius,-a,-um   *serious*
ministerium,-ī [n.]   *service*
adcommodō,-āre,-āvī,-ātum [1]   *fit, adapt, suit*
hōrum: gen.pl. of 'hic, haec, hoc'
fābula,-ae [f.]   *tale, story*
tener,-era,-erum   *tender*
rudis,-e   *impressionable*
imbuō,-ere, imbuī, imbūtum [3]   *fill, taint*
pēnsī habeō,-ēre   *care a jot* (genitive of value: *hold/regard as a* 'pēnsum')
cōram [+ abl.]   *in the presence of*

2.   Greek methods of argument were studied and games with logic practised – to the point
of ridicule:

mūs syllaba est. mūs autem cāseum rōdit; syllaba ergō
cāseum rōdit. verendum est nē, sī neglegentior fuerō,
cāseum liber comedat.

Seneca, Moral Epistles 48.6

mūs, mūris [m.]   *mouse*
syllaba,-ae [f.]   *syllable*
autem   *but, now* (not the temporal '*now*' but explanatory)
cāseus,-ī [m.]   *cheese*
rōdō,-ere, rōsī, rōsum [3]   *gnaw, nibble*
verendum est   *it is to be feared, it is a matter of concern*
neglegēns   *neglectful, careless*
fuerō: future perfect of 'sum, esse'
liber,-brī [m.]   *book*
comedō,-ere, comēdī, comēsum [3]   *gobble up* ('comedat': subjunctive after a verb of
    fearing)

3.   As the empire grew, it evolved into a bureaucratic state with a need for literate people outside the old senatorial elite. By the time of Petronius (mid-first century AD), freedmen as lavish as his fictional character Trimalchio had more than enough wealth to educate their children – and even pet slaves:

puerum bāsiāvī frūgālissimum, nōn propter fōrmam, sed quia frūgī est; decem partēs dīcit, librum ab oculō legit.

Petronius, Satyricon 75

bāsiō,-āre,-āvī,-ātum [1]   *kiss*
frūgālis,-e   *worthy*
propter [+ acc.]   *because of*
frūgī [an idiom where the dative of 'frūx, frūgis' (*fruit, success*) is used like an adjective]   *worthy, virtuous*
decem partēs dīcit   *he can do division*
oculus,-ī [m.]   *eye* ('ab oculō' = *at sight*)
legō,-ere, lēgī, lēctum [3]   *read*

4.   If your parents could afford it you probably had a tutor to yourself, or perhaps shared one with another pupil. Quintilian recommended a little competition.

doceātur alius cui invideat; contendat interim et saepius vincere sē putet: praemiīs etiam, quae capit illa aetās, ēvocētur.

Quintilian, Elements of Oratory 1.1.20

doceātur: 3rd person pres. subj. passive of 'doceō,-ēre' [2] (*teach*)
invideat: subjunctive expressing purpose, of 'invideō,-ēre' [2; + dat.] (*envy*)
contendō,-ere, contendī, contentum [3]   *compete*
interim   *sometimes*
capit: here *takes to, enjoys*
ēvocō,-āre,-āvī,-ātum [1]   *call out, bring out, encourage*

5.   Or you might share a tutor with several other families, so creating a 'school'. Pliny took a close interest in the affairs of his home town of Comum in northern Italy, where he gave money to pay for a teacher:

proximē cum in patriā meā fuī, vēnit ad mē salūtandum municipis meī fīlius praetextātus. huic ego 'studēs?' inquam. respondit: 'etiam.'
'ubī?'
'Mediolānī.'
'cūr nōn hīc?' et pater eius – erat enim ūnā atque etiam ipse addūxerat puerum: 'quia nūllōs hīc praeceptōrēs habēmus.'

Pliny, Letters 4.13

proximē   *recently*
patriā: i.e. his hometown
ad mē salūtandum   *for me to be greeted, to greet me* (i.e. pay respect as a client)
mūniceps,-ipis [m./f.]   *fellow citizen*
praetextātus,-a,-um   *wearing a toga praetexta, young* (i.e. too young to wear a full toga)
huic: dative of 'hic, haec, hoc'
studeō,-ēre, studuī [2]   *study*
inquam   *I say*
respondeō,-ēre, respondī, respōnsum [2]   *reply*
etiam   *also, even, yes*
Mediolānī: locative (Mediolānum is now Milan)
ūnā   *at the same place, together*
ipse [nom.]   *he himself*
addūcō,-ere, addūxī, adductum [3]   *lead to, bring along*
praeceptor,-ōris [m.]   *teacher, instructor*

6. A school would be small, usually only one class, and privately run by a freedman or similar. He would rent some space in the forum or busy street, and start the day early before the bustle and crowds distracted his pupils; too early for Martial:

vīcīnī somnum nōn tōtā nocte rogāmus:
    nam vigilāre leve est, pervigilāre grave est.
discipulōs dīmitte tuōs. vīs, garrule, quantum
    accipis ut clāmēs, accipere ut taceās?
Martial, Epigrams 9.68.9–12

vīcīnus,-ī [m.]   *neighbour*
somnus,-ī [m.]   *sleep*
(per)vigilō,-āre,-āvī,-ātum [1]   *be awake (all night)*
levis,-e   *light, trifling, not serious*
discipulus,-ī [m.]   *student*
dīmitte: imperative
vīs: 2nd person sing. of 'volō, velle'
garrulus,-a,-um   *chatterbox*
quantus,-a,-um   *how much*
clāmō,-āre,-āvī,-ātum [1]   *shout*
taceō,-ēre, tacuī, tacitum [2]   *be quiet, silent*
Word order for translation of the final sentence: 'vīs accipere ut taceās quantum accipis
    ut clāmēs?'

7. Parents had high expectations, and teachers, with their traditional background as slaves and freedmen, were not greatly respected.

sed vōs saevās impōnite lēgēs,
ut praeceptōrī verbōrum rēgula cōnstet,

ut legat historiās, auctōrēs nōverit omnēs
tamquam unguēs digitōsque suōs.

Juvenal, *Satires* 7.229–32

vōs: i.e. parents
impōnite: imperative of 'impōnō,-ere' (*impose*), used here with sarcasm (*go on, impose . . .*)
rēgula,-ae [f.]   *rule* ('verbōrum rēgula' = *rules of grammar*)
cōnstet [subjunctive in indirect command after 'ut']   *be established, well known*
auctor,-ōris [m.]   *author*
nōverit: perfect subjunctive of 'nōscō,-ere, nōvī, nōtum' (*come to know*)
tamquam   *as if, just as*
unguis,-is [m.]   *nail*
digitus,-ī [m.]   *finger*

8.   Teachers' fees were not always forthcoming, and annual earnings were no more than
     the prize money for a charioteer or fighter winning a single competition:

'haec,' inquit, 'cūrēs, et cum sē verterit annus,
accipe, victōrī populus quod postulat, aurum.'

Juvenal, *Satires* 7.242–3

inquit   *says (a parent)*
cūrō,-āre,-āvī,-ātum [1]   *look after, see to*
vertō,-ere, vertī, versum [3]   *turn*
accipe: imperative
quod: for its position see Reading notes of Ch.16
postulō,-āre,-āvī,-ātum [1]   *demand*
aurum,-ī [n.]   *gold*

9.   Educated slaves were put to work as teachers, copyists and secretaries. Cicero's slave
     Tiro (at some point freedman) was trusted to look after his library, and we probably have
     him to thank for the survival of so much of Cicero's work after his death. This letter to
     Tiro reveals Cicero's respect for his man's literary talent:

pangis aliquid Sophocleum? fac opus appāreat.

Cicero, *Letters to Friends and Family* 16.18

pangō,-ere, pepigī, pactum [3]   *compose*
Sophocleus,-a,-um   *in the style of Sophocles* (Athenian dramatist, fifth century BC)
fac [imperative of 'faciō,-ere']   *see that* ('ut' is understood)
appāreō,-ēre [2]   *appear*

10. Despite glimpses of more educated women in the late Republic and afterwards, the idea
     of a female holding forth with opinions on literature still raised a laugh in the second
     century AD [16.3]. Education beyond the basics remained unusual for daughters of even
     the grander families. We know that Pliny's wife enjoyed her reading; for he praised her
     taste in books (or, his own):

meōs libellōs habet, lectitat, ēdiscit etiam.

Pliny, *Letters* 4.19

lecticō,-āre,-āvī,-ātum [1]   *read repeatedly*
ēdiscō,-ere, ēdidicī [3]   *learn thoroughly*

11. Writers from Cato to Pliny warned parents to keep a close eye on their children's
    education. Some went to great lengths to get the best available. Horace's father, a modest
    but proud freedman, managed to find the fees for his son to go to a school in Rome and
    so avoid the rougher facility closer to home:

nōluit in Flāvī lūdum mē mittere, magnī
quō puerī magnīs ē centuriōnibus ortī,
sed puerum est ausus Rōmam portāre.

Horace, *Satires* 1.6.72–3,76

nōlō, nōlle, nōluī   *be unwilling* (created from 'nōn' + 'volō')
Flāvī: Flavus was the local schoolmaster
lūdus,-ī [m.]   *game, place of practice, school*
magnī . . . magnīs: tongue-in-cheek
centuriō,-ōnis [m.]   *centurion*
ortus,-a,-um   *born*
est ausus: from 'audeō,-ēre', which is deponent in the perfect, i.e. looks passive but with
    an active meaning

12. For older students time spent with a *rhetor* away from parental eyes could be pleasant
    enough. Cicero's son completed his education with *rhetores* such as Cassius and Bruttius
    in Athens, from where he writes to Tiro:

praetereā dēclāmitāre Graece apud Cassium īnstituī;
Latīnē autem apud Bruttium exercērī volō.

Cicero, *Letters to Friends and Family* 16.21

praetereā   *moreover*
dēclāmitō,-āre,-āvī,-ātum [1]   *declaim, practise declamation*
Graece   *in Greek*
apud [+ acc.]   *with*
īnstituō,-ere, īnstituī, īnstitūtum [3]   *undertake, begin*
Latīnē   *in Latin*
exercērī [passive infinitive of 'exerceō,-ēre']   *to be exercised, trained*

13. The young man was anxious to show how seriously he was taking his studies; so seriously
    that he needed help with some of the duties involved:

sed petō ā tē, ut quam celerrimē mihi librārius mittātur,
maximē quidem Graecus; multum mihi enim ēripiētur
operae in exscrībendīs hypomnēmatīs.

Cicero, *Letters to Friends and Family* 16.21

librārius,-ī [m.]   *clerk, secretary*
maximē   *especially*
mihi [dative of (dis)advantage, see p. 338]   *from me*
ēripiētur: future passive of 'ēripiō,-ere'   *(take away)*
opera,-ae [f.]   *work, effort* ('multum operae' = *much of the effort*)
in exscrībendīs hypomnēmatīs   *in writing out notes*

Exercises 19b

1.   Translate:
(a)   nihil est dulcius carmine illō.
(b)   quid servō magis convenit quam fessus labōribus esse?
(c)   lībertus, vir vīlissimus, vīllam odōre obscēnō implēvit.
(d)   Narcissus sē plūs quam ūllam deam amāvit.
(e)   quis tibi est cārior Nerōne?

2.   Identify any adverbs in each sentence, and translate:
(a)   Ītaliam nōn sponte sequor.
(b)   Augustus ipse iūs dīxit assiduē.
(c)   nōn minus līber sum quam vōs!
(d)   citius ē mundō genus hominum quam Cicerō cēdet.

3.   Give the case, number and gender of each underlined adjective, and translate:
(a)   sī **neglegentiōrēs** fuerimus, bellum in Britanniā erit.
(b)   quae mē ad **maiōra** reservō?
(c)   numquam **fōrmōsior** mihi vīsa est domina.
(d)   pars malī servī **pessima** est lingua.
(e)   Coriolānus prīmum **multō** obstinātior adversus lacrimās muliebrēs erat.

4.   Why are
(a)   'dīcat' and 'faciat' [19.1] and
(b)   'comedat' [19.2] in the subjunctive?

5.   Think of three adjectives each to describe
(a)   war (i.e. 'bellum est . . . . .')
(b)   the gods (i.e. 'deī sunt . . . . .')
(c)   yourself ('ego sum . . . . .')

6.   Find Latin words in this chapter which are related to *computer, digital, invidious, native, rodent, total* and *vile*.

— 20 —

Life at work

Past participles

Past participles are created from the fourth principal part of a verb, and have endings like the adjective **bonus,-a,-um**:

> amō, amāre, amāvī, **amātum**   (i.e. **amātus,-a,-um**)

The past participle is passive: **puella amāta** = *the loved girl, the girl who was loved.*

Like an adjective, the participle agrees with a noun or pronoun. This (pro)noun may be in any case, depending on its function in the sentence. The participle **trucīdātum** below agrees with **Servium**, which is accusative as it is the object of the verb:

> dominae <u>Servium</u> **trucīdātum** ostendit
> *s/he shows the <u>murdered Servius</u> to the mistress* [2.2]

The past participle with **est, sunt** or other part of the verb **esse** creates the perfect passive tenses. When so, the participle is always nominative while the gender and number match the subject:

> Servius **trucīdātus est**
> *Servius <u>was murdered</u>*

All past participles are passive, except those of deponent verbs.

Past participles of deponent verbs
Deponent verbs are exceptions to the above rule. Like their other forms they have a passive look but an active meaning:

> Germānōs Caesar **aggressus** maximīs affēcit clādibus
> *Caesar, <u>having attacked</u> the Germani, afflicted them with very great disasters* [7.11]

Claudiam dūxit uxōrem ac, **simultāte** cum Fulviā socrū **ortā**, dīmīsit intāctam
*he took as his wife Claudia, and <u>with animosity having arisen</u> with his mother-in-law Fulvia, he
dismissed her untouched* [10.7]

Practice 20a

1. Here are some past participles. Identify the present infinitive active
    of each verb: e.g. missus . . . **mittere**
    (a) audītus
    (b) acceptus
    (c) dictus
    (d) occīsus
    (e) ductus
    (f) inventus
    (g) āctus
    (h) dēlātus

2. Explain the case of each underlined past participle:
    (a) dictātūram mihi **dēlātam** et ā populō et ā senātū nōn recēpī.
    (b) Germānōs Caesar **aggressus** maximīs affēcit clādibus.
    (c) hominēs membra **trucīdātī** cīvis vidēre poterant.

The ablative absolute

Where the noun or pronoun in the participial phrase is *not* an integral part of the sentence,
(i.e. not the subject or object, etc), the (pro)noun and participle will be in the ablative, forming
a separate clause. This is called the ablative absolute ('absolute' = disengaged):

> **audītā vōce** gaudium fuit
> <u>*with the voice having been heard*</u> *there was joy* [4.3]
> (*after the voice of the herald had been heard* . . .)

Grammatically the sentence could function without the ablative absolute, even though it may
miss an important part of the meaning:

> gaudium fuit
> *there was joy*

See how these ablative absolutes are grammatically independent of the main body of their
sentences:

> cēterī, cum catēnātī prōdūcerentur, **imperātōre Antōniō** honōrificē **salūtātō**, hunc
> foedissimō convītiō cōram prōscidērunt
> *the rest of the prisoners, when they were brought forward in chains, <u>with the general Antony having been
> respectfully saluted</u>, this man they reviled to his face with the foulest abuse* [10.8]

Caesar, **implōrātō** Cicerōnis **testimōniō**, nē Curiō praemia darentur, effēcit
Caesar, with Cicero's evidence having been called upon, managed to prevent the payments being made to Curius [7.2]

The past participle of a deponent verb may also appear in an ablative absolute, but with an active meaning:

Caesar uxōrem, simultāte **ortā**, dīmīsit   (orior, orīrī, ortus sum = *rise, arise*)
with animosity having arisen Caesar dismissed his wife [10.7]

Practice 20b
Identify the participle in the ablative absolute in each sentence, and translate:
(a)   dīvus habēbitur Augustus adiectūs Britannīs imperiō gravibusque Persīs.
(b)   ausa est asperās serpentēs tractāre dēlīberātā morte ferōcior.

Present participles

The present participle has endings like the adjective **ingens** (see p. 89). They all except the 1st conjugation have an 'e' in the ending:

amō,-āre	habeō,-ēre	mittō,-ere	audiō,-īre	capiō,-ere
amāns	**habēns**	**mittēns**	**audiēns**	**capiēns**
amant-	habent-	mittent-	audient-	capient-

The present participle, like the past, is functionally an adjective, but differs from the past participle in three respects:

• the endings are like **ingēns**, not **bonus**
• it usually describes something happening at the same time as the main verb (not before it)
• it is active, not passive

The participle **fluēns** below is nominative agreeing with the subject ('he' or 'she'):

linquēbat habēnās ad terram nōn sponte **fluēns**
slipping involuntarily to the ground s/he let go of the reins [1.4]

(fluō,-ere [3] = *flow*)

	M/F	N
N.	**fluēns**	fluēns
A.	fluentem	fluēns
G.	fluentis	fluentis
D.	fluentī	fluentī
Ab.	fluentī/e	fluentī/e

This present participle agrees with a noun in the dative:

Caesar **Brūtō irruentī** dīxit: 'kai su teknon?'
Caesar said to Brutus rushing in: 'And you my child?' [9.4]

(irruō,-ere [3] = *rush in, attack*)

	M/F	N
N.	irruēns	irruēns
A.	irruentem	irruēns
G.	irruentis	irruentis
D.	**irruentī**	irruentī
Ab.	irruentī/e	irruentī/e

A 'present' participle is not necessarily happening 'now' as with an ordinary verb in the present tense; but at the same time as the action of the main verb. In the two examples above, she was slipping as she let go of the reins, and Brutus was rushing in as Caesar was speaking. Likewise below, the action of the present participle **profugientēs** is simultaneous with the action of the verb **adiūvit**:

Atticus familiārēs Antōniī ex urbe **profugientēs** adiūvit
Atticus helped the friends of Antony as they were fleeing from the city [10.4]

The present participle of a deponent verb has an active meaning like an ordinary verb:

iam nimis multōs audiō Corinthī et Athēnārum ōrnāmenta laudantēs **mīrantēs**que
these days I hear too many people praising and admiring the ornaments of Corinth and Athens [4.7]   (laudō,-āre = *praise*; mīror,-ārī [deponent] = *admire*)

> ### Practice 20c
> Give the principal parts of the verb behind each underlined participle, and translate:
>
> Antōnius **fugientis** rēgīnae quam **pugnantis** mīlitis suī comes esse māluit.

Present participles in ablative absolutes

Any participle may appear in an ablative absolute – present, past or future. The ablative singular of the present participle usually ends **-ī**, but if it is part of an ablative absolute it ends **-e**:

quippe indīgnātur veterī pārēre clientī
quodque aliquid poscās et quod **sē stante** recumbās
to be sure he thinks it demeaning to obey an old client and (is resentful) because you ask for something and because you recline with him standing (while he stands) [14.2]

The simple verb *to be* does not have a present participle. It is taken as understood in certain ablative phrases:

nōn Caesare et Bibulō, sed Iūliō et Caesare cōnsulibus
not in the consulship of Caesar and Bibulus but of Julius and Caesar
(lit. *not with Caesar and Bibulus being consuls but Julius and Caesar*) [7.7]

fēminā duce
under a woman as leader
(lit. *with a woman being leader*) [23.8]

Participles with dependent nouns

A participle functions like an adjective but it also retains properties of a verb. The participles
below have dependent nouns or objects:

nōbīs **rem pūblicam**
gubernantibus, nōnne togae arma
cessērunt?
*with us governing the Republic did not
arms give way to the toga?* [6.9]

(gubernō,-āre [1] = *govern*)

pl.	M/F	N
N.	gubernantēs	gubernantia
A.	gubernantēs	gubernantia
G.	gubernantium	gubernantium
D.	gubernantibus	gubernantibus
Ab.	**gubernantibus**	gubernantibus

Antōnium, **condiciōnēs pācis**
temptantem, ad mortem adēgit
he drove Antony, (who was) proposing conditions of peace, to his death [11.9]

trecentī ad āram **Dīvō Iūliō** extructam mactātī sunt
three hundred men were sacrificed at an altar constructed for Divine Julius [10.11]

Practice 20d

Fill each gap with the present participle, and translate:

(a)   quis cīvēs ē urbe .... {fugiō,-ere} adiuvābit?

(b)   taurus poētam epistulam .... {scrībō,-ere} vīdit.

(c)   nōnne nōs fēlīcēs sumus Augustō rem pūblicam ....
     {gubernō,-āre}?

Future participles

The future participle is active, with endings like **bonus,-a,-um**. It looks like the past
participle except for the extra syllable **-ūr-** just before the ending, e.g. **vīsūrus, vīsūra,
vīsūrum** *(about to see)*.

amō,-āre	habeō,-ēre	mittō,-ere	audiō,-īre	capiō,-ere
amātūrus	**habitūrus**	**missūrus**	**audītūrus**	**captūrus**

The verb *to be* may not have a present participle in Latin, but it does have a future one. In fact it has given English the word *future*: **futūrus,-a,-um** = *about to be*.

As with the present and past participles, the timing of a future participle is governed by its relation to the main verb. A future participle refers to something which will happen at some point *after* the action of the main verb (while the present participle is *simultaneous* and the past participle happens *before* it):

> illa **peritūrae** īgnōscit Elissae
> *she forgives Elissa (who is) about to die* [16.3]

> ā philosophiā eum māter āvertit monēns **imperātūrō** contrāriam esse
> *his mother turned him away from philosophy advising it to be counter-productive for one about to rule* [17.11]

Every now and then a present participle is used where you might expect a past one:

> Hylan pantomīmum, **querente praetōre**, in ātriō domūs suae flagellīs verberāvit
> *as the praetor was complaining, he had Hylas, the pantomime artist, beaten with whips in the atrium of his own home* [20.8]

Strictly speaking the complaints of the praetor must have arisen before the punishment, not at the same time.

Practice 20e
Fill each gap with the future participle, and translate:
(a) nōs .... {pereō, perīre} nōn tē timēmus.
(b) Clōdia in amphitheātrō sedēbat gladiātōrēs .... {videō,-ēre}.
(c) omnēs Brūtum filiōs .... {occīdō,-ere} spectābant.

Participles as nouns
In the example with **imperātūrō** above, no noun appears with the participle.
Like an adjective a participle can stand alone, with the person or thing implied:

> cūncta plēbs Catilīnae **incepta** probābat
> *all the ordinary people approved of the things begun of Catiline (Catiline's initiatives)* [6.5]

Summary: participles

Participles are adjectives created from verbs. They can be present (**amāns, amant-**), future (**amātūrus,-a,-um**) or past (**amātus,-a,-um**). Present and future participles are active, while past participles are passive (with the exception of deponent verbs).

Practice 20f

Translate:

(a) Britannīs imperiō adiectīs dux ad urbem discessit.
(b) prīmum venit Discordia, Bellōnā sequente.
(c) obscēnō strepitū audītō agricola servum ē vīllā fugāvit.
(d) ego secūtus in Graeciam nōn dēseram Pompēium.

Translating participles

The different ways we might translate participles were introduced on p. 51. Sometimes we can translate them literally, and they transfer comfortably enough into English:

> iam nimis multōs audiō Corinthī et Athēnārum ōrnāmenta **laudantēs mīrantēs**que
> *these days I hear too many people <u>praising</u> and <u>admiring</u> the ornaments of Corinth and Athens* [4.7]

> servus, ut praemium **prōmissum** indicī habēret, manūmissus est
> *the slave was freed so that he might have the reward <u>promised</u> to an informer* [5.10]

But if a literal translation seems awkward there are other ways to translate them, depending on the context ('while . . .', 'after . . .', 'when . . .', 'once . . .', 'who . . .', 'which . . .', 'because . . .', 'although . . .' and more). Some participles may be translated as an additional main verb:

> cohortēs **decimātās** hordeō pāvit
> <u>*he decimated*</u> *the troops and fed them with barley*
> (lit. *he fed the having-been-decimated troops with barley*)   [12.12]

Or even as a noun:

> nōbīs rem pūblicam **gubernantibus**, nōnne togae arma cessērunt?
> *during our <u>leadership</u> of the Republic did not arms give way to the toga?* [6.9]

This sentence quoted earlier in the chapter might be translated in different ways:

> Caesar, **implōrātō** Cicerōnis **testimōniō**, nē Curiō praemia darentur, effēcit
> *Caesar, after Cicero's evidence had been called upon, managed to . . .*
> *After appealing for Cicero's evidence, Caesar managed to . . .*
> *Caesar appealed for Cicero's evidence and managed to . . .*

Practice 20g

1. Translate and include 'while . . .':
   nōbīs rem pūblicam gubernantibus, nōnne togae arma cessērunt?
2. Translate and include 'after . . .':
   audītā vōce praecōnis gaudium fuit.
3. Translate and include 'although . . .':
   (a) Graecia capta ferum victōrem cēpit.
   (b) dictātūram mihi dēlātam nōn recēpī.
4. Translate and include 'who . . .' or 'which . . .':
   vix hominēs sine lacrimīs intuērī trucīdātī membra cīvis poterant.

Latin has no active past participle (except deponents), only passive ones. English on the other hand does have an active past participle, and if the passive seems heavy in English, then you can switch to the active, provided you keep the meaning:

Caesar, **implōrātō** Cicerōnis testimōniō, . . .
(lit. *Caesar, with the evidence of Cicero <u>having been called upon</u>, . . .*)
Caesar, <u>having called upon</u> the evidence of Cicero, . . . [7.2]

Vocabulary 20

Find eight past participles which appear in the readings of Chapter 7, and four present participles which appear in the readings of Chapter 11. Identify the principal parts of each verb.

Look online for more participles which appear in the course (see p. 393).

These two verbs share the same past participle (and perfect stem). We have a similarly eccentric sharing in English with the use of *been* in *to go* and *to be*:

> sufferō, sufferre, **sustulī, sublātum**   *suffer*
> tollō,-ere, **sustulī, sublātum**   *raise, elevate, do away with*

Exercises 20a

1. Translate:
(a) fīliī Brūtī ad pālum dēligātī sunt.
(b) Cicerō epistulā Atticī acceptā forum relīquit.
(c) nimis multōs audiō Clōdiam mīrantēs.
(d) Cloeliam, puellīs ad propinquōs restitūtīs, omnēs cīvēs laudāvērunt.

(e)   agricola servō ē silvā retractō flagellum quaesiit.
(f)   vōce cōnsulis audītā omnēs tacuērunt.
(g)   testāmentīs mūtātīs clientēs frūstrā manēbant.

2.   Identify the case, gender and number of each underlined participle, and say whether it is part of an ablative absolute:
(a)   **scissā gaudēns** vādit Discordia pallā.
(b)   Caesar, socerō generōque **suffrāgantibus**, Galliās ēlēgit.
(c)   tū calcās lūce **reversā** coniugis ūrīnam magnōs **vīsūrus** amīcōs.

3.   Give the principal parts of each verb whose participle is underlined, and translate:
(a)   **audītā** vōce praecōnis gaudium fuit.
(b)   frūgēsne in Graeciā **inventae** sunt?
(c)   corpus Caesaris in terrā **iacēns** vīdimus.
(d)   senātōrēs tribūnum ē forō **fugientem** occīdērunt.
(e)   Clōdiō **mortuō** Cicerō erat laetus.

Life at work

Men and women from poorer backgrounds worked as bakers, bath attendants, blacksmiths, builders, butchers, innkeepers, laundresses, midwives, nurses, shopkeepers, toolmakers and in all the other inevitable occupations. There is precious little about ordinary people in the literature, which was mostly written by and for the upper class. There are glimpses in writers like Plautus, Petronius and Martial, and brief cameos of daily chores in the imagery of poets, but much of what we know about the day-to-day lives of the majority of people has come to light from the study of archaeology.

The careers of higher-ranking Roman males were narrowed to law, military duty and government. They left it to slaves and freedmen to work as accountants, architects, artists, doctors, engineers, librarians and teachers. Women from wealthier families did not follow careers in business or politics, but managed the **familia**, which included all the slaves and other dependants as well as the immediate family.

Reading notes

Here are typical contractions of 1st conjugation verbs like **amō,-āre**:

repudiāsset for **repudiāvisset** [7.4] (repudiō,-āre)
nōminārit for **nōmināverit** [15.11] (nōminō,-āre)
putāstī for **putāvistī** [15.15] (putō,-āre)
iūrārunt for **iūrāvērunt** [20.9] (iūrō,-āre)
vocāssēs for **vocāvissēs** [21.13] (vocō,-āre)
appellāstī for **appellāvistī** [22.10] (appellō,-āre)

1.   During the early Republican period senators performed duties as magistrates, judges, diplomats, military officers and priests – and also farmed their own land.

in agrīs erant tum senātōrēs.

Cicero, On Old Age 16.56

tum   then, in those times

2.   Commercial activity was thought to be demeaning for senators, and they were discouraged from involvement in business. In 218 BC the consul Gaius Flaminius made himself unpopular by supporting a law which denied senators the opportunity to make money from trade overseas. No ship could carry more than 300 amphoras:

id satis habitum est ad frūctūs ex agrīs vectandōs. quaestus omnis patribus indecōrus vīsus.

Livy, History of Rome 21.63

satis   enough
habitum est: habeō,-ēre can mean consider, deem, as here
frūctus,-ūs [m.]   fruit, produce
ad frūctūs ex agrīs vectandōs   for produce to be transported from (their own) estates
quaestus,-ūs [m.]   profit, business
indecōrus,-a,-um   unseemly, unbecoming
vīsus: understand 'est'

3.   Senators had other opportunities for self-enrichment: spoils of war, backhanders in office, other gifts and revenues. A guest at Trimalchio's dinner grumbles about a crooked magistrate:

sed quārē nōs habēmus aedīlem trium cauniārum, quī sibi māvult assem quam vītam nostram. itaque domī gaudet, plūs in diē nummōrum accipit, quam alter patrimōnium habet. iam sciō, unde accēperit dēnāriōs mīlle aureōs. sed sī nōs cōleōs habērēmus, nōn tantum sibi placēret.

Petronius, Satyricon 44

quārē   why
aedīlis,-is [m.]   aedile (superintendent of public works)
cauniae,-ārum [f.]   figs
trium cauniārum: genitive of value (worth three figs)
māvult   s/he prefers
as, assis [m.]   penny, copper coin
itaque   and so
domī   at home
gaudeō,-ēre [2]   rejoice
nummus,-ī [m.]   coin (pl. money)
alter [nom.]   another (person)
patrimōnium: (as) an inheritance
accēperit: perfect subjunctive
cōleus,-ī [m.]   sack, scrotum
sī nōs cōleōs habērēmus   if we had any balls

tantum   *so much, so greatly*
placēret [placeō,-ēre]   *it would be pleasing*

4. Many senators sidestepped the indignity of commerce by employing business agents to act on their behalf. Some amassed huge fortunes, from estate-farming (no ships needed) as well as construction and import/export. By Cicero's time, making money from commerce was all right, provided you made a lot of it.

mercātūra autem, sī tenuis est, sordida putanda est; sīn magna et cōpiōsa, nōn est vituperanda. omnium autem rērum ex quibus aliquid acquīritur, nihil est agrī cultūrā melius, nihil ūberius, nihil dulcius, nihil homine līberō dignius.

Cicero, On Duties 1.151

mercātūra,-ae [f.]   *trade, business*
tenuis,-e   *insignificant*
putandus,-a,-um   *to be thought, to be reckoned*
sīn   *but if*
cōpiōsus,-a,-um   *abundant*
vituperandus,-a,-um   *to be disparaged*
acquīrō,-ere, acquīsīvī, acquīsītum [3]   *obtain*
cultūra,-ae [f.]   *tilling, cultivation*
ūber   *fruitful, productive*
dignus,-a,-um [+ abl.]   *worthy of*

5. The cherished memory of citizens farming their own land lived long in people who themselves left the business of getting hands dirty to others. Cato tried and failed to resist advancing sophistication and the relaxation of old-fashioned virtues, but he remained a symbol of the good old days. He was once asked what he thought was the best occupation:

'bene pāscere'; quid secundum: 'satis bene pāscere'; quid tertium: 'male pāscere'; quid quārtum: 'arāre'; et cum ille, quī quaesierat, dīxisset: 'quid faenerārī?', tum Catō: 'quid hominem,' inquit, "occīdere?"

Cicero, On Duties 2.89

pāscō,-ere, pāvī, pāstum [3]   *raise livestock*
secundus,-a,-um   *following, second*
tertius,-a,-um   *third*
quārtus,-a,-um   *fourth*
arō,-āre,-āvī,-ātum [1]   *plough, grow crops*
faenerāror,-ārī   *lend money*

6. The fantasy of rural life is a frequent theme in literature, not least in ancient Rome, even if its charms lived largely in the imagination of city-dwellers. Farming was a tough business. Its hardships were faced by gangs of slaves and by hired workers. Varro offered practical advice for the deployment of staff:

neque enim senēs neque puerī callium difficultātem ac montium arduitātem atque asperitātem facile ferunt.

Varro, On Agriculture 2.10.3

senex,-is [m.]   *old man*
callis,-is [f.]   *footpath*
difficultās,-tātis [f.]   *difficulty*
callium, montium: genitive plurals
arduitās,-tātis [f.]   *steepness*
asperitās,-tātis [f.]   *unevenness*
ferō, ferre, tulī, lātum   *carry, bear, endure*

7. The influx of conquered but resourceful Greeks, with their much-prized cultural background, provoked an inferiority complex which writers often touch upon. Juvenal grumbles that locals are displaced or outshone by cleverer immigrants:

grammaticus, rhētor, geometrēs, pictor, alīptēs, augur, schoenobatēs, medicus, magus, omnia nōvit Graeculus ēsuriēns.

Juvenal, Satires 3.76–8

geometrēs,-ae [m.*]   *geometrician, surveyor*
pictor, pictōris [m.]   *painter*
alīptēs,-ae [m.*]   *masseur*
augur,-ūris [m.]   *soothsayer*
schoenobatēs,-ae [m.*]   *rope-dancer, tightrope artist*
medicus,-ī [m.]   *doctor*
magus,-ī [m.]   *sorcerer*
nōvit: the perfect of 'nōscō,-ere' *(come to know) = know*
Graeculus: the diminutive suffix '-ulus' could be affectionate or sneery
ēsuriō,-īre [4]   *be hungry, ravenous*
* nouns borrowed from Greek (nom. -ēs, acc. -ēn, gen. -ae, dat. -ae, abl. -ē)

8. Actors were often Greek, and so too singers, athletes and performers of various kinds. As elsewhere, actors might become stars and celebrities. But the traditional Roman viewed them as dodgy sorts. Hylas, a comic actor, provoked the displeasure of Augustus:

Hylan pantomīmum, querente praetōre, in ātriō domūs suae nēmine exclūsō flagellīs verberāvit.

Suetonius, Life of Augustus 45

Hylan [acc.]:   *Hylas* (a Greek name)
pantomīmus,-ī [m.]   *pantomime artist*
queror, querī [deponent, but its present participle works as any other]   *complain*
praetor,-ōris [m.]   *praetor, magistrate*
ātrium,-ī [n.]   *hall*
suae: normally refers to the subject but here to 'Hylas' (see p. 290)
nēmō,-inis   *no one*
exclūdō,-ere, exclūsī, exclūsum [3]   *shut out, exclude*
nēmine exclūsō: i.e. everyone was watching
verberō,-āre,-āvī,-ātum [1]   *beat, whip* (it is unlikely he did it himself, so *'had him whipped'*)

9. Pliny the Elder (the letter-writing Pliny's uncle) recorded a warning from Cato to his son to avoid Greek doctors:

iūrārunt inter sē barbarōs necāre omnēs medicīnā. nōs quoque dictitant barbarōs. interdīxī tibi dē medicīs.

Pliny the Elder, *Natural History* 29.14

iūrārunt = iūrāvērunt (iūrō,-āre [1] = *swear*)
inter sē: they have sworn amongst each other, i.e. conspired
barbarus,-ī [m.]   *foreigner* (i.e. non-Greeks, including Romans)
medicīna,-ae [f.]   *medicine, treatment*
dictitō,-āre,-āvī,-ātum [1]   *say often, call*
interdīcō,-ere, interdīxī, interdictum [3; + dat.]   *banish, forbid*

10. By Martial's time medical services were well established. He once found himself (or imagined himself) at the mercy of a doctor and his crowd of students.

languēbam: sed tū comitātus prōtinus ad mē
    vēnistī centum, Symmache, discipulīs.
centum mē tetigēre manūs aquilōne gelātae:
    nōn habuī febrem, Symmache, nunc habeō.

Martial, *Epigrams* 5.9

langueō,-ēre [2]   *feel weak*
prōtinus   *immediately, at once*
comitātus,-a,-um   *attended*
Symmachus: a doctor
tangō,-ere, tetigī, tāctum [3]   *touch* ('tetigēre' = 'tetigērunt')
aquilō,-ōnis [m.]   *north wind*
gelō,-āre,-āvī,-ātum [1]   *freeze, chill*
febris,-is [f.]   *fever*

Exercises 20b

1. Why are
(a) 'accēperit' [20.3] and
(b) 'dīxisset' [20.5] in the subjunctive?

2. Give the case, gender and number of each underlined participle:
(a) Lāocoōn **ardēns** summā dēcurrit ab arce.
(b) servus, ut praemium **prōmissum** indicī habēret, manūmissus est.
(c) Augustus aedēs sacrās vetustāte **collāpsās** refēcit.
(d) Caesar Catullum **satisfacientem** eādem diē adhibuit cēnae.
(e) tum Trōiānus caput **ōrantis** nēquīquam dēturbat terrae.
(f) timeō Danaōs et dōna **ferentīs**.
(g) ā philosophiā eum māter āvertit **monēns imperātūrō** contrāriam esse.

3. Translate, and include the English word in brackets:
(a) nātōs pater nova bella moventēs ad poenam vocābit.   (*because*)
(b) Tiberiī Gāīque et Claudiī ac Nerōnis rēs flōrentibus ipsīs ob metum falsae compositae sunt.   (*while*)

4. Identify two ablative absolutes in this sentence, and translate:

Caesar Hylan pantomīmum, querente praetōre, in ātriō domūs suae nēmine exclūsō flagellīs verberāvit.

5. Fill each gap with two words, one of them a participle:
(a) Cleopātra .... {*after dismissing the slaves*} venēnum bibit. (dīmittō,- ere, dīmīsī, dīmissum = *dismiss*)
(b) ō domine, ... {*after attending you*} nunc aliquid ex tē exspectō. (sequor, sequī, secūtus [deponent] = *attend, follow*)
(c) ō Clōdia, ego .... {*Caelius sitting*} in tuō lectō vīdī. (sedeō,-ēre, sēdī, sessum = *sit*)

6. Translate:

ō puer, dīc mihi quī salūtātōrēs adsint?
— advēnērunt pictor, rhētor, tōnsor, cōpō, poēta, pantomīmus et duo medicī.
heu! dīmitte omnēs quam celerrimē praeter medicōs. tē moritūrus iubeō.

— 21 —

Life at leisure

Conditional clauses

A conditional clause (i.e. an 'if' clause) is introduced by **sī** (*if*) or **nisi/nī** (*unless*)

> flet **sī** lacrimās cōnspexit amīcī
> *he weeps if he has seen the tears of a friend* [4.12]

> nec minus līber sum quam vōs, etiam **sī** pauperem pater mē relīquit
> *I am no less a free man than yourselves, even if my father did leave me a pauper* [18.13]

Where in English we use a present tense, or what appears to be a present tense, Latin often uses the future or future perfect:

> sī **dīxeris** 'aestuo,' sūdat
> *if you say (will have said) 'I am hot,' he sweats* [4.12]

> **sī** ponticulum **trānsierimus**, omnia armīs agenda erunt
> *if we cross the little bridge, everything will have to be resolved by armed conflict* [8.6]

Practice 21a
Translate:
(a) sī lacrimās tuās cōnspexerō, ego ipse nōn flēbō.
(b) sī domum vēnerō, cēnam meam afferam.
(c) Caesar sī Antōnium vīcerit, dominus mundī erit.

Conditional clauses with the subjunctive
The verb in the conditional clause is indicative if it represents something which is possible, which could happen or has happened, as in the examples above.

But if a conditional is hypothetical and impossible to fulfil, or unlikely and implausible, then the subjunctive is used:

nūllī sē dīcit mulier mea nūbere mālle / quam mihi, nōn sī sē Iuppiter ipse **petat**
my girl says that she prefers to marry no one other than me, not even if Jupiter himself <u>were to ask</u> her
[15.8]

The present subjunctive refers to something unlikely to happen in the future, the imperfect subjunctive to something that might be happening now (but is not) and the pluperfect to something in the past (again hypothetical and imaginary):

sī tamen aut vēlōcitāte equōrum aut hominum arte **traherentur, esset** ratiō nōn nūlla
however, if <u>they were attracted</u> by the speed of the horses or by the skill of the men, <u>there would be</u> some justification (in watching the races) [21.11]

sī gladiātōrēs dēcrepitōs **sufflāssēs, cecidissent**
if you <u>had blown</u> upon the decrepit gladiators, they <u>would have fallen down</u> [21.9]

The subjunctive is used in both clauses. The pluperfect subjunctive in a conditional is usually translated *if X had . . ., Y would have. . .*:

Domine, sī **fuissēs** hīc, nōn **esset mortuus** frāter meus
Master, if you <u>had been</u> here, my brother <u>would</u> not <u>have died</u> [26.5]

Practice 21b
Translate:
(a)   sī omnēs taurōs fugiās, īnsānus sīs.
(b)   taurus sī fugāvisset vōs cēpisset.
(c)   sī ego Marius essem, omnēs senātōrēs contemnerem.

Conditionals mixing subjunctive and indicative
Regular conditionals have both verbs, the main verb and the verb in the if-clause, in the same mood, i.e. indicative or subjunctive. A few bend this rule and have one verb in the indicative and the other in the subjunctive, mixing an open statement with something hypothetical or implausible for a particular effect. Below, the indicative **eris** (*you will be*) gives Marcellus a stronger presence in life. The regular construction would have **sīs** (*if you were to . . . . you would be . . .*)

heu, miserande puer, **sī** quā fāta aspera **rumpās**, / tū Mārcellus **eris**
alas, pitiable boy, if by some way you <u>were to break</u> the harsh fates, you <u>will be</u> Marcellus [14.13]

Unless and *if not*

Nisi and **nī** mean *unless* or *if not*:

> **nisi** mē frūstrantur oculī, māter tibi coniūnxque et līberī adsunt
> *unless my eyes deceive me, your mother, wife and children are here* [17.2]

Sī nōn is also used, to negate a particular word or idea:

> ego autem **sī** causās **nōn** agō, in domūsiōnem tamen litterās didicī
> *now if I do not practise law myself, I have nonetheless learned literature for use at home* [21.1]

Nisi, which means *except* as well as *unless*, typically provides a qualification or exception to the main statement:

> malum; **nisi** peius est haec sufferre et perpetī
> *bad, yes; except suffering and enduring these (losses) is worse* [3]

Practice 21c

Translate:
(a) ō domina, poēta nōn aliam quam tē dūcet uxōrem, nōn sī Venus ipsa sē petat.
(b) ō domina, poēta nōn aliam quam tē dūcet uxōrem, nisi Venus ipsa sē petat.

Translating conditionals

In English we use *were* or what appears to be a past tense to express an impossible present or implausible future conditional:

> *if I were as rich as you, I'd retire tomorrow*
> *if they came/were to come to the beach with us there would be no room in the tent*

The partitive genitive

The 'partitive' genitive is so called because it is used to describe a part of something. In English we do not always need to translate this with *of* :

> **quid** ille nōbīs **bonī** fēcit?
> *what good* (lit. *what of good*) *has that man done for us?* [21.9]

> mīror tot **mīlia virōrum** cupere currentēs equōs vidēre
> *I am surprised that so many thousands of men want to see galloping horses* [21.11]

> **quid** enim **dēlectātiōnis** habent sescentī mūlī?
> *for what pleasure* (lit. *what of pleasure*) *do six hundred mules bring?* [21.2]

The partitive question (*What bit of . . . ?*) in **quid dēlectātiōnis** above is quite emphatic: not the slightest pleasure. The word appears again below, this time without a partitive genitive and more along the lines of the English expression:

> **quae** potest hominī esse polītō **dēlectātiō**?
> *what pleasure can there be for a person of refinement?* [21.5]

Irregular verbs: volō, nōlō, mālō

Nōlō (*I am unwilling, do not wish*) is a combination of the negative with **volō**, and **mālō** (*I prefer, wish rather*) of **magis** with **volō**:

infinitive	**velle**	**nōlle**	**mālle**
	to wish	*to be unwilling*	*to prefer*
I . . .	**volō**	**nōlō**	**mālō**
you [s.] *. . .*	**vīs**	**nōn vīs**	**māvīs**
s/he, it . . .	**vult**	**nōn vult**	**māvult**
we . . .	**volumus**	**nōlumus**	**mālumus**
you [pl.] *. . .*	**vultis**	**nōn vultis**	**māvultis**
they . . .	**volunt**	**nōlunt**	**mālunt**

The future endings of all three are **-am, -ēs, -et**, etc.
The imperfect endings are **volēbam, nōlēbam, mālēbam**, etc.
The perfect endings are **voluī, nōluī, māluī**, etc.

> **nōluit** in Flāvī lūdum mē mittere
> *he did not want to send me to Flavus' school* [19.11]

> **māvīs**, Rūfe, cocum scindere quam leporem
> *Rufus, you prefer to cut up the cook than the hare* [18.1]

> **vīs**, garrule, quantum / accipis ut clāmēs, accipere ut taceās?
> *are you willing, you chatterbox, to receive as much as you receive to make this din – to shut up?* [19.6]

Irregular verb: fīō

The verb **fīō** (*become, be made, happen, come to pass, be*) stands for the passive of **faciō,-ere** (*make*). It has only a present, future and imperfect. The perfect tenses are represented by **factus** with **sum** etc, the perfect passive of **faciō,-ere**.

> deus **fīō**
> *I am becoming a god* [24.16]

present
fīō
fīs
fit
fīmus
fītis
fīunt

The future is **fīam, fīēs, fīet**, etc, and the imperfect **fīēbam, fīēbās**, etc. The present infinitive **fierī** (*to be, become, be done*) is common:

aliquis dē dīs nōn trīstibus optat / sīc **fierī** turpis
one of the cheery gods desires <u>to become</u> thus disgraced [24.5]

Vocabulary 21
Words with fixed endings are sometimes called 'particles'. These include prepositions, adverbs, conjunctions (**aut, et, sed, sī, ut**, etc), enclitics and exclamations.

Enclitics	Exclamations
-ne introduces a question	**ecce** *look, see*
-que *and* (**-que . . . -que** = *both . . . and*)	**ēheu** *oh no, alas!*
-ve *or* (**-ve . . . -ve** = *either . . . or*)	**hercle** (**hercule**) *indeed, by Hercules!*
	heu *oh! alas!*
Conjunctions which appear in conditionals	**immō** *on the contrary, by no means, no, to be more accurate*
nī *unless, if not*	
nisi *unless, if not, except*	**pol** *indeed, truly, by Pollux!*
seu . . . seu (**sīve . . . sīve**) *whether . . . or*	**vae** *alas, oh dear*
sī *if*	
sīn *but if*	
-ve *or* (enclitic, like '-que')	

One common verb which has not appeared in the course readings is **habitō,-āre** [1], which means *to live* as in to live somewhere, to dwell, whereas **vīvō,-ere** [3] usually means *to live* in the sense of being alive.

Look online for a review of 1st declension nouns which appear in the course (see p. 393).

Exercises 21a
1.   Translate:
(a)   ēheu, sī līber essem, in tuā vīllā nōn habitārem.
(b)   vīsne, ō Lesbia, mihi convīctor fierī? — immō, hodiē cum Caeliō discumbere mālō.
(c)   patrōnusne mē audiat, sī ego canam?
(d)   quis in Britanniā Galliāve habitāre vult?
(e)   sī nōbīs sunt tantī amīcī, nōn est dēspērandum.
(f)   ecce, sī illud flūmen trānsieris, castra hostium vidēbis.
(g)   Porsenna urbem Rōmam cēpisset, nī ūnus vir fuisset, Horātius Cōcles.
(h)   mī fīlī, sī medicus ille ad tē languentem veniat, eum dīmitte!

2. Identify the tense and mood (indicative or subjunctive) of each underlined verb, and translate:
(a) ō miser, sī ad cēnam **veniās**, aliquod vīnum affer!
(b) ego, si mē invītāvissēs, nōn **vēnissem**.
(c) Antōnius, si verba Cicerōnis audiat, **sūdet**.
(d) ēheu cūr mē **fugās** velut taurus?
(e) Carthāgō hercule, sī Hannibal Rōmam **vīcisset**, nunc domina mundī **esset**.

3. Fill each gap with the correct Latin word:
(a) ō Discordia, ... {*may you be absent*}!
(b) ō rēgīna, sī meum carmen audīveris, vix lacrimās tenēre .... {*you will be able*}
(c) patrōnus, sī quem clientem ornamenta Athēnārum laudantem .... {*he had heard*}, ē vīllā .... {*he would have chased*}.

Life at leisure

1. The question of how a man should live his days was a popular topic of discussion among those with the freedom and time to discuss it. The majority of people had precious little *otium* (free time). Their daily routine would be a long list of chores. Men like Cicero and Pliny would spend their leisure time reading and writing (or hearing and dictating). Anyone with the ease to devote himself to the study of literature or philosophy was considered a man fulfilled. Such learning, or the appearance of it, was a token of respectability. By Nero's time, Trimalchio, the fictional freedman who had done very well for himself, presented his credentials thus:

> **Reading notes**
> Enclitic particles (**-que**, **-ne** and **-ve**) are treated as additional syllables with regard to stress accent, e.g. **meliúsve** [22.6]. For more on stress and pronunciation see p. 352, and on reading verse p. 393.

ego autem sī causās nōn agō, in domūsiōnem tamen litterās didicī. et nē mē putēs studia fastīdītum, duās bybliothēcās habeō, ūnam Graecam, alteram Latīnam.

Petronius, Satyricon 48

non causās agō   *I do not plead cases*, i.e. *practise law*
in domūsiōnem   *for domestic purposes, for use at home*
tamen   *yet at least, nonetheless*
discō, discere, didicī [3]   *learn*
fastīdītus,-a,-um   *despising, disdainful of*
bybliothēca,-ae [f.]   *library*

2. Public theatre had a lively tradition in Italy, if never reaching the heights of the classical Athenian drama of Aeschylus, Euripides and Sophocles. People flocked to watch farces, mimes and plays, which fed on Greek precedents in a vigorous fusion of the two cultures. For the discerning, this entertainment was too rough and low-brow. They avoided the

noisy populous theatres and preferred to hear readings of Greek plays or Latin imitations within their own homes. Ironically the Greek plays they prized so much had derived much of their strength from a universal appeal across the community. But popular plays in Italy were too showy for the refined tastes of someone like Cicero:

quid enim dēlectātiōnis habent sescentī mūlī in
Clytaemnēstrā?

Cicero, Letters to Friends and Family 7.1.2

dēlectātiō,-ōnis [f.]   delight, pleasure
sescentī,-ae,-a   six hundred
mūlus,-ī [m.]   mule
Clytaemnēstra: the title of the play, named after the wife of Agamemnon, who led the
   Greeks against Troy

3.   The comedies of Plautus and Terence were modelled on Greek originals. Terence was more conscious of his literary models and for a while his adaptations of Greek plays were better received in private houses than public theatres. In 160 BC he experienced a miserable first night for his play *The Mother-in-Law*, and so he added a new prologue to the second attempt five years later:

Hecyram ad vōs referō, quam mihi per silentium
numquam agere licitumst: ita eam oppressit calamitās.

Terence, The Mother-in-Law, Second Prologue

hecyra,-ae [f.]   mother-in-law (title of the play)
licitum (e)st   it was allowed
opprimō,-ere, oppressī, oppressum [3]   crush, overwhelm
calamitās,-tātis [f.]   mischief, misfortune

4.   Those who disdained public theatres still had a taste for the violence you would expect in an amphitheatre. At their dinner parties they would hear readings which were invariably more bloodthirsty than the Greek plays they were modelled on. In Seneca's *Oedipus*, at the point Oedipus realizes he has killed his father and married his mother, the Roman author doesn't let symbolism stand in the way of guts and gore:

rigat ōra foedus imber et lacerum caput
largum revulsīs sanguinem vēnīs vomit.

Seneca, Oedipus 978–9

rigō,-āre,-āvī,-ātum [1]   soak
ōs, ōris [n.]   face, facial feature
foedus,-a,-um   foul
imber,-bris [m.]   shower
lacer,-era,-erum   mutilated
largus,-a,-um   abundant

revellō,-ere, revellī, revulsum [3]   *pull, tear*
sanguis,-inis [m.]   *blood*
vēna,-ae [f.]   *vein*
vomō,-ere, vomuī, vomitum [3]   *pour forth*

5.   The amphitheatre is perhaps the most strikingly unpleasant feature of ancient Rome. In these infamous arenas, built all over the empire, gladiators, slaves, prisoners and social miscreants died horrible deaths in front of wildly applauding spectators. Derived from funeral rites, the shows presented beasts eating humans and animals slaughtered in 'hunts'. Criminals were routinely executed, gladiators fought duels, and even sea battles were enacted in flooded arenas. Traders grew rich from importing lions, bears, bulls, elephants and all sorts of other animals into Rome. Some animals fought each other, a bull against a bear perhaps, while others were drawn against human challengers, whose prospects were somewhere between poor (armed fighters) and certain death (prisoners and criminals).

sed quae potest hominī esse polītō dēlectātiō, cum aut
homō imbēcillus ā valentissimā bēstiā laniātur, aut
praeclāra bēstia vēnābulō trānsverberātur?

Cicero, *Letters to Friends and Family* 7.1.3

polītus,-a,-um   *refined*
imbēcillus,-a,-um   *weak*
valēns   *powerful*
bēstia,-ae [f.]   *beast*
laniō,-āre,-āvī,-ātum [1]   *mangle, tear in pieces*
praeclārus,-a,-um   *magnificent*
vēnābulum,-ī [n.]   *hunting spear*
trānsverberō,-āre,-āvī,-ātum [1]   *transfix*

6.   The inhumanity of the amphitheatre seemed largely lost on the moralists of the time. Many thought these games were distasteful, but few had sympathy for the victims. One reason for this insensitivity may have been the long-standing practice of dramatic criticism to measure artistic quality by its moral impact upon an audience. This had been central to Aristotle's criticism of drama, and remained influential long after him, with a wider application to shows and spectacles of all kinds. Thus there was discussion of the rights and wrongs of the amphitheatre, but it had very little to do with the suffering of the participants. The principal question was its value as a spectacle:

nihil vērō tam damnōsum bonīs mōribus quam in aliquō
spectāculō dēsidēre.

Seneca, *Moral Epistles* 7.2

damnōsus,-a,-um   *harmful*
spectāculum,-ī [n.]   *spectator's seat, seat at a show, show*
dēsideō,-ēre, dēsēdī, dēsessum [2]   *sit idly*

7. There was no end to the slaughter. A man deserved to die in the arena if he himself was a killer, but who deserved to watch it?

quia occīdit ille, meruit ut hoc paterētur; tū quid meruistī miser, ut hoc spectēs? 'occīde, verberā, ūre! quārē tam timide incurrit in ferrum? quārē parum audācter occīdit? quārē parum libenter moritur?' intermissum est spectāculum: 'interim iugulentur hominēs, nē nihil agātur.'

Seneca, Moral Epistles 7.5

mereō,-ēre, meruī, meritum [2]   *deserve*
paterētur: imperfect subjunctive of 'patior, patī' (*suffer*)
spectō,-āre,-āvī,-ātum [1]   *watch*
ūrō,-ere [3]   *burn*
incurrō,-ere [3]   *run (into or on to), attack*
ferrum,-ī [n.]   *iron, blade*
parum   *not . . . enough*
audācter   *boldly*
libenter   *willingly*
intermissum est   *(it) has an interval*
iugulō,-āre,-āvī,-ātum [1]   *cut the throat*

8. The games were sponsored by local dignitaries keen to earn popular favour. Below, Trimalchio's dinner guests discuss the merits of different shows. Someone called Glyco has donated his steward, a slave, to be fed to wild beasts, for sleeping with his wife.

Titus habet mulierem essedāriam et dispēnsātōrem Glycōnis, quī dēprehēnsus est, cum dominam suam dēlectārētur. Glycō, sēstertiārius homō, dispēnsātōrem ad bēstiās dedit. quid servus peccāvit, quī coāctus est facere? sed quī asinum nōn potest, strātum caedit.

Petronius, Satyricon 45

Titus: the show's producer
essedārius,-ī [m.]   *chariot fighter* (here the feminine form)
dispēnsātor,-ōris [m.]   *steward*
dēprehendō,-ere, dēprehendī, dēprehēnsum [3]   *catch, arrest*
dēlector,-ārī, dēlectātus [1; deponent]   *please, delight, give pleasure to*
sēstertiārius,-a,-um   *worth twopence*
peccō,-āre,-āvī,-ātum [1]   *offend, do wrong, make a mistake*
coāctus: from 'cōgō,-ere'
asinus,-ī [m.]   *donkey*
strātum,-ī [n.]   *saddle*
caedō,-ere, cecīdī, caesum [3]   *strike, beat*
quī . . . potest: understand 'caedere' after 'potest'

9.   Another show failed to impress:

quid ille nōbīs bonī fēcit? dedit gladiātōrēs sēstertiāriōs
iam dēcrepitōs, quōs sī sufflāssēs, cecidissent; iam meliōrēs
bēstiāriōs vīdī.

Petronius, Satyricon 45

ille: the show's producer, Norbanus
dēcrepitus,-a,-um   *decrepit*
sufflō,-āre,-āvī,-ātum [1]   *blow upon* ('sufflāssēs' = 'sufflāvissēs')
cadō,-ere, cecidī, cāsum   *fall over*
iam   *before now*
bēstiārius,-ī [m.]   *animal fighter*

10.   There were entertainments closer to our own. Trimalchio played with a ball with his
      slaves before dinner. If he dropped it, someone else was expected to pick it up or provide
      a new one.

nec amplius pilam repetēbat quae terram contigerat, sed
aliam servus sufficiēbat lūdentibus.

Petronius, Satyricon 27

amplius   *further, again*
pila,-ae [f.]   *ball*
repetō,-ere, repetīvī, repetītum [3]   *seek again, return to*
contingō,-ere, contigī, contāctum [3]   *touch*
sufficiō,-ere, suffēcī, suffectum [M.]   *provide, supply*
lūdō,-ere [3]   *play*

11.   Racing was arguably the most popular of all the different entertainments, and successful
      drivers were the sporting celebrities of their day. Rome's largest amphitheatre, the
      Colosseum, had room for 50,000 spectators. The Circus Maximus, where the horses
      were raced, could entertain five times as many. Charioteers belonged to one of four
      teams represented by the colours white, red, blue and green. People were passionately
      committed to a particular colour. Pliny was an exception:

mīror tot mīlia virōrum tam pueriliter identidem cupere
currentēs equōs, īnsistentēs curribus hominēs vidēre. sī
tamen aut vēlōcitāte equōrum aut hominum arte
traherentur, esset ratiō nōn nūlla; nunc favent pannō,
pannum amant, et sī in ipsō cursū mediōque certāmine
hic color illūc ille hūc trānsferātur, studium favorque
trānsībit, et repente agitātōrēs illōs equōs illōs, quōrum
clāmitant nōmina, relinquent.

Pliny, Letters 9.6

mīror tot . . . cupere . . . vidēre   *I am surprised that so many . . . want to see*

pueriliter   *childishly*

identidem   *again and again, repeatedly*

īnsistō,-ere, īnstitī [3; + dat.]   *stand on*

vēlōcitās,-tātis [f.]   *speed, swiftness*

trahō,-ere, traxī, tractum [3]   *draw, attract*

ratiō,-ōnis [f.]   *reason, justification*

nōn nūlla: i.e. *some*

nunc   *now, as it is*

faveō,-ēre, fāvī, fautum [+ dat.]   *favour, support*

pannus,-ī [m.]   *rag, piece of cloth*

cursus,-ūs [m.]   *course*

color,-ōris [m.]   *colour*

studium,-ī [n.]   *eagerness, enthusiasm*

favor,-ōris [m.]   *favour, support*

trānsībit: future of 'trānseō,-īre'

repente   *suddenly*

agitātor,-ōris [m.]   *driver, charioteer*

clāmitō,-āre,-āvī,-ātum [1]   *cry aloud, bawl (the names of)*

12. At the end of the same letter Pliny makes a play on the word *otium*:

per hōs diēs libentissimē ōtium meum in litterīs collocō, quōs aliī ōtiōsissimīs occupatiōnibus perdunt. valē.

Pliny, Letters 9.6

libentissimē: superlative of 'libenter'

ōtium,-ī [n.]   *leisure, free time*

collocō,-āre,-āvī,-ātum [1]   *occupy*

quōs: the antecedent is 'diēs'

ōtiōsus,-a,-um   *idle*

occupātiō,-ōnis [f.]   *occupation*

valē   *farewell*

13. Public baths were the place to take exercise, bathe, be cleaned and catch up with your social life. Martial here complains that Cotta will not invite anyone for dinner unless he has been to the baths with him.

invītās nūllum nisi cum quō, Cotta, lavāris,
     et dant convīvam balnea sōla tibi.
mīrābar quārē numquam mē, Cotta, vocāssēs:
     iam sciō mē nūdum displicuisse tibi.

Martial, Epigrams 1.23

lavāris: 2nd person sing., present passive of 'lavō,-āre' (*wash, bathe*), which is passive because Cotta would not be washing himself

convīva,-ae [m.]   *table companion, guest*
balneum,-ī [n.]   *bath*
mīrābar: imperfect (*I used to wonder*)
vocāssēs: for 'vocāvissēs' (subjunctive in indirect question after 'mīrābar quārē . . .')
mē . . . displicuisse   *myself to have displeased, that I displeased*
nūdus,-a,-um   *naked*

Exercises 21b

1.   Why are
(a)   'sufflāssēs' [21.9] and
(b)   'vocāssēs' [21.13] in the subjunctive?

2.   Identify the four principal parts of:
(a)   occīdit [21.7]
(b)   agātur [21.7]
(c)   dedit [21.8]
(d)   fēcit [21.9]
(e)   vīdī [21.9]
(f)   relinquent [21.11]
(g)   perdunt [21.12]
(h)   invītās [21.13]

3.   Translate:
(a)   quid rēs pūblica nōbis bonī fēcit?
(b)   quārē ille servus, sī nōn peccāvit, ad bēstiās retinētur?
(c)   sī pila terram contigerit, quīdam aliam sufficiet.
(d)   sī mē centum manūs tetigerint febrem habēbō.
(e)   sī mulierem essedāriam et bēstiās et dispēnsātōrem Glycōnis habēmus, fīet spectāculum
      praeclārum – immō hercle ego nōlō adesse.

4.   Explain the case of each underlined word, and translate:
      quid hodiē in harēnā vīdistī?
            — vīdimus valentissimum taurum quōsdam servōs fugantem.
      ēheu, nōnne iam spectāvimus nimium **multōs** taurōs fugantēs illōs miserōs?
            — sed etiam duās essedāriās elephantum **agitantēs**.

5.   Find Latin ancestors in this chapter of *amplify, lacerate* and *reverberate*.

— 22 —

Fugit irreparabile tempus

Infinitives

Latin infinitives are usually translated into English with 'to' in front of the verb:

amāre   *to love*

Infinitives are used after verbs like **volō** (*I want*), **mālō** (*I prefer*), **cupiō** (*I desire*), **possum** (*I am able*), **debeō** (*I ought*), **iubeō** (*I order*), **sciō** (*I know* [*how*]) **videor** (*I seem*):

ego tamen Antōnī amīcitiam **retinēre** sānē volō
for all that I certainly want <u>to keep</u> the friendship of Antony [9.11]

ille mī pār **esse** deō vidētur
that fellow seems to me <u>to be</u> equal to a god [15.7]

In some circumstances Latin infinitives can be translated as gerunds (*-ing*) or nouns:

<u>**vigilāre**</u> leve est
<u>to lie awake</u> is no matter/<u>lying awake</u> is no matter [19.6]

<u>**pārēre**</u> necesse est
it is necessary <u>to obey</u>/<u>to obey</u> is necessary/<u>obedience</u> is necessary [13.15]

Practice 22a
Identify the infinitive in each sentence, and translate:
(a)   melius sānam est, mulier, mentem sūmere.
(b)   gravia loca ūtilius est mercēnāriīs colere quam servīs.
(c)   dēsine mēque tuīs incendere tēque querēlīs.

Reported speech, thoughts and feelings

When writers describe what people say or think they sometimes quote directly what was said:

'nisi mē frūstrantur,' inquit, 'oculī, māter tibi coniūnxque et līberī adsunt'
'unless my eyes deceive me,' he said, 'your mother, wife and children are here' [17.2]

It is more usual for the words or thoughts of a character to be expressed indirectly, with the help of a construction called 'the accusative and infinitive'.

The accusative and infinitive

We have seen examples of a verb of saying or thinking followed by an accusative-and-infinitive:

silvīs **tē** ferās **agitāre** putāstī?
did you suppose <u>that you were hunting</u> (lit. yourself to be hunting) wild beasts in the woods? [15.15]

This construction is also called 'reported speech' or 'indirect statement'. An indirect statement may be introduced by a verb of saying, thinking, feeling or knowing (e.g. 'Marcus knows that . . .'), with the subject of what would be the direct speech in the accusative and the verb in the infinitive:

Mārcus dīcit **taurum** in vīllā **esse**
Marcus says that the bull is in the villa (lit. *M. says <u>the bull to be</u> in the villa*)

Infinitives: present, past and future

You have met the present infinitive active. It is the second of the four principal parts:

amō, **amāre** (*to love*), amāvī, amātum

There are more infinitives, six altogether, present, future and perfect in both active and passive. Here are shown the infinitives of 1st conjugation verbs like **amō,-āre** (the infinitives of all conjugations are online in the Grammar tables – see p. 393):

	present	future	perfect
active	**amāre** *to love*	**amātūrus* esse** *to be about to love*	**amāvisse** *to have loved*
passive	**amārī** *to be loved*	**amātum īrī** *to be about to be loved*	**amātus* esse** *to have been loved*

* the forms **amātūrus,-a,-um** and **amātus,-a,-um** are the future and past participles, which are combined with **esse** to create the infinitives. Thus they have endings like **bonus,-a,-um** and agree with the subject of the infinitive, which in the accusative-and-infinitive construction will be in the accusative:

Pompēius cōnfirmat **Clōdium** nihil **esse factūrum** contrā mē
Pompey reassures (me) that Clodius will do nothing against me [7.5]

Antōnius **adoptiōnem** avunculī stuprō **meritum esse** rettulit
Antony related that the adoption had been obtained through the lust of his uncle [13.10]

Remember that a deponent verb looks passive but has an active meaning:

nec vitia nostra nec remedia **patī** possumus (present infinitive of 'patior')
we are able to endure neither our vices nor the remedies [6.3]

Practice 22b

With help from the first conjugation above, give (i) the future infinitive active, (ii) perfect infinitive active and (iii) perfect infinitive passive of

(a) videō,-ēre, vīdī, vīsum
(b) dūcō,-ere, dūxī, ductum
(c) audiō,-īre, audīvī, audītum
(d) capiō,-ere, cēpī, captum

Translating the accusative and infinitive

If the verb of saying or thinking is past, we express the infinitive in English in one (further) step into the past to keep the English sequence of tenses:

Mārcus **dīcit** taurum in vīllā **esse**
Marcus says that the bull is in the villa

Mārcus **dīxit** taurum in vīllā **esse**
Marcus said that the bull was in the villa (he actually said '*The bull is in . . .*')

and with a past infinitive

Mārcus **dīcit** taurum in vīllā **fuisse**
Marcus says that the bull has been/was in the villa

Mārcus **dīxit** taurum in vīllā **fuisse**
Marcus said that the bull had been in the villa

and with a future infinitive

Mārcus **dīcit** taurum in vīllā **futūrum esse**
Marcus says that the bull will be in the villa

Mārcus **dīxit** taurum in vīllā **futūrum esse**
Marcus said that the bull would be in the villa

Practice 22c

Translate:
(a) Mārcus dīcit multās fēminās in forō fuisse.
(b) Mārcus dīcit multās fēminās in forō esse.
(c) Mārcus dīxit multās fēminās in forō fuisse.
(d) Mārcus dīcit multās fēminās in forō futūrās esse.
(e) Mārcus dīxit multās fēminās in forō futūrās esse.
(f) Mārcus dīxit multās fēminās in forō esse.

To say that . . . not

The Latin verb for *to say . . . not* or *deny* is **negō,-āre** [1]:

esse **negās** coctum leporem
you say that the hare has not been cooked [18.1]

adulteria exercuisse nē amīcī quidem
negant
not even his friends deny that he practised adultery
[12.9]

tē **negat** lassō iānitor esse domī
the doorkeeper says to the weary (me) that you are not at home [14.4]

Practice 22d

Translate:
(a) Semprōnia negāvit Clōdiam cum aliīs fēminīs adesse.
(b) Cicerō negāvit Caelium umquam Clōdiam amāvisse.

The 'other party' subjunctive

The subjunctive is used to show that thoughts or words are not the writer's own but those of his character(s), i.e. an 'other party'. This is a deft construction, for it allows the author to show that a reason offered for something (e.g. after **quod**) is not his own but expressed by the person(s) he is describing. In English we need additional words to make the distinction:

> Mārcus domum relīquit quod tristis **erat**
> *Marcus left home because he was sad*   (the writer's reason)

> Mārcus domum relīquit quod tristis **esset**
> *Marcus left home because he was sad*   (Marcus' reason: *because, so he said, he was sad*)

The 'other party'[1] subjunctive is particularly useful for historians, whose narratives mix their own explanations with the reasons or thoughts of their characters. You have met this subjunctive already:

> Augustus, quod Thallus prō epistulā prōditā dēnāriōs quīngentōs **accēpisset**, crūra eī frēgit
> *Augustus, because Thallus had received five hundred denarii in return for a disclosed letter, broke his legs* [12.14]

The subjunctive clarifies that the reason given for breaking the legs is Augustus' own and not merely the writer's offered explanation. The writer below is responding to criticism of his substituting names. The verb is subjunctive because it is following the line of thought of his critics, not his own:

> eādem igitur operā accūsent Catullum, quod Lesbiam prō Clodiā **nōminārit**
> *then by the same token they may as well accuse Catullus, because (so their logic dictates) he used the name Lesbia in place of Clodia* [15.11]
>> ('nōminārit' for 'nōmināverit', perf. subj. of 'nōminō,-āre')

The subjunctive is used similarly in subordinate clauses in indirect speech, to indicate that the speech or thought belongs to the character (here, Augustus) rather than the writer:

> iūre est glōriātus urbem marmoream sē relinquere, quam laterīciam **accēpisset**
> *with justification he boasted that he was leaving the city made of marble, which he had inherited in brick* [12.8]

More on the reflexive pronoun and adjective: sē and suus

The reflexive pronoun **sē** was introduced on p. 173. Along with the reflexive adjective **suus,-a, -um,** it refers to the subject of the sentence:

---

1 Traditionally called the 'subjunctive of oblique discourse'.

Catullus Lesbiam plūs quam **sē** atque **suōs** amāvit omnēs
Catullus loved Lesbia more than <u>himself</u> and all <u>his</u> people [15.9]

When **sē** is used in the accusative-and-infinitive, it refers to the subject of saying or thinking:

nūllī **sē** dīcit **mulier** mea nūbere mālle quam mihi, nōn sī **sē** Iuppiter ipse petat
my <u>woman</u> says that <u>she</u> prefers to marry no one other than me, not if Jupiter himself were to ask <u>her</u> [15.8]

The rule is that **sē** refers to the subject. However, the second **sē** above reveals a grey area, for Jupiter is not seeking himself. The context should clarify which subject is meant.

Occasionally the reflexive does not refer to the subject but the person uppermost in mind (which nine times out of ten is the subject):

quem dīgnitās **sua** dēfendet?
what man will <u>his</u> rank defend? [18.7]

The grammatical subject is **dīgnitās**, but **sua** refers to **quem**, the object. Similarly below:

Hylan pantomīmum, querente praetōre, in ātriō domūs **suae** flagellīs verberāvit
as the praetor was complaining, he (Augustus) had Hylas, the pantomime artist, beaten with whips in the hall of <u>his own</u> house [20.8]

The reflexive adjective **suae** would normally be taken to mean the house of the subject (i.e. Augustus). But Hylas, first word to appear, is the most prominent person in this sentence, and **suae** is used (not **eius**, which could mean the praetor's house) to underline the humiliation taking place in his own hallway.

Nonetheless, departures from the reflexive referring to the subject are few.

Vocabulary 22
Verbs of saying, reporting or thinking which introduce the accusative-and-infinitive:

audiō,-īre, audīvī (-iī), audītum [4]   *hear*
cognōscō,-ere, cognōvī, cognitum [3]   *become acquainted with, learn*
cōnfirmō,-āre, cōnfirmāvī, cōnfirmātum [1]   *establish, confirm*
cōnstituō,-ere, cōnstituī, cōnstitūtum [3]   *determine, decide*
crēdō,-ere, crēdidī, crēditum [3; + dat.]   *believe, trust*
dīcō,-ere, dīxī, dictum [3]   *say, tell*
ferō, ferre, tulī, lātum   *bear, tell, say*
iubeō,-ēre, iussī, iussum [2]   *order, tell (instruct)*
mīror,-ārī, mīrātus [1; deponent]   *be surprised, be amazed*
negō,-āre, negāvī, negātum [1]   *say that . . . not, deny*
nuntiō,-āre, nuntiāvī, nuntiātum [1]   *announce*

putō,-āre, putāvī, putātum [1]   *think, consider, reflect, suppose*
referō, referre, rettulī, relātum   *report*
reor, rērī, ratus [3; deponent]   *think, imagine, suppose*
sciō,-īre, scīvī, scītum [4]   *know*
testor,-ārī, testātus [1; deponent]   *declare, give evidence*
trādō,-ere, trādidī, trāditum [3]   *hand over, pass on, record*
videō,-ēre, vīdī, vīsum [2]   *see*

Look online for a review of 2nd declension nouns which appear in the course (see p. 393).

Exercises 22a

1.   Translate:
(a)   putāsne mē servum esse?
(b)   nunc Lesbia negat sē umquam mē amātūra esse.
(c)   Fulvia dīcēbat Antōnium semper illum senātōrem contempsisse.
(d)   tribūnus nuntiāvit omnēs captīvōs in amphitheātrum ductum īrī.
(e)   agricola multōs Rōmānōs in silvā trucīdātōs esse rettulit.
(f)   māter philosophiam imperātūrō contrāriam esse monuit.
(g)   mīror Clōdium patī uxōrem eius prōcurrere in pūblicum.

2.   Identify the infinitive in each sentence, and translate:
(a)   māvīs, Rūfe, cocum scindere quam leporem.
(b)   ferre potēs dominam salvīs tot restibus ūllam?
(c)   Augustum ipsum adulteria exercuisse nē amīcī quidem negant.

3.   Fill each gap with the correct word to complete the imagined actual words or thoughts:
(a)   Pompēius cōnfirmat Clōdium nihil esse factūrum contrā mē.
      'Clōdius nihil contrā tē .... {*will do*}.'
(b)   Coriolānō nuntiātum est adesse ingēns mulierum agmen.
      'ingēns mulierum agmen .... {*is present*}.'
(c)   iam sciō mē nūdum displicuisse tibi.
      'ego nūdus tibi .... {*I have displeased*}.'

4.   Explain why the underlined verb is subjunctive:
      servus indīgnātur veterī pārēre clientī quodque sē stante **recumbās**.

Fugit irreparabile tempus

What were the dates of 'Classical' Rome? Scholars in the twentieth century and earlier defined a brief span: the half-century lapping the last decades of the Republic with the beginning of Augustus' principate. Why so brief? Because students were expected to write Latin with careful attention to classical models, and the models had to be black and white with a minimum of grey. A student could never squeal that his phrasing was actually all right because it was found in a later writer like Tacitus. For the subject to function in schools there had to be a right and wrong. Model texts were narrowed to Cicero, Caesar, Sallust and Livy (though even these authors were by no means uniform). For many hundreds of years their Latin has set the standard, and their language has been upheld as the Latin model for almost everyone since. That definition has now loosened up a bit. We say the classical period starts with Cicero and Catullus and ends with Juvenal in the first half of the second century AD. This is almost 200 years, a long time in the history of a people and their language.

We think of ancient Rome as a model not only of language, but in all kinds of ways, architecture, engineering, law, literary form, political administration and more. But this role as a model can distort our view. What sometimes gets lost in our recall of this period is a sense of the present, of change and life evolving. Learners of Latin come across this sooner or later. A 'dead' language is not subject to ongoing evolution as a living one inevitably is. The language rules of Latin are fixed. On closer inspection, however, we find words used in unusual ways, there are exceptions to grammatical norms, variable spellings, evidence of evolving sounds and a sense of language at change.

Changes in history are more obvious, certainly from a linear viewpoint as we skip through the lives and dates of political groundbreakers like Julius Caesar, Augustus, and the emperors who followed. Social change is also evident, whether documented or unearthed by archaeologists. We sometimes think of Romans as Romulus' community of owner-occupiers farming and fighting for seven hills, of sturdy yeomen who broke free of Etruscan domination and built an empire on the strength of their qualities of courage and self-sufficiency. The truth is that by the classical period such a picture had changed beyond recognition. We think of it though because classical Romans themselves took pride in such a view. But the poets and historians who cherished old Roman values themselves enjoyed privileges of a very different social structure, with its elaborate dependencies on patrons, clients, provincials, freedmen and slaves.

Reading notes

In poetry the ending of the 3rd person plural of the perfect active (**-ērunt**) is often written **-ēre** to shorten the final syllable and so fit the metre (the **-nt** ending restricted a poet to a long syllable, in fact a succession of them). This 'poetic licence' suggests the sound of the final syllable **-unt** was not strong, and the sounds of the two endings were not so far apart: the **-nt** 3rd person plural has faded in Romance languages. Once poets had made a habit of the new ending, so did later prose writers like Tacitus:

fūgēre for **fūgērunt** [22.4]; **subiēre** for **subiērunt** [22.4]; **dōnāvēre** for **dōnāvērunt** [22.6]; **perculēre** for **perculērunt** [23.5]; **sūmpsēre** for **sūmpsērunt** [23.8]; **iacuēre** for **iacuērunt** [24.5]; **rīsēre** for **rīsērunt** [24.5]; **posuēre** for **posuērunt** [24.9].

---

1.   Roman poets often touch upon 'the times-they-are-a-changin'' motif, served with a dash of melancholy.

sed fugit intereā, fugit irreparābile tempus.

Virgil, *Georgics* 3.284

irreparābilis,-e   *irrecoverable, irretrievable*

2.   Times seldom seem to be changing for the better. The good old days is a recurrent theme in Roman literature and poets long for a simpler, more rural past.

beātus ille quī procul negōtiīs,
    ut prīsca gēns mortālium,
paterna rūra bōbus exercet suīs
    solūtus omnī faenore;
libet iacēre modo sub antīquā īlice,
    modo in tenācī grāmine.

Horace, Epodes 2.1–4, 23–4

beātus,-a,-um   *blest, happy*
procul [+ abl.]   *far, remote*
negōtium,-ī [n.]   *business affair*
ut: with the indicative means *when* or *as*
prīscus,-a,-um   *ancient, of former times*
gēns, gentis [f.]   *clan, race*
mortālis,-e [m.]   *mortal*
rūs, rūris [n.]   *country, land, estate*
bōs, bovis ['bōbus' = dat.pl./abl.pl.]   *ox*
solvō,-ere, solvī, solūtum [3]   *loosen, release*
faenus,-oris [n.]   *interest payment*
libet   *it is pleasing*
iaceō,-ēre [2]   *lie*
modo . . . modo   *now . . . now*
īlex,-icis [f.]   *oak tree*
tenāx [like 'fēlīx']   *clinging*
grāmen,-inis [n.]   *grass*

3.   Roman mythology of prehistory has a similar feel of deterioration. The first age was golden, and all was well:

aurea prīma sāta est aetās, quae vindice nūllō,
sponte suā, sine lēge fidem rēctumque colēbat.
poena metusque aberant.

Ovid, Metamorphoses 1.89–91

serō,-ere, sēvī, sātum [3]   *sow, cause, bring forth*
vindex,-icis [m.]   *protector, enforcer*
sponte suā   *of its own free will*
rēctum,-ī [n.]   *virtue, uprightness*

4.   Things took gradual turns for the worse. Second came the age of silver, then bronze, and finally the age of iron, when . . .

fūgēre pudor vērumque fidēsque.
in quōrum subiēre locum fraudēsque dolusque
īnsidiaeque et vīs et amor scelerātus habendī.

Ovid, *Metamorphoses* 1.129–31

fūgēre: for 'fūgērunt'
pudor,-ōris [m.]   *decency, sense of shame*
vērum,-ī [n.]   *truth*
subiēre: for 'subiērunt' ('subeō,-īre,-iī' = *steal into, creep*)
fraus, fraudis [f.]   *cheating, deceit*
dolus,-ī [m.]   *trick, trickery, malice*
īnsidiae,-ārum [f.]   *treachery*
vīs: could be the noun meaning *violence* or the verb *you want*
scelerātus,-a,-um   *wicked, pernicious*
habendī   *of having (things), of gain*

5.   This fourth age served a reminder of life during the civil wars.

nōn hospes ab hospite tūtus,
nōn socer ā generō, frātrum quoque grātia rāra est;
imminet exitiō vir coniugis, illa marītī,
lūrida terribilēs miscent aconīta novercae,
fīlius ante diem patriōs inquīrit in annōs:
victa iacet pietās.

Ovid, *Metamorphoses* 1.144–9

hospes,-itis [m.]   *host, guest*
tūtus,-a,-um   *safe*
grātia,-ae [f.]   *favour, esteem, affection*
est, imminet, miscent, inquirit, iacet: translate these verbs as past (for the 'historic present' see p. 303)
immineō,-ēre [2; + dat.]   *watch for, long for*
exitium,-ī [n.]   *destruction, ruin*
lūridus,-a,-um   *ghastly, lurid*
terribilis,-e   *dreadful*
aconītum,-ī [n.]   *poison*
noverca,-ae [f.]   *stepmother*
ante diem: i.e. *before due time* (in the hope they will die early)
patrius,-a,-um   *belonging to a father, a father's*
inquīrō,-ere, inquīsīvī, inquīsītum [3]   *inquire into*
pietās,-tātis [f.]   *piety, sense of duty, dutiful conduct*

6.   Augustus' literary team pick up the note of optimism for the peace he brought the Roman world, the here-and-now, a better future. But even this is described in terms of the past – a golden age.

quō nihil maius meliusve terrīs
fāta dōnāvēre bonīque dīvī,
nec dabunt, quamvīs redeant in aurum
    tempora prīscum.

Horace, Odes 4.2.37–40

quō   than whom, than him (i.e. than Augustus)
-ve: enclitic like '-que' (or)
terrīs: in the plural lands or the world, earth
fāta: the subject along with 'bonī dīvī'
dōnō,-āre, dōnāvī, dōnātum [1]   give as a present ('dōnāvēre' for 'dōnāvērunt')
quamvīs   even if

7. In the century after Augustus, Rome's power and riches grew even more. Juvenal pins the blame for moral collapse on this expansion, which brought in foreign ways:

prīma peregrīnōs obscēna pecūnia mōrēs
intulit, et turpī frēgērunt saecula luxū
dīvitiae mollēs.

Juvenal, Satires 6.298–300

peregrīnus,-a,-um   foreign, strange
intulit: perfect of 'īnferō, īnferre'
frangō,-ere, frēgī, frāctum [3]   break, corrupt
luxus,-ūs [m.]   extravagance, excess
dīvitiae,-ārum [f.]   riches, wealth
mollis,-e   soft, unmanly

8. Juvenal doesn't have a good word to say about the Greeks, for all their cultural importance (see 20.7). The 'Greece' below is anywhere where Greek was spoken, in other words all around the eastern Mediterranean.

quae nunc dīvitibus gēns acceptissima nostrīs
et quōs praecipuē fugiam, properābo fatērī,
nec pudor obstābit. nōn possum ferre, Quirītēs,
Graecam Urbem. quamvīs quota portio faecis Achaeī?
iam prīdem Syrus in Tiberim dēfluxit Orontēs
et linguam et mōrēs et cum tībīcine chordās
oblīquās nec nōn gentīlia tympana sēcum
vēxit et ad circum iussās prōstāre puellās.

Juvenal, Satires 3.58–65

quae gēns acceptissima nostrīs dīvitibus: understand *is*
dīvitibus nostrīs   *to our rich men*, i.e. *to wealthy Romans*
acceptus,-a,-um   *pleasing*
praecipuē   *especially*
properō,-āre,-āvī,-ātum [1]   *hurry, be quick*
fateor,-ērī, fassus [2; deponent]   *indicate, make plain*
pudor,-ōris [m.]   *shame, embarrassment*
obstō,-āre [1]   *stand in the way, stop*
Quirītēs   *fellow Romans* (see footnote on p. 214)
Graecam Urbem: he means the city of Rome hankering after Greek ways
quamvīs   *and yet*
quotus,-a,-um   *how many, how few, how small*
portio,-ōnis [f.]   *share, portion*
faex, faecis [f.]   *dregs*
Achaeī: '*Greeks proper*', '*real Greeks*'; the 'Achaeans' had been a name for the Greeks from
    Homeric times; Achaea was now a Roman province covering all the Greek peninsula
    south of Thessaly
iam prīdem   *for a long time now*
Syrus,-a,-um   *Syrian*
Orontēs: river in Syria
dēfluō,-ere, dēfluxī [3]   *flow down*
tībīcen,-inis [m.]   *flute-player, piper*
chorda,-ae [f.]   *string*
oblīquus,-a,-um   *sideways, slanting* (chordās oblīquās: *oriental harps*)
nec nōn   *and also*
gentīlis,-e   *belonging to their race, native*
tympanum,-ī [n.]   *drum, tambourine*
prōstō,-āre, prōstitī [1]   *stand for sale*

9.   All kinds of beliefs and cults found their way to the empire's capital. Tacitus notes how
      one cult took hold in the city (which later would spread across the Roman world):

repressaque in praesēns exitiābilis superstitiō rūrsum
ērumpēbat, nōn modo per Iūdaeam, orīginem eius malī,
sed per urbem etiam quō cūncta undique atrōcia aut
pudenda cōnfluunt celebranturque.

Tacitus, *Annals* 15.44

reprimō,-ere, repressī, repressum [3]   *curb, keep in check*
in praesēns   *for the time being*
exitiābilis,-e   *deadly*
superstitiō,-ōnis [f.]   *superstition*
rūrsum   *again*
ērumpō,-ere, ērūpī, ēruptum [3]   *break out*
nōn modo   *not only*

orīgō,-inis [f.]   *origin*
urbem: i.e. Rome
quō   *to where*
undique   *from all sides*
pudendus,-a,-um   *shameful*
cōnfluō,-ere, cōnfluxī [3]   *flow together*
celebrō,-āre,-āvī,-ātum [1]   *practise*

10. We speak of writers in the first century BC like Catullus, Cicero, Horace and Virgil as
'Roman', even though all four were born in other parts of Italy. In the next century
Martial came from Spain, Seneca from a Spanish family, and Tacitus was born in
southern Gaul. Even emperors would soon emerge from the provinces. The testy
concept of citizenship so fought over by Italians in the first century BC was extended in
time to the whole empire. By the fourth and fifth centuries the idea of Roman citizenship
was so diluted it meant little more than a person living in the empire.

  The status of **civis** still carried enough weight in the first century AD for Saint Paul,
who came from Tarsus in what is now southern Turkey, to claim the right to face his
accusations in Rome.

'Iūdaeīs nōn nocuī, sīcut tū melius nōstī. sī enim nocuī, aut
dīgnum morte aliquid fēcī, nōn recūsō morī: sī vērō nihil
est eōrum quae hī accūsant mē, nēmō potest mē illīs
dōnāre. Caesarem appellō.' tunc Festus, cum conciliō
locūtus, respondit: 'Caesarem appellāstī? ad Caesarem
ībis.'

Luke, *Acts of the Apostles* 25.11–12

Iūdaeī,-ōrum [m.]   *Jews*
noceō,-ēre, nocuī, nocitum [+ dat.]   *harm, injure*
sīcut   *as, just as*
melius   *better (than anyone), quite well*
nōstī: for 'nōvistī' (*you know*)
dīgnus,-a,-um [+ abl.]   *worthy of, deserving*
recūsō,-āre,-āvī,-ātum [1]   *refuse*
morī: present infinitive of 'morior' (deponent)
eōrum [gen.pl. of 'is, ea, id']: with 'nihil' = *nothing of (in) those things* 'quae . . .'
Caesarem: i.e. Nero
appellō,-āre,-āvī,-ātum [1]   *call (upon), appeal to*
tunc   *then, next*
Festus: Roman procurator of Judaea
appellāstī: for 'appellāvistī'
ībis: future of 'eō,-īre'

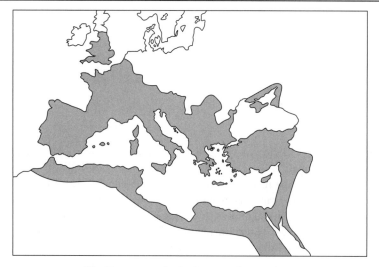

The Roman empire in the second century AD

Exercises 22b

1. In 22.8 and 22.9, Juvenal and Tacitus use different compounds of the same verb to describe social deterioration. What is the simple verb?

2. Identify the infinitive in each sentence and give its tense (present, future or perfect) and voice (active or passive):
(a) Antōnius adoptiōnem avunculī stuprō meritum esse rettulit.
(b) īnsidiātōrī vērō et latrōnī quae potest īnferrī iniūsta nex?
(c) trādidērunt quīdam Caesarem Mārcō Brūtō irruentī dīxisse: 'kai su teknon?'
(d) Pompēius cōnfirmat Clōdium nihil esse factūrum contrā mē.
(e) Latīnē autem apud Bruttium exercērī volō.

3. Translate this sentence, which includes *two* accusative-and-infinitives:
crēdō tē audīsse cum veste muliebrī Clōdium dēprehēnsum esse domī Caesaris.

4. Complete the indirect statements by filling each gap with a single word (using the direct statement to guide you). Then translate both the indirect and direct statements:
(a) Lāocoōn dīcit sē Danaōs et dōna ferentīs .... {timeō,-ēre, timuī}. ['timeō Danaōs et dōna ferentīs.']
(b) Plinius dīcit sē eadem omnibus .... {pōnō,-ere, posuī, positum}. ['eadem omnibus pōnō.']
(c) familiārium quīdam Coriolānō dīxit .... {māter,-tris} coniugemque et līberōs eius .... {adsum, adesse, affuī}. ['māter tibi coniūnxque et līberī adsunt.']

5. Translate:
ego audiī dominam Catullī amīcam omnium potius quam cuiusquam inimīcam esse.

6. Find Latin ancestors in this chapter of *appeal, celebrate, eruption* and *prostitute*.

On the edge of the world

Gerunds

An English gerund looks very like an English participle, and indeed both gerunds and participles are created from verbs. The difference is that a gerund is a noun and a participle an adjective:

> *you can stay healthy by <u>walking</u>* (gerund)
> <u>*walking*</u> *into the wall, he broke his glasses* (participle)
> <u>*walking*</u> *into the wall is not wise* (gerund)

In the first, *walking* is doing the work of a noun. In the second, *walking* is a participle, an adjective dependent on the subject *he*. In the third *walking* is a noun once more, a gerund, the subject of the verb *is*.

Practice 23a
Is the underlined word a gerund or participle?
(a) Who is the girl <u>talking</u> in the classroom?
(b) <u>Talking</u> in the classroom is not allowed.
(c) When was <u>smoking</u> banned in bars?
(d) I did not see the man <u>smoking</u> behind the tree.
(e) She does not like <u>flying</u>.
(f) <u>Flying</u> into a rage he smashed the bottle.

Latin gerunds
Like its English counterpart, a Latin gerund is a noun formed from a verb. It teams up with the infinitive to provide for all the cases:

N.	**vidēre**	*to see, seeing*
A.	**vidēre, videndum**	*to see, seeing*
G.	**videndī**	*of seeing*
D.	**videndō**	*for seeing*
Ab.	**videndō**	*by seeing*

The infinitive is used when the verbal noun is the subject or simple object:

vidēre est **crēdere**
to see is to believe/seeing is believing

pārēre necesse est
to obey/obeying/obedience is necessary [13.15]

In other cases or with prepositions the gerund is used:

ad **resistendum** mē parō   (accusative)
I am preparing myself for resisting [7.5]

amor scelerātus **habendī**   (genitive)
the wicked love of having (things), i.e. *of material gain* [22.4]

ūnus homō nōbīs **cūnctandō** restituit rem   (ablative)
one man recovered the situation for us by delaying [3.7]

The five conjugations are very similar. As with present participles, the 1st conjugation shows an 'a' in the stem while the others have an 'e':

amandum, habendum, mittendum, audiendum, capiendum

Practice 23b

1.   Translate:
    (a)   quis cūnctandō vincit?
    (b)   omnibus gladiātōribus erat vincendī amor.

2.   Translate the underlined words into a single Latin gerund from the verb given:
    (a)   a fear of losing. (careō,-ēre)
    (b)   by resisting we will win. (resistō,-ere)
    (c)   a love of drinking. (bibō,-ere)

Gerundives

English has no single-word equivalent to a Latin gerundive:

a bull not to be chased
the wine is to be drunk

The gerundive has a name like the gerund because of a similarity not in meaning but in appearance:

> taurus nōn **fugandus**
> vīnum est **bibendum**

The gerundive is passive (a gerund is active), and an adjective (a gerund is a noun). A gerundive has the same form as a gerund[1] but with *all* the endings of **bonus,-a,-um** (a gerund's endings are limited to **-um, -ī**, and **-ō**).

> multārum rērum exempla **imitanda** posterīs trādidī
> *I passed on to posterity examples of many things <u>to be imitated</u> (for imitation)* [12.6]

> mercātūra, sī tenuis est, sordida **putanda** est
> *if an enterprise is small it is <u>to be (should be) considered</u> demeaning* [20.4]

> dē quā ego nihil dīcam nisi **dēpellendī** crīminis causā
> *about her I shall say nothing except for the purpose of the charge <u>to be thrown out</u> (of having the charge thrown out)* [8.1]

> populus mē triumvirum reī pūblicae **cōnstituendae** creāvit
> *the people appointed me triumvir for the state <u>to be managed</u> (to manage the state)* [10.5]

A gerundive often carries a sense of obligation or inevitability:

> sī ponticulum trānsierimus, omnia armīs **agenda** erunt
> *if we cross the little bridge, everything is <u>to be (must be) resolved</u> by armed conflict* [8.6]

As a gerundive is passive, it often comes with an agent, i.e. the person responsible for the action of a passive verb (*the house was cleaned <u>by me</u>*). The agent with a gerundive is unusual, for it is not in the ablative as we might expect, but the dative (called the dative of agent). For instance, **armīs** above and **mihi** below are datives of agent:

> culpa silenda **mihi** erat
> *the offence had to be kept quiet <u>by me</u>* [13.6]

A gerundive is an adjective, and like other adjectives it can stand alone without a noun:

> cūncta atrōcia aut **pudenda** cōnfluunt
> *all things sleaze-ridden or <u>to be ashamed of</u> (shameful) ooze together* [22.9]

A gerundive is passive, like the past participle (**agendus** = *to be done*, **āctus** = *having been done*). However, with deponent verbs, the past participle has an active meaning (**secūtus** = *having followed*). The gerundive of a deponent verb does not switch like this but remains passive (**ille est sequendus** = *he is to be followed*).

Generally you will meet more gerundives than gerunds. Remember that a gerundive is passive, an adjective, and has the same endings as **bonus,-a,-um**.

---

1 Most gerunds and gerundives have the stem **-and-** or **-end-**. A common exception is the gerund **eundum** (*going*) from **eō, īre**, which is also used in the gerundive (and passive) with compound verbs that take a direct object, like **subeō,-īre** (*go under, creep up to*).

Practice 23c

1. Give the first two principal parts of the verb from which the gerundive is formed:
    (a) faciendus,-a,-um
    (b) agendus,-a,-um
    (c) putandus,-a,-um
    (d) retinendus,-a,-um
    (e) patiendus,-a,-um
    (f) scrībendus,-a,-um

2. Identify the gerundive from each verb:
    (a) ferō, ferre
    (b) videō, vidēre
    (c) doceō, docēre
    (d) bibō, bibere
    (e) loquor, loquī
    (f) habeō, habēre

3. Translate:
    (a) estne Catullus poēta mīrandus?
    (b) Clōdiane est putanda īnfēlīx?
    (c) domina tua est laudanda ōrnanda dīmittenda.

Vocabulary 23

Interrogative words:

cūr	*why*	**quid***	*what, why*
quā	*by what way*	**quis***	*who*
quālis*	*of what sort*	**quō**	*to where*
quam	*how*	**quot**	*how many*
quandō	*when*	**quotiēns**	*how often, how many times*
quantus*	*how great, how many*	**ubī (ubi)**	*where, when*
quārē	*why, for what reason*	* these have variable endings	

Many interrogative words can also be used as relatives or in an exclamatory way, where they do not ask a question, e.g. **quam** = *how!, than, as*; **quālis** = *of such a kind*; **quotiēns** = *how many times!, as often as*. **Quandō** can mean *when?*, or as a conjunction *when* or *since*, or as an adverb *at any time*.

Look online for a review of 2nd declension neuter nouns appearing in the course (see p. 393).

Exercises 23a

1. Gerund or gerundive? Give the case.
(a) cūncta atrōcia aut **pudenda** cōnfluunt.
(b) ūnus homō nōbīs **cūnctandō** restituit rem.
(c) istīc nunc, **metuende**, iacē.
(d) mercātūra, sī tenuis est, sordida **putanda** est.
(e) nihil aequē amōrem incitat et accendit quam **carendī** metus.
(f) sī ponticulum trānsierimus, omnia armīs **agenda** erunt.
(g) sit vōbīs cūra **placendī**!

2. Translate:
(a) quārē servus tuus manūmittendus est?
(b) quandō rogātus adest servus?
(c) ecce, ego modum discendī novum invēnī!
(d) quotiēns taurum fugāre cōnātus es!
(e) scīlicet spectāculum, sī tenue est, sordidum putandum est; sīn nōbīs erunt hae bēstiae et ille grammaticus garrulus, nōn est dēspērandum.

3. Identify a girl's name from the gerundive of each verb:
(a) amō, amāre
(b) mīror, mīrārī

4. Identify an English word derived from the gerundive of each verb:
(a) addō,-ere.
(b) agō,-ere.
(c) dīvidō,-ere.
(d) referō, referre.
(e) revereor, reverī.

5. Identify a word derived from (a) the ablative of the gerund of **innuō,-ere** (*nod*); (b) the neuter plural of the gerundive of **prōpāgō,-āre** (*extend, spread*).

On the edge of the world

Britannia was a not greatly valued island to the north of Gaul, with a bland, unwelcoming climate. Little prospect of much, a few slaves, some lead and tin to be mined, and perhaps a little gold and silver for those energetic enough to look for it. But there it was, ripe for acquisition, something empire-builders such as the Romans do not overlook. Caesar had whetted the appetite with his forays in 55 and 54 BC, and traders were already coming and going. Romans were curious

Reading notes

The present tense is sometimes used instead of the past (called the 'historic present') to lend variety or vividness. We have a similar thing when describing a past event in English, e.g. 'Would you believe it, he comes in, helps himself to a drink . . .'. This occurs in 22.5, 23.7 and 25.10. The Latin historic present is usually translated into English as a past tense.

to see what they perceived to be the world's most northern point, and Caesar had political reasons for invasion—to quell any support or refuge British tribes might give disaffected parties on the mainland. But politics at the capital would soon distract him. Shortly after Caesar's exploratory visits, Rome was plunged into a civil war from which he would emerge as dictator. It was another hundred years before a serious campaign to annex Britain was launched under the emperor Claudius.

1. Caesar describes the people he finds in Britain. The further inland they were the less they were like their Gallic neighbours. They did not grow crops but lived off milk and meat, and dressed in animal skins. They even dyed their faces and wore moustaches. Their marital arrangements were communal, but with strings attached.

> omnēs vērō sē Britannī vitrō īnficiunt, quod caeruleum efficit colōrem, atque hōc horridiōrēs sunt in pugnā aspectū; capillōque sunt prōmissō atque omnī parte corporis rāsā praeter caput et labrum superius. uxōrēs habent dēnī duodēnīque inter sē commūnēs et maximē frātrēs cum frātribus parentēsque cum līberīs; sed quī sunt ex hīs nātī, eōrum habentur līberī, quō prīmum virgō quaeque dēducta est.

> Caesar, *De Bello Gallico* 5.14

vitrum,-ī [n.]   *woad*
īnficiō,-ere, īnfēcī, īnfectum [M.]   *stain*
efficiō,-ere, effēcī, effectum [M.]   *make, produce*
horridus,-a,-um   *rough, frightening*
pugna,-ae [f.]   *battle*
aspectus,-ūs [m.]   *appearance*
capillus,-ī [m.]   *hair*
capillō . . . parte: ablatives of 'quality' (*they are with hair . . ., i.e. they have their hair . . .*)
prōmittō,-ere, prōmīsī, prōmissum [3]   *send forth, let grow*
rādō,-ere, rāsī, rāsum [3]   *shave*
praeter [+ acc.]   *except, besides*
labrum,-ī [n.]   *lip*
superius: comparative of 'superus,-a,-um' (*above, higher*)
dēnī duodēnīque   *in tens and twelves*
commūnis,-e   *in common, shared*
quō   *to where, to whose home*
quaeque: nom. fem. of 'quisque' (*each*)
dēdūcō,-ere dēdūxī, dēductum [3]   *escort, marry*

2. Cicero, whose brother was on Caesar's staff, passes on information about Britain to Atticus:

> neque argentī scrīpulum est ūllum in illā īnsulā neque ūlla spēs praedae nisi ex mancipiīs.

> Cicero, *Letters to Atticus* 4.17

scrīpulum,-ī [n.]   *small weight, scrap*
īnsula,-ae [f.]   *island*

3. Tacitus' comment on British weather shows little has changed:

caelum crēbrīs imbribus ac nebulīs foedum; asperitās
frīgorum abest.

Tacitus, Agricola 12

crēber,-bra,-brum   *frequent*
imber, imbris [m.]   *rain, shower*
nebula,-ae [f.]   *mist, fog*
foedus,-a,-um   *dirty*
asperitās,-tātis [f.]   *harshness*

4. Claudius' invasion force landed in AD 43 and within five years most of southern Britain was under Roman control. One chieftain, Caratacus (also spelt Caractacus), continued to resist. He dodged attempts to catch him by heading north where the Romans had fewer friends, or so he thought. He took refuge with Cartimandua, queen of the Brigantes tribe, who sensed an opportunity more valuable than inter-tribal friendship: she clapped him in chains and sold him to the Romans. Caratacus was taken to Rome, where at the end of a triumphal procession he was due to be customarily strangled. Before execution he is said to have made a speech that so impressed Claudius he was freed:

habuī equōs, virōs, arma, opēs: quid mīrum, sī haec
invītus āmīsī? nam sī vōs omnibus imperitāre vultis,
sequitur ut omnēs servitūtem accipiant?

Tacitus, Annals 12.37

ops, opis [f.]   (in plural) *resources, wealth*
mīrus,-a,-um   *extraordinary, surprising*
invītus,-a,-um   *unwilling*
imperitō,-āre,-āvī,-ātum [1; + dat.]   *command, rule over*
servitūs,-tūtis [f.]   *slavery, servitude*
accipiō,-ere, accēpī, acceptum [3]   *receive, welcome*

5. Meanwhile back in Britain, Romanization was in progress. The new province started to prosper as traders took advantage of the new roads and settlements. Money was provided to support developments and keep new subjects acquiescent. Whether this money was a gift or a loan was not always clear – at least to the Britons, who may not have been aware of a difference.

The Britons were characterized as somewhat naïve. Imperial economics was a world beyond them. Cassius Dio, who wrote his history in Greek, tells us that after his release Caratacus wandered around the city marvelling at the buildings of stone, and that he asked his hosts why they coveted his modest resources in Britain.

Some Britons welcomed Roman occupation, others less so. The issue was not simply freedom or servitude but, for many, choice of ruler. Relations between the different *nationes* (tribes) had been made worse by hostile immigrants escaping from Roman control on the mainland. Life was anything but secure. Gradually they learned to deal with officers and agents from Rome, and with each other.

From earliest days Roman expansion was achieved by conquest and coercion, but there were less brutal instruments in their favour too: diplomacy, military support, 'liberation', a huge trading network, roads, towns, houses, and all the refinements of the Roman world. The empire, Cairo to Carlisle, could never have grown and lasted as it did without a degree of giving as well as all the taking. By and large Romans were flexible to local ways, often merging Roman and indigenous practices, even religious ones.

But there were frequent trouble spots, some of which flared into full-scale wars. By the end of the 50s the Romans were bent on suppressing the British Druids, who were spiritual leaders with a reputation for sacrificing Roman prisoners. Their stronghold was on the modern island of Anglesey, then called Mona, off the north-west tip of Wales. The governor of Britain, Gaius Suetonius Paulinus, took a force into Wales and stormed the island.

Druidae, precēs dīrās sublātīs ad caelum manibus fundentēs, novitāte aspectūs perculēre mīlitem.

Tacitus, *Annals* 14.30

prex, precis [f.] *prayer*
dīrus,-a,-um *fearful*
tollō, tollere, sustulī, sublātum [3] *raise, take up, lift up*
fundō,-ere, fūdī, fūsum [3] *pour forth, utter*
percellō,-ere, perculī, perculsum [3] *strike, discourage* ('perculēre' for 'perculērunt')
mīlitem: singular for plural, each individual was struck with fear

6. While Suetonius was in Wales a thunderous rebellion blew up in the south-east. The tribe which started it was the Iceni whose domain approximated to modern Norfolk in East Anglia. The two surviving sources give different causes: Tacitus writes that Prasutagus, king of the Iceni, named the Romans in his will as co-heirs with his wife and daughters. This was not unusual. Territory on the fringe of the empire might be left as a client kingdom prior to full annexation.

rēx Icēnōrum Prasutagus, longā opulentiā clārus, Caesarem hērēdem duāsque fīliās scrīpserat, tālī obsequiō ratus rēgnum et domum suam procul iniūriā fore.

Tacitus, *Annals* 14.31

longus,-a,-um *long, longstanding*
opulentia,-ae [f.] *wealth*
Caesarem: Nero
hērēs, hērēdis [m./f.] *heir, successor*
tālis,-e *such*
obsequium,-ī [n.] *compliance, submission*
reor, rērī, ratus [deponent] *think, reckon* (translate past participle 'ratus' as *thinking*)
fore: an alternative form of the future infinitive of 'sum, esse'
iniūria,-ae [f.] *harm*

7. When Prasutagus died the Romans helped themselves to all his property, not just the half they had been promised. After all, the kingship had continued only with their approval and was now vacant, or so they thought. And so when the dead king's wife started to cause trouble it was time these new provincials learned who was in charge.

prīmum uxor eius Boudicca verberibus affecta et fīliae stuprō violātae sunt; praecipuī quīque Icēnōrum, quasi cūnctam regiōnem mūnerī accēpissent, avītīs bonīs exuuntur, et propinquī rēgis inter mancipia habēbantur.

Tacitus, *Annals* 14.31

Boudicca,-ae: also known as Boudica or Boadicea
verber, verberis [n.]   *blow, lash*
violō,-āre, violāvī, violātum [1]   *violate, outrage*
praecipuus,-a,-um   *especial* ('praecipuus,-ī' = *leading man, chief*)
quīque [nom. pl.]   *each and every*
quasi   *as if*
mūnerī: the 'predicative' dative (see. p. 339), translate *as a gift*
accēpissent: the Romans are the subject, and the subjunctive is used to express their justification for taking all the estate (other-party subjunctive, see p. 289)
avītus,-a,-um   *ancestral*
exuō,-ere, exuī, exūtum [3]   *strip, deprive* (translate as a past tense; for the 'historic present' see p. 303)
propinquus,-ī [m.]   *relative*
inter mancipia habēbantur   *were treated like slaves*

8. The other source, Cassius Dio, does not mention Prasutagus or his will but puts the resentment down to Romans demanding money in the form of taxes, interest on 'gifts', and even the return of the original capital. Cassius states that Seneca, the writer and tutor to Nero, demanded back 40 million sesterces, a huge sum of money, enough to qualify a hundred men for the exclusive class of equestrians. Either way, both sources agree that the immediate cause of resentment was the Romans taking property that the British thought was theirs. And then came the humiliation of their women.

The idea of a woman in political authority was alien to the Romans. The Celts on the other hand were as comfortable being ruled by a queen as by a king. Centuries later in the early Celtic monasteries we find women in charge of male monastic communities. Even today there is a discernible pattern of greater equality in public life – in attitude at least – the further north you are in Europe.

fēminā duce (neque enim sexum in imperiīs discernunt) sūmpsēre ūniversī bellum.

Tacitus, *Agricola* 16

fēminā duce: ablative absolute, with the verb 'to be' understood
sexus,-ūs [m.]   *sex*
discernō,-ere, discrēvī, discrētum [3]   *divide*
sūmpsēre: for 'sūmpsērunt'

9. Britons swarmed to Boudicca's support. They burned three settlements, Camulodunum (Colchester), Londinium (London) and Verulamium (St Albans), and killed all their inhabitants. Suetonius hurried back from north Wales to prevent a complete collapse of the province, but was unable to save the settlements, either because he failed to get there in time or he thought it too risky to try. The final battle for Boudicca's army was fought somewhere between London and Birmingham (the site is still unknown), probably close to Watling Street, the Roman road running from the south-east to the north-west (today the A5).

    Both Cassius and Tacitus imagine speeches for leaders going into battle, in line with the historiographical tradition. These speeches convey the most articulate expression of a cause, a retrospective political PR statement, one for their own side and one for the enemy. Cassius creates a lengthy speech for Boudicca, closing with a prayer to the British goddess Andraste: 'I pray for the preservation of life and liberty against men who are violent, vicious, insatiable, impious; that is if we have to call those people "men" who wash in warm water, eat artificial dainties, drink unmixed wine, smear themselves with myrrh, sleep on soft couches with boys for company – boys past their prime at that – and are slaves to a lyre-player and a rubbish one too.'[1]

    Tacitus' speech for Boudicca is shorter, but just as sharp, ending with a plea to the men to join her in a woman's work:

Boudicca, currū fīliās prae sē vehēns, solitum quidem Britannīs fēminārum ductū bellāre testābātur; vincendum illā aciē vel cadendum esse; id mulierī dēstinātum: vīverent virī et servīrent.

Tacitus, Annals 14.35

prae [+ abl.]   *before, in front of*
ductus,-ūs [m.]   *leadership*
bellō,-āre,-āvī,-ātum [1]   *fight a war*
testor,-ārī, testātus [1; deponent]   *invoke, declare*
solitus,-a-um   *customary* (understand 'esse' with 'solitum' as an accusative-and-infinitive after 'testabātur')
vincendum . . . : Boudicca is still speaking (lit. *it had to be conquered*)
aciēs,-ēī [f.]   *battle-line, battle*
dēstinō,-āre,-āvī,-ātum [1]   *establish, determine*
serviō,-īre, servīvī, servītum [4]   *be a slave*
vīverent, servīrent: imperfect subjunctive, which in Boudicca's direct speech would be present subjunctive ('vīvant et serviant')

10. Tacitus tells us the result was a slaughter of the Britons with one estimate of casualties at 80,000 Britons and 400 Romans, and he adds that Boudicca took her own life with poison. Cassius says that the battle was less decisive; that Boudicca died shortly afterwards through sickness, and that the rebellious Britons melted away to their homes.

    It wasn't long before the province settled down peacefully again, although there were still parts of the island, especially its northern tip, which remained outside Rome's control. In the early 80s, the governor Agricola marched against the Caledonian tribesmen and defeated them at Mons Graupius (another unknown site), where they had gathered under the chieftain Calgacus. Tacitus married Agricola's daughter and so came to write his biography. Before the battle he imagines a rousing speech for his father-in-law; but he reserves his best for Calgacus.

quotiēns causās bellī et necessitātem nostram intueor,
magnus mihi animus est hodiernum diem cōnsēnsumque
vestrum initium lībertātis tōtī Britanniae fore.

Tacitus, Agricola 30

quotiēns   *how many times, as many times as, as often as*
necessitās,-tātis [f.]   *necessity, need*
intueor,-ērī, intuitus [2; deponent]   *look upon, consider*
animus,-ī [m.]   *mind, thought, feeling*
hodiernus,-a,-um   *of this day, today's*
cōnsēnsus,-ūs [m.]   *agreement, unanimity*
fore: the future infinitive of 'sum, esse' is part of the accusative-and-infinitive after 'magnus mihi animus est'

11. This apparent even-handedness of the historians is a lesson for many a writer since. There are of course nuances which give away their standpoint and show, if proof were needed, that the speeches were Roman in origin. The most striking is Calgacus' belief that Britons lived on the edge of the known world. The British, of course, lived in the middle of their world just as we each live in the middle of ours.

nōs terrārum ac lībertātis extrēmōs recessus ipse ac sinus fāmae in hunc diem dēfendit.

Tacitus, Agricola 30

extrēmōs [agrees with 'nōs']   *on the edge (of the world and of liberty)*
recessus,-ūs [m.]   *corner, retreat, remote position*
sinus,-ūs [m.]   *bosom*
sinus fāmae: lit. *the bosom of (our) fame*, i.e. *the protection of (provided by) our reputation*

12.   Tacitus has Calgacus say that Romans used the name of empire to conceal their destructive ways.

ubī sōlitūdinem faciunt, pācem appellant.

Tacitus, Agricola 30

sōlitūdō,-inis [f.]   *loneliness, desert*

13.   Tacitus' talking up of the British cause was not all down to a historian's sense of fair play. There were things about imperial Rome which he despised, the corruption and cruelty of some in authority. Tacitus was not anti-imperialist in the modern sense, but believed in 'imperium' so long as it was in the hands of people like his father-in-law, and not emperors like Tiberius, Nero or Domitian. Neither Tacitus nor his wife, Julia Agricola, were with Agricola when he died, which saddened them both.

sī quis piōrum mānibus locus, sī, ut sapientibus placet, nōn cum corpore exstinguuntur magnae animae, placidē quiēscās.

Tacitus, Agricola 46

mānēs, mānium [m.]   *spirits*
pius,-a,-um   *dutiful, conscientious, just*
placet [+ dat.]   *it pleases, it is the opinion of*
exstinguō,-ere, exstinxī, exstinctum [3]   *extinguish* (in the passive: *perish*)
placidē   *calmly, peacefully*
quiēscō,-ere, quiēvī, quiētum [3]   *rest*

14.   Britons came to accept their provincial status, and the Roman occupation of Britain lasted over four hundred years – one-fifth of the island's entire documented history. Business picked up as traders exploited the plentiful supply of cattle, of slaves and the mining of metals, especially tin. But with its sullen climate and uncivilized traditions Britain remained second choice as an overseas posting. Hadrian's Wall would be built a few decades after Agricola, and there at Vindolanda archaeologists have discovered fragments of letters and other writings which open a little window on the lives of soldiers and others moving around the empire.
      The Britons continued to follow their religious beliefs, in some cases alongside the Roman pantheon. Local cults were merged with Roman ones, such as the worship of the British goddess Sul at Bath where she became identified with Diana. And many Britons learned to speak Latin, a symptom of their moral collapse says Tacitus:

quī modo linguam Rōmānam abnuēbant, ēloquentiam
concupīscēbant. paulātimque dēscēnsum ad dēlēnīmenta
vitiōrum, porticūs et balinea et convīviōrum ēlegantiam.
idque apud imperitōs hūmānitās vocābātur, cum pars
servitūtis esset.

Tacitus, *Agricola* 21

modo   *recently*
abnuō,-ere, abnuī, abnuitum [3]   *reject*
ēloquentia,-ae [f.]   *eloquence, fluency*
concupīscō,-ere, concupīvī, concupītum [3]   *desire, aspire to*
paulātim   *little by little*
dēscēnsum (est): lit. *it was descended*, i.e. *there was a decline*
dēlēnīmentum,-ī [n.]   *allurement*
porticus,-ūs [f.]   *colonnade*
balineum,-ī [n.]   *bath*
ēlegantia,-ae [f.]   *refinement*
imperitus,-a,-um   *inexperienced, ignorant*
hūmānitās,-tātis [f.]   *civilization*

Exercises 23b

1.   Translate:
(a)   labrum superius nōn est rādendum.
(b)   culpa dominae tibi silenda erit.
(c)   quārē Britannīs est pugnandī amor?
(d)   servitūsne timenda est?
(e)   Britannī clāmābant rēgīnam Icēnōrum nōn esse vituperandam.

2.   Identify the noun with which each underlined gerundive agrees, and translate:
(a)   ipse multārum rērum exempla **imitanda** posterīs trādidī.
(b)   dē Clōdiā ego nihil dīcam nisi **dēpellendī** crīminis causā.
(c)   populus mē triumvirum reī pūblicae **cōnstituendae** creāvit.

3.   Translate:
(a)   sī tua domina est fīlia tōnsōris vel cōpōnis vel cocī vel laniī, certē est vituperanda; sīn ē
    magnīs orta, est mīranda.
        — minimē! mea domina semper est laudanda, quae neque ūllum argentum neque ūllās
        imāginēs habet. nihil illī est nisi sua probitās!
(b)   ego ratus sum ūnam navem satis esse ad novōs servōs in Italiam vectandōs.
        — ūnam? quantī tibi servī?
(c)   dominus mē servum pedibus lavandīs creāvit.
        — tū es fēlīx. ille cloācam lavāre mē iussit.

4.   The phrase *mutatis mutandis* is still used from time to time in English. It is, or was, an
    ablative absolute, both words from 'mūtō, mūtāre' (*change*). What does the phrase mean?

5.   Find Latin ancestors in this chapter of *acquiescent, deduct, discernible* and *extinction*.

— 24 —

Gods and spirits

Impersonal verbs

Most of the verbs you have met have been 'personal', where the subject is an identifiable person or thing.

> **Romulus** centum creat senātōrēs
> *Romulus appoints a hundred senators* [1.8]

A few verbs are 'impersonal'. They appear in the 3rd person singular: (*it . . .*):

licet (*it is lawful, allowed*) + dative and infinitive:

> **licet** nōbīs dare tribūtum Caesarī?
> *is it lawful for us to give tribute to Caesar?* [26.2]

libet (*it is pleasing, agreeable*) + dative and infinitive:

> **libet** mihi iacēre in grāmine
> *it pleases me to lie on the grass* [22.2]

oportet (*it is necessary, proper*) + accusative and infinitive:

> illōs ad iūdicium veluti aegrōs ad medicum dūcī **oportet**
> *it is proper that those men are brought to trial like the sick (are taken) to a doctor* [26.10]

placet (*it pleases, seems good, right*) + dative:

> sī, ut sapientibus **placet**, nōn cum corpore exstinguuntur animae, placidē quiēscās
> *if, as (it) seems right to wise men, souls do not perish with the body, may you rest in peace* [23.13]

iuvat (*it is helps, pleases, delights*) + accusative and infinitive:

> quid tē **iuvat** indulgēre dolōrī?
> *what does it help you (why does it please you) to yield to grief?* [17.8]

convenit (*it is suitable for, it is agreed between, there is like-mindedness between*) + dative and infinitive:

> quid virō bonō magis **convenit** quam abesse ā cīvīlibus contrōversiīs?
> *what is more suitable for a good man than to be far from political quarrels?* [8.9]

> **convenit** Māmurrae Caesarīque
> *Mamurra and Caesar are suited* (lit. *there is like-mindedness between . . .*) [13.1]

Some of these verbs can be rendered as personal ones in an English translation:

> illōs ad iūdicium velutī aegrōs ad medicum dūcī **oportet**
> *those men should be brought to trial like the sick are taken to a doctor* [26.10]

And some are used in Latin as personal verbs too, e.g. **iuvō,-āre** (*please, help*) and **conveniō, -īre** (*come together, meet*).

Practice 24a

Translate:
(a) hodiē nōn licet taurōs in forum dūcere.
(b) convenitne mihi cum uxōre Caesaris discumbere?
(c) nunc mihi placet discumbere versūsque tuōs audīre.

Transitive and intransitive verbs

Verbs which can take a direct object are called transitive verbs and those which cannot – but may take an indirect one – are intransitive, e.g.

> he *prepares* the meal   (transitive verb)
> she *sulks* in the kitchen   (intransitive verb)

A transitive verb switches easily into the passive, where the direct object becomes the subject of the passive verb (*the meal is prepared*). An intransitive verb, which cannot take a direct object, is less adaptable: in English you cannot say 'it was sulked'. Latin, however, does have an impersonal use of intransitive verbs in the passive (many involving past participles or gerundives, which are both passive):

> ubī ad castra **ventum est**, nuntiātum Coriolānō est adesse ingēns mulierum agmen
> *when they came* (lit. *it was come*) *to the camp, it was announced to Coriolanus that a large crowd of women was present* [17.2]

> in Perusīnōs **saevītum est**
> *brutal treatment* (lit. *it was raged against*) *was inflicted upon the people of Perusia* [10.10]

paulātim **dēscēnsum est** ad dēlēnīmenta vitiōrum
little by little there was a decline (lit. *it was descended . . .*) *to the allurements of vices* [23.14]

verendum est nē cāseum liber comedat
there is concern (lit. *it is to be feared*) *that a book may gobble up the cheese* [19.2]

sī Pompēium et Caesarem habēmus, nōn **est dēspērandum**
if we have Pompey and Caesar (on our side), it is not to be despaired [7.13]

Some compounds of intransitive verbs take direct objects and so are transitive, e.g.
venio,-īre (*come*) is intransitive, but **circumveniō,-īre** (*surround*) and **inveniō,-īre** (*find, discover*) both take direct objects and so can be used in the passive:

in Graeciā prīmum hūmānitās, litterae, etiam frūgēs **inventae sunt**
in Greece first of all civilization, literature and even crops were discovered [4.4]

English phrasal verbs

Some English phrasal verbs which you might expect to be intransitive in Latin are in fact
transitive with their objects in the accusative:

haec **cūrēs**
you should look after these things
[19.8]

aliquid **poscis**
you call for something [14.2]

+ object in the accusative
conquīrō,-ere [3]   *search for*
cūrō,-āre [1]   *care for, see to, look after*
exerceō,-ēre [2]   *work at*
intueor,-ērī [2; deponent]   *gaze at, look at, upon*
poscō,-ere [3]   *call for*
rīdeō,-ēre [2]   *laugh at*

Poscō,-ere is one of a handful of verbs which can govern *two* accusatives, typically
verbs of teaching, asking, demanding or begging, i.e. to beg X (accusative) for a Y (also
accusative): **doceō,-ēre** = *teach*; **ōrō,-āre** = *beg (for)*; **poscō,-ere** = *call for, demand*;
rogō,-āre = *ask (for)*.

Practice 24b
Translate:
(a)   captīvus frūstrā victōrem vītam ōrāvit.
(b)   illa mulier semper tribūnum auxilium rogābat.
(c)   līberōsne Fulviae Octāvia cūrābat?

Revision of the uses of the subjunctive

Here is a review of the uses of the subjunctive (see Chapters 15 and 16):

in a main clause
- expressing wishes, exhortations, commands, ironic sighs
- asking rhetorical questions (2nd and 3rd person) and deliberative questions (1st person)

in a subordinate clause
- after **ut** (= *that, so that*)
- after **nē** (= *that . . . not*)
- after **cum** (= *when, since, although*)
- to express a purpose/intention or result/consequence
- in an indirect command or indirect question
- after a verb of fearing (**nē** = *that*, **ut** = *that . . . not*)
- in an impossible or unlikely 'if' clause (**sī**)
- for another party's reasons or thoughts (and not the writer's)

There is a degree of overlap. On p. 205 we saw how a fearing clause (**nē** . . .) can be similar to a negative purpose clause. The sentence below has a verb of 'effecting', with a clause which is partly purpose and partly one of result:

Caesar nē Curiō praemia darentur effēcit
Caesar managed to prevent the payments being made to Curius [7.2]

Practice 24c

The underlined words in both sentences are subjunctive for the same reason. What is it?
(a) in prīmīs ā tē petō ut tē videam, ut tuō cōnsiliō, grātiā, dīgnitāte, ope omnium rērum ūtī <u>possim</u> [8.7];
(b) Cleopātrae, quam servātam triumphō magnopere cupiēbat, etiam psyllōs admōvit, quī venēnum <u>exsūgerent</u> [11.10]

Vocabulary 24

How many prepositions can you find in this course? Include the case (or cases) each governs.

Look online for all the prepositions which appear in the course (see p. 393).

Exercises 24a

1. Translate:
(a) nōs prō patriā bene loquī oportet.
(b) dominō dominaeque bene convenit.
(c) ēheu, nunc nōbīs est cadendum.
(d) nōnne nōbīs dolēre licet?
(e) mihi placet cum lībertīs bibere.
(f) mē illa superba rīdet raedamque velut servum poscit.
(g) licetne nōbīs cum līberīs ac coniugibus adesse?
(h) tōtōsne servōs praefectī ad supplicium dūcī oportēbat?

(i)   poēta numquam Clōdiam cēnam ōrābit.
(j)   utinam dea nōs omnēs cūret.

2.   Translate into Latin:
(a)   I like to hear the poems. (*use* 'libet')
(b)   Who will teach me Greek letters?

3.   Translate:
Octāvia quaesiit quārē Claudiō placēret tibi parcere.
—ego locūtus cōram multīs senātōribus adeō Claudium mōvī ut lībertātem accēperim.

Gods and spirits

Gods and goddesses are central figures in Roman mythology. They pull the strings and steer the action, controlling the lives of mortals, and are themselves depicted almost entirely like humans. Venus, goddess of love, is loving, flirtatious, deceitful; Juno, the wife of all-powerful Jupiter, is embittered by his many romances elsewhere; Diana, goddess of the woods, nimble, aloof and vengeful; Bacchus is the god of booze, of party-going and ritual madness; Apollo serves as the god of many things, including the sun, prophecy, archery, healing and music; we've already seen Mars, the grim god of war; and Vulcan, smouldering in his forge deep beneath a mountain.

Most of these gods were Roman in origin but by the time we meet them, in the stories of Virgil and Ovid, their personalities had been almost entirely twinned with the gods of Greek literature. Thus Venus assumed the personality and function of Aphrodite, Juno of Hera, Diana of Artemis, Bacchus of Dionysos, Mars of Ares, Vulcan of Hephaistos and so on.

A few differences and native characteristics remained. The Greek goddess Athena, patron of Athens, was much worshipped by Athenians; you hear less about her Roman counterpart, Minerva. Saturn was identified with the Greek god Kronos and so was the father of Jupiter, but he never loses his deeply Italian character. The cult of Apollo arrived in Italy much earlier than his brothers and sisters: he is one of the few to keep his Greek name in Latin.

In the myths and stories gods shape the course of events. They are depicted as puppeteers, pursuing their own goals, sometimes in competition with each other. In Virgil's *Aeneid* the gods appear to be running the show and yet the cleverness of the storyteller reveals human characters who, despite being pushed and pulled by the gods, act in convincingly human ways.

1.   Aeneas' mother is Venus. When he is shipwrecked on the Carthaginian coast, she arranges for Dido to fall in love with him. The goddess Juno, bent on stopping Aeneas from reaching Italy, suggests a long-term match:

'ardet amāns Dīdō, traxitque per ossa furōrem.
commūnem hunc ergō populum paribusque regāmus
auspiciīs; liceat Phrygiō servīre marītō,
dōtālisque tuae Tyriōs permittere dextrae.'

Virgil, *Aeneid* 4.101–4

ardeō,-ēre [2]   *burn, glow, be on fire*

trahō,-ere, traxī, tractum [3]   *draw, drag, take on*

os, ossis [n.]   *bone*

furor,-ōris [m.]   *rage, passion*

commūnis,-e   *in common, as one*

regāmus: subjunctive *let us . . ., why don't we . . .*

auspicia,-ōrum [n.]   *auspices* (i.e. sign-reading from the flight of birds; to be 'under the same auspices' was to belong to a single group of people sharing the same divine signs)

liceat [subjunctive]   *may it be allowed* (understand *to her*)

Phrygius,-a,-um: i.e. *Trojan* (Phrygia was a kingdom close to Troy, so translate as *Trojan*)

dōtālis,-e   *as a dowry* ('dōtālīs' = acc.pl.)

tuae: Venus, as the parent of Aeneas, would have an interest in any dowry

Tyrius,-ī [m.]   *Tyrian* (Dido had settled in north Africa having escaped from Tyre, a city on the coast of modern Lebanon)

dextra,-ae [f.]   *right hand*, i.e. *control*

2.   Venus knows the destiny planned for her son, but avoids a confrontation with Juno.

sīc contrā est ingressa Venus: 'quis tālia dēmēns
abnuat, aut tēcum mālit contendere bellō?'

Virgil, Aeneid 4.107–8

ingredior, ingredī, ingressus [deponent]   *go forward, proceed*

tālia: neuter plural of 'tālis,-e'

abnuat: subjunctive as it is a rhetorical question (see p. 187)

mālit: present subjunctive of 'mālō, mālle'

3.   Does Jupiter want the Trojans to settle with the Carthaginians? Venus already knows the answer. Perhaps Juno might first check with her husband.

'tū coniūnx tibi fās animum temptāre precandō.
perge; sequar.' tum sīc excēpit rēgia Iūnō:
'mēcum erit iste labor.'

Virgil, Aeneid 4.113–15

tū coniūnx: treat as a separate clause, i.e. *you are his wife and . . .*

temptō,-āre [1]   *make trial of, test, sound out*

precandō: gerund from 'precor,-ārī' (*ask, entreat*)

pergō,-ere, perrēxī, perrēctum [3]   *go, proceed*

sequar: 1st person of either present subjunctive or future indicative of 'sequor, sequī'

excipiō,-ere, excēpī, exceptum [M.]   *come next, follow*

rēgius,-a,-um   *royal*

4.   Venus' method with male gods was more direct. After Aeneas leaves Carthage he faces a struggle to settle in Italy. So she uses her supernatural talents to persuade her husband Vulcan, god of the forge, to make her son some new weapons (including the shield already seen).

dīxerat et niveīs hinc atque hinc dīva lacertīs
cūnctantem amplexū mollī fovet. ille repente
accēpit solitam flammam.

Virgil, Aeneid 8.387–9

dīxerat: the subject is Venus
niveus,-a,-um   *snow-white*
hinc atque hinc   *from one side then the other*
lacertus,-ī [m.]   *arm*
cūnctor,-ārī, cūnctātus [1; deponent]   *hesitate*
amplexus,-ūs [m.]   *embrace*
foveō,-ēre, fōvī, fōtum [2]   *warm*
solitus,-a,-um   *familiar*

5.   Marriage to the goddess of sex had its downside. In a myth as old as Homer, Vulcan took umbrage at her affair with Mars, god of war, and with his metal-working skills caught the two together in a trap. He then invited the other gods to view them:

Lemnius extemplō valvās patefēcit eburnās
immīsitque deōs; illī iacuēre ligātī
turpiter, atque aliquis dē dīs nōn trīstibus optat
sīc fierī turpis; superī rīsēre diūque
haec fuit in tōtō nōtissima fābula caelō.

Ovid, Metamorphoses 4.185–9

Lemnius: i.e. Vulcan; the island of Lemnos was sacred to Hephaistos (Vulcan's Greek
    counterpart)
extemplō   *immediately, without delay*
valvae,-ārum [f.]   *(folding) door*
patefaciō,-ere, patefēcī, patefactum [M.]   *reveal, open*
eburnus,-a,-um   *(made) of ivory*
immittō,-ere, immīsī, immissum [3]   *send in, let in*
illī: Mars and Venus
iacuēre: for 'iacuērunt'
ligō,-āre,-āvī,-ātum [1]   *tie, bind together*
aliquis dē dīs   *one of the gods*
nōn trīstibus: i.e. *cheerful, full of mirth*
optō,-āre,-āvī,-ātum [1]   *pray, express a wish*
superī,-ōrum [m.; noun from 'superus,-a,-um']   *those above, gods*
rīsēre: for 'rīsērunt'

nōtus,-a,-um *known*
fābula,-ae [f.] *story*

6. Women were barely visible in historical and political writing; but in the more internalized view of life in fictional narratives they are fully drawn characters – if by men – as powerful, vulnerable, attractive, frightening, and at moments vicious. Goddesses had no less a role than the gods. At times their power seems more chilling, for in many of the myths they appear closer to the action than the males. Gods are though a reflection of humans themselves, and even goddesses have moments of vulnerability.

> dum Prōserpina lūcō
> lūdit et aut violās aut candida līlia carpit,
> dumque puellārī studiō calathōsque sinumque
> implet et aequālēs certat superāre legendō,
> paene simul vīsa est dīlectaque raptaque Dītī.
>
> Ovid, Metamorphoses 5.391–5

Prōserpina: (Greek – Persephone) virginal daughter of the goddess Ceres
lūcus,-ī [m.] *wood, grove*
lūdit, carpit, implet, certat: the present is regularly used after 'dum' (*while*), which we translate as if imperfect
viola,-ae [f.] *violet*
candidus,-a,-um *fair, white*
līlium,-ī [n.] *lily*
carpō,-ere [3] *pluck, pick*
puellāris,-e *girlish*
calathus,-ī [m.] *basket*
sinus,-ūs [m.] *fold of a garment, bosom* (the flowers will tumble out as she is snatched away)
aequālis,-e *equal* (as a noun, *comrade* or *companion*)
certō,-āre,-āvī,-ātum [1] *strive, compete*
legendō: gerund (*in picking*)
paene *nearly, almost*
Dītī [abl.]: Dis was the god of the underworld, identified with Greek Pluto

7. Venus and Juno manipulate the action of the *Aeneid*, yet there is no question who is ultimately the boss: Jupiter *omnipotens* never loses his perch as the paterfamilias.

> dīvōsque mortālīsque turmās
> imperiō regit ūnus aequō.
>
> Horace, Odes 3.4.47–8

The subject of 'regit' is Jupiter
turma,-ae [f.] *troop, crowd, throng*
ūnus: i.e. *alone, singly*
aequus,-a,-um *equal, impartial*

8. The powers and functions of the gods are revealed in everyday descriptions of life. Their names were sometimes used as words for the feelings, activities or natural phenomena they represented: Venus for love, Bacchus for drinking wine, Mars for war, Dis or Orcus for the underworld, and so on. Jupiter was leader of the gods, and also looked after the weather and the sky. Here a huntsman is too excited by the chase to return home to his tender wife:

> manet sub Iove frīgidō
> vēnātor tenerae coniugis immemor.

Horace, Odes 1.1.25–6

frīgidus,-a,-um   *cold, chilly*
vēnātor,-ōris [m.]   *huntsman*
immemor   *heedless, forgetful*

9. The richness of the stories, the statues and temples, the mythology that has been ingrained over centuries, all this would excuse anyone for thinking these gods were at the centre of ancient belief. They were not. At least they were not alone. Behind the facade of these personality-gods lay a much deeper array of spirits who were ever-present in a world full of superstitious uncertainty. Spirits were identified in all things which could affect human life. Some have appeared already, e.g. Discordia and Bellona [13.5]. Here are some more, whom Aeneas passes on his way down to the underworld. Their dwelling-place at the entrance to hell gives handy access to the world above.

> vestibulum ante ipsum prīmīs in faucibus Orcī
> Lūctus et ultrīcēs posuēre cubīlia Cūrae;
> pallentēs habitant Morbī trīstisque Senectus,
> et Metus et malesuāda Famēs ac turpis Egestās,
> terribilēs vīsū fōrmae, Lētumque Labōsque.

Virgil, Aeneid 6.273–7

vestibulum,-ī [n.]   *hall*
faucēs, faucium [f.]   *throat, opening, mouth*
Orcus,-ī [m.]   *Hades, hell* (Orcus: another name for the god of the underworld)
lūctus,-ūs [m.]   *grief*
ultrīx   *avenging*
posuēre: for 'posuērunt'
cubīle, cubīlis [n.]   *couch, bed*
Cūra,-ae [f.]   *(spirit of) care, anxiety*
pallēns   *pallid-making*
morbus,-ī [m.]   *(spirit of) disease*
senectūs, senectūtis [f.]   *(spirit of) old age*
malesuādus,-a,-um   *evil-counselling*

famēs, famis [f.]   (*spirit of*) *hunger*
egestās, egestātis [f.]   (*spirit of*) *necessity, poverty*
vīsū: the supine (a part of a verb not yet seen) of 'videō,-ēre' meaning *to see*
fōrma,-ae [f.]   *shape*
lētum,-ī [n.]   *death*
labōs, labōris [m.]   *toil*

10. *Terribiles visu formae* says Virgil, although the physical representation of these spirits was far less clear-cut than that of the Olympian gods. In some ways these shadowy half-drawn figures exert a greater degree of menace. *Fama*, the spirit of rumour, hears of the love-making of Dido and Aeneas (inspired by Juno and Venus) and turns a quiet whisper into hot gossip:

extemplō Libyae magnās it Fāma per urbēs,
Fāma, malum quā nōn aliud vēlōcius ūllum.

Virgil, Aeneid 4.173–4

Libya,-ae [f.]   *Libya, north Africa*
it: from 'eō, īre'
quā: ablative of comparison (*than which*)
vēlōx [like 'fēlīx']   *rapid, quick*

11. People prayed to all kinds of spirits in the hope that the activity or condition each spirit represented would turn out to their advantage. Their desires and fears energized daily rituals in private homes or state ceremonies. Sacrifices were commonplace, which merged the smell and noise of an abattoir with the solemnity of a church.

Religious belief and ritual pervaded all ancient life. Romans planned their lives around a calendar of religious festivals, not least because they were holidays. The spirits *Lares* (the hearth) and *Penates* (foodstore) were worshipped as much as any god, with rituals and sacrifices in private homes. There were similar ceremonies in public, where Jupiter was celebrated as the protector of the state.

Priests in ancient Rome were not moral or spiritual counsellors, but honorary officials who performed public rituals. The *pontifex maximus* (chief pontiff) supervised state ceremonies and also monitored the calendar. Augurs were responsible for reading omens and interpreting the will of the gods (with a useful if dubious political influence); and the *flamines* looked after the worship of individual gods and their temples. According to legend, priesthoods were set up by Numa Pompilius, king of Rome after Romulus.

flāminem Iovī adsiduum sacerdōtem creāvit īnsignīque
eum veste et curūlī rēgiā sellā adōrnāvit. huic duōs
flāminēs adiēcit, Martī ūnum, alterum Quirīnō,
virginēsque Vestae lēgit.

Livy, History of Rome 1.20

The subject is Numa

flāmen,-inis [m.]   *flamen, priest* (devoted to a particular god)
adsiduus,-a,-um   *continually present, attending, devoted*
sacerdōs,-dōtis [m./f.]   *priest/priestess*
īnsignis,-e   *distinguished*
curūlis sella   *curule chair* (an official seat for magistrates)
Quirīnus: i.e. Romulus, after he was deified
Vesta,-ae [f.]   *Vesta* (goddess of the hearth and home, and of the hearth of the city; in
   her temple the Vestal Virgins kept the flame of Vesta always burning)

12. The possibility of life after death was much thought about, as everywhere. Poetic
narrative presents the underworld of Hades, the shadowy realm of fluttering spirits,
ruled by the god Orcus/Dis and his goddess-wife Proserpina, who after an uncertain
start (p. 319) settles as a forbidding figure in the world below. Aeneas was one of a very
few who visited this world and returned above. The Sibyl, his guide, says what a
challenge that is:

> facilis dēscēnsus Avernō:
> noctēs atque diēs patet ātrī iānua Dītis;
> sed revocāre gradum superāsque ēvādere ad aurās,
> hoc opus, hic labor est.

Virgil, Aeneid 6.126–9

dēscēnsus,-ūs [m.]   *descent, way down*
Avernus,-a,-um   *belonging to the underworld* (here used as a noun)
noctēs atque diēs: accusative of duration of time
pateō,-ēre [2]   *lie open*
āter, ātra, ātrum   *black, gloomy*
iānua,-ae [f.]   *door, entrance*
ēvādō,-ere, ēvāsī, ēvāsum [3]   *go out, come out, escape*
aura,-ae [f.]   *air, breeze, fresh air*

13. At the very end of the *Aeneid*, Aeneas angrily plunges his weapon into Turnus, whose
resentful soul slips away to the world below.

> vītaque cum gemitū fugit indīgnāta sub umbrās.

Virgil, Aeneid 6.952

indīgnātus,-a,-um   *resentful, in anger* (from 'indīgnor,-ārī')
sub: with the accusative = *to the . . . below*
umbra,-ae [f.]   *shadow, shade*

14. People like Cicero would no doubt participate in state and private rituals, but he himself
had no fixed belief about the next life:

nam sī suprēmus ille diēs nōn exstinctiōnem, sed
commūtātiōnem affert locī, quid optābilius? sīn autem
perimit ac dēlet omnīnō, quid melius quam in mediīs vītae
labōribus obdormīscere?

Cicero, Tusculan Disputations 1.117

suprēmus,-a,-um   *highest, extreme, last* (superlative of 'superus,-a,-um')
exstinctiō,-ōnis [f.]   *extinction*
commūtātiō,-ōnis [f.]   *change*
afferō, afferre, attulī, allātum   *bring*
optābilis,-e   *desirable*
perimō,-ere, perēmī, peremptum [3]   *destroy*
dēleō,-ēre, dēlēvī, dēlētum [3]   *annihilate*
omnīnō   *entirely, in entirety*
obdormīscō,-ere [3]   *fall asleep*

15. A few rejected religious beliefs out of hand, such as Lucretius, a poet-philosopher and
     contemporary of Cicero:

quippe ita formīdō mortalīs continet omnīs,
quod multa in terrīs fierī caelōque tuentur
quōrum operum causās nūllā ratiōne vidēre
possunt ac fierī dīvīnō nūmine rentur.

Lucretius, On the Nature of Things 1.151–4

quippe   *indeed, to be sure*
formīdō,-inis [f.]   *fear, dread*
mortālīs . . . omnīs: both accusative plural
contineō,-ēre, continuī, contentum [2]   *contain, restrain*
quod   *that, namely that*
multa: acc.pl., part of an accusative-and-infinitive with 'fierī'
tueor,-ērī, tuitus [2; deponent]   *behold, look upon*
opus, operis [n.]   *work, action, event*
ratiō,-ōnis [f.]   *reckoning, (rational) explanation*
rentur: from 'reor, rērī'

16. Many emperors when they died were awarded divine status. Not all took this too
     seriously. Just before his death Vespasian was heard to say:

'vae,' inquit, 'putō deus fīō.'

Suetonius, Life of Vespasian 23

vae   *alas, oh dear*
putō . . . fīō   *I think I'm becoming* (we might expect an accusative-and-infinitive, but
    colloquial Latin did not follow all the literary rules)

Exercises 24b

1.   Translate:
(a) Graecās litterās tibi licet discere sed nōn philosophiam.
(b) Cleopātrae fīlium appellāre nōmine Caesaris placēbat.
(c) cūr, ō Hannibal, tē in montibus manēre iuvat?
(d) poētam oportuit cum ille patrōnum salūtāret dominum dīcere.
(e) ō amīcī, sī Atticus nōs iuvat, nōn est dēspērandum.
(f) Clōdiō placēbat in forum venīre cum uxōre.

2.   Identify the case of each underlined word, and translate:
(a) **nōbīs** verendum est nē Porsenna urbem capiat.
(b) cūr **dominae** libet mē exclūdere perferentem frīgora noctis?
(c) quārē placuit **Cicerōnī** Catilīnam dēfendere?
(d) deinde familiārium quīdam quaesiit quid **dominae** placēret.
(e) ego nōn Iūdaeīs nocuī, nec **Britannīs**, nec Gallīs, nec Graecīs; sed tū, ō Rōmāne, quid fēcistī?
(f) **mulierēs** forō sē et contiōne abstinēre oportet.

3.   Translate:
(a) tōtīne prīncipēs crēdidērunt sē factūrōs esse deōs?
(b) facilis est dēscēnsus Avernō; sed nē Prōserpina quidem ad aurās superās ēvādere potuit.
(c) puellīs libet lūdere in lūcō et candida līlia carpere.
(d) mātremne Dīs rogāvit num fīliam rapere licēret?
(e) dolēre nōs oportet nec tamen suprā modum.
(f) mī libet sub Iove frīgidō iacēre.

4.   Find Latin ancestors in this chapter of *gradually*, *lethal* and *operation*.

— 25 —

Rough justice

Words working in pairs

On p. 218 appeared correlative pronouns, which are used in pairs to balance a sentence, e.g.

> <u>illa</u> tamen gravior, **quae** laudat Vergilium
> *yet more troublesome is <u>that woman who</u> praises Virgil* [16.3]

and in some examples with the antecedent missing (here added in brackets)

> **quī** modo linguam Rōmānam abnuēbant, (**eī**) ēloquentiam concupīscēbant
> *<u>those</u> <u>who</u> recently rejected the Roman language wanted to be fluent* [23.14]

Adverbs and conjunctions also serve in pairs to balance expressions (**aut** . . . **aut, et** . . . **et, neque** . . . **neque**, etc).

Practice 25a
Identify the two words in each sentence which work together to balance two clauses or phrases: (e.g. prīmō **magis** ambitiō **quam** avāritia animōs hominum exercēbat).
(a)   nec minus līber sum quam vōs
(b)   seu plūrīs hiemēs seu tribuit Iuppiter ultimam
(c)   meī tam suspiciōne quam crīmine carēre dēbent
(d)   libet iacēre modo sub antīquā īlice, / modo in tenācī grāmine
(e)   cum in administrātiōne tum in victōriā bellī
(f)   nihil aequē amōrem incitat et accendit quam carendī metus

---

Some of these words may have different meanings when used singly, e.g. **cum, quam, nec/neque** – as **nec** in (a) above.

In the final two chapters we revisit the case-endings and review their functions.

The nominative case reviewed

The nominative is used for the subject

> **populus** mē triumvirum creāvit
> *the people appointed me triumvir* [10.5]

> exiit **ēdictum** ā Caesare Augustō
> *a decree went out from Caesar Augustus* [12.13]

> prīmō magis **ambitiō** quam **avāritia** animōs hominum exercēbat
> *at first ambition rather than greed exercised the minds of men* [6.1]

and for the complement of the subject

> tua est Lāvīnia **coniūnx**
> *Lavinia is your wife* [1.5]

> senātūs cōnsultō **Augustus** appellātus sum.
> *I was named Augustus by decree of the senate* [12.1]

Practice 25b

1. Give the genitive singular of each of the underlined nouns in the examples above (**populus . . . Augustus**).
2. What are the possible cases (and state singular or plural) of (a) opus (b) gradus (*or* gradūs) (c) virtūs
3. Identify ten 3rd declension nouns, each with a different ending in the nominative singular.

The accusative case reviewed

The principal function of the accusative is to indicate the object of the verb

> centum creat **senātōrēs**
> *he appoints a hundred senators* [1.8]

> dēfendī **rem pūblicam**
> *I defended the Republic* [9.12]

and it is used with some prepositions (e.g. **ad, ante, in,**[1] **trāns, per, sub**)

---

1 Some prepositions (e.g. **in, sub**) take either the accusative or the ablative. See p. 13.

Cloelia omnēs ad **propinquōs** restituit
Cloelia restored everyone to their <u>relatives</u> [2.8]

pete rēgna per **undās**
seek the lands over <u>the waves</u> [3.12]

īnsepultus in **flūmen** prōiectus est
he was thrown unburied into <u>the river</u> [5.1]

Iugurtha ante **currum** ductus est
Jugurtha was led before <u>the chariot</u> [5.7]

and as an object of motion sometimes with no preposition

Caesar Pompēium fugientem **Alexandrēam** persecūtus est
Caesar pursued Pompey as he fled to <u>Alexandria</u> [8.10]

and to express duration of time or distance

noctēs atque **diēs** patet ātrī iānua Dītis
<u>*night*</u> *and <u>day</u> the door of gloomy Dis lies open* [24.12]

and to express other kinds of extent, sometimes with neuter adjectives (the 'adverbial accusative')

quid **tantum** īnsānō iuvat indulgēre dolōrī?
what help is it to yield <u>so much</u> to your demented grief? [17.8]

and frequently in an indirect statement (the accusative and infinitive)

Pompēius cōnfirmat **Clōdium** nihil esse factūrum contrā mē
Pompey reassures (me) that <u>Clodius</u> will do nothing against me [7.5]

and less frequently as the 'accusative of respect'

ille simul manibus tendit dīvellere nōdōs
perfūsus saniē **vittās** ātrōque venēnō
at the same time he struggles to prise apart the coils with his hands, spattered <u>with respect to his ribbons</u>
(i.e. *his ribbons spattered*) *with gore and with black poison* [25.11]

This accusative of respect appears to represent an object of a passive verb. Something similar happens in Greek, and that probably reinforced the use in Latin. The accusative of respect also surfaces in uses of **quid** and **quod** (see p. 217).

Another use of the accusative is the 'accusative of exclamation', where a wail of woe or expression of joy is phrased in the accusative, usually a noun or pronoun with an adjective. At some earlier point these accusatives may have been objects of verbs indicating feeling or distress, but the verbs were lost in the emotion of the moment:

nōs fēlīcēs!
how fortunate we are!

mē miserum!
how wretched I am!

Practice 25c

1. What are the possible cases (and state singular or plural) of (a) venēnum (b) patrum?
2. Give all the possible functions (i.e. case, gender and number) of (a) bona (or bonā) (b) gravia.
3. Identify a word that ends **-e** in the accusative.
4. Identify five nouns each with a different ending in the accusative plural (**-ās, -ēs**, etc).

The genitive case reviewed

The genitive was introduced as a case typically translated as *of . . .*

and is used to show ownership/possession/belonging, usually dependent on another noun

cōnsulis līberī
the children of <u>the consul</u> [2.9]

contempsī **Catilīnae** gladiōs
I scorned the swords of <u>Catiline</u> [9.12]

or to describe a part of something or quantity (the partitive genitive)

scrīptōrum cōpia
an abundance of <u>writers</u> [4.8]

quid ille nōbīs **bonī** fēcit?
what of <u>good</u> (what good) has that man done for us? [21.9]

or as an objective genitive to describe the object of another noun (often used to express feelings about something or someone)

metū **Mārcī Antōnī**
from fear of <u>Mark Antony</u> [9.5]

prīmō **pecūniae**, deinde **imperiī**, cupīdō crēvit
at first there grew a love of <u>money</u>, then of <u>power</u> [6.2]

or to describe value (called the 'genitive of value')

quantī lībertās cōnstet mihi tanta, requīris?
do you want to know (at) how much such licence is costing me? [14.6]

omnēs **ūnīus** aestimēmus **assis**
let us value them all at one as [15.6]

and you will meet other uses of the genitive, such as the descriptive genitive:

puella **annōrum** decem
a girl of ten years

Practice 25d

1. Give the nominative forms (singular or plural as they appear) of: lacrimās, competitōrem, hominum, clādibus, crīminis, proeliō, administrātiōne, metū.
2. Give the genitive singular of: carmen, exercitus, honestās, discidium, rēs, homō, facinus, vultus, crux, carcer, bēstia.

Vocabulary 25

These word-pairs balance sentences:

alter* . . . alter*   *one . . . the other*

aut . . . aut   *either . . . or*

cum . . . tum   *as . . . so . . .; both . . . and; not only . . . but also*

et . . . et   *both . . . and*

id* . . . quod* (and other pronouns with **quī, quae, quod**)   *that . . . which*

ita . . . ut [+ subjunctive]   *so/in such a way . . . that*

modo . . . modo   *sometimes . . . sometimes, now . . . now*

neque . . . neque (nec . . . nec)   *neither . . . nor*

nōn sōlum/tantum . . . sed/vērum etiam   *not only . . . but also*

quantus* . . . tantus*   *as much/many as . . . so much/many*

-que . . . -que   *both . . . and*

quot . . . tot   *as many . . . . so many*

seu . . . seu (sīve . . . sīve)   *whether . . . or*

sīc . . . ut   *so . . . as*

simul . . . simul   *while . . . at the same time*

tālis* . . . quālis*   *of such a kind . . . as*

tam . . . quam   *as (much) . . . as*

ut . . . ita   *as . . . so*

vel . . . vel   *either . . . or*

* variable endings

Many of these words also appear singly, some with different meanings.

Look online to see adverbs and conjunctions which appear in the course (see p. 393).

Exercises 25a

1.   Translate:
(a)   nec minus fōrmōsa sum quam tū.
(b)   est difficile dominōque dominaeque servīre: alter saevus, altera īnsāna est.
(c)   nihil vērō tam damnōsum bonīs mōribus quam taurum fugāre.
(d)   nihil aequē avāritiam incitat quam habendī nihil metus.
(e)   quī fugat, ipse fugātur.
(f)   miserōs servōs! facilius est dominum eōs verberāre quam ipsum labōrāre.
(g)   quī modo convīvia rīdēbant, nunc amīcitiam meam concupīscunt.

2.   Give the gender of each underlined word and identify another word in the sentence which helps you identify that gender:
(a)   **cohortēs**, sī quae locō cessissent, decimātās hordeō pāvit.
(b)   **urbem** novam ipse aliam sub Albānō **monte** condidit.
(c)   audītā **vōce** praecōnis, gaudium fuit.
(d)   aliquam in tuīs litterīs **grātulātiōnem** exspectāvī.
(e)   Germānōs, quī trāns Rhēnum incolunt, Caesar prīmus Rōmānōrum **ponte** fabricātō aggressus maximīs adfēcit clādibus.
(f)   ita relātum est caput ad Antōnium iussūque eius inter duās **manūs** in rōstrīs positum est.
(g)   Augustus **aedēs** sacrās vetustāte collāpsās aut incendiō absūmptās refēcit.

3.   Translate each phrase into two Latin words:
(a) an abundance of slaves (b) the daughters of the consul (c) the leaders of the army

4.   Translate:

ēheu, illud est grave quod Clōdia iānitōrī imperat ut mē exclūdat.
— ille tamen gravior est quī semper queritur amīcam sē exclūdere.

Rough justice

How much your future was predestined and to what extent you could influence that yourself was a question which loomed large in ancient thought. Greek tragedies of the fifth century BC had drawn on the tension between the inevitability of the gods' will expressed in well-known stories with inescapable outcomes and a more humanistic outlook that people make their own moral choices

Reading notes
An historic infinitive has already appeared in 9.9:

deinde Brūtus, multīs audientibus, Servīliā, Tertullā, Porciā, **quaerere** quid placēret
then Brutus, with many listening, including Servilia, Tertulla and Porcia, _asked_ what I recommended

where the present infinitive is used in place of a past tense to shorten a verb to almost note form to give a description more punch. You will see it again in 25.9.

(and dig their own graves). The world of oracles, omens and prophecies had collided with the pursuit of reason and rational decision-making. In Roman literature a similar tension appears. For instance, in Virgil's story of Aeneas, his future actions are fixed by his destiny which not even the goddess Juno can prevent, and yet there is a sense all the way through that he makes his own tough decisions. The same uncertainty was picked up later by Christian thinkers: how we take responsibility for our actions if everything we do is predestined by God.

1. Possibly the most worshipped of all the ancient spirits was *Fortuna*, the personification of luck. She was perceived as a divine agent playfully unravelling the future.

> Fortūna saevō laeta negōtiō et
> lūdum īnsolentem lūdere pertināx
>   trānsmūtat incertōs honōrēs,
>   nunc mihi, nunc aliī benigna.

Horace, Odes 3.29.49–52

laetus,-a,-um   *cheerful, revelling*
negōtium,-ī [n.]   *business, work*
lūdus,-ī [m.]   *game*
īnsolēns   *haughty, high-handed*
pertināx [like 'fēlīx']   *determined*
trānsmūtō,-āre,-āvī,-ātum [1]   *transfer, switch*
incertus,-a,-um   *uncertain, wavering*
honor,-ōris [m.]   *honour, favour*
aliī: dative singular of 'alius,-a,-ud'

2. *Fortuna* was still at large at the end of the fifth century. Boethius, writing his *Consolation of Philosophy* in prison, struggled to ignore her. The spirit *Philosophia* encouraged him to look beyond her material charms in order to reach an understanding of goodness and God. Boethius himself was a Christian, though his *Consolatio* is imbued with pagan touches, not least the spirits themselves, *Philosophia* and *Fortuna*.

> nōn illa miserōs audit aut cūrat flētūs;
> ultrōque gemitūs dūra quōs fēcit rīdet.

Boethius, Consolation of Philosophy 2.1

illa: Fortūna
ultrō   *even, actually*

3. The philosophical school of Stoics took the view that *Fortuna* should not be feared. Their goal was to endure calmly whatever she brought:

tolerābimus damna et dolōrēs, ignōminiās, locōrum
commūtātiōnēs, orbitātēs, discidia, quae sapientem, etiam
sī ūniversa circumveniant, nōn mergunt.

Seneca, The Steadfastness of the Wise 8.3

tolerō,-āre,-āvī,-ātum [1]   *endure*
damnum,-ī [n.]   *loss*
dolor,-ōris [m.]   *pain, suffering*
orbitās,-tātis [f.]   *bereavement*
discidium,-ī [n.]   *divorce*
ūniversus,-a,-um   *as one, all together*
circumveniō,-īre [4]   *come around, surround, oppress*
mergō,-ere, mersī, mersum [3]   *sink, overwhelm*

4. The Epicurean school of philosophy argued that gods, if they existed at all, had little
    bearing on people's lives:

nōs tē, / nōs facimus, Fortūna, deam caelōque locāmus.

Juvenal, Satires 10.365–6

5. Stoicism was a refuge for senators who suffered under bullying emperors, and a useful
    ideology for military disciplinarians. If the Stoic way was to tough out life's troubles,
    Epicureans preferred to go with the breeze. Epicureans prized the Greek concept of
    ataraxia (freedom from stress), which in its extreme form meant no marriage, family,
    career, business or anything else which might upset the peace. Horace had a liking for its
    unambitious values:

petentibus multa / dēsunt multa.

Horace, Odes 3.16.42–3

petentibus: dative
dēsum, dēesse   *be lacking*

6. People looked for signs and portents from the study of animals' entrails, the flight of
    birds, the weather and dreams. There were astrologers available for consultation, for a
    fee of course. Horace had little time for them and below tells a girlfriend not to fret over
    the future, but enjoy the moment (with him). The ode has undertones of both Stoicism
    (endure whatever the gods bring) and Epicureanism (make the most of it).

tū nē quaesierīs, scīre nefās, quem mihi, quem tibi
fīnem dī dederint, Leuconoē, nec Babylōniōs
temptārīs numerōs. ut melius quicquid erit patī,
seu plūrīs hiemēs seu tribuit Iuppiter ultimam,
quae nunc oppositīs dēbilitat pūmicibus mare
Tyrrhēnum. sapiās, vīna liquēs, et spatiō brevī

spem longam resecēs. dum loquimur, fūgerit invida
aetās: carpe diem, quam minimum crēdula posterō.

Horace, Odes 1.11

quaesierīs, temptārīs: perfect subjunctives, see p. 203
fīnis,-is [m.]   *end*
Leuconoē: a girlfriend of Horace, possibly a substitute name
Babylōniōs numerōs: i.e. astrologers' numbers
ut: here means *how* in an exclamatory sense
patī: infinitive of the deponent verb 'patior, patī'
seu . . . seu   *whether . . . or*
plūrīs: for 'plūrēs'
hiems, hiemis [f.]   *winter*
tribuō,-ere, tribuī, tribūtum [3]   *grant, give*
ultimam: 'hiemem' is understood
oppōnō,-ere, opposuī, oppositum [3]   *place opposite*
dēbilitō,-āre,-āvī,-ātum [1]   *weaken, wear out*
pūmex,-icis [f.]   *rock*
mare, maris [n.]   *sea*
Tyrrhēnum mare: the Tyrrhenian Sea is enclosed by Sardinia to the west, Sicily to the
    south and the Italian mainland to the north-east
sapiō,-ere [M.]   *be wise*
liquō,-āre,-āvī,-ātum [1]   *decant, strain*
spatium,-ī [n.]   *space*
resecō,-āre, resecuī, resectum [1]   *cut back*
loquimur: 1st person plural (*we . . .*), present indicative of deponent verb 'loquor,
    loquī'
fūgerit: future perfect
invidus,-a,-um   *begrudging, hateful*
aetās,-tātis [f.]   *time*
carpō,-ere [3]   *pluck, enjoy*
quam minimum: see p. 250
crēdulus,-a,-um [+ dat.]   *trusting* (feminine agreeing with the subject of the imperative,
    i.e. Leuconoë)
posterō   *coming after* (understand 'diēī' with 'posterō')

7.   However firm the conviction that everything we do is predetermined, it is universally
      assumed that the choices we make influence our lives. Otherwise we exist as robotic
      instruments of some divine plan, with a moral licence to do as we please. Rome, no
      different from anywhere else, could not afford such a view. Good or bad behaviour is
      observed in the oldest literatures, and it was generally thought that the gods punished
      wicked actions and rewarded good ones. *Hubris* – the Greek concept of man getting
      above himself – resurfaces in Roman thinking. Horace uses the myth of Daedalus and
      Icarus (who took to the air, fatally for Icarus) to illustrate the folly of overreaching
      ambition:

caelum ipsum petimus stultitiā neque
  per nostrum patimur scelus
īracunda Iovem pōnere fulmina.

Horace, Odes 1.3.38–40

stultitia,-ae [f.]   *folly, foolishness*
patimur: 1st person plural (*we . . .*), present indicative of deponent verb 'patior, patī'
īracundus,-a,-um   *wrathful*
pōnō,-ere, posuī, positum [3]   *put (aside, down)*
fulmen,-inis [n.]   *thunderbolt*

8. The one word that sums up wickedness is *nefas*, which means sinful, contrary to divine
    will. Aeneas is challenged by the boatman as he approaches the Styx on his visit to the
    underworld:

'umbrārum hic locus est, somnī noctisque sopōrae:
corpora vīva nefās Stygiā vectāre carīnā.'

Virgil, Aeneid 6.390–1

sopōrus,-a,-um   *sleepy, sleep-bringing*
nefās: understand 'est'
Stygius,-a,-um   *of the Styx, Stygian*
vectō,-āre,-āvī,-ātum [1]   *carry, convey*
carīna,-ae [f.]   *boat*

9. In the underworld Aeneas is shown the treatment reserved for sinners:

  stat ferrea turris ad aurās,
Tīsiphonēque sedēns pallā succincta cruentā
vestibulum exsomnis servat noctēsque diēsque.
hinc exaudīrī gemitūs et saeva sonāre
verbera, tum strīdor ferrī tractaeque catēnae.

Virgil, Aeneid 6.554–8

stō, stāre, stetī, statum [1]   *stand*
ferreus,-a,-um   *of iron*
turris,-is [f.]   *tower*
Tīsiphonē [nom.]: one of the three Furies
succingō,-ere, succinxī, succinctum [3]   *gird up, tuck up*
cruentus,-a,-um   *bloody*
exsomnis,-e   *without sleep, wide awake*
servō,-āre,-āvī,-ātum [1]   *keep, guard*
-que . . . -que   *both . . . and*
exaudīrī, sonāre: for historic infinitives see p. 330 ('exaudīrī' is the present passive
    infinitive)

exaudiō,-īre, exaudīvī, exaudītum [4] *hear clearly*
sonō,-āre,-āvī,-ātum [1] *resound*
strīdor,-ōris [m.] *rattling, clanking*
ferrī: genitive
tractae [nom. with 'catēnae']: from 'trahō,-ere, traxī, tractum' [3]
catēna,-ae [f.] *chain*

10. A mortal would feel the heat of the gods' wrath not only after a moral misdemeanour but also if they felt in some way slighted. Thus people could account for life's highs and lows: if things were tough, the gods had taken against you.

The story of Actaeon is morally ambiguous. Did he mean to sneak up on the goddess Diana as she bathed naked in her forest pool? In Ovid's version he seems to reach the pool by accident, but once there cannot take his eyes off her. Diana, enraged and vindictive, turns him into a deer, whereupon his own dogs have him for dinner:

undique circumstant, mersīsque in corpore rōstrīs
dīlacerant falsī dominum sub imāgine cervī,
nec nisi fīnītā per plūrima vulnera vītā
īra pharētrātae fertur satiāta Diānae.

Ovid, Metamorphoses 3.249–52

circumstō,-āre [1] *stand in a circle around, surround*
mersīs: from 'mergō,-ere'
rōstrum,-ī [n.] *snout, muzzle*
dīlacerō,-āre,-āvī,-ātum [1] *tear apart*
cervus,-ī [m.] *deer, stag*
Word order for last two lines: 'nec īra pharētrātae Diānae fertur satiāta (esse) nisi vītā fīnītā per plūrima vulnera'
nisi fīnītā vītā lit. *except with his life having been ended* (i.e. *until his life was ended*)
plūrimus,-a,-um *most, very many*
pharētrātus,-a,-um *quiver-carrying*
fertur: here means *report, say* (in the present passive)
satiō,-āre,-āvī,-ātum [1] *satisfy, appease* (understand 'esse' with 'satiāta' = *to have been appeased*)

11. The killing of Laocoön and his sons is as rough a piece of justice as you'll find. One minute he is trying to save his comrades from the Greeks hidden within the wooden horse, the next he and his two sons are being crushed to death by a pair of serpents sent by Neptune (after some minor offence against the sea-god).

To describe Laocoön's desperate wrestling with the snakes the poet uses the simile of a sacrifice which has gone wrong, something easily imagined by his contemporaries. For many of us today, however, the simile is almost as remote as the scene it describes:

ille simul manibus tendit dīvellere nōdōs
perfūsus saniē vittās ātrōque venēnō,
clāmōrēsque simul horrendōs ad sīdera tollit:

quālīs mūgītūs, fūgit cum saucius āram
taurus et incertam excussit cervīce secūrim.

Virgil, Aeneid 2.220–4

simul . . . simul   *while . . . at the same time*
tendō,-ere, tetendī, tentum [3]   *stretch, struggle*
dīvellō,-ere, dīvellī, dīvulsum [3]   *tear apart, prise apart*
nōdus,-ī [m.]   *knot* (i.e. the coils of the serpents crushing his sons)
perfundō,-ere, perfūdī, perfūsum [3]   *sprinkle, spatter*
saniēs,-ēī [f.]   *gore*
vitta,-ae [f.]   *ribbon* (worn around the head by religious officials)
perfūsus vittās: see p. 327
horrendus,-a,-um   *fearful, dreadful*
sīdus,-eris [n.]   *star, group of stars,* (pl.) *sky*
quālis,-e   *such as*
mūgītus,-ūs [m.]   *bellowing*
quālīs mūgītūs: accusative plural to correspond with 'clāmōrēs'
saucius,-a,-um   *wounded*
excutiō,-ere, excussī, excussum [M.]   *remove, shake off*
cervīx, cervīcis [f.]   *neck*
secūris,-is [f.]   *axe* ('secūrim' = acc.)

12. Adversity and misfortune might well befall a person who inadvertently overlooked some respectful ritual, or so it was thought. In this ode commemorating a sacrifice to the fountain of Bandusia, Horace's thoughts turn to the victim:

ō fōns Bandūsiae, splendidior vitrō,
dulcī dīgne merō nōn sine flōribus,
    crās dōnāberis haedō,
        cui frōns turgida cornibus
prīmīs et venerem et proelia dēstinat.
frūstrā: nam gelidōs īnficiet tibi
    rubrō sanguine rīvōs
        lascīvī subolēs gregis.

Horace, Odes 3.13.1–8

fōns, fontis [m.]   *spring, fountain*
Bandūsiae: in the Italian countryside
splendidus,-a,-um   *bright*
vitrum,-ī [n.]   *glass, crystal*
dīgnus,-a,-um [+ abl.]   *deserving* ('dīgne' is vocative, agreeing with 'fōns')
merum,-ī [n.]   *wine*
crās   *tomorrow*
dōnāberis: 2nd person sing, future passive of 'dōnō,-āre' (*present*)
haedus,-ī [m.]   *young goat, kid*

frōns, frontis [f.]   *forehead*
turgidus,-a,-um   *swollen* (the growing horns show that the young goat is coming of age)
cornū,-ūs [n.]   *horn*
venus, veneris [f.]   *love*
venerem et proelia [both acc.]   *mating and jousts*
dēstinō,-āre,-āvī,-ātum [1]   *foretell*
frūstrā   *in vain*
īnficiō,-ere, īnfēcī, īnfectum [M.]   *stain, colour*
ruber,-bra,-brum   *red*
sanguis,-inis [m.]   *blood*
rīvus,-ī [m.]   *stream*
lascīvus,-a,-um   *playful*
subolēs,-is [f.]   *offspring*
grex, gregis [m.]   *flock*

Exercises 25b

1. Why are (a) 'circumveniant' [25.3], (b) 'quaesierīs' [25.6] and (c) 'dederint' [25.6] in the subjunctive?

2. Identify the case of the underlined word:
(a) nam lingua **malī** pars pessima servī.
(b) frūmentāriam rem ex **senātūs** cōnsultō tollam.
(c) Caesar in **Cornēliae** autem locum Pompēiam dūxit.
(d) neque / per nostrum patimur **scelus** / īracunda Iovem pōnere fulmina.
(e) Druidae, precēs dīrās sublātūs ad caelum manibus fundentēs, novitāte **aspectūs** perculēre mīlitem.
(f) Tīsiphonē vestibulum exsomnis servat **noctēs**que diēsque.

3. Translate into Latin:
(a) Antony said that Octavius was a boy.
(b) Caesar took the daughter of the consul as his wife.
(c) Octavius may praise Cicero, but it is to be feared that his words may be contrary to his actions.
(d) Fulvia said that she valued all Cicero's words at one as.
(e) If the consul sees (*say* will have seen) the children he will weep.
(f) I fear Romans carrying arms.
(g) Diana was cruel to the huntsman, Neptune to the priest.
(h) Antony saw his mother-in-law wide-awake sitting in the villa.
(i) I have made you a goddess, Clodia, and I have been wrong!

4. Find Latin ancestors in this chapter of *incredulous, liquid, submerge* and *tractor*.

— 26 —

Christianity

The dative case reviewed

The dative was introduced as a case typically translated with '*to*' or '*for*'. So far we have seen it used . . .

as an indirect object

> Caesar rēgnum Aegyptī **Cleopātrae frātrīque** eius permīsit
> *Caesar entrusted the kingdom of Egypt to <u>Cleopatra</u> and to her <u>brother</u>* [8.11]

to show possession (typically with 'to be')

> **mihi** nova nōbilitās est
> *high rank for <u>me</u> is new (my high rank . . .)* [5.6]

to describe someone (dis)pleased, gratified, obeyed, or put at (dis)advantage:

> ad āram **Dīvō Iūliō** extructam
> *at an altar built to (in honour of) <u>Divine Julius</u>* [10.11]

as an object of violence[1]

> Catilīna īnsidiās parābat **Cicerōnī**
> *Catiline was preparing an ambush for <u>Cicero</u>* [6.6]

as an object of believing, trusting or forgiving

> carpe diem, quam minimum crēdula **posterō**
> *enjoy the moment, trusting as little as possible in <u>tomorrow</u>* [25.6]

as 'agent' (where you might expect **ab** + ablative), typically with gerundives

> omnia **armīs** agenda erunt
> *everything will have to be resolved <u>by armed conflict</u>* [8.6]

---

1 There is a degree of overlap between these grammatical descriptions; for example, an object of violence could be considered a dative of disadvantage.

sometimes in poetry in place of **ad** or **in** + accusative

> caput dēturbat **terrae**
> *he severs the head <u>on to the ground</u>* [14.10]

for a person interested or concerned (often a personal pronoun)

> iam **mihi** lībertās illa paterna valē
> *now, <u>as for me</u>, farewell that liberty of my fathers* [15.13]

for the object of certain verbs, personal and impersonal

> parcere **subiectīs**
> *to spare <u>the conquered</u>* [4.10]

> quid **virō bonō** convenit?
> *what is suitable for <u>a good man</u>?* [8.9]

in place of a nominative or accusative after verbs like **sum, esse** (*am, serve <u>as</u>*), **habeō,-ēre** (*consider <u>as</u>*) or below **accipiō,-ere** (*receive <u>as</u>*), called the 'predicative dative'

> quasi cūnctam regiōnem **mūnerī** accēpissent, avitīs bonīs exuuntur
> *they were stripped of their ancestral property, as if they (the Romans) had received the entire region <u>as a gift</u>* [23.7]

and with some adjectives

> Clōdius inimīcus **nōbīs** est
> *Clodius is hostile to <u>us</u>* [7.5]

> nunc **mihi**, nunc **aliī** benigna
> *now kind to <u>me</u>, now (kind) to <u>another</u>* [25.1]

Practice 26a

1. Give the nominative forms of the words underlined in the examples above (**Cleopātrae** . . . **aliī**) singular or plural as they appear, and if an adjective same gender.

2. Give the dative singular of
    (a) corpus,-oris
    (b) dīgnitās,-tātis
    (c) mulier,-is
    (d) nōmen,-inis
    (e) praeda,-ae
    (f) rēs, reī

(g)   rosa,-ae
(h)   scelus,-eris
(i)   socer,-erī
(j)   socrus,-ūs
(k)   uxor,-ōris
(l)   vestīgium,-ī
(m)   vir,-ī
(n)   virtūs,-tūtis

3.   Give the dative plural of
(a)   crīmen,-inis
(b)   diēs,-iēī
(c)   fīlius,-ī
(d)   lacrima,-ae
(e)   mīles,-itis
(f)   rēgnum,-ī
(g)   senātor,-ōris

The ablative case reviewed

The ablative was introduced as a case typically translated with *in*, *on*, *by*, *with* or *from*. So far we have seen it used . . .

to describe the place or position of something (usually with **in**)

> libet iacēre in **tenācī grāmine**
> *it pleases to lie on <u>the clinging grass</u>* [22.2]

to describe the agent

> ab **optimātibus** occīsus est
> *he was killed by <u>aristocrats</u>* [5.1]

to describe separation or departure

> ē **mundō** genus hominum cēdet
> *the human race will fade from <u>the world</u>* [12.21]

> **patriā** profugus
> *a fugitive from <u>his own country</u>* [4.5]

to explain <u>how</u> (manner, method or instrument of something)

> **ingentī**que urbem **obsidiōne** premēbat
> *and he pressed the city with <u>a huge blockade</u>* [2.6]

dēsine mēque **tuīs** incendere tēque **querēlīs**
stop distressing both me and you with your complaints [3.11]

to describe a cause or source of something

in Perusīnōs magis **īrā** mīlitum quam **voluntāte** saevītum ducis
there were atrocities inflicted upon the people of Perusia more through the anger of the soldiers than the intention of the leader [10.10]

ex **omnī** prōvinciārum **cōpiā**
from the entire supply of provinces [7.10]

to describe someone or something in accompaniment

Iugurtha cum **duōbus fīliīs** ante currum ductus est
Jugurtha was led in front of the chariot with his two sons [5.7]

to describe the point of a comparison

rē pūblicā nihil mihi est cārius
nothing is dearer to me than the Republic [8.8]

to create the ablative absolute, a participial phrase which grammatically stands on its own within the sentence

dēlīberātā morte
with death decided upon [11.14]

to describe a quality or characteristic of someone or something

capillōque sunt **prōmissō** atque **omnī parte** corporis **rāsā** praeter caput et labrum superius
and they are with hair grown long (i.e. they have . . .) and with every part of the body shaved except the head and upper lip [23.1]

to describe a point of time (as opposed to duration, which is accusative) or 'time within which' (e.g. **duōbus annīs** *within three days*)[1]

nōnō diē
on/by the ninth day [3.2]

hōc tempore
at this time [6.4]

---

1 The ablative of time is used in 19.6 where you might expect the accusative of duration: **vīcīnī somnum nōn tōtā nocte rogāmus** (*we neighbours do not ask for sleep all night long*). This is the ablative of 'time within which' and embraces both extremities of the period and all in between (i.e. from beginning to end).

to describe the measure or amount of difference

> prīmum **multō** obstinātior adversus
> lacrimās muliebrēs erat
> *at first he was (by) much more resistant to the tears
> of the women* [17.2]

as object of one or two verbs

> **suspīciōne** carēre
> *to lack suspicion* [7.4]

after one or two adjectives (e.g. **dīgnus,-a,-um**)

> dīgnum **morte** aliquid fēcī
> *I have done something deserving death* [22.10]

after prepositions, many of which appear in other
categories already described[1]

> sine **īrā** et **studiō**
> *without anger and favour* [13.12]

> prō **meritō meō**
> *in return for my service* [12.1]

Practice 26b

1. Give the ablative singular of
   (a) urbs, urbis
   (b) nōmen,-inis
   (c) vīlla,-ae
   (d) tempus,-oris
   (e) senex, senis
   (f) rēs pūblica
   (g) grātia,-ae
   (h) exercitus,-ūs
   (i) magister,-trī
   (j) flagellum,-ī

2. Give the ablative plural of
   (a) prex, precis
   (b) mōns, montis
   (c) manus,-ūs
   (d) mōs, mōris
   (e) senātor,-ōris
   (f) praemium,-ī
   (g) habēna,-ae
   (h) puer,-ī

Vocabulary 26

A number of Latin verbs have their objects in the dative, not the accusative. Many describe a
service (or disservice), an act of (un)kindness or (dis)favour, revealing a difference in rank or
power between the subject and the object in the dative (ordering, obeying, serving, etc):

faveō,-ēre [2] *favour*	**noceō,-ēre** [2] *harm, injure*
īgnōscō,-ere [3] *forgive, excuse*	**parcō,-ere** [3] *spare*
imperō,-āre [1] *command*	**pāreō,-ēre** [2] *obey*
indulgeō,-ēre [2] *gratify, yield*	**prōsum, prōdesse, prōfuī** *be of use to*
interdīcō,-ere [3] *banish, forbid*	**serviō,-īre** [4] *be a slave (to), serve*
invideō,-ēre [2] *envy, begrudge*	

Very few verbs have their objects in the ablative:

careō,-ēre [2] *be without, lack, lose*	**ūtor,-ī** [3; deponent] *use, profit by, benefit from*

---

1 Prepositions are sometimes left out in verse; and are not used with names of cities or towns or **domus** (*house,
home*), **humus** (*ground, soil*) or **rūs** (*countryside*).

Exercises 26a

1. Fill the gaps, and translate:
(a) ego cum meā .... {**socrus,-ūs**} nōn habitō.
(b) cūr .... {**tū, tuī**} serviō? ego tibi nōn servus sum.
(c) ego vīllam .... {**vetustās**} collāpsam refēcī.
(d) infēlīx servus dē .... {**pōns, pontis**} dēiciendus est.
(e) .... {**audītus,-a,-um**} vōce praefectī tacuimus.
(f) litterās discere Latīnās .... {**ego, meī**} placet.
(g) dux militem .... {**praeda,-ae**} pellexit.
(h) rēgīna fūnus .... {**imperium,-ī**} parābat.
(i) quis .... {**Catullus,-ī**} Clōdiam reconciliāvit?

2. Translate into Latin:
(a) Who will care for me?
(b) My friend, what does it please you to do?
(c) Why do you never obey your wife?
(d) Let us kill Brutus and Cassius!
(e) Surely I lack suspicion?

3. Identify the meaning of these words, and give the principal parts of the verbs from which they were once formed [e.g. amāns, amantis = *lover* (**amō, amāre, amāvī, amātum**)]:
(a) factum,-ī
(b) respōnsum,-ī
(c) ācta, āctōrum
(d) quaesītus,-a,-um
(e) tribūtum,-ī

Reading notes

Words have been introduced in this course according to the eightfold parts of speech: noun, verb, adjective, pronoun, adverb, conjunction, preposition, and exclamation or interjection. Every word in a sentence has the function of one of these parts of speech.

During the course you will have noticed that some words are able to serve as more than one part of speech:

*   Adjectives (including participles) either agree with a noun or pronoun, or themselves serve as nouns where they stand alone

    in illō numerō sunt **bonī**
    there are in that number good (men) [4.11]

    pilam servus sufficiēbat **lūdentibus**
    a slave provided a ball for those playing [21.10]

- Some adjectives and participles were used so much as nouns that they were recognized as such (e.g. **amāns, amantis; nātus,-ī; Rōmānus,-ī**)

- Participles are adjectives, yet are created from verbs and retain certain functions of a verb, e.g. take an object (**persecūtus <u>taurum</u>** = *having pursued <u>the bull</u>*)

- Some prepositions serve as adverbs (e.g. **contrā, ultrā**) where they appear without nouns

- Pronouns may appear alone

  <u>hic</u> tamen vīvit
  yet <u>this (man)</u> lives [6.7]

- Or as adjectives with nouns

  Lesbia nostra, Lesbia **<u>illa</u>**
  our Lesbia, <u>that</u> Lesbia [15.9]

- And some adverbs serve as conjunctions, and vice versa, depending on their role in the sentence (e.g. **etiam, quandō**).

When reading you do not need to define the part of speech for every word, but it is important to be receptive to their flexible and changeable roles.

Christianity

1. The Roman empire came into contact with many different religions and cults, some of which found their way back to the capital. These were only restricted or persecuted if they were considered anti-social or at odds with state worship. One such cult was sufficiently unpopular to be used by Nero as a scapegoat for the fire of Rome in AD 64, to quash rumours that he himself had started it.

ergō abolendō rūmōrī Nerō subdidit reōs et quaesītissimīs poenīs affēcit quōs per flāgitia invīsōs vulgus Christiānōs appellābat. auctor nōminis eius Christus Tiberiō imperitante per prōcūrātōrem Pontium Pīlātum suppliciō affectus erat.

Tacitus, *Annals* 15.44

aboleō,-ēre, abolēvī, abolitum [2]   *destroy*
rūmor,-ōris [m.]   *rumour*
subdō,-ere, subdidī, subditum [3]   *substitute, introduce falsely*
reus,-ī [m.]   *defendant, scapegoat*

quaesītus,-a,-um   *select, special*
flāgitium,-ī [n.]   *crime*
invīsus,-a,-um   *hateful, hated*
vulgus,-ī [n.]   *crowd* (one of very few neuter nouns which decline like 'servus-ī')
Christiānus,-a,-um   *Christian*
auctor,-ōris [m.]   *founder*
Christus,-ī [m.]   *Christ*
Tiberiō imperitante: ablative absolute
per prōcūrātōrem   *by order of the procurator*

2.   Romans were capable of brutal treatment but seldom as an act of religious suppression.
      Few global empires have been as tolerant in that respect. In some places Romans let their
      own cults be merged with provincial ones to promote a feeling of partnership. Persecution,
      when it happened, was motivated by politics, not theological difference. The Druids in
      Britain (p. 306) were suppressed for stirring rebellion and sacrificing prisoners. In Judaea
      the close-knit society of Jews rebelled in the first century AD and they were then crushed.
      The provocation of the sub-Jewish cult of Christianity was their refusal to practise rituals
      other than their own or to accept any god other than the one God. They appeared to be
      rejecting the authority of Rome, which the enemies of Christ had tried to exploit:

'magister, scīmus quia rēctē dīcis et docēs: licet nōbīs dare
tribūtum Caesarī, an nōn?' cōnsīderāns autem dolum
illōrum, dīxit ad eōs: 'quid mē temptātis? ostendite mihi
dēnārium: cuius habet imāginem et īnscrīptiōnem?'
respondentēs dīxērunt: 'Caesaris.' et ait illīs: 'reddite ergo
quae Caesaris sunt, Caesarī: et quae Deī sunt, Deō.' et
nōn potuērunt verbum eius reprehendere cōram plēbe: et
mīrātī in respōnsō eius, tacuērunt.

Luke, Gospel 20.21–6 (Trans. Jerome)[1]

quia: *because*; in later Latin, as here, *that*
tribūtum,-ī [n.; a noun created from 'tribuō,-ere,-uī, tribūtum']   *tribute*
an   *or*
cōnsīderō,-āre,-āvī,-ātum [1]   *reflect on, consider, be cautious about*
reprehendō,-ere, reprehendī, reprehēnsum [3]   *find a fault with, catch out*
respōnsum,-ī [n.; a noun created from 'respondeō,-ēre, respondī, respōnsum']   *reply,
   response*

3.   Compromise was impossible for Christians. They would not worship any other deities
      alongside their one God. Saint Augustine of Hippo would later ridicule the plurality of
      paganism:

1   The gospels were initially translated piecemeal from Greek into Latin, and it was not until the early fifth century
    that the first full translation of the Bible appeared in Latin, by the monk and scholar Saint Jerome. His work is
    known as the Vulgate (*vulgare* means to spread abroad, make accessible).

ūnum quisque domuī suae pōnit ōstiārium, et quia homō
est, omnīnō sufficit: trēs deōs istī posuērunt, Forculum
foribus, Cardeam cardinī, Līmentīnum līminī. ita nōn
poterat Forculus simul et cardinem līmenque servāre.

Augustine, City of God 4.8

ōstiārius,-ī [m.]   *doorkeeper*
omnīnō   *entirely*
sufficiō,-ere, suffēcī, suffectum [M.]   *supply, be enough*
istī [nom.pl.]   *those people*, i.e. pagans
Forculus: spirit of the door
forēs, forium [f.]   *gate, door*
Cardea: spirit of the hinge
cardō,-inis [m.]   *hinge*
Līmentīnus: spirit of the threshold

4.   The first Christians in Rome were thought to be secretive and exclusive. Their teaching
      had limited appeal to anyone comfortably off, in fact seemed biased in favour of social
      misfits.

et iterum dīcō vōbīs: facilius est camēlum per forāmen
acūs trānsīre quam dīvitem intrāre in rēgnum caelōrum.

Matthew, Gospel 19.24 (Trans. Jerome)

iterum   *a second time, again*
camēlus,-ī [m.]   *camel*
forāmen,-inis [n.]   *hole, opening*
acus,-ūs [f.]   *needle*
dīves,-itis [m.]   *rich man*
intrō,-āre,-āvī,-ātum [1]   *enter*

5.   In time the message that hardship in this world would win a foothold in the next won
      over hearts in all corners of the Roman empire. Stories in the gospels struck a chord
      with people everywhere, such as the failure of Jesus to prevent the death of Lazarus: in
      his very human moment of grief, Jesus uses all his divine power to bring the dead man
      back to life:

Marīa ergo, cum vēnisset ubī erat Iēsus, vidēns eum,
cecidit ad pedēs eius, et dīxit eī: 'Domine, sī fuissēs hīc,
nōn esset mortuus frāter meus.' Iēsus ergo, ut vīdit eam
plōrantem, et Iūdaeōs quī vēnerant cum eā plōrantēs,
fremuit spīritū, et turbāvit sē ipsum, et dīxit: 'ubī posuistis
eum?' dīcunt eī 'Domine venī et vidē.' et lacrimātus est
Iēsus. dīxērunt ergo Iūdaeī: 'ecce quōmodo amābat eum.'

John, Gospel 11.32–6 (Trans. Jerome)

Marīa: sister of Lazarus
cadō,-ere, cecidī, cāsum [3] *fall*
plōrō,-āre,-āvī,-ātum [1] *weep*
ut: with the indicative means *as* or *when*
Iūdaeī,-ōrum [m.] *Jews*
fremō,-ere, fremuī, fremitum [3] *growl, groan deeply* (the Greek word is 'enebrimēsato',
    used to describe the groan of a horse; the description of his human emotions are
    sealed with an animal metaphor)
turbō,-āre,-āvī,-ātum [1] *disturb, trouble* ('turbāvit sē' = *he got himself worked up*)
posuistis: 2nd person pl., perfect, of 'pōnō,-ere'
venī, vidē: imperatives
lacrimor,-ārī, lacrimātus [1; deponent] *weep*
ecce *behold, see*
quōmodo *how*

6. Half a century after Nero's fire the writer Pliny was in charge of the province Bithynia
    (north-west Turkey). He sent a number of letters to the emperor Trajan seeking political
    guidance, including what to do with the Christians. Until he heard from the emperor, he
    would treat them as follows:

interim in iīs, quī ad mē tamquam Christiānī dēferēbantur,
hunc sum secūtus modum. interrogāvī ipsōs an essent
Christiānī. cōnfitentēs iterum ac tertiō interrogāvī
supplicium minātus. perseverantēs dūcī iussī. neque enim
dubitābam pertināciam certē et īnflexibilem obstinātiōnem
dēbēre pūnīrī.

Pliny, Letters 10.96

interim *meanwhile*
iīs: for 'eīs', dat.pl./abl.pl. of 'is, ea, id'
tamquam *as if, on a charge of being*
modus,-ī [m.] *method, procedure*
ipsōs: *them (in person)*
an *whether*
cōnfiteor,-ērī, cōnfessus [2; deponent] *admit*
minor,-ārī, minātus [1; deponent] *threaten*
perseverō,-āre,-āvī,-ātum [1] *persist*
dūcī: present passive infinitive of 'dūcō,-ere' (i.e. *to be taken to their execution*)
dubitō,-āre,-āvī,-ātum [1] *doubt*
pertinācia,-ae [f.] *stubbornness*
certē *surely, certainly*
īnflexibilis,-e *inflexible*
obstinātiō,-ōnis [f.] *persistence*
pūnīrī: present passive infinitive

7. Pliny found the Christians to be secretive and superstitious, but not threatening serious harm. He learned this through the torture of some believers (it was routine to torture slaves for their evidence):

necessārium crēdidī ex duābus ancillīs, quae ministrae dīcēbantur, quid esset vērī et per tormenta quaerere. sed nihil aliud invēnī, quam superstitiōnem prāvam, immodicam.

Pliny, Letters 10.96

necessārius,-a,-um   *indispensable, necessary*
crēdidī: perfect of 'crēdō,-ere'
ministra,-ae [f.]   *deaconess*
vērī: partitive genitive with 'quid', i.e. *what truth*
tormentum,-ī [n.]   *torture*
prāvus,-a,-um   *depraved, weird*
immodicus,-a,-um   *excessive, unrestrained*

8. The emperor Trajan's reply to Pliny:

conquīrendī nōn sunt. sī dēferantur et arguantur, pūniendī sunt.

Pliny, Letters 10.97

conquīrō,-ere, conquīsīvī, conquīsītum [3]   *search for*
arguō,-ere, arguī, argūtum [3]   *convict*

9. Christians rejected any notion that human suffering was divinely caused. Theirs was an altogether different view: suffering would open the way to salvation, and this would give them the strength to put aside fear of persecution. The optimism with which Christians faced their tormentors was something others thought bizarre. The ancient world had long embraced the idea of heroic sacrifice, but religious martyrdom was for many implausible and disturbing.
    If trouble and suffering were not divinely caused, this left Christian thinkers challenged – as it still does – to explain the source of such negative things: if God is only good, and God is behind everything, how can there be bad? Boethius tackles this head-on in his *Consolation of Philosophy*. Under torture in the prison where he would shortly die, he imagines *Philosophia* lighting up his dark moments with the comfort of rational argument. *Philosophia* uses methods well practised in antiquity to explain how evil cannot exist at all:

'num igitur Deus facere malum potest?'
'minimē,' inquam.
'malum igitur,' inquit, 'nihil est, cum id facere ille nōn possit, quī nihil nōn potest.'

'lūdisne,' inquam, 'mē inextrīcābilem labyrinthum
ratiōnibus texēns?'

Boethius, *Consolation of Philosophy* 3.12

minimē   *no, not in the least*
inquam   *I say*
cum   *since*
ille: i.e. God
inextrīcābilis,-e   *inextricable*
labyrinthus,-ī [m.]   *labyrinth*
ratiō,-ōnis [f.]   *argument*
texō,-ere, texī, textum [3]   *weave*

10.   *Philosophia* persuades Boethius that goodness must be identified with happiness, that
despite his circumstances if he has goodness he must therefore have happiness. It is not
the victims of evil but the perpetrators who need to be pitied for their weakness and flaws:

quōs nōn ab īrātīs sed ā propitiīs potius miserantibusque
accūsātōribus ad iūdicium veluti aegrōs ad medicum dūcī
oportēbat.

Boethius, *Consolation of Philosophy* 4.4

quōs [acc.]   *those men,* i.e. wicked people
īrātus,-a,-um   *angry*
propitius,-a,-um   *kindly*
miserāns [from 'miseror,-ārī']   *pitying*
accūsātor,-ōris [m.]   *prosecutor, accuser*
iūdicium,-ī [n.]   *judgement, trial*
veluti   *just as*
aeger,-gra,-grum   *sick*

11.   For centuries Boethius' *Consolatio* was second only to the Bible as the most copied and
translated work in Europe. But *Philosophia*'s rational consoling has not put to bed the
central questions. Her argument that wickedness is its own punishment is short of
compelling:

sīcut igitur probīs probitās ipsa fit praemium ita improbīs
nēquitia ipsa supplicium est.

Boethius, *Consolation of Philosophy* 4.3

sīcut   *just as*
(im)probus,-a,-um   *good (wicked)*
probitās,-tātis [f.]   *uprightness, goodness*
fit [3rd person singular of 'fīō, fierī']   *is, becomes*
nēquitia,-ae [f.]   *wickedness*

12. Debates such as these injected a fresh stimulus to intellectual life, and the lack of straightforward answers enveloped the spreading faith in a sense of mystery. The identification of God lay at the root of this. A pagan divinity had been identified with the phenomenon which it represented. Light, for example, was a mystery to pagans, and they explained it in terms of a sun-god. Christians now inverted the formula: God was the mystery, and light the metaphorical representation. To frame this new and complex theology, intellectuals borrowed from previous philosophers, especially Plato, whose theory of forms begins (or ends) with corporeal images and leads to the absolute form from which all things are derived.

Mysteries of course lead to different interpretations, and in due course to conflict. The concept of trinity – three in one – stretched even the most capable minds, and its brush with plurality (three gods?) would stoke feelings to the point of bloodshed. Boethius himself was imprisoned for lining up with the traditional three-in-one believers against Arian's teaching to separate and relegate the son and the spirit to lesser roles.

pater fīlius spīritus sānctus ūnus nōn trēs diī.

Boethius, *On the Trinity* 1

diī: for 'deī'

13. Christianity did not remain forever the religion of the poor: by the end of the fourth century, a century before Boethius, it had become established as the state religion. Soon stories of the amoral antics of pagan gods would be frowned upon. Converts like Saints Augustine and Jerome, who were well versed in classical literature, joined the call for its exclusion. Jerome wrote of a dream in which his loyalties were tested:

interrogātus condiciōnem, Christiānum mē esse respondī: et ille quī residēbat, 'mentīris,' ait, 'Cicerōniānus es, nōn Christiānus; ubī thēsaurus tuus, ibī et cor tuum.'

Jerome, *Letters* 22.30

condiciō,-ōnis [f.]   *state, position*
resideō,-ēre [2]   *sit, be seated* (in judgment)
mentīris: 2nd person sing., present indicative, of deponent 'mentior,-īrī' (*lie*)
thēsaurus,-ī [m.]   *treasure*
cor, cordis [n.]   *heart, soul*

Jerome's quarrel was not really with the books but with the pagans who upheld them, and after their opposition receded, classical writings returned to favour as allegorical tales. In fact it was the monks in the monasteries who kept classical literature alive for the next thousand years with their careful copying and inkwork.

The momentum of Christianity overcame paganism and arguably the empire too. Roman administration had been founded on a Greek idea which the Romans put into wider practice: the partly self-governing municipality. In towns all over the empire local magistrates were elected to supervise local government, including a portion of the taxes. In later years a combination of corruption, mismanagement and the influx of immigrants from the east prompted central government to replace local elections with magistrates of their own choosing, who were obliged to collect the taxes for central government to spend. The ensuing vacuum in popular representation was filled by the leaders of the church, who soon earned more favour than the magistrates: bishops were preferable to bailiffs. In this way the church replaced the forum as the centre of local affairs, and the self-administered towns began to disappear. It was not very long of course before the bishop became the bailiff too, sharing power with the local lord in a manner that underpinned the political structure of the medieval era to follow.

Christianity had swept across Europe with its uncompromising monotheism and radical outlook on faith and ethics. There was no halfway conciliatory status: you either joined or you did not. And yet in some ways the transition was seamless. The new religion slipped into the shoes of the old empire, absorbing various parts of the pagan world. Religious festivals continued to be observed, now re-aligned in honour of Christian saints; even the stones of the old temples would be recycled in the construction of new churches.

The political unity of the empire and a shared language helped the new faith to spread all the more quickly. As the empire weakened Christianity continued to thrive. Whether or not the religion was a principal cause of the empire's decline is a well-chewed bone of contention beyond the scope of this book. What is remarkable is not that the empire came to a close, but how long it survived. The end arrived for a variety of reasons, arguably over some hundreds of years. And the works of writers were thereafter preserved; not quite all their writings, for there are gaps in what has survived, but the insights they give us are richly detailed and remain the main prop of our historical enquiry.

Without them the visible remains of the Roman world, its fragmentary and picturesque ruins, would offer only a tantalizing glimpse of their time. These writings are not all historically secure and reliable of course, but they share that with every other literate society. We are drawn in by the records of ancient lives and at the same time learn to step back and exercise our sense of enquiry and judgement. The myths and stories told by poets arguably reflect an even more revealing and honest view of humanity, lighting up their world and engaging our feelings and responses all these centuries later; while the act of reading their language, itself a process of re-imagining, is at the heart of that historical experience.

Exercises 26b

Translate:

> quid maximē tibi placet?
>   — bene latīne dēclāmitāre.
> quid secundum?
>   — satis bene latīne dēclāmitāre.
> quid tertium?
>   — male dēclāmitāre. citius ē mundō genus hominum quam lingua latīna cēdet.

The pronunciation of classical Latin

A guide to letter sounds

a   short 'a' sound, between the 'u' in *cup* and the 'a' in *cap*; as in *ă-ha!*

ā   long as in *father*

ae somewhere between *pine* and *pain*; the latter was the sound in spoken Latin, certainly after the classical period and probably before it;[1] scholars cannot entirely agree over the classical sound

au as in *house*; in speech tendency towards Latin **ō**

b   as in English (**bs** and **bt** are pronounced 'ps' and 'pt')

c   as in *cat* (not *chair* or *ceiling*)

ch like English 'k', with a sharper expulsion of breath

d   as in English

e   (short) as in *ef* (the name of the English letter)

ē   (long) as in *may*

ei can be two syllables, e.g. **de-ī**, or a diphthong (where two vowels together create a single syllable), e.g. **deinde**, with a sound not far from a cockney London accent in 'playin football')

eu usually two syllables, as in **meus**; in a few words, a diphthong ('e-oo' run together as a monosyllabic sound), e.g. **heu**

f   as in English, always soft

g   similar to a hard English 'g' (never as in *George*); in certain words less closure . . . a fading sound in **magister, fugit, ego**

gn at the beginning of a word as 'n' (the **g** is like English 'k' in *knee*); in the middle of a word between *hangnail* and *Bolognese*

h   as in English, although there was a tendency to ignore an initial **h** in speech

i   a short vowel, as in *lip*

ī   a long vowel, as in *keep*

i   a consonant (sometimes written as a 'j') like English 'y'. In some words the vowel and consonant would have been vocalized similarly: e.g. **mulier** (vowel) and **etiam** (consonant); the consonant-vowel distinction mattered in verse which was regulated by the number of syllables (the vocalic **i** in **mulier** counts as a syllable, whereas the consonantal **i** in **etiam** does not)

l   as in English

m   as in English at the beginning or in the middle of words; a final 'm' is a fading sound which should be pronounced with the lips open, as a nasalization of the preceding vowel

n   as in English, except below

---

1 'classical' – This broadly includes the first centuries BC and AD, and the first few decades of the second century AD (i.e. from Cicero to Juvenal); the traditional definition is much narrower (Cicero, Caesar, Sallust and Livy).

nf a preceding vowel is always long (**īnferō**)

ng as in *anger* (not *hangar*)

ns a preceding vowel is always long (**īnsula**); the **n** is nasalized and less solid than an English 'n' (closer to *instigate* than in *inspect*)

o as in *not*

ō as in *note* (as pronounced by Scots and Welsh)

oe as in *boil* or as a Scotsman might say '*oy!*'

p as in English but with quicker completion and less 'h'

ph as in 'p', with a sharper expulsion of breath

qu closer to *queen* than *quarter*); **qu** makes the sound of a single consonant, so less of the 'w' sound than in English ('k*w*')

r trilled with the tip of the tongue

s as in *gas* (never voiced as in *has*)

t as in English but with quicker completion and less 'h'

th as in 't', with a sharper expulsion of breath

u as in *pull*

ū as in *pool*

ui usually two syllables (e.g. **graduī, fuī**); in a few words, a diphthong like French 'oui' (e.g. **huic, cui**);

v in the first century BC like an English 'w' (Cicero, Catullus, Virgil, etc.); but developed to a 'v' sound in the first century AD; note that **v** is sometimes written as **u**.

x as in English

y (short) as in French *tu*

ȳ (long) as in French *sur*

z as in English

With double letters extend the sound of the doubled-up consonant:

currus, reddere, posse, committere, supplicium

Quantity: vowels and syllables

The length or 'quantity' of a vowel is the duration of its sound. A 'long' vowel is roughly twice the length of a 'short' one. In this course a long vowel is shown with a macron, a short one without.

A syllable too may be long or short.[1] A syllable is long if it contains a long vowel (**amāre**); or if it contains a diphthong (two vowels together creating one sound), e.g. **praemium**; or if a short vowel is followed by two consonants (e.g. **mittere**). For more on quantity see Poetic Metres, available online with other supports for this course (p. 393).

---

1 Some scholars refer to them as 'heavy' and 'light' syllables to avoid confusion with long and short vowels; but this has not gained widespread use, perhaps because of the suggestion of weight or emphasis (i.e. stress), which quantity should not imply. Think of length as lingering, or even lazy, and shortness as brief or rapid.

Stress

A long syllable is not necessarily stressed (though they often are). That depends on the syllable's position in the word. Latin had a stress accent similar to our own: the second last syllable (penultimate) of a word is stressed if it is long

amāre   habēnās   incéndunt   virúmque

but if the penultimate syllable is short, then the previous (antepenultimate) syllable is stressed

práemium   míttere   dóminus   cóndidit   mílitēs

A word of only two syllables should have the first syllable stressed, even if it is a short syllable (e.g. the first syllable of **erat** would carry a light stress, that of **dīvus** would be a little heavier). Some monosyllabic words may carry stress if the sense demands it, e.g. **ī!** (*go!*); but words like **ad, est** and **et** carry hardly any stress. Polysyllabic words may have a secondary stress (as in English, e.g. *ínformátion*):

condidḗrunt   *they founded*

The pluperfect tense of the same verb is

condíderant   *they had founded*

On the page the difference between the two is one vowel. But because of the change in quantity, the stress of the pluperfect form moves back a syllable to create a perceptibly different sound. Variations such as this were no doubt important to the spoken language, in which the role of inflexion (word-endings) tended to diminish.

Practice

Say aloud: agenda, amāre, bonus, centum, deinde, deus, equus, fugit, ignis, īnsula, laudāre, māter, mittere, pater, pervāsit, puellae, recipe, vēnī vīdī vīci.

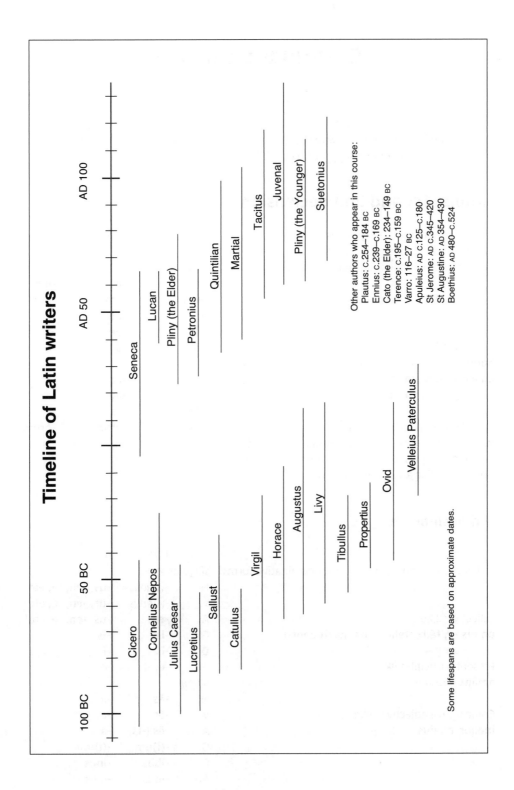

Timeline of Latin writers

100 BC — 50 BC — AD 50 — AD 100

Cicero

Cornelius Nepos

Julius Caesar

Lucretius

Sallust

Catullus

Virgil

Horace

Augustus

Livy

Tibullus

Propertius

Ovid

Velleius Paterculus

Seneca

Lucan

Pliny (the Elder)

Petronius

Quintilian

Martial

Tacitus

Juvenal

Pliny (the Younger)

Suetonius

Other authors who appear in this course:
Plautus: c.254–184 BC
Ennius: c.239–c.169 BC
Cato (the Elder): 234–149 BC
Terence: c.195–c.159 BC
Varro: 116–27 BC
Apuleius: AD c.125–c.180
St Jerome: AD c.345–420
St Augustine: AD 354–430
Boethius: AD 480–c.524

Some lifespans are based on approximate dates.

Grammar summary

Full tables of grammatical endings for this course (with both US and UK case listings) are available with other online supports: see p. 393.

Nouns: 1st and 2nd declensions

		Masculine	Feminine	Neuter
1st declension nouns **-a (puella)**				
2nd declension nouns **-us (servus)**	*singular*			
2nd declension nouns **-er (puer, magister)**	N.	**-us (-er)**	**-a**	**-um**
	V.	**-e (-ī)**	**-a**	**-um**
2nd declension neuter nouns **-um (vīnum)**	A.	**-um**	**-am**	**-um**
	G.	**-ī**	**-ae**	**-ī**
	D.	**-ō**	**-ae**	**-ō**
Adjectives like	Ab.	**-ō**	**-ā**	**-ō**
bonus (m.), **bona** (f.), **bonum** (n.)	*plural*			
miser, misera, miserum	N.	**-ī**	**-ae**	**-a**
noster, nostra, nostrum	V.	**-ī**	**-ae**	**-a**
	A.	**-ōs**	**-ās**	**-a**
Superlatives like **trīstissimus,-a,-um**	G.	**-ōrum**	**-ārum**	**-ōrum**
Past participles like **amātus,-a,-um**	D.	**-īs**	**-īs**	**-īs**
Future participles like **futūrus,-a,-um**	Ab.	**-īs**	**-īs**	**-īs**
Gerundives like **addendus,-a,-um**				

3rd declension

		M/F	N
3rd declension nouns with various nominative forms.	*singular*		
	N.	*-various*	**-us, -en, -e**, etc
	V.	*-various*	**-us, -en, -e**, etc
Adjectives like	A.	**-em**	**-us, -en, -e**, etc
omnis,-e, fēlīx (fēlīc-), ingēns (ingent-)	G.	**-is**	**-is**
	D.	**-ī**	**-ī**
Present participles like	Ab.	**-e, -ī**	**-e, -ī**
amāns (amant-)	*plural*		
	N.	**-ēs**	**-a**
Comparative adjectives like	V.	**-ēs**	**-a**
melior, melius	A.	**-ēs (-īs)**	**-a**
	G.	**-(i)um**	**-(i)um**
	D.	**-ibus**	**-ibus**
	Ab.	**-ibus**	**-ibus**

4th declension

	M/F	N
singular		
N.	**-us**	**-ū**
V.	**-us**	**-ū**
A.	**-um**	**-ū**
G.	**-ūs**	**-ūs**
D.	**-uī**	**-ū**
Ab	**-ū**	**-ū**
plural		
N.	**-ūs**	**-ua**
V.	**-ūs**	**-ua**
A.	**-ūs**	**-ua**
G.	**-uum**	**-uum**
D.	**-ibus**	**-ibus**
Ab	**-ibus**	**-ibus**

5th declension

singular	
N.	**-ēs**
V.	**-ēs**
A.	**-em**
G.	**-eī**
D.	**-eī**
Ab	**-ē**
plural	
N.	**-ēs**
V.	**-ēs**
A.	**-ēs**
G.	**-ērum**
D.	**-ēbus**
Ab	**-ēbus**

Regular verbs: indicative active

Conjugation	1	2	3	4	Mixed
Verbs	amō,-āre	habeō,-ēre	mittō,-ere	audiō,-īre	capiō,-ere
Stem	**am-**	**hab-**	**mitt-**	**aud-**	**cap-**

Present	*I love, am loving, etc*				
I	-ō	-eō	-ō	-iō	-iō
you [s.]	-ās	-ēs	-is	-īs	-is
s/he, it	-at	-et	-it	-it	-it
we	-āmus	-ēmus	-imus	-īmus	-imus
you [pl.]	-ātis	-ētis	-itis	-ītis	-itis
they	-ant	-ent	-unt	-iunt	-iunt

Future	*I shall love, etc*				
I	-ābō	-ēbō	-am	-iam	-iam
you [s.]	-ābis	-ēbis	-ēs	-iēs	-iēs
s/he, it	-ābit	-ēbit	-et	-iet	-iet
we	-ābimus	-ēbimus	-ēmus	-iēmus	-iēmus
you [pl.]	-ābitis	-ēbitis	-ētis	-iētis	-iētis
they	-ābunt	-ēbunt	-ent	-ient	-ient

Imperfect	*I was loving, used to love, loved, etc*				
I	-ābam	-ēbam	-ēbam	-iēbam	-iēbam
you [s.]	-ābās	-ēbās	-ēbās	-iēbās	-iēbās
s/he, it	-ābat	-ēbat	-ēbat	-iēbat	-iēbat
we	-ābāmus	-ēbāmus	-ēbāmus	-iēbāmus	-iēbāmus
you [pl.]	-ābātis	-ēbātis	-ēbātis	-iēbātis	-iēbātis
they	-ābant	-ēbant	-ēbant	-iēbant	-iēbant

Perfect tenses   Perfect: *I (have) loved*, etc
Future perfect: *I shall have loved*, etc
Pluperfect: *I had loved*, etc

		Perfect	*Fut. Perf.*	*Pluperfect*
amāv-	*I*	-ī	-erō	-eram
habu-	*you* [s.]	-istī	-eris	-erās
mīs-	*s/he, it*	-it	-erit	-erat
audī(v)-	*we*	-imus	-erimus	-erāmus
cēp-	*you* [pl.]	-istis	-eritis	-erātis
	they	-ērunt	-erint	-erant

Regular verbs: indicative passive (and deponent verbs)

Conjugation	**1**	**2**	**3**	**4**	**Mixed**
Verbs	amor,-ārī	habeor,-ērī	mittor,-ī	audiō,-īrī	capiō,-ī
Stem	**am-**	**hab-**	**mitt-**	**aud-**	**cap-**

Present   *I am loved*, etc

I	-or	-eōr	-or	-ior	-ior
you [s.]	-āris	-ēris	-eris	-īris	-eris
s/he, it	-ātur	-ētur	-itur	-ītur	-itur
we	-āmur	-ēmur	-imur	-īmur	-imur
you [pl.]	-āminī	-ēminī	-iminī	-īminī	-iminī
they	-antur	-entur	-entur	-iuntur	-iuntur

Future   *I shall be loved*, etc

I	-ābor	-ēbor	-ar	-iar	-iar
you [s.]	-āberis *	-ēberis *	-ēris *	-iēris *	-iēris *
s/he, it	-ābitur	-ēbitur	-ētur	-iētur	-iētur
we	-ābimur	-ēbimur	-ēmur	-iēmur	-iēmur
you [pl.]	-ābiminī	-ēbiminī	-ēminī	-iēminī	-iēminī
they	-ābuntur	-ēbuntur	-entur	-ientur	-ientur

Imperfect   *I was (being) loved, I used to be loved*, etc

I	-ābar	-ēbar	-ēbar	-iēbar	-iēbar
you [s.]	-ābāris *	-ēbāris *	-ēbāris *	-iēbāris *	-iēbāris *
s/he, it	-ābātur	-ēbātur	-ēbātur	-iēbātur	-iēbātur
we	-ābāmur	-ēbāmur	-ēbāmur	-iēbāmur	-iēbāmur
you [pl.]	-ābāminī	-ēbāminī	-ēbāminī	-iēbāminī	-iēbāminī
they	-ābantur	-ēbantur	-ēbantur	-iēbantur	-iēbantur

Perfect tenses   Perfect: *I was (have been) loved*, etc
Future perfect: *I shall have been loved*, etc
Pluperfect: *I had been loved*, etc

* These second person sing. forms have the alternative ending **-re** for **-ris**

amātus/a/um	*Perfect*	*Fut. Perf.*	*Pluperfect*
habitus/a/um	sum,	erō,	eram,
missus/a/um	es,	eris,	erās,
audītus/a/um	est,	erit,	erat,
captus/a/um	*etc*	*etc*	*etc*

Regular verbs: subjunctive active

Conjugation	**1**	**2**	**3**	**4**	**Mixed**
Verbs	amō,-āre	habeō,-ēre	mittō,-ere	audiō,-īre	capiō,-ere
Stem	**am-**	**hab-**	**mitt-**	**aud-**	**cap-**

Present   *I may love*, etc

I	-em	-eam	-am	-iam	-iam
you [s.]	-ēs	-eās	-ās	-iās	-iās
s/he, it	-et	-eat	-at	-iat	-iat
we	-ēmus	-eāmus	-āmus	-iāmus	-iāmus
you [pl.]	-ētis	-eātis	-ātis	-iātis	-iātis
they	-ent	-eant	-ant	-iant	-iant

Imperfect   *I might love*, etc

I	-ārem	-ērem	-erem	-īrem	-erem
you [s.]	-ārēs	-ērēs	-erēs	-īrēs	-erēs
s/he, it	-āret	-ēret	-eret	-īret	-eret
we	-ārēmus	-ērēmus	-erēmus	-īrēmus	-erēmus
you [pl.]	-ārētis	-ērētis	-erētis	-īrētis	-erētis
they	-ārent	-ērent	-erent	-īrent	-erent

Perfect tenses   Perfect: *I (may have) loved*, etc
                 Pluperfect: *I had loved*, etc

		Perfect	*Pluperfect*
	I	-erim	-issem
amāv-	*you* [s.]	-erīs	-issēs
habu-	*s/he, it*	-erit	-isset
mīs-	*we*	-erīmus	-issēmus
audī(v)-	*you* [pl.]	-erītis	-issētis
cēp-	*they*	-erint	-issent

Regular verbs: subjunctive passive (and deponent verbs)

Conjugation	**1**	**2**	**3**	**4**	**Mixed**
Verbs	amor,-ārī	habeor,-ērī	mittor,-ī	audiō,-īrī	capiō,-ī
Stem	**am-**	**hab-**	**mitt-**	**aud-**	**cap-**

Present	*I may be loved,* etc				
I	-er	-ear	-ar	-iar	-iar
you [s.]	-ēris *	-eāris *	-āris *	-iāris *	-iāris *
s/he, it	-ētur	-eātur	-ātur	-iātur	-iātur
we	-ēmur	-eāmur	-āmur	-iāmur	-iāmur
you [pl.]	-ēminī	-eāminī	-āminī	-iāminī	-iāminī
they	-entur	-eantur	-antur	-iantur	-iantur

Imperfect	*I might be loved,* etc				
I	-ārer	-ērer	-erer	-īrer	-erer
you [s.]	-ārēris *	-ērēris *	-erēris *	-īrēris *	-erēris *
s/he, it	-ārētur	-ērētur	-erētur	-īrētur	-erētur
we	-ārēmur	-ērēmur	-erēmur	-īrēmur	-erēmur
you [pl.]	-ārēminī	-ērēminī	-erēminī	-īrēminī	-erēminī
they	-ārentur	-ērentur	-erentur	-īrentur	-erentur

* These second person sing. forms have the alternative ending **-re** for **-ris**

Perfect tenses   Perfect: *I may have been loved,* etc
Pluperfect: *I had been loved,* etc

		Perfect	*Pluperfect*
amātus/a/um		sim,	essem,
habitus/a/um		sīs,	essēs,
missus/a/um		sit,	esset,
audītus/a/um		*etc*	*etc*
captus/a/um			

Irregular verbs: indicative active

Infinitives	**esse**	**posse**	**velle**	**īre**	**ferre**
Present	*I am*	*I am able*	*I wish*	*I go*	*I carry*
I	sum	possum	volō	eō	ferō
you [s.]	es	potes	vīs	īs	fers
s/he, it	est	potest	vult	it	fert
we	sumus	possumus	volumus	īmus	ferimus
you [pl.]	estis	potestis	vultis	ītis	fertis
they	sunt	possunt	volunt	eunt	ferunt

Future	*I shall be*, etc				
I	erō	poterō	volam	ībō	feram
you [s.]	eris	poteris	volēs	ībis	ferēs
s/he, it	erit	poterit	volet	ībit	feret
we	erimus	poterimus	volēmus	ībimus	ferēmus
you [pl.]	eritis	poteritis	volētis	ībitis	ferētis
they	erunt	poterunt	volent	ībunt	ferent

Imperfect	*I was (being)*, etc				
I	eram	poteram	volēbam	ībam	ferēbam
you [s.]	erās	poterās	volēbās	ībās	ferēbās
s/he, it	erat	poterat	volēbat	ībat	ferēbat
we	erāmus	poterāmus	volēbāmus	ībāmus	ferēbāmus
you [pl.]	erātis	poterātis	volēbātis	ībātis	ferēbātis
they	erant	poterant	volēbant	ībant	ferēbant

Perfect tenses	*I was (have been)*, etc	Perfect stem + regular perfect, future perfect or pluperfect endings			
I (perfect)	fuī	potuī	voluī	iī	tulī
	etc	*etc*	*etc*	*etc*	*etc*

Irregular verbs: subjunctive active

Infinitives	**esse**	**posse**	**velle**	**īre**	**ferre**

Present	*I may be*, etc				
I	sim	possim	velim	eam	feram
you [s.]	sīs	possīs	velīs	eās	ferās
s/he, it	sit	possit	velit	eat	ferat
we	sīmus	possīmus	velīmus	eāmus	ferāmus
you [pl.]	sītis	possītis	velītis	eātis	ferātis
they	sint	possint	velint	eant	ferant

Imperfect	*I might be*, etc				
I	essem	possem	vellem	īrem	ferrem
you [s.]	essēs	possēs	vellēs	īrēs	ferrēs
s/he, it	esset	posset	vellet	īret	ferret
we	essēmus	possēmus	vellēmus	īrēmus	ferrēmus
you [pl.]	essētis	possētis	vellētis	īrētis	ferrētis
they	essent	possent	vellent	īrent	ferrent

Perfect tenses	*I may have been*, etc	Perfect stem + regular perfect or pluperfect subjunctive endings			
I (perfect)	fuerim	potuerim	voluerim	ierim	tulerim
I (plupf.)	fuissem	potuissem	voluissem	iissem	tulissem

1st and 2nd person pronouns

	I/me	*you* (s.)	*we/us*	*you* (pl.)
N.	ego	tū	nōs	vōs
A.	mē	tē	nōs	vōs
G.	meī	tuī	nostrum/trī	vestrum/trī
D.	mihi	tibi	nōbīs	vōbīs
Ab.	mē	tē	nōbīs	vōbīs

3rd person pronouns

is, ea, id = *this, that, he, she, it*
hic, haec, hoc = *this (man, woman, thing), he, she*
ille, illa, illud = *that (man, woman, thing), he, she*

	Masculine	Feminine	Neuter
singular			
N.	is, hic, ille	ea, haec, illa	id, hoc, illud
A.	eum, hunc, illum	eam, hanc, illam	id, hoc, illud
G.	eius, huius, illīus	eius, huius, illīus	eius, huius, illīus
D.	eī, huic, illī	eī, huic, illī	eī, huic, illī
Ab.	eō, hōc, illō	eā, hāc, illā	eō, hōc, illō
plural			
N.	eī, hī, illī	eae, hae, illae	ea, haec, illa
A.	eōs, hōs, illōs	eās, hās, illās	ea, haec, illa
G.	eōrum, hōrum, illōrum	eārum, hārum, illārum	eōrum, hōrum, illōrum
D.	eīs, hīs, illīs	eīs, hīs, illīs	eīs, hīs, illīs
Ab.	eīs, hīs, illīs	eīs, hīs, illīs	eīs, hīs, illīs

Emphatic and reflexive pronouns

ipse = *-self* (emphatic)
sē = *himself, herself, itself, themselves* (reflexive)

	M	F	N	All genders
singular				
N.	ipse	ipsa	ipsum	—
A.	ipsum	ipsam	ipsum	sē
G.	ipsīus	ipsīus	ipsīus	suī
D.	ipsī	ipsī	ipsī	sibi
Ab.	ipsō	ipsā	ipsō	sē
plural				
N.	ipsī	ipsae	ipsa	**sē** can be
A.	ipsōs	ipsās	ipsa	singular or
G.	ipsōrum	ipsārum	ipsōrum	plural
D.	ipsīs	ipsīs	ipsīs	
Ab.	ipsīs	ipsīs	ipsīs	

Interrogative/relative/indefinite pronouns

quis/quī = *who, what, which, any*

	M	F	N
singular			
N.	quis/quī	quis/quae/qua	quid/quod
A.	quem	quam	quid/quod
G.	cuius	cuius	cuius
D.	cui	cui	cui
Ab.	quō	quā	quō
plural			
N.	quī	quae	quae/qua
A.	quōs	quās	quae/qua
G.	quōrum	quārum	quōrum
D.	quibus	quibus	quibus
Ab.	quibus	quibus	quibus

Index of examples

This index gives the page numbers of those Latin passages which reappear in the course as illustrations of language points.

Index of grammar

Abbreviations

a., acc.	accusative
ab., abl.	ablative
AD	after Christ
adj.	adjective
adv.	adverb
alt.	alternative
BC	before Christ
c.	about (circa)
d., dat.	dative
e.g.	for example
f., fem.	feminine
ff.	and following
fut.	future
g., gen.	genitive
i.e.	that is
imperf.	imperfect
indic.	indicative
lit.	literally
M.	mixed conjugation
m., masc.	masculine
mod.	modern
n., neut.	neuter
n. (in a table)	nominative
nom.	nominative
perf.	perfect
p.	page
pp.	pages
pl.	plural
prep.	preposition
pres.	present
s., sing.	singular
subj.	subjunctive
v., voc.	vocative

Latin to English vocabulary

The principal meanings are given along with particular uses which arise in the texts. Beyond this course you may find one or two words have additional meanings to what has been stated here. A few of the less common words given in the text vocabularies may not be included here. Numerals are listed in Additional vocabulary (online – see p. 393).

ab (ā) [+ abl.]   *by, from, away from*
abdūcō,-ere, abdūxī, abductum [3]   *lead away, take away*
abeō,-īre, abiī (-īvī), abitum   *go away*
abnuō,-ere, abnuī, abnuitum [3]   *reject*
aboleō,-ēre, abolēvī, abolitum [2]   *destroy*
abstineō,-ēre,-uī, abstentum [2]   *hold back, abstain*
absum, abesse, āfuī   *be absent, be far from*
absūmō,-ere, absūmpsī, absūmptum [3]   *consume, exhaust*
ac   *and*
Acca,-ae [f.]   *Acca*
accendō,-ere, accendī, accēnsum [3]   *inflame, stimulate*
acceptus,-a,-um   *pleasing*
accipiō,-ere, accēpī, acceptum [M.]   *receive, take, get, welcome*
accūsātor,-ōris [m.]   *prosecutor, accuser*
accūsō,-āre,-āvī,-ātum [1]   *accuse*
acerbus,-a,-um   *bitter, sour, harsh*
Achaeī,-ōrum [m.pl.]   *Greeks*
aciēs,-ēī [f.]   *battle-line, battle*
aconītum,-ī [n.]   *poison*
acquīrō,-ere, acquīsīvī, acquīsītum [3]   *obtain*
ācrius   *rather keenly, too keenly*
ācta,-ōrum [n.pl.]   *actions, public acts, decrees*
acus,-ūs [f.]   *needle*
ad [+ acc.]   *to, towards, at*
adcommodō,-āre,-āvī,-ātum [1]   *fit, adapt, suit*
addīcō,-ere, addīxī, addictum [3]   *resign to, give assent to, become subject to*
addō,-ere, addidī, additum [3]   *put to, add to*
addūcō,-ere, addūxī, adductum [3]   *lead to, bring along*
adeō   *so much, to such an extent*
adeō,-īre, adiī (-īvī), aditum   *approach, go to*
adhibeō,-ēre,-uī, adhibitum [2]   *bring, summon, invite*

adhūc   *still, yet*
adiciō,-ere, adiēcī, adiectum [M.]   *throw to, add*
adigō,-ere, adēgī, adāctum [3]   *drive to, push to*
adiungō,-ere, adiūnxī, adiūnctum [3]   *join, attach*
adiuvō,-āre, adiūvī, adiūtum [1]   *help, support*
administrātiō,-ōnis [f.]   *government, administration*
admīrābilis,-e   *admirable, unusual*
admoveō,-ēre, admōvī, admōtum [2]   *move to, bring in*
adoptiō,-ōnis [f.]   *adoption*
adoptō,-āre,-āvī,-ātum [1]   *adopt*
adōrnō,-āre,-āvī,-ātum [1]   *decorate*
adsiduus,-a,-um   *continually present, attending, devoted*
adsum, adesse, adfuī   *be present, at hand*
adulēscēns,-entis [m./f.]   *young man/woman*
adulterium,-ī [n.]   *act of adultery*
adveniō,-īre, advēnī, adventum [4]   *arrive*
adventus,-ūs [m.]   *arrival*
adversārius,-ī [m.]   *opponent*
adversum,-ī [n.]   *calamity, misfortune*
aedēs,-is [f.]   *shrine*
aedīlis,-is [m.]   *aedile*
aeger,-gra,-grum   *sick*
aegrē   *with difficulty*
Aegyptius,-a,-um   *Egyptian*
Aegyptus,-ī [m.]   *Egypt*
aequālis,-e   *equal*
aequē   *equally, in like manner, as much*
aequus,-a,-um   *equal, impartial*
aestimō,-āre,-āvī,-ātum [1]   *value*
aestuō,-āre,-āvī,-ātum [1]   *be hot*
aetās,-tātis [f.]   *age, era, time, lifetime*
aethēr,-eris [m.]   *sky, heaven*
afferō, afferre, attulī, allātum   *bring*
afficiō,-ere, affēcī, affectum [M.]   *treat, affect, afflict*

ager,-grī [m.]   *field, estate*

aggredior, aggredī, aggressus [M.; dep.]   *attack, approach*

agitātor,-ōris [m.]   *driver, charioteer*

agitō,-āre,-āvī,-ātum [1]   *rouse, stir up, drive, hunt*

agmen,-inis [n.]   *crowd, throng, troop*

agō,-ere, ēgī, āctum [3]   *do, lead, act, perform*

agrestis,-e   *rustic, uncultivated*

agricola,-ae [m.]   *farmer*

ait, aiunt   *s/he says, they say, say yes*

Alexandrēa,-ae [f.]   *Alexandria*

aliēnus,-a,-um   *other, strange, foreign*

alīptēs,-ae [m.]   *masseur*

aliquis, aliqua, aliquid   *some(one/thing), any(one/thing)*

aliter   *otherwise, by another way*

alius, alia, aliud   *other, another*

Alpēs,-ium [f.]   *Alps*

alter, altera, alterum   *one (of two), the other (of two), another*

altus,-a,-um   *high, deep*

amāns, amantis [m./f.]   *one who loves, a lover*

ambitiō,-ōnis [f.]   *ambition*

āmēns   *crazed, demented*

amīca,-ae [f.]   *female friend, girlfriend*

amīcitia,-ae [f.]   *friendship*

amiculum,-ī [n.]   *cloak*

amīcus,-a,-um   *friendly*

amīcus,-ī [m.]   *a (male) friend*

āmittō,-ere, āmīsī, āmissum [3]   *lose*

amō,-āre,-āvī,-ātum [1]   *love, like*

amor,-ōris [m.]   *love, passion*

amphitheātrum,-ī [n.]   *amphitheatre*

amplexus,-ūs [m.]   *embrace*

amplius   *further, again, more so*

an   *or, whether*

anagnōstēs,-ae [m.]   *reader*

Anchīsēs, Anchīsis [m.]   *Anchises*

ancilla,-ae [f.]   *servant*

angiportum,-ī [n.]   *alley*

anima,-ae [f.]   *spirit, soul, breath*

animal,-ālis [n.]   *animal*

animus,-ī [m.]   *mind, intention, feeling, courage*

annus,-ī [m.]   *year*

ante [+ acc.]   *before, in front of*

antehāc   *before this, hitherto*

Antiochus,-ī [m.]   *Antiochus*

antīquus,-a,-um   *ancient, longstanding*

apparātus,-ūs [m.]   *preparation*

appāreō,-ēre,-uī,-itum [2]   *appear*

appellō,-āre,-āvī,-ātum [1]   *name, call, call upon*

apud [+ acc.]   *in the presence of, near, with, among*

aqua,-ae [f.]   *water*

aquilō,-ōnis [m.]   *north wind*

āra,-ae [f.]   *altar*

arbitrium,-ī [n.]   *will, bidding, authority*

ārdeō,-ēre, ārsī, ārsum [2]   *be on fire, burn, be passionate*

arduitās,-tātis [f.]   *steepness*

argentum,-ī [n.]   *silver*

arguō,-ere, arguī, argūtum [3]   *convict*

arma,-ōrum [n.pl.]   *weapons, forces*

arō,-āre,-āvī,-ātum [1]   *plough, grow crops*

ars, artis [f.]   *art, skill, practice*

artus,-ūs [m.]   *limb*

arvum,-ī [n.]   *ploughed field, plain*

arx, arcis [f.]   *citadel*

as, assis [m.]   *as, a copper coin*

Ascanius,-ī [m.]   *Ascanius*

asinus,-ī [m.]   *donkey*

aspectus,-ūs [m.]   *appearance*

asper,-era,-erum   *harsh, rough, bitter*

asperitās,-tātis [f.]   *harshness*

aspiciō,-ere, aspexī, aspectum [M.]   *look upon, consider*

aspis, aspidis [f.]   *viper, asp*

asportō,-āre,-āvī,-ātum [1]   *carry away, bring away*

assiduē   *busily, constantly*

at   *but, but indeed, and indeed*

āter, ātra, ātrum   *black, gloomy*

atque   *and*

ātrium,-ī [n.]   *hall*

atrōx   *fierce, repulsive*

auctor,-ōris [m.]   *author*

auctōritās,-tātis [f.]   *power, authority*

audāciā,-ae [f.]   *boldness, presumption*

audācter   *boldly*

audeō, audēre, ausus [2; semi-dep.]   *dare*

audiō, audīre, audīvī (-iī), audītum [4]   *hear*

auferō, auferre, abstulī, ablātum   *take away, steal*

augur,-uris [m.]   *soothsayer*

Augustus,-ī [m.]   *Augustus*

aura,-ae [f.]   *air, breeze, fresh air*

aurō,-āre,-āvī,-ātum   *gild, decorate in gold*

aureus,-a,-um   *golden*

aurum,-ī [n.]   *gold*

Ausonia,-ae [f.]   *Ausonia, Italy*

auspicia,-ōrum [n.pl.]   *auspices*

aut, aut . . . aut   *or, either . . . or*

autem   *however, but, now*

auxilium,-ī [n.]   *help, aid*

avāritia,-ae [f.]   *greed*

Avernus,-a,-um   *belonging to the underworld*

āvertō,-ere, āvertī, āversum [3]   *turn away, deflect*
avītus,-a,-um   *ancestral*
avunculus,-ī [m.]   *uncle, great-uncle*
Bactra,-ōrum [n.pl.]   *Bactra*
bal(i)neum,-ī [n.]   *bath*
barbarus,-ī [m.]   *foreigner*
bāsiō,-āre,-āvī,-ātum [1]   *kiss*
beātus,-a,-um   *blest, happy*
bellō,-āre,-āvī,-ātum [1]   *fight a war*
Bellōna,-ae [f.]   *Bellona*
bellum,-ī [n.]   *war*
bene   *well*
benignus,-a,-um   *kind*
bēstia,-ae [f.]   *beast*
bēstiārius,-ī [m.]   *animal fighter*
bibō, bibere, bibī [3]   *drink*
bona,-ōrum [n.]   *goods, property*
bonus,-a,-um   *good*
bōs, bovis [m./f.]   *ox*
Boudicca,-ae [f.]   *Boudic(c)a, Boadicea*
brevis,-e   *short, brief*
Britannī,-ōrum [m.pl.]   *Britons*
Britannia,-ae [f.]   *Britain*
Brundusium,-ī [n.]   *Brindisi*
Brūtus,-ī [m.]   *Brutus*
bybliothēca,-ae [f.]   *library*
caballus,-ī [m.]   *horse*
cadō,-ere, cecidī, cāsum [3]   *fall, fall down*
caedēs,-is [f.]   *killing, murder*
caedō,-ere, cecīdī, caesum [3]   *strike, beat*
caelātus,-a,-um   *engraved*
caelum,-ī [n.]   *heaven, sky*
Caesar,-aris [m.]   *Caesar*
Caesariō,-ōnis [m.]   *Caesarion*
calamitās,-tātis [f.]   *mischief, misfortune*
calathus,-ī [m.]   *basket*
calcō,-āre,-āvī,-ātum [1]   *tread on, in*
calidus,-a,-um   *warm, hot*
cālīgō,-āre [1]   *cover with darkness, be dark, gloomy*
cālīgō,-inis [f.]   *darkness, mist*
callis,-is [f.]   *footpath*
calx, calcis [f.]   *heel*
camēlus,-ī [m.]   *camel*
candidus,-a,-um   *fair, white*
canis, canis [m./f.]   *dog*
canō,-ere, cecinī, cantum [3]   *sing*
capillus,-ī [m.]   *hair*
capiō,-ere, cēpī, captum [M.]   *take, capture*
Capitōlium,-ī [n.]   *the Capitol*
captīvus,-ī [m.]   *captive, prisoner*
caput, capitis [n.]   head
carcer,-is [m.]   *prison*

cardō,-inis [m.]   *hinge*
careō,-ēre,-uī,-itum [2; + abl.]   *be without, lack, lose*
carīna,-ae [f.]   *boat*
carmen,-inis [n.]   *poem, song*
carpō,-ere, carpsī, carptum [3]   *pluck*
Carthāgō,-inis [f.]   *Carthage*
cārus,-a,-um   *dear, loved*
cāseus,-ī [m.]   *cheese*
castra,-ōrum [n.pl.]   *(military) camp*
castus,-a,-um   *pure, chaste*
cāsus,-ūs [m.]   *chance, accident, misfortune*
catēna,-ae [f.]   *chain*
catēnō,-āre,-āvī,-ātum [1]   *chain, put in chains*
Catilīna,-ae [m.]   *Catiline*
caulis,-is [m.]   *cabbage stalk*
cauniae,-ārum [f.pl.]   *figs*
causa,-ae [f.]   *case, cause*
cēdō,-ere, cessī, cessum [3]   *give way, go, submit*
celebrō,-āre,-āvī,-ātum [1]   *practise*
celer   *quick*
cella,-ae [f.]   *cellar*
cēna,-ae [f.]   *dinner*
centum   *hundred*
centuriō,-ōnis [m.]   *centurion*
cēra,-ae [f.]   *writing tablet*
certāmen,-inis [n.]   *battle, conflict, competition*
certē   *surely, certainly*
certō,-āre,-āvī,-ātum [1]   *strive, compete*
cervīx, cervīcis [f.]   *neck*
cervus,-ī [m.]   *deer, stag*
cēterus,-a,-um   *the other, remaining*
chorda,-ae [f.]   *string*
Cicerō,-ōnis [m.]   *Cicero*
cinaedus,-ī [m.]   *sodomite*
cinis,-eris [m.]   *ashes*
circā (circum)   [adverb or prep. + acc.] *near, around*
circumferō, circumferre, circumtulī, circumlātum   *carry around*
circumstō,-āre, circumstetī [1]   *stand around*
circumveniō,-īre, circumvēnī, circumventum [4]   *surround*
citius   *more quickly*
cīvīlis,-e   *civil, political, public*
cīvis,-is [m./f.]   *citizen*
clādēs,-is [f.]   *disaster*
clāmitō,-āre,-āvī,-ātum [1]   *cry aloud, shout, bawl*
clāmō,-āre,-āvī,-ātum [1]   *cry, shout*
clāmor,-ōris [m.]   *shout, cry, noise*
clārus,-a,-um   *bright, clear, famous, distinguished*
clēmentia,-ae [f.]   *kindness*

Cleopātra,-ae [f.]   *Cleopatra*

cloāca,-ae [f.]   *sewer*

Clōdia,-ae [f.]   *Clodia*

Clōdius,-ī [m.]   *Clodius*

Clytaemnēstra,-ae [f.]   *Clytaemnestra*

cocus,-ī [m.]   *cook* (alt. spelling of 'coquus,-ī')

coepī   *I began, have begun*

coerceō,-ēre,-uī, coercitum [2]   *restrain*

cōgitō,-āre,-āvī,-ātum [1]   *consider, contemplate*

cognātus,-ī [m.]   *kinsman*

cognōscō,-ere, cognōvī, cognitum [3]   *become acquainted with, learn, recognize*

cōgō,-ere, coēgī, coāctum [3]   *compel, force*

cohors,-ortis [f.]   *troop*

cōleus,-ī [m.]   *sack, scrotum*

collāpsus,-a,-um   *fallen, collapsed*

collocō,-āre,-āvī,-ātum [1]   *occupy, place, settle in marriage*

colō,-ere, coluī, cultum [3]   *cultivate, worship*

color,-ōris [m.]   *colour*

combibō,-ere, combibī [3]   *drink entirely*

comedō,-ere, comēdī, comēsum [3]   *gobble up*

comes,-itis [m./f.]   *companion*

comitātus,-a,-um   *attended*

commendō,-āre,-āvī,-ātum [1]   *enhance*

commoveō,-ēre, commōvī, commōtum [2]   *excite, disturb*

commūnis,-e   *in common, shared, as one*

commūtātiō,-ōnis [f.]   *change*

cōmō,-ere, cōmpsī, cōmptum   *adorn, embellish*

competitor,-ōris [m.]   *rival, competitor*

compōnō,-ere, composuī, compositum [3]   *arrange, settle, record, write*

concēdō, concēdere, concessī, concessum [3]   *retire, concede, allow*

concipiō,-ere, concēpī, conceptum [M.]   *conceive*

concupīscō,-ere, concupīvī, concupītum [3]   *desire, aspire to*

condiciō,-ōnis [f.]   *condition, term, state*

condō,-ere, condidī, conditum [3]   *found, establish*

cōnficiō,-ere, cōnfēcī, cōnfectum [M.]   *complete, finish*

cōnfirmō,-āre,-āvī,-ātum [1]   *establish, reassure*

cōnfiteor, cōnfitērī, cōnfessus [2; dep.]   *admit, confess*

cōnfluō,-ere, cōnflūxī [3]   *flow together*

cōnfodiō,-ere, cōnfōdī, cōnfossum [M.]   *pierce, stab*

coniugium,-ī [n.]   *union, marriage*

coniūnx, coniugis [m./f.]   *husband, wife*

coniūrātus,-ī [m.]   *conspirator*

coniūrō,-āre,-āvī,-ātum [1]   *swear together, bind together by oath*

cōnor, cōnārī, cōnātus [1; dep.]   *try*

conquīrō,-ere, conquīsīvī (-iī), conquīsītum [3]   *search for, procure*

cōnsēnsus,-ūs [m.]   *agreement, unanimity*

cōnsīderō,-āre,-āvī,-ātum [1]   *reflect on, consider*

cōnsilium,-ī [n.]   *intention, plan, advice*

cōnspiciō,-ere, cōnspexī, cōnspectum [M.]   *catch sight of, see*

cōnstāt (from 'cōnstō,-āre')   *be well-known, be fixed, cost*

cōnsternō,-āre,-āvī,-ātum [1]   *dismay, terrify*

cōnstituō,-ere, cōnstituī, cōnstitūtum [3]   *determine, decide, manage*

cōnstō,-āre, cōnstitī [1]   *stand firm, be established*

cōnsul,-is [m.]   *consul*

cōnsulātus,-ūs [m.]   *consulship*

cōnsultum,-ī [n.]   *decree, resolution*

contemnō,-ere, contempsī, contemptum [3]   *despise, scorn*

contendō,-ere, contendī, contentum [3]   *compete*

contentus,-a,-um (from 'contineō,-ēre')   *satisfied*

contineō,-ēre,-uī, contentum [2]   *contain, hold together, restrain*

contingō,-ere, contigī, contāctum [3]   *touch*

contiō,-ōnis [f.]   *assembly*

contrā   [prep. + acc.] *opposite, against;* [adv.] *opposite*

contrārius,-a,-um   *opposite, contrary, counter-productive*

contrōversia,-ae [f.]   *quarrel, dispute*

conveniō,-īre, convēnī, conventum [4]   *meet, agree*

convenit (from 'conveniō,-īre')   *it is suitable for, agreed between, there is like-mindedness between*

convīctor,-ōris [m.]   *table companion, fellow diner*

convītium,-ī [n.]   *abuse*

convīva,-ae [m.]   *table companion, guest*

convīvium,-ī [n.]   *banquet, dinner-party*

cōpia,-ae [f.]   *abundance, supply*

cōpiōsus,-a,-um   *abundant*

cōpō,-ōnis [m.]   *barman, innkeeper* (alt. spelling of 'caupō,-ōnis')

coquō,-ere, coxī, coctum [3]   *cook*

cor, cordis [n.]   *heart, soul*

cōram   [prep. + abl.] *in the presence of;* [adv.] *openly, in public*

Corinthus,-ī [m.]   *Corinth*

cornū,-ūs [n.]   *horn*

corpus,-oris [n.]   *body*

crās   *tomorrow*

crēber,-bra,-brum *frequent*

crēdō,-ere, crēdidī, crēditum [3; + dat.] *believe, trust*

crēdulus,-a,-um [+ dat.] *trusting*

creō,-āre, creāvī, creātum [1] *choose, appoint, elect*

crēscō,-ere, crēvī, crētum [3] *grow*

crīmen,-inis [n.] *crime, charge, accusation*

cruentus,-a,-um *bloody*

crūs, crūris [n.] *leg*

crux, crucis [f.] *cross*

cubīle, cubīlis [n.] *couch, bed*

culpa,-ae [f.] *blame, mistake, transgression*

cultūra,-ae [f.] *tilling, cultivation*

cultus,-ūs [m.] *cultivation*

cum [prep. + ablative] *with, together with*; [conjunction] *when, since, as soon as, whereas, although*

cum . . . tum *both . . . and*

cūnctātiō,-ōnis [f.] *delay*

cūnctor, cūnctārī, cūnctātus [1; dep.] *hesitate, delay*

cūnctus,-a,-um *all, whole, entire*

cupīdō,-inis [f.] *desire, longing*

cupiō,-ere, cupīvī (-iī), cupītum [M.] *desire*

cūr *why*

cūra,-ae [f.] *attention, care, anxiety*

cūrō,-āre,-āvī,-ātum [1] *care for, see to, look after*

currō,-ere, cucurrī, cursum [3] *run*

currus,-ūs [m.] *chariot*

cursus,-ūs [m.] *course*

curūlis,-e *of a chariot, curule*

damnō,-āre,-āvī,-ātum [1] *condemn*

damnōsus,-a,-um *destructive, harmful*

damnum,-ī [n.] *loss*

Danaī,-ōrum [m.pl.] *Greeks*

dē [+ abl.] *from, down from, concerning*

dea,-ae [f.] *goddess*

dēbellō,-āre,-āvī,-ātum [1] *subdue*

dēbeō,-ēre,-uī, dēbitum [2] *owe, ought*

dēbilitō,-āre,-āvī,-ātum [1] *weaken*

dēcēdō,-ere, dēcessī, dēcessum [3] *go away, withdraw, die*

decem *ten*

dēcernō,-ere, dēcrēvī, dēcrētum [3] *decide, make a judgment*

decimō,-āre,-āvī,-ātum [1] *decimate, execute every tenth man*

decimus,-a,-um *tenth*

dēclāmitō,-āre,-āvī,-ātum [1] *declaim*

decōrus,-a,-um *fitting, proper*

dēcrepitus,-a,-um *decrepit*

dēcurrō,-ere,-cucurrī [3] *run down*

dēdūcō,-ere dēdūxī, dēductum [3] *lead away, bring down, take as a bride*

dēfendō,-ere, dēfendī, dēfēnsum [3] *defend*

dēferō, dēferre, dētulī, dēlātum *offer, bring down, accuse*

dēficiō,-ere, dēfēcī, dēfectum [M.] *desert, fail, revolt*

dēfluō,-ere, dēfluxī [3] *flow down*

dēiciō,-ere, dēiēcī, dēiectum [M.] *throw down*

deinde (dein) *then, next, afterwards*

dēlectātiō,-ōnis [f.] *delight, pleasure*

dēlector, dēlectārī, dēlectātus [1; dep.] *delight, give pleasure to*

dēlēgō,-āre,-āvī,-ātum [1] *commit, entrust*

dēlēnīmentum,-ī [n.] *allurement*

dēleō,-ēre, dēlēvī, dēlētum [3] *destroy*

dēlīberō,-āre,-āvī,-ātum [1] *decide, resolve*

dēlictum,-ī [n.] *fault, offence, wrong*

dēligō,-āre,-āvī,-ātum [1] *tie, bind*

dēmēns *mad, crazy, foolish*

dēnārius,-ī [m.] *denarius*

dēnsus,-a,-um *thick*

dēpellō,-ere, dēpulī, dēpulsum [3] *remove, expel*

dēpōnō,-ere, dēposuī, dēpositum [3] *put aside*

dēprehendō,-ere, dēprehendī, dēprehēnsum [3] *catch, arrest*

dēprōmō,-ere,-prompsī,-promptum [3] *bring forth, draw out*

dēripiō,-ere, dēripuī, dēreptum [M.] *tear down*

dēscendō,-ere, dēscendī, dēscēnsum [3] *go down, descend*

dēscēnsus,-ūs [m.] *descent, way down*

dēscrībō,-ere, dēscrīpsī, dēscrīptum [3] *describe, register*

dēserō,-ere, dēseruī, dēsertum [3] *abandon*

dēsideō,-ēre, dēsēdī, dēsessum [2] *sit idly*

dēsinō,-ere, dēsiī, dēsitum [3] *stop, cease*

dēsistō,-ere, dēstitī [3] *stop, cease*

dēspērō,-āre,-āvī,-ātum [1] *have no hope, despair*

dēstinō,-āre,-āvī,-ātum [1] *establish, determine, foretell*

dēstitūtus,-a,-um *lonely*

dēsum, dēesse, dēfuī *be lacking*

dēturbō,-āre,-āvī,-ātum [1] *beat down, cut off*

deus,-ī [m.] *god*

dextra,-ae [f.] *right hand*

dīcō,-ere, dīxī, dictum [3] *say, tell*

dictātūra,-ae [f.] *dictatorship*

dictitō,-āre,-āvī,-ātum [1] *say often, call*

diēs, diēī [m./f.] *day*

difficilis,-e *difficult*

difficultās,-tātis [f.] *difficulty*

digitus,-ī [m.]   *finger*
dīgnitās,-tātis [f.]   *prestige, rank, authority*
dīgnus,-a,-um [+ abl.]   *worthy of, deserving*
dīlacerō,-āre,-āvī,-ātum [1]   *tear apart*
dīligō,-ere, dīlēxī, dīlēctum [3]   *value, love*
dīmittō,-ere, dīmīsī, dīmissum [3]   *dismiss, release*
Dīra,-ae [f.]   *Fury*
dīrus,-a,-um   *fearful*
Dīs, Dītis [m.]   *Pluto*
discēdō,-ere, discessī, discessum [3]   *depart*
discernō,-ere, discrēvī, discrētum [3]   *divide*
discidium,-ī [n.]   *divorce*
discipulus,-ī [m.]   *student*
discō,-ere, didicī [3]   *learn, study*
discordia,-ae [f.]   *disagreement, strife, acrimony*
discumbō,-ere, discubuī, discubitum [3]   *recline at table*
dispēnsātor,-ōris [m.]   *steward*
displiceō,-ēre,-uī [2; + dat.]   *displease*
dissimulō,-āre,-āvī,-ātum [1]   *make a pretence*
diū   *for a long time*
dīvellō,-ere, dīvellī, dīvulsum [3]   *tear apart, prise apart*
dīves,-itis   [adj.] *rich*; [noun] *rich man*
dīvidō,-ere, dīvīsī, dīvīsum [3]   *divide, part*
dīvitiae,-ārum [f.pl.]   *riches, wealth*
dīvus,-a,-um   *divine*
dīvus,-ī (dīva,-ae)   *god(dess)*
dō, dare, dedī, datum [1]   *give*
doceō,-ēre,-uī, doctum [2]   *teach, show*
documentum,-ī [n.]   *example, demonstration*
doleō,-ēre,-uī, dolitum [2]   *grieve*
dolor,-ōris [m.] *pain, grief, suffering*
dolus,-ī [m.]   *trick, malice*
domina,-ae [f.]   *lady, mistress*
dominicus,-a,-um   *belonging to a master*
dominus,-ī [m.]   *lord, master*
domus,-ūs [f.]   *house, home, family*
dōnec   *while, as long as, until*
dōnō,-āre,-āvī,-ātum [1]   *give as a present*
dōnum,-ī [n.]   *gift*
dormiō,-īre, dormīvī (-iī), dormītum [4]   *sleep*
dōtālis,-e   *as a dowry*
dubitō,-āre,-āvī,-ātum [1]   *hesitate, doubt*
dūcō,-ere, dūxī, ductum [3]   *lead, bring*
ductus,-ūs [m.]   *leadership*
dulcēdō,-inis [f.]   *sweetness, pleasantness*
dulcis,-e   *sweet, pleasant, charming*
dum   *while, for as long as, until*
duo   *two*
dūrus,-a,-um   *unfeeling, cruel*
dux,-cis [m.]   *commander, leader, guide*

ē (ex) [+ abl.]   *out of, from, away from*
ēbrius,-a,-um   *drunk, sated*
eburnus,-a,-um   *of ivory*
ecce   *behold, see*
ecquis, ecquid   *is there anyone (thing) who (which)*
ēdictum,-ī [n.]   *decree*
ēdiscō,-ere, ēdidicī [3]   *learn thoroughly*
ēdō,-ere, ēdidī, ēditum [3]   *utter, bring forth, give birth*
ēdūcō,-ere, ēdūxī, ēductum [3]   *bring out, lead out, bring up, educate*
efficiō,-ere, effēcī, effectum [M.]   *effect, produce, bring about, accomplish*
effigiēs,-ēī [f.]   *image*
egestās,-tātis [f.]   *necessity, poverty*
ego   *I*
ēgregius,-a,-um   *outstanding*
ēheu   *alas, oh no*
ēlegantia,-ae [f.]   *refinement*
elephantus,-ī [m.]   *elephant*
ēligō,-ere, ēlēgī, ēlectum [3]   *pick out, choose*
Elissa,-ae [f.]   *Dido*
ēloquentia,-ae [f.]   *eloquence, fluency*
ēmittō,-ere, ēmīsī, ēmissum [3]   *send out*
emō,-ere, ēmī, emptum [3]   *buy*
enim   *for, I mean, in fact, to be sure*
eō, īre, iī (īvī) itum   *go*
Ēpīrōtae,-ārum [m.]   *the Epirotes, the people of Epirus*
epistula,-ae [f.]   *letter*
eques, equitis [m.]   *horseman, equestrian*
equitō,-āre,-āvī,-ātum [1]   *ride*
equus,-ī [m.]   *horse*
ergō (ergo)   *therefore, so, accordingly, then*
ēripiō,-ere, ēripuī, ēreptum [M.]   *snatch, take away*
errō,-āre,-āvī,-ātum [1]   *wander, make a mistake*
error,-ōris [m.]   *mistake*
ērumpō,-ere, ērūpī, ēruptum [3]   *break out*
erus,-ī [m.]   *master*
essedārius,-ī [m.], essedāria,-ae [f.]   *chariot fighter*
ēsuriō,-īre [4]   *be hungry*
et   *and, even, and also*
et . . . et   *both . . . and*
etiam   *also, (and) even, yes*
etsī   *although, albeit*
ēvādō,-ere, ēvāsī, ēvāsum [3]   *go out, come out, escape*
ēveniō,-īre, ēvēnī, ēventum [4]   *happen*
ēvocō,-āre,-āvī,-ātum [1]   *call out, bring out, encourage*
exaudiō,-īre, exaudīvī (-iī), exaudītum [4]   *hear clearly*

excipiō,-ere, excēpī, exceptum [M.]   *take, take the place of*

exclūdō,-ere, exclūsī, exclūsum [3]   *shut out, exclude*

excolō,-ere, excoluī, excultum [3]   *tend, improve*

excutiō,-ere, excussī, excussum [M.]   *remove*

exemplum,-ī [n.]   *example, precedent*

exeō,-īre, exiī (-īvī), exitum   *go out*

exerceō,-ēre,-uī, exercitum [2]   *keep busy, occupy, exercise*

exercitus,-ūs [m.]   *army*

exhibeō,-ēre,-uī, exhibitum [2]   *hold forth, present, show*

exilium,-ī [n.]   *exile*

exitiābilis,-e   *deadly*

exitium,-ī [n.]   *destruction, ruin*

exōrnō,-āre,-āvī,-ātum [1]   *equip, adorn*

expediō,-īre, expedīvī (-iī), expedītum [4]   *disengage, set free*

expellō,-ere, expulī, expulsum [3]   *banish*

expugnō,-āre,-āvī,-ātum [1]   *storm, capture*

exquīrō,-ere, exquīsīvī, exquīsītum [3]   *search out, discover*

exsomnis,-e   *without sleep, wide awake*

exspectō,-āre,-āvī,-ātum [1]   *expect*

exstinctiō,-ōnis [f.]   *extinction*

exstinguō,-ere, exstinxī, exstinctum [3]   *kill, extinguish*

exsūgō,-ere, exsūxī, exsūctum [3]   *suck out*

extemplō   *immediately, without delay*

extendō,-ere, extendī, extentum [3]   *overreach*

extrēmus,-a,-um   *final, furthest*

extruō,-ere, extruxī, extructum [3]   *build up*

exuō,-ere, exuī, exūtum [3]   *lay aside, cast off, deprive*

fabricō,-āre,-āvī,-ātum [1]   *build, construct*

fābula,-ae [f.]   *tale, story*

faciēs,-ēī [f.]   *face, shape*

facile   *easily*

facilis,-e   *easy*

facinus,-oris [n.]   *deed, misdeed, crime, outrage*

faciō,-ere, fēcī, factum [M.]   *do, make*

factum,-ī [n.]   *deed, action, thing done*

faenerāror, faenerārī, faenerātus [1; dep.]   *lend money*

faenus,-oris [n.]   *interest payment*

faex, faecis [f.]   *dregs*

fallō,-ere, fefellī, falsum [3]   *deceive, escape the notice of*

falsus,-a,-um   *false, deceptive, spurious*

fāma,-ae [f.]   *rumour*

famēs, famis [f.]   *hunger*

familia,-ae [f.]   *household, family*

familiāris,-e   *domestic, family, private*

famula,-ae [f.]   *maidservant*

fās [n.]   *what is proper, right*

fascēs, fascium [m.pl.]   *fasces*

fastīdītus,-a,-um   *despising, disdainful of*

fateor, fatērī, fassus [2; dep.]   *speak, confess, make plain*

fātum,-ī [n.]   *fate*

faucēs, faucium [f.pl.]   *throat, opening, mouth*

faveō,-ēre, fāvī, fautum [2; + dat.]   *favour, support*

favor,-ōris [m.]   *favour, support*

fax, facis [f.]   *torch*

febris,-is [f.]   *fever*

fēcunditās,-tātis [f.]   *fruitfulness, fertility*

fēlēs,-is [f.]   *cat*

fēlīx   *fortunate, successful*

fēmina,-ae [f.]   *woman*

fenestra,-ae [f.]   *window*

fera,-ae [f.]   *wild animal*

ferē   *almost, nearly*

feretrum,-ī [n.]   *bier, stretcher*

ferō, ferre, tulī, lātum   *bear, carry, say*

ferōx   *bold, defiant, headstrong*

ferreus,-a,-um   *of iron*

ferrum,-ī [n.]   *iron instrument, knife, sword*

ferus,-a,-um   *wild, uncultivated*

fessus,-a,-um   *exhausted, weary*

fēstīvus,-a,-um   *agreeable, pleasant*

Festus,-ī [m.]   *Festus*

fidēs,-eī [f.]   *faith, loyalty, trust*

fīdus,-a,-um   *faithful, loyal*

fīlia,-ae [f.]   *daughter*

fīlius,-ī [m.]   *son*

fingō,-ere, finxī, fictum [3]   *make, fashion*

finiō,-īre, finīvī (-iī), finītum [4]   *finish, limit*

finis,-is [m.]   *boundary, limit, end*

fiō, fierī, factus   *be, become, happen, be done*

flagellum,-ī [n.]   *whip*

flāgitium,-ī [n.]   *shameful act, disgrace, crime*

flagrō,-āre,-āvī,-ātum [1]   *burn, blaze*

flāmen,-inis [m.]   *flamen, priest*

Flāvus,-ī [m.]   *Flavus*

flectō,-ere, flexī, flexum [3]   *bend, turn*

fleō,-ēre, flēvī, flētum [2]   *weep*

flētus,-ūs [m.]   *weeping, tears*

flōreō,-ēre,-uī [2]   *blossom, flourish*

flōs, flōris [m.]   *flower*

flūmen,-inis [n.]   *river*

fluō,-ere, fluxī, fluxum [3]   *flow, fall down*

foedus,-a,-um   *foul, dirty, detestable*

fōns, fontis [m.]   *spring, fountain*

for, fārī, fātus [1; dep.]   *speak, utter*
forāmen,-inis [n.]   *hole, opening*
forās   *out of doors*
forēs, forium [f.]   *gate, door*
fōrma,-ae [f.]   *beauty, shape*
formīdō,-inis [f.]   *fear, dread*
fōrmōsus,-a,-um   *beautiful, shapely*
forte   *by chance*
fortis,-e   *brave, strong*
fortūna,-ae [f.]   *fortune, luck*
forum,-ī [n.]   *forum*
foveō,-ēre, fōvī, fōtum [2]   *warm*
frangō,-ere, frēgī, frāctum [3]   *break, corrupt*
frāter,-tris [m.]   *brother*
fraus, fraudis [f.]   *cheating, deceit*
fremō,-ere, fremuī, fremitum [3]   *growl*
frīgidus,-a,-um   *cold, chilly*
frīgus,-oris [n.]   *cold, chill*
frōns, frontis [f.]   *forehead*
frūctus,-ūs [m.]   *fruit, produce*
frūgālis,-e   *worthy, virtuous, thrifty*
frūmentārius,-a,-um   *relating to the corn supply, of
   the corn supply*
frūstrā   *in vain*
frūstror, frūstrārī, frūstrātus [1; dep.]   *deceive,
   elude, frustrate*
frūx, frūgis [f.]   *fruit, crop, produce*
fuga,-ae [f.]   *escape, flight*
fugiō,-ere, fūgī, fugitum [M.]   *flee, escape*
fugō,-āre,-āvī,-ātum [1]   *chase, put to flight*
fulmen,-inis [n.]   *thunderbolt*
fundāmentum,-ī [n.]   *foundation*
fundō,-ere, fūdī, fūsum [3]   *pour, scatter, pour forth,
   utter*
fūnus,-eris [n.]   *death, funeral*
furiōsus,-a,-um   *mad, in a rage*
furō,-ere, furuī [3]   *rave, rage*
furor,-ōris [m.]   *rage, passion*
futuō,-ere, futuī, futūtum [3]   *make love (to), fuck*
Gallia,-ae [f.]   *Gaul*
garrulus,-a,-um   *talkative*
gaudeō,-ēre, gāvīsus [2; semi-dep.]   *rejoice*
gaudium,-ī [n.]   *joy*
gelidus,-a,-um   *icy cold*
gelō,-āre,-āvī,-ātum [1]   *freeze, chill*
gemitus,-ūs [m.]   *groan*
gemō,-ere, gemuī, gemitum [3]   *groan*
gener,-ī [m.]   *son-in-law*
gēns, gentis [f.]   *clan, race*
gentīlis,-e   *belonging to their race, native*
genus,-eris [n.]   *race, stock, offspring*
geometrēs,-ae [m.]   *geometrician, surveyor*

Germānī,-ōrum [m.pl.]   *Germans*
Germānicus,-ī [m.]   *Germanicus*
gerō,-ere, gessī, gestum   *carry, wear, perform,
   manage*
gladius,-ī [m.]   *sword*
glōrior, glōriārī, glōriātus [1; dep.]   *boast*
glūbō,-ere [3]   *pick off, rob*
gradus,-ūs [m.]   *step*
Graecia,-ae [f.]   *Greece*
Graeculus,-a,-um   *Greek, Grecian*
Graecus,-a,-um   *Greek*
Graecus,-ī [m.]   *a Greek*
grāmen,-inis [n.]   *grass*
grammaticus,-ī [m.]   *teacher*
grātia,-ae [f.]   *gratitude, goodwill, affection, influence*
grātulātiō,-ōnis [f.]   *congratulation, good wish*
gravis,-e   *heavy, serious, important*
gravitās,-tātis [f.]   *weight, seriousness*
grex, gregis [m.]   *flock*
gubernō,-āre,-āvī,-ātum [1]   *be at the helm, steer,
   govern*
habēna,-ae [f.]   *rein, strap*
habeō,-ēre,-uī, habitum [2]   *have, hold, consider*
habitō,-āre,-āvī,-ātum [1]   *live, dwell*
hāctenus   *thus far*
haedus,-ī [m.]   *young goat, kid*
haereō,-ēre, haesī, haesum [2]   *cling to*
Hannibal,-is [m.]   *Hannibal*
harēna,-ae [f.]   *arena*
hasta,-ae [f.]   *spear*
hauriō,-īre, hausī, haustum [4]   *drain, drink up*
hecyra,-ae [f.]   *mother-in-law*
hercle (hercule)   *indeed, by Hercules!*
hērēs, hērēdis [m./f.]   *heir, successor*
heu   *oh! alas!*
hīc   *here*
hic, haec, hoc   *this, he, she, it*
hiems, hiemis [f.]   *winter*
hinc   *from here, on this side*
historia,-ae [f.]   *history, story*
hodiē   *today*
hodiernus,-a,-um   *of this day, today's*
homō,-inis [m.]   *man, person*
honestās,-tātis [f.]   *reputation*
honestus,-a,-um   *honourable*
honor,-ōris [m.]   *public honour, respect, favour*
honōrificē   *respectfully*
Horātius,-ī   *Horatius, Horace*
hordeum,-ī [n.]   *barley*
horrendus,-a,-um   *fearful, dreadful*
horridus,-a,-um   *rough, frightening*
hospes,-itis [m.]   *host, guest*

hostia,-ae [f.] *sacrificial victim*

hostis,-is [m.] *foe, enemy*

hūc *to here, hither*

hūmānitās,-tātis [f.] *civilization*

humilis,-e *insignificant, humble*

humus,-ī [f.] *earth, ground, soil*

iaceō,-ēre,-uī, iacitum [2] *lie*

iaciō,-ere, iēcī, iactum *throw, hurl*

iam *now, already*

iānitor,-ōris [m.] *doorkeeper*

iānua,-ae [f.] *door, entrance*

ibi *there*

ictus,-ūs [m.] *blow, thrust*

īdem, eadem, idem *the same*

identidem *again and again, repeatedly*

Īdūs, Īduum [f.pl.] *Ides*

igitur *therefore, then, accordingly*

ignāvia,-ae [f.] *worthlessness, idleness*

ignis,-is [m.] *fire, firewood*

īgnōscō,-ere, ignōvī, ignōtum [3; + dat.] *forgive, excuse*

īgnōtus,-a,-um *unknown*

īlex,-icis [f.] *oak tree*

ille, illa, illud *that, he, she, it*

illīc *in that place, over there*

illiterātus,-a,-um *uneducated*

illūc *to that place, thither*

imāgō,-inis [f.] *portrait, likeness, bust*

imbēcillus,-a,-um *weak*

imber, imbris [m.] *rain, shower*

imbuō,-ere, imbuī, imbūtum [3] *fill, taint*

imitor, imitārī [1; dep.] *imitate, copy*

immemor *heedless, forgetful*

immergō,-ere, immersī, immersum [3] *plunge, dip*

immineō,-ēre [2; + dat.] *hang over, watch for*

immittō,-ere, immīsī, immissum [3] *send in, let in*

immō *on the contrary, by no means, no*

immodicus,-a,-um *excessive, unrestrained*

impedīmenta,-ōrum [n.pl.] *baggage*

imperātor,-ōris [m.] *commander, emperor*

imperitō,-āre,-āvī,-ātum [1; + dat.] *command, rule over*

imperitus,-a,-um *inexperienced, ignorant*

imperium,-ī [n.] *power, empire*

imperō,-āre,-āvī,-ātum [1; + dat.] *order*

impleō,-ēre, implēvī, implētum [2] *fill*

implōrō,-āre,-āvī,-ātum [1] *invoke, entreat*

impōnō,-ere, imposuī, impositum [3] *place on, establish, impose*

improbus,-a,-um *shameless, wicked*

imprūdēns *unaware, without realizing*

impudēns *shameless*

impūnitās,-tātis [f.] *impunity*

īmus,-a,-um *last, at the bottom of*

in [+ acc.] *into, onto, against;* [+ abl.] *in, on*

incendium,-ī [n.] *fire*

incendō,-ere, incendī, incēnsum [3] *set fire to, inflame, distress*

incertus,-a,-um *uncertain, wavering*

incipiō,-ere, incēpī, inceptum [M.] *begin, undertake*

incitō,-āre,-āvī,-ātum [1] *arouse*

incolō,-ere, incoluī [3] *inhabit, live*

increpō,-ere,-uī,-itum [3] *rebuke*

incultus,-a,-um *uncultivated, unrefined*

incurrō,-ere, in(cu)currī [3] *run (into or on to), attack*

inde *then, after that, from that place*

indecōrus,-a,-um *unseemly, unbecoming*

index,-icis [m.] *informer, witness*

indicium,-ī [n.] *information, evidence*

indīgnor, indīgnārī, indīgnātus [1; dep.] *think demeaning, resent*

indīgnus,-a,-um *unworthy, demeaning*

indūcō,-ere, indūxī, inductum [3] *draw upon, spread over*

indulgeō,-ēre, indulsī, indultum [2; + dat.] *gratify, yield to*

industria,-ae [f.] *diligence*

ineō,-īre, iniī (-īvī), initum *go in, enter*

inextrīcābilis,-e *inextricable*

īnfāns, īnfantis [m./f.] *infant*

īnfēlīx *unfortunate, unhappy*

īnferō, īnferre, intulī, illātum *bring in, put on, cause*

īnficiō,-ere, īnfēcī, īnfectum [M.] *colour, stain, infect*

īnflexibilis,-e *inflexible*

ingemō,-ere, ingemuī, ingemitum [3] *groan over, sigh at*

ingēns *huge, immense*

ingredior, ingredī, ingressus [M.; dep.] *go forward*

īniciō,-ere, īniēcī, īniectum [M.] *throw on, in*

inimīcus,-a,-um *hostile, unfriendly*

initium,-ī [n.] *beginning*

iniūria,-ae [f.] *harm*

iniūstus,-a,-um *unjust*

inquam *I say*

inquīrō,-ere, inquīsīvī, inquīsītum [3] *inquire into*

inquit *(s/he) says, said* (present or perfect)

īnsānia,-ae [f.] *madness*

īnsānus,-a,-um *insane, mad, raging*

īnscendō,-ere, īnscendī, īnscēnsum [3] *climb on, up*

īnscrīptiō,-ōnis [f.] *inscription*

īnsepultus,-a,-um *unburied*

īnsidiae,-ārum [f.pl.] *treachery, ambush, trap*

īnsidiātor,-ōris [m.] *cut-throat, mugger*

īnsignis,-e *distinguished*

īnsistō,-ere, īnstitī [3; + dat.] *stand on*

īnsociābilis,-e *unshareable*

īnsolēns *haughty*

īnstituō,-ere, īnstituī, īnstitūtum [3] *undertake, begin*

īnstrātus,-a,-um *covered*

īnsula,-ae [f.] *island*

intāctus,-a,-um *untouched, chaste*

intellegō,-ere, intellēxī, intellēctum [3] *understand*

inter [+ acc.] *among, between*

interdīcō,-ere, interdīxī, interdictum [3; + dat.] *banish, forbid*

intereā *meanwhile*

interficiō,-ere, interfēcī, interfectum [3] *kill*

interim *sometimes, meanwhile*

intermittō,-ere,-mīsī,-missum [3] *pause, suspend*

interrogō,-āre,-āvī,-ātum [1] *ask, interrogate*

intestīnus,-a,-um *private*

intrō,-āre,-āvī,-ātum [1] *enter*

intueor, intuērī, intuitus [2; dep.] *look upon, consider*

inundātiō,-ōnis [f.] *flood*

inveniō,-īre, invēnī, inventum [4] *discover, find*

invideō,-ēre, invīdī, invīsum [2; + dat.] *begrudge, cheat, envy*

invidus,-a,-um *envious, jealous, begrudging*

inviolātus,-a,-um *unhurt, unharmed*

invīsus,-a,-um *hateful, hated*

invītō,-āre,-āvī,-ātum [1] *invite*

invītus,-a,-um *unwilling*

ipse, ipsa, ipsum *(my/your/him/her/it)self*

īra,-ae [f.] *anger*

īracundus,-a,-um *wrathful*

īrātus,-a,-um *angry*

irreparābilis,-e *irrecoverable, irretrievable*

irruō,-ere, irruī [3] *rush in*

is, ea, id *that, he, she, it*

iste, ista, istud *that (of yours)*

istīc *there*

ita *so, in such a way, thus*

Ītalia,-ae [f.] *Italy*

Ītalicus,-a,-um *Italian*

Italus,-ī [m.] *an Italian*

itaque *and so, therefore, for that reason*

iter, itineris [n.] *route, way*

iterum *again, a second time*

iubeō,-ēre, iussī, iussum [2] *order, tell*

Iūdaea,-ae [f] *Judaea*

Iūdaeī,-ōrum [m.] *Jews*

iūdex,-icis [m.] *judge, juror*

iūdicium,-ī [n.] *court, trial, judgement*

iugulō,-āre,-āvī,-ātum [1] *kill, cut a throat*

iugum,-ī [n.] *summit, ridge*

Iugurtha,-ae [m.] *Jugurtha*

iūmentum,-ī [n.] *pack animal*

Iuppiter, Iovis [m.] *Jupiter, Jove*

iūre *rightly, justifiably*

iūrō,-āre,-āvī,-ātum [1] *swear*

iūs, iūris [n.] *justice*

iussū *on the order, by command*

iuventa,-ae [f.] *youth*

iuvō,-āre, iūvī, iūtum [1] *help, please*

labor (labōs),-ōris [m.] *toil, exertion*

labōrō,-āre,-āvī,-ātum [1] *work, toil*

labrum,-ī [n.] *lip*

labyrinthus,-ī [m.] *labyrinth*

lacer,-era,-erum *mutilated*

lacertus,-ī [m.] *arm*

lacrima,-ae [f.] *tear*

lacrimor, lacrimārī, lacrimātus [1; dep.] *weep*

laetitia,-ae [f.] *joy, rejoicing, cheerfulness*

laetus,-a,-um *delighted, gladdened, cheerful*

langueō,-ēre [2] *feel weak*

laniō,-āre, laniāvī, laniātum [1] *tear into pieces*

lanius,-ī [m.] *butcher*

Lāocoōn, Lāocoontis [m.] *Laocoön*

lapidārius,-a,-um *stone-carrying*

largus,-a,-um *abundant*

lascīvus,-a,-um *playful, wanton*

lassus,-a,-um *tired, exhausted*

laterīcius,-a,-um *made of bricks*

Latīnus,-a,-um *Latin*

Latium,-ī [n.] *Latium*

latrō,-ōnis [m.] *robber*

lātus,-a,-um *broad, wide*

laudō,-āre,-āvī,-ātum [1] *praise*

Lāvīnia,-ae [f.] *Lavinia*

Lāvīnus,-a,-um *Lavinian*

lavō,-āre, lāvī, lautum [1] *wash, bathe*

lectīca,-ae [f.] *litter*

lecticō,-āre,-āvī,-ātum [1] *read repeatedly*

lectus,-ī [m.] *bed, couch*

lēgātiō,-ōnis [f.] *embassy*

lēgātus,-ī [m.] *commander, commissioned officer*

legiō,-ōnis [f.]   *legion*

legō,-ere, lēgī, lectum [3]   *pick, select, read*

leō,-ōnis [m.]   *lion*

lepus,-oris [m.]   *hare*

lētum,-ī [n.]   *death*

levis,-e   *light, superficial*

lēx, lēgis [f.]   *law*

libellus,-ī [m.]   *little book*

libenter   *willingly*

liber,-brī [m.]   *book*

līber,-era,-erum   *free*

līberī,-ōrum [m.pl.]   *children*

līberō,-āre,-āvī,-ātum [1]   *set free, release*

lībertās,-tātis [f.]   *freedom*

lībertus,-ī [m.]   *freedman*

libet [+ dat.]   *it is agreeable, pleasing*

librārius,-ī [m.]   *clerk, secretary*

Libya,-ae [f.]   *Libya, north Africa*

licet (licitum est) [+ dat.]   *it is (was) lawful, permitted*

ligō,-āre,-āvī,-ātum [1]   *tie, bind*

līlium,-ī [n.]   *lily*

līmen,-inis [n.]   *threshold, doorway*

lingua,-ae [f.]   *tongue, speech*

linquō,-ere, līquī [3]   *let go*

liquō,-āre,-āvī,-ātum [1]   *decant, strain*

littera,-ae [f.]   *letter*

lītus,-oris [n.]   *shore*

locō,-āre,-āvī,-ātum [1]   *set, arrange, contract*

locus,-ī [m.]   *place*

longus,-a,-um   *long*

loquor,-ī, locūtus [3; dep.]   *speak*

Lucrētia,-ae [f.]   *Lucretia*

lūctuōsus,-a,-um   *sorrowful*

lūctus,-ūs [m.]   *grief*

lūcus,-ī [m.]   *wood, grove*

lūdō,-ere, lūsī, lūsum [3]   *play, tease*

lūdus,-ī [m.]   *school, game*

lūmen,-inis [n.]   *light, eye*

lūridus,-a,-um   *ghastly, lurid*

lūx, lūcis [f.]   *light, daylight*

luxus,-ūs [m.]   *extravagance, excess*

Macedonicus,-a,-um   *Macedonian*

mactō,-āre,-āvī,-ātum [1]   *sacrifice*

magis   *more, rather*

magister,-trī [m.]   *master*

magnanimus,-a,-um   *highminded*

magnopere   *greatly, very much*

magnus,-a,-um   *great, large*

magus,-ī [m.]   *sorcerer*

maiestās,-tātis [f.]   *greatness, dignity*

maior, maius [comparative of 'magnus']   *greater*

maiōrēs,-um [m.]   *ancestors*

male   *badly*

maledictum,-ī [n.]   *abuse*

malesuādus,-a,-um   *evil-counselling*

mālō, mālle   *prefer, wish rather*

malus,-a,-um   *bad*

mancipium,-ī [n.]   *slave*

mandō,-āre,-āvī,-ātum [1]   *instruct, order*

māne   *early, in the morning*

maneō,-ēre, mānsī, mānsum [2]   *remain*

mānēs,-ium [m.pl.]   *spirits*

manūmittō,-ere,-mīsī,-missum [3]   *set free*

manus,-ūs [f.]   *hand*

mare, maris [n.]   *sea*

marītus,-ī [m.]   *husband*

marmor,-oris [n.]   *marble*

marmoreus,-a,-um   *made of marble*

māter,-tris [f.]   *mother*

mātrimōnium,-ī [n.]   *marriage*

mātrōna,-ae [f.]   *lady, matron*

mātūrus,-a,-um   *ready, ripe*

Māvors,-ortis [m.]   *Mars*

maximē   *especially, very, most*

medicīna,-ae [f.]   *medicine, treatment*

medicus,-ī [m.]   *doctor*

medius,-a,-um   *mid, in the middle of*

membrum,-ī [n.]   *limb*

memorābilis,-e   *memorable*

memorō,-āre,-āvī,-ātum [1]   *relate, tell*

mēns, mentis [f.]   *mind*

mēnsa,-ae [f.]   *table*

mentior, mentīrī, mentītus [4; dep.]   *lie*

mentula,-ae [f.]   *penis*

mercātūra,-ae [f.]   *trade, business*

mercēnārius,-ī [m.]   *mercenary, hired hand*

mereō,-ēre,-uī, meritum [2]   *deserve, obtain*

meretrīx,-īcis [f.]   *prostitute*

mergō,-ere, mersī, mersum [3]   *sink, overwhelm*

meritum,-ī [n.]   *service, worth*

merum,-ī [n.]   *wine*

metuō,-ere, metuī [3]   *fear, be apprehensive*

metus,-ūs [m.]   *fear*

meus,-a,-um   *my*

micturiō,-īre [4]   *urinate*

migrō,-āre,-āvī,-ātum [1]   *move*

mīles,-itis [m.]   *soldier, army*

mīlitāris,-e   *military*

mīlitō,-āre,-āvī,-ātum [1]   *fight*

minimē   *least, not at all, no*

minister,-trī [m.]   *servant, attendant*

ministerium,-ī [n.]   *service*

ministra,-ae [f.]   *deaconess*

minor, minārī, minātus [1; dep.]   *threaten*

minus   *less*

mīrābilis,-e   *wonderful, extraordinary*

mīror, mīrārī, mīrātus [1; dep.]   *be surprised, amazed*

mīrus,-a,-um   *extraordinary, surprising*

misceō,-ēre,-uī, mixtum [2]   *mix, mingle*

miser,-era,-erum   *wretched, unhappy*

miseror, miserārī, miserātus [1; dep.]   *pity, feel compassion for*

mittō,-ere, mīsī, missum [3]   *send*

moderātiō,-ōnis [f.]   *moderation*

modo   *only, recently*

modo . . . modo   *sometimes . . . sometimes, now . . . now*

modus,-ī [m.]   *extent, manner, method*

moenia,-ōrum [n.pl.]   *city-walls*

mollis,-e   *soft*

moneō,-ēre,-uī, monitum [2]   *advise, warn*

mōns, montis [m.]   *mountain*

mōnstrō,-āre,-āvī,-ātum [1]   *show*

mora,-ae [f.]   *delay*

morbus,-ī [m.]   *disease*

morior, morī, mortuus [M.; dep.]   *die*

moror, morārī, morātus [1; dep.]   *delay, wait*

mors, mortis [f.]   *death*

morsus,-ūs [m.]   *bite*

mortālis,-e   *mortal*

mōs, mōris [m.]   *fashion, custom, conduct*

moveō,-ēre, mōvī, mōtum [2]   *move, stir*

mox   *soon, afterwards, presently*

mūgītus,-ūs [m.]   *bellowing*

muliebris,-e   *womanly, of a woman*

mulier,-is [f.]   *woman*

multitūdō,-inis [f.]   *crowd*

multus,-a,-um   *much, many*

mūlus,-ī [m.]   *mule*

mundus,-ī [m.]   *world*

mūniceps,-ipis [m./f.]   *fellow citizen*

mūnus,-eris [n.]   *gift, service, public show*

mūs, mūris [m.]   *mouse*

mūtō,-āre,-āvī,-ātum [1]   *change*

nam   *for, in fact*

nātus,-a,-um   *born*

nātus,-ī [m.]   *son*

navālis,-e   *naval*

nāvis,-is [f.]   *ship*

nē   *lest, that . . . not, do not . . .*

nebula,-ae [f.]   *mist, fog*

nec (as 'neque')

necessārius,-a,-um   *indispensable, necessary*

necesse   *necessary, unavoidable*

necessitās,-tātis [f.]   *necessity, need*

necō,-āre,-āvī,-ātum [1]   *kill*

nefās [n.]   *wrong, sacrilege*

neglegō,-ere, neglexī, neglectum [3]   *disregard*

negō,-āre,-āvī,-ātum [1]   *deny, say that . . . not*

negōtium,-ī [n.]   *business, occupation*

nēmō,-inis   *no one*

nepōs,-ōtis [m./f.]   *descendant*

neptis,-is [f.]   *granddaughter*

neque   *and . . . not, but . . . not*

neque . . . neque   *neither . . . nor*

nēquīquam   *in vain, fruitlessly*

nēquitia,-ae [f.]   *wickedness*

nex, necis [f.]   *death, murder*

nigrēscō,-ere [3]   *grow dark, become black*

nihil   *nothing*

nimis   *too, too much, excessively*

nisi   *unless, if not, except*

nītor, nītī, nīsus [3; dep.]   *strive*

niveus,-a,-um   *snow-white*

nix, nivis [f.]   *snow*

nōbilis,-e   *noble, well-born*

nōbilitās,-tātis [f.]   *high rank, nobility*

noceō,-ēre,-uī, nocitum [2; + dat.]   *harm, injure*

nōdus,-ī [m.]   *knot*

nōlō, nōlle, nōluī   *be unwilling*

nōmen,-inis [n.]   *name*

nōminō,-āre,-āvī,-ātum [1]   *call by name, give a name to*

nōn   *not*

nōndum   *not yet*

nōnne   *surely*

nōs   *we, us*

nōscō,-ere, nōvī, nōtum [3]   *get knowledge of, come to know ('nōvī' = I know)*

noster,-tra,-trum   *our*

nota,-ae [f.]   *social grading*

nōtus,-a,-um   *known, familiar, notorious*

noverca,-ae [f.]   *stepmother*

novitās,-tātis [f.]   *newness, novelty*

novus,-a,-um   *new*

nox, noctis [f.]   *night*

nūbilis,-e   *marriageable*

nūbō,-ere, nūpsī, nūptum [3; + dat.]   *marry*

nūdus,-a,-um   *naked*

nūllus,-a,-um   *no, not any*

num   *surely not, whether*

nūmen,-inis [n.]   *nod, divine will, god*

numerus,-ī [m.]   *number*

nummus,-ī [m.]   *coin*

numquam   *never*

nunc   *now*

nuntiō,-āre,-āvī,-ātum [1]   *announce*

nūper   *recently, not long ago*

ob [+ acc.]   *because of*

obdormīscō,-ere [3]   *fall asleep*

obnoxius,-a,-um [+ dat.]   *liable to*

obscēnus,-a,-um   *obscene, foul*

obsequium,-ī [n.]   *compliance, submission*

observō,-āre,-āvī,-ātum [1]   *watch, observe*

obsidiō,-ōnis [f.]   *siege, blockade*

obstinātiō,-ōnis [f.]   *persistence*

obstinātus,-a,-um   *determined, stubborn*

obstipēscō,-ere, obstipuī [3]   *be amazed*

obstō,-āre, obstitī [1]   *stand in the way, obstruct*

occidō,-ere, occidī, occāsum [3]   *fall, die*

occīdō,-ere, occīdī, occīsum [3]   *kill*

occulō,-ere,-uī, occultum [3]   *hide, cover*

occupātiō,-ōnis [f.]   *occupation*

occupō,-āre,-āvī,-ātum [1]   *take, seize*

oculus,-ī [m.]   *eye*

ōdium,-ī [n.]   *hatred, ill-feeling*

odor,-ōris [m.]   *smell*

ōlim   *once, previously*

omnīnō   *entirely, in entirety*

omnis,-e   *all, every*

onus,-eris [n.]   *burden*

opera,-ae [f.]   *task, effort*

oportet   *it is necessary, proper*

oppōnō,-ere, opposuī, oppositum [3]   *place opposite*

opprimō,-ere, oppressī, oppressum [3]   *crush, overwhelm*

ops, opis [f.]   *strength; [in plural] resources, wealth*

optābilis,-e   *desirable*

optimātēs,-ium [m.]   *aristocrats*

optō,-āre,-āvī,-ātum [1]   *pray, wish*

opulentia,-ae [f.]   *wealth*

opulentus,-a,-um   *lavish, rich*

opus,-eris [n.]   *work, action, task*

ōra,-ae [f.]   *shore, land*

orbis,-is [m.]   *circle, world*

orbitās,-tātis [f.]   *bereavement*

Orcus,-ī [m.]   *hell, god of the underworld*

Oriēns, Orientis   *the east*

orīgō,-inis [f.]   *origin*

orior, orīrī, ortus [4; dep.]   *rise, arise*

ōrnāmentum,-ī [n.]   *ornament*

ōrnō,-āre,-āvī,-ātum [1]   *adorn, equip, honour*

ōrō,-āre,-āvī,-ātum [1]   *beg (for), plead*

ōs, ōris [n.]   *face, mouth*

os, ossis [n.]   *bone*

ostendō,-ere, ostendī, ostentum [3]   *show*

ōstiārius,-ī [m.]   *doorkeeper*

ostrīnus,-a,-um   *purple*

ōtiōsus,-a,-um   *idle, at leisure*

ōtium,-ī [n.]   *leisure, free time, peace*

pācō,-āre,-āvī,-ātum [1]   *pacify*

paene   *nearly, almost*

palla,-ae [f.]   *cloak*

pālus,-ī [m.]   *stake, pole*

pangō,-ere, pepigī, pactum [3]   *compose*

pannus,-ī [m.]   *rag, cloth*

pantomīmus,-ī [m.]   *pantomime artist*

pār   *equal*

parcō,-ere, pepercī, parsum [3; + dat.]   *spare*

parēns, parentis [m./f.]   *parent*

pāreō,-ēre,-uī, pāritum [2; + dat.]   *obey*

pariter   *equally, in equal degree*

parō,-āre,-āvī,-ātum [1]   *prepare*

pars, partis [f.]   *part*

parum   *too little, not enough*

parvus,-a,-um   *small*

pāscō,-ere, pāvī, pāstum [3]   *feed, pasture*

passim   *everywhere*

patefaciō,-ere, patefēcī, patefactum [M.]   *reveal, open*

pateō,-ēre,-uī [2]   *stand open, lie open*

pater,-tris [m.]   *father, patrician, senator*

paternus,-a,-um   *belonging to one's father*

pathicus,-a,-um   *lustful*

patior, patī, passus [M.; dep.]   *allow, suffer*

patria,-ae [f.]   *one's own country*

patrimōnium,-ī [n.]   *inheritance*

paucus,-a,-um   *few*

paulātim   *little by little, gradually*

paulum   *briefly, little*

pauper,-is [m.]   *poor man*

pāx, pācis [f.]   *peace, treaty*

peccō,-āre,-āvī,-ātum [1]   *offend, do wrong, make a mistake*

pectus,-oris [n.]   *breast, heart, courage*

pecūnia,-ae [f.]   *money*

pedes,-itis [m.]   *walker, footsoldier*

pēdīcō,-āre [1]   *sodomize*

peior, peius [comp. of 'malus']   *worse*

pelliciō,-ere, pellexī, pellectum [3]   *win over, entice*

pellō,-ere, pepulī, pulsum [3]   *drive, beat, strike*

Penātēs,-ium [m.]   *spirits of the household*

pēnsum,-ī [n.]   *weight (of wool), importance*

per [+ acc.]   *by means of, through, on account of, across, for, by*

percellō,-ere, perculī, perculsum [3]   *strike, discourage*

perdō,-ere, perdidī, perditum [3]   *ruin, waste*

peregrīnus,-a,-um   *foreign, strange*

pereō,-īre, periī (-īvī), peritum   *perish, die*
perferō, perferre, pertulī, perlātum   *endure, suffer*
perfundō,-ere, perfūdī, perfūsum [3]   *pour over, sprinkle, moisten*
pergō,-ere, perrēxī, perrēctum [3]   *go, proceed*
perīculōsus,-a,-um   *dangerous*
perimō,-ere, perēmī, peremptum [3]   *destroy*
permittō,-ere, permīsī, permissum [3]   *let go, give up, entrust*
perpetior, perpetī , perpessus [M.; dep.]   *endure*
persequor, persequī, persecūtus [3; dep.]   *pursue*
persevēranter   *steadfastly*
persevērō,-āre,-āvī,-ātum [1]   *persist*
pertimēscō,-ere [3]   *fear*
pertinācia,-ae [f.]   *stubbornness*
pertināx   *determined, stubborn*
pervādō,-ere, pervāsī, pervāsum [3]   *spread through, reach*
perveniō,-īre, pervēnī, perventum [4]   *reach*
pēs, pedis [m.]   *foot*
petō,-ere, petīvī (-iī), petītum [3]   *seek, ask, strive for, attack*
pharetrātus,-a,-um   *quiver-carrying*
philosophia,-ae [f.]   *philosophy*
pictor, pictōris [m.]   *painter*
pietās,-tātis [f.]   *piety, sense of duty, dutiful conduct*
pila,-ae [f.]   *ball*
Pīsō,-ōnis [m.]   *Piso*
pius,-a,-um   *dutiful, devoted*
placeō,-ēre,-uī, placitum [2; + dat.]   *please, satisfy*
placet [+ dat.]   *it pleases, seems good, right*
placidē   *calmly, peacefully*
plāga,-ae [f.]   *blow, lash, wound*
plēbs, plēbis [f.]   *common people*
plōrō,-āre,-āvī,-ātum [1]   *weep*
plūrimus,-a,-um   *most, very many*
plūs   *more*
poena,-ae [f.]   *punishment*
poēta [m.]   *poet*
pol   *indeed, truly, by Pollux!*
polītus,-a,-um   *refined*
pōnō,-ere, posuī, positum [3]   *put, place, put down, set up*
pōns, pontis [m.]   *bridge*
ponticulus,-ī [m.]   *little bridge*
populus,-ī [m.]   *people*
Porsenna,-ae [m.]   *Porsenna*
porta,-ae [f.]   *gate*
porticus,-ūs [f.]   *entrance, colonnade*
portiō,-ōnis [f.]   *share, portion*
poscō, poscere, poposcī [3]   *demand, desire, beg*

possessor,-ōris [m.]   *owner*
possum, posse, potuī   *be able*
post [+ acc.]   *after, behind*
posterus,-a,-um   *coming after*
postis,-is [m.]   *doorpost*
postquam   *after*
postulō,-āre,-āvī,-ātum [1]   *demand*
potestās,-tātis [f.]   *power, authority*
potis,-e   *capable, able*
potius   *more, rather, preferably*
pōtō,-āre,-āvī,-ātum [1]   *drink*
prae [+ abl.]   *before, in front of*
praebeō,-ēre,-uī, praebitum [2]: contraction of 'praehibeō,-ēre'
praeceptor,-ōris [m.]   *teacher, instructor*
praecipuē   *especially, chiefly*
praecipuus,-a,-um   *special, principal*
praeclārus,-a,-um   *magnificent*
praecō,-ōnis [m.]   *herald*
praeda,-ae [f.]   *loot, plunder*
praedicō,-āre,-āvī,-ātum [1]   *proclaim, say publicly*
praedō,-ōnis [m.]   *robber, pirate*
praefectus,-ī [m.]   *commander, prefect*
praefixus,-a,-um   *stuck, impaled*
praegnō,-āre [1]   *be pregnant*
praehibeō,-ēre,-uī, praehibitum [2]   *hold forth, furnish, offer, supply*
praemium,-ī [n.]   *reward*
praesēns   *here and now*
praesentiō,-īre, praesēnsī, praesēnsum [4]   *feel beforehand*
praesidium,-ī [n.]   *defence, protection, guard*
praeter [+ acc.]   *except, besides*
praetereā   *moreover*
praetor,-ōris [m.]   *praetor, magistrate, governor*
prāvus,-a,-um   *depraved*
precor, precārī, precātus [1; dep.]   *ask, entreat*
premō,-ere, pressī, pressum [3]   *press*
pretium,-ī [n.]   *price, value*
prex, precis [f.]   *prayer*
prīdem   *long ago, long since*
prīmum, prīmō   *at first*
prīmus,-a,-um   *first*
prīnceps,-ipis [m.]   *princeps, leading citizen, emperor*
prīncipātus,-ūs [m.]   *principate, reign*
prīscus,-a,-um   *ancient, of former times*
prīvātus,-a,-um   *private, stripped of one's rank*
prīvīgna,-ae [f.]   *stepdaughter*
prō [+ abl.]   *in place of, in return for, for the sake of*
probitās,-tātis [f.]   *uprightness, goodness, honesty*
probō,-āre,-āvī,-ātum [1]   *cherish, commend*

probus,-a,-um *good*

procul [prep. + abl.] *far from*; [adv.] *far off, distant*

prōcurrō,-ere,-(cu)currī,-cursum [3] *rush forth*

prōditus,-a,-um *disclosed*

prōdūcō,-ere, prōdūxī, prōductum [3] *lead forth, bring before*

proelium,-ī [n.] *combat, battle*

profugiō,-ere, prōfūgī [M.] *flee away*

profugus,-ī [m.] *fugitive*

profundō,-ere, profūdī, profūsum [3] *pour forth*

prōiciō,-ere, prōiēcī, prōiectum [M.] *throw, throw forth, throw down*

prōmittō,-ere, prōmīsī, prōmissum [3] *send forth, let hang down, promise*

prope *almost*

properō,-āre,-āvī,-ātum [1] *hurry, be quick*

propinquus,-ī [m.] *relative*

propitius,-a,-um *kindly*

propter [+ acc.] *because of*

prōscindō,-ere, prōscidī, prōscissum [3] *revile*

Proserpina,-ae [f.] *Proserpina*

prosperus,-a,-um *favourable*

prōsum, prōdesse, prōfuī [+ dat.] *be of use to*

prōtegō,-ere, prōtexī, prōtectum [3] *protect*

prōtinus *immediately, at once*

prōvincia,-ae [f.] *province, provincial command*

prōvolvō,-ere,-volvī,-volūtum [3] *roll forward*

proximus,-a,-um *nearest, next*

prūdēns *knowing, experienced, wise*

prūdentia,-ae [f.] *good sense*

psyllī,-ōrum [m.] *serpent charmers*

pūblicō,-āre,-āvī,-ātum [1] *confiscate*

pūblicus,-a,-um *public*

pudendus,-a,-um *shameful, scandalous*

pudēns *modest, bashful*

pudor,-ōris [m.] *decency, shame, embarrassment*

puella,-ae [f.] *girl*

puer,-ī [m.] *boy*

pugna,-ae [f.] *battle*

pugnō,-āre,-āvī,-ātum [1] *fight*

pulcher,-chra,-chrum *beautiful, noble, glorious*

pulchrē *well, splendidly*

pūmex,-icis [f.] *rock*

Pūnicus,-a,-um *Carthaginian*

pūniō,-īre, pūnīvī (-iī), pūnītum [4] *punish*

putō,-āre,-āvī,-ātum [1] *think, consider, reflect, suppose*

Pyrrhus,-ī [m.] *Pyrrhus*

quā *by what way, by any way*

quadrāns,-ntis [m.] *coin, ¼ of an as*

quaerō,-ere, quaesīvī (-iī) quaesītum [3] *ask, inquire, look for, seek*

quaestus,-ūs [m.] *profit, business*

quālis,-e *of what sort, of such a sort, such as*

quam *as, than*; [acc.fem.] *whom, which*

quam ob rem *why*

quamquam *although*

quamvīs *although, and yet, even if*

quandō *when, since, as, at any time*

quantus,-a,-um *how much*

quārē *why, for what reason*

quārtus,-a,-um *fourth*

quasi *as if*

querēla,-ae [f.] *complaint, wailing*

queror, querī, questus [3; dep.] *complain*

quī, quae, quod *who, which, what, any(one/thing)*

quia *because, that*

quid *what, which, why, any(thing)*

quīdam, quaedam, quiddam *a certain (person)*

quidem *indeed, certainly, even*

quiēscō,-ere, quiēvī, quiētum [3] *rest*

quiētus,-a,-um *inactive, quiet*

quīnque *five*

quīntus,-a,-um *fifth*

quippe *indeed, to be sure*

quis, quid (n.) *who?, which?, what? any(one/thing)*

quisquam, quidquam *anyone at all*

quisque, quaeque, quodque *each, every*

quisquis, quidquid *whoever, whichever, whatever*

quō *to where*; abl. of 'quis/quī'

quod *because, that, that which, in that, which, any, what*

quōmodo *how*

quondam *formerly*

quoniam *since*

quoque *also, too*

quotiēns *how many times, as often as*

quotus,-a,-um *how many, how few, how small*

rādō,-ere, rāsī, rāsum [3] *shave*

raeda,-ae [f.] *carriage*

rapiō,-ere, rapuī, raptum [M.] *seize, take, plunder, rape*

ratiō,-ōnis [f.] *argument, reason, justification, procedure*

recēns *fresh, recent*

recessus,-ūs [m.] *corner, retreat*

recipiō,-ere, recēpī, receptum [M.] *take, accept, recover*

reconciliō,-āre,-āvī,-ātum [1] *reconcile, appease*

rēctē *properly, correctly*

rēctum,-ī [n.] *virtue, uprightness*

recumbō,-ere, recubuī [3]   *recline*
recūsō,-īre,-āvī,-ātum [1]   *refuse*
reddō,-ere, reddidī, redditum [3]   *give back*
redeō,-īre, rediī, reditum   *return*
redimō,-ere, redēmī, redemptum [3]   *redeem, buy back*
redūcō,-ere, redūxī, reductum [3]   *bring back, lead back*
refellō,-ere, refellī [3]   *refute, challenge*
referō, referre, rettulī, relātum   *bring back, report, refer*
reficiō,-ere, refēcī, refectum [M.]   *make again, restore*
refugiō,-ere, refūgī [M.]   *flee back, away*
rēgia,-ae [f.]   *palace*
rēgīna,-ae [f.]   *queen*
rēgius,-a,-um   *royal*
rēgnātor,-ōris [m.]   *ruler*
rēgnō,-āre,-āvī,-ātum [1]   *reign, rule*
rēgnum,-ī [n.]   *territory, dominion*
regō,-ere, rēxī, rēctum [3]   *rule*
regredior, regredī, regressus [M.; dep.]   *go back*
rēgula,-ae [f.]   *rule*
relinquō,-ere, relīquī, relictum [3]   *leave, abandon*
remedium,-ī [n.]   *cure*
remittō,-ere, remīsī, remissum [3]   *let go back, send back*
Remus,-ī [m.]   *Remus*
reor, rērī, ratus [3; dep.]   *think, imagine, reckon, suppose*
repellō,-ere, reppulī, repulsum [3]   *drive back*
repente   *recently, suddenly*
repetō,-ere, repetīvī (-iī), repetītum [3]   *seek again, return to*
repōnō,-ere, reposuī, repos(i)tum [3]   *put away, put down*
reprehendō,-ere, reprehendī, reprehēnsum [3]   *find a fault with, catch out*
reprimō,-ere, repressī, repressum [3]   *curb, keep in check*
repudiō,-āre,-āvī,-ātum [1]   *reject, divorce*
requīrō,-ere, requīsīvī (-iī), requīsītum [3]   *seek to know*
rēs pūblica, reī pūblicae [f.]   *the Republic*
rēs,-eī [f.]   *thing, matter, business, issue*
rescindō,-ere,-scidī,-scissum [3]   *repeal, cancel*
resecō,-āre, resecuī, resectum [1]   *cut back*
reservō,-āre,-āvī,-ātum [1]   *keep back*
resideō,-ēre, resēdī [2]   *be seated, reside*
resistō,-ere, restitī [3]   *resist*
respondeō,-ēre, respondī, respōnsum [2]   *answer, reply*

respōnsum,-ī [n.]   *reply, response*
restis,-is [f.]   *rope*
restituō,-ere, restituī, restitūtum [3]   *bring back, restore*
retineō,-ēre,-uī, retentum [2]   *keep, restrain*
retrahō,-ere, retraxī, retractum [3]   *drag back, bring back*
reus,-ī [m.]   *defendant*
revellō,-ere, revellī, revulsum [3]   *pull, tear*
rēvereor,-ērī, reveritus [2; dep.]   *be in awe of, revere*
revertor,-ī, reversus [3; dep.]   *return, come back, turn back*
revīsō,-ere, revīsī [3]   *revisit, rejoin*
revocō,-āre,-āvī,-ātum [1]   *recall, restore*
rēx, rēgis [m.]   *king*
Rhēnus,-ī [m.]   *Rhine*
rhētor,-oris [m.]   *professor*
rīdeō,-ēre, rīsī, rīsum [2]   *laugh (at)*
rigō,-āre,-āvī,-ātum [1]   *soak*
rīvus,-ī [m.]   *stream*
rōdō,-ere, rōsī, rōsum [3]   *gnaw, nibble*
rogō,-āre,-āvī,-ātum [1]   *ask (for)*
Rōma,-ae [f.]   *Rome*
Rōmānus,-a,-um   *Roman*
Romulus,-ī [m.]   *Romulus*
rosa,-ae [f.]   *rose*
rōstrum,-ī [n.]   *snout, muzzle, beak of a ship;* [pl.] *speaker's platform*
ruber,-bra,-brum   *red*
rudis,-e   *raw, rough*
ruīna,-ae [f.]   *ruin, destruction*
rūmor,-ōris [m.]   *rumour, gossip*
rumpō,-ere, rūpī, ruptum [3]   *break*
rūrsum (rūrsus)   *again*
rūs, rūris [n.]   *country, land, estate*
Sabīnus,-a,-um   *Sabine*
sacer,-cra,-crum   *sacred*
sacerdōs,-dōtis [m./f.]   *priest/priestess*
saeculum,-ī [n.]   *generation, lifetime;* [pl.] *age, times*
saepe   *often*
saepiō,-īre, saepsī, saeptum [4]   *fence in, barricade*
saeviō,-īre, saeviī, saevītum [4]   *rage, vent one's fury*
saevitia,-ae [f.]   *cruelty*
saevus,-a,-um   *cruel, harsh, mean*
salūs, salūtis [f.]   *safety, well-being*
salūtātor,-ōris [m.]   *visitor, caller*
salūtō,-āre,-āvī,-ātum [1]   *greet, salute*
salvus,-a,-um   *safe, unharmed*
Samnītēs,-(i)um [m.pl.]   *Samnites*
sānctus,-a,-um   *sacred, holy*
sānē   *certainly*

sanguineus,-a,-um *bloody, bloodstained*

sanguis,-inis [m.] *blood*

saniēs,-ēī [f.] *gore*

sānus,-a,-um *healthy, sound*

sapiēns *wise, judicious*

sapiō,-ere [M.] *taste, have good taste, be wise*

satiō,-āre,-āvī,-ātum [1] *appease, satisfy*

satis *enough*

satisfaciō,-ere,-fēcit,-factum [M.] *satisfy, apologize*

Sāturnus,-ī [m.] *Saturn*

saucius,-a,-um *wounded*

scelerātus,-a,-um *wicked, pernicious*

scelus,-eris [n.] *evil deed, wicked act, crime*

scīlicet *no doubt, to be sure, of course*

scindō,-ere, scidī, scissum [3] *tear, cut up*

sciō,-īre, scīvī (-iī), scītum [4] *know*

scītē *elegantly, tastefully*

scrībō,-ere, scrīpsī, scrīptum [3] *write*

scrīptor,-ōris [m.] *writer*

scrīpulum,-ī [n.] *small weight, scrap*

sē *himself, herself, itself, themselves*

secō,-āre, secuī, sectum [1] *cut*

secundus,-a,-um *following, second*

secūris,-is [f.] *axe*

secūritās,-tātis [f.] *security, safety*

sed *but*

sedeō,-ēre, sēdī, sessum [2] *sit*

sēditiō,-ōnis [f.] *rebellion*

sēdūcō,-ere, sēdūxī, sēductum [3] *lead apart, separate*

sella,-ae [f.] *chair, seat*

sēmita,-ae [f.] *narrow path, narrow track*

semper *always*

senātor,-ōris [m.] *senator*

senātus,-ūs [m.] *senate*

senectūs,-tūtis [f.] *old age*

senex, senis [m.] *old man*

sequor, sequī, secūtus [3; dep.] *follow*

sera,-ae [f.] *bar*

serēnus,-a,-um *calm*

sērius,-a,-um *serious*

serō,-ere, sēvī, sātum [3] *sow, cause, bring forth*

serpēns,-entis [f.] *serpent*

sērus,-a,-um *late, belated*

serva,-ae [f.] *slave (female)*

serviō,-īre, servīvī (-iī), servītum [4; + dat.] *be a slave to, serve*

servitūs,-tūtis [f.] *slavery, servitude*

servō,-āre,-āvī,-ātum [1] *save, keep, guard*

servus,-ī [m.] *slave*

seu . . . seu *whether . . . or*

sevērus,-a,-um *serious, grave, stern*

sexus,-ūs [m.] *sex, gender*

sī *if*

Sibylla,-ae [f.] *the Sibyl*

sīc *so, thus, in this way, just so, yes*

sīcut *as, just as*

sīdus,-eris [n.] *star, [pl.] sky*

signum,-ī [n.] *sign, standard*

silentium,-ī [n.] *silence*

sileō,-ēre, siluī [2] *keep silent, be silent*

silva,-ae [f.] *wood*

simul *at the same time, together*

simul . . . simul *while . . . at the same time*

simultās,-tātis [f.] *quarrel, enmity, animosity*

sīn *but if*

sine [+ abl.] *without*

sinō,-ere, sīvī, situm [3] *allow*

sinus,-ūs [m.] *fold of a garment, bosom*

seu . . . seu (sīve . . . sīve) *whether . . . or*

socer,-ī [m.] *father-in-law*

societās,-tātis [f.] *political alliance, pact, partnership*

socius,-ī [m.] *colleague, comrade*

socrus,-ūs [f.] *mother-in-law*

soleō,-ēre [2] *be accustomed*

sōlitūdō,-inis [f.] *loneliness, desert*

solitus,-a,-um *familiar, customary*

sōlum [adv.] *only*

sōlus,-a,-um *only, alone*

solvō,-ere, solvī, solūtum [3] *loosen, release*

somnus,-ī [m.] *sleep*

sonō,-āre,-āvī,-ātum [1] *resound*

sōpiō,-īre, sōpīvī (-iī), sōpītum [4] *put to sleep, lull*

sopōrus,-a,-um *sleepy, sleep-bringing*

sordidus,-a,-um *demeaning, vulgar, vile*

soror,-ōris [f.] *sister*

sospes [gen. 'sospitis'] *safe, safe and sound*

spatium,-ī [n.] *space*

spectāculum,-ī [n.] *show, a seat at a show*

spectō,-āre,-āvī,-ātum [1] *watch*

spērō,-āre,-āvī,-ātum [1] *hope (for)*

spēs,-ēī [f.] *hope*

spīritus,-ūs [m.] *breath, spirit*

splendidus,-a,-um *bright*

spoliō,-āre,-āvī,-ātum [1] *rob, deprive*

sponte *willingly, of one's own initiative*

statim *immediately*

stō,-āre, stetī, stātum [1] *stand, be stationary*

strepitus,-ūs [m.] *noise*

strīdor,-ōris [m.] *rattling, clanking*

studeō,-ēre,-uī [2] *study, strive after, pursue*

studiōsus,-a,-um *eager, devoted, supportive*

studium,-ī [n.] *eagerness, inclination, study*

stultitia,-ae [f.]   *folly, foolishness*

stuprum,-ī [n.]   *lust, defilement*

Stygius,-a,-um   *of the Styx, Stygian*

sub [+ acc./abl.]   *beneath, under*

subdō,-ere, subdidī, subditum [3]   *substitute, introduce falsely*

subdomō,-āre [1]   *tame, break in*

subeō,-īre, subiī (-īvī), subitum   *go under, draw near, creep up to*

subiciō,-ere, subiēcī, subiectum [M.]   *throw under, subject, subdue*

subinde   *then*

subolēs,-is [f.]   *offspring, descendant*

subvertō,-ere, subvertī, subversum [3]   *overthrow, upset, ruin*

succēdō,-ere, successī, successum [3]   *enter, approach, succeed*

succingō,-ere, succinxī, succinctum [3]   *gird up, tuck up*

sūdō,-āre,-āvī,-ātum [1]   *sweat*

sufferō, sufferre, sustulī, sublātum   *suffer*

sufficiō,-ere, suffēcī, suffectum [M.]   *provide, supply, be enough*

sufflō,-āre,-āvī,-ātum [1]   *blow upon*

suffrāgor, suffrāgārī, suffrāgātus [1; dep.]   *support, vote for*

Sulla,-ae [m.]   *Sulla*

sum, esse, fuī   *be*

summus,-a,-um   *top of, uppermost, utmost, extreme*

sūmō,-ere, sūmpsī, sūmptum [3]   *take, take up*

super   [prep. + acc./abl.] *on, upon*; [adv.] *above*

superbus,-a,-um   *proud, arrogant*

superō,-āre,-āvī,-ātum [1]   *overcome, surpass*

superstitiō,-ōnis [f.]   *superstition*

superus,-a,-um   *above, on high*

supplex,-icis [m.]   *supplicant*

supplicium,-ī [n.]   *punishment*

suprā [+ acc.]   *beyond*

surgō,-ere, surrexī, surrectum [3]   *rise*

suscitō,-āre,-āvī,-ātum [1]   *arouse*

suspīciō,-ōnis [f.]   *suspicion*

sustentō,-āre,-āvī,-ātum [1]   *maintain, preserve*

suus,-a,-um   *his own, her own, their own*

syllaba,-ae [f.]   *syllable*

taberna,-ae [f.]   *shop*

taceō,-ēre,-uī, tacitum [2]   *be silent*

tacitus,-a,-um   *silent, quiet, secret*

tālis,-e   *such, of such a kind*

tam   *so*

tam . . . quam   *as (much) . . . as*

tamen   *nevertheless, yet, still, for all that, however*

tamquam   *as if*

tangō,-ere, tetigī, tāctum [3]   *touch*

tantum   [adv.] *only, just, so much*

tantus,-a,-um   *so great, so much, so many*

Tarquinius,-ī [m.]   *Tarquin*

taurus,-ī [m.]   *bull*

temptō,-āre,-āvī,-ātum [1]   *try, make trial of, test*

tempus,-oris [n.]   *time*

tenāx   *persisting, holding fast*

tendō,-ere, tetendī, tentum [3]   *stretch, reach, march*

tenebrae,-ārum [f.pl.]   *darkness, gloom*

teneō,-ēre,-uī, tentum [2]   *hold, control, restrain*

tener,-era,-erum   *tender, delicate, soft*

tenuis,-e   *narrow, small, insignificant*

tepeō,-ēre [2]   *be lukewarm*

terra,-ae [f.]   *ground, land, earth*

terribilis,-e   *dreadful, terrible*

terror,-ōris [m.]   *terror, fear*

testāmentum,-ī [n.]   *will*

testimōnium,-ī [n.]   *evidence*

testis,-is [m./f.]   *witness*

testor, testārī, testātus [1; dep.]   *declare, give evidence*

texō,-ere, texī, textum [3]   *weave*

thēsaurus,-ī [m.]   *treasure*

Tiber,-is [m.]   *Tiber*

tībīcen,-inis [m.]   *flute-player, piper*

timeō,-ēre,-uī [2]   *fear*

timide   *timidly, fearfully*

timidus,-a,-um   *fearful, cowardly*

toga,-ae [f.]   *toga*

tolerō,-āre,-āvī,-ātum [1]   *endure*

tollō,-ere, sustulī, sublātum [3]   *take up, lift up, remove*

tōnsor,-ōris [m.]   *barber*

tormentum,-ī [n.]   *torture*

tot   *so many*

tōtus,-a,-um   *whole, entire*

tractō,-āre,-āvī,-ātum [1]   *touch, handle*

trādō,-ere, trādidī, trāditum [3]   *hand over, pass on, record*

trahō,-ere, traxī, tractum [3]   *draw, drag*

trānō,-āre,-āvī,-ātum [1]   *swim across*

trāns [+ acc.]   *across*

trānsdūcō,-ere,-dūxī,-ductum [3]   *transfer, bring across*

trānseō,-īre, trānsiī (-īvī), trānsitum   *go across, pass through*

trānsferō, trānsferre, trānstulī, trānslātum   *transfer*

trānsgredior, trānsgredī, trānsgressus [M.; dep.]   *go across, cross* trānsmūtō,-āre,-āvī,-ātum [1]   *transfer*

trānsverberō,-āre,-āvī,-ātum [1]   *transfix*

trēs, tria   *three*

tribūnus,-ī [m.]   *tribune*

tribuō,-ere, tribuī, tribūtum [3]   *grant, give*

tribūtum,-ī [n.]   *tribute*

trīstis,-e   *sad, grim, gloomy*

triumphus,-ī [m.]   *triumph*

triumvir,-ī [m.]   *triumvir*

Trōiānus,-a,-um   *Trojan*

trucīdō,-āre,-āvī,-ātum [1]   *slaughter, cut down*

tū   *you* (s.)

tueor, tuērī, tuitus [2; dep.]   *look upon, regard, protect*

tum   *then, at that time*

tumultus,-ūs [m.]   *uproar, insurrection*

tunc   *then, at that time, thereupon*

tunica,-ae [f.]   *under-garment, tunic*

turba,-ae [f.]   *crowd*

turbō,-āre,-āvī,-ātum [1]   *disturb, trouble*

turgidus,-a,-um   *swollen*

turma,-ae [f.]   *troop, throng*

turpis,-e   *disgraceful*

turpiter   *disgracefully*

turris,-is [f.]   *tower*

tūtus,-a,-um   *safe, secure*

tuus,-a,-um   *your* (s.)

tympanum,-ī [n.]   *drum, tambourine*

Tyrrhēnus,-a,-um   *Etruscan*

ūber [gen. 'ūberis']   *fruitful, productive*

ubī (ubi)   *where, when*

ubīque   *everywhere*

ūllus,-a,-um   *any*

ultimus,-a,-um   *last, farthest, remote*

ultor,-ōris [m.]   *avenger*

ultrā   [prep. + acc.] *above, beyond, more than;* [adv.] *beyond*

ultrīx   *avenging*

ultrō   *moreover, even, actually*

umbra,-ae [f.]   *shadow, shade*

umquam   *ever*

ūnā   *together, at the same time*

unda,-ae [f.]   *wave*

unde   *from where*

undique   *from all sides*

unguis,-is [m.]   *nail*

ūnicē   *especially, above all*

ūniversus,-a,-um   *whole, entire, as one*

ūnus,-a,-um   *one, single, alone*

urbs, urbis [f.]   *city*

ūrīna,-ae [f.]   *urine*

ūrō,-ere, ussī, ustum [3]   *burn*

ut (utī)   [+ subjunctive] *that, so that, in order that, with the result that;* [+ indicative] *as, when, how*

ūtilis,-e   *useful, suitable, profitable*

utinam   *if only*

ūtor, ūtī, ūsus [3; dep.; + abl.]   *use, profit by, benefit from*

utrum   *whether*

uxor,-ōris [f.]   *wife*

vādō,-ere [3]   *go, walk*

vae   *alas, oh dear*

valē   *farewell*

valeō,-ēre,-uī,-itum [2]   *be well, fit, powerful*

validus,-a,-um   *healthy, strong*

vectō,-āre,-āvī,-ātum [1]   *bear, carry*

vehō,-ere, vēxī, vectum [3]   *carry, bring, ride, travel*

vel   *or, or if you will*

vel . . . vel   *either . . . or*

vēlōcitās,-tātis [f.]   *speed, swiftness*

vēlōx   *rapid, quick*

velut(ī)   *just as, like*

vēna,-ae [f.]   *vein*

vēnābulum,-ī [n.]   *hunting spear*

vēnātor,-ōris [m.]   *huntsman*

venēnum,-ī [n.]   *poison*

veniō,-īre, vēnī, ventum [4]   *come*

ventus,-ī [m.]   *wind*

venus, veneris [f.]   *love, mating*

verber, verberis [n.]   *blow, lash*

verberō,-āre,-āvī,-ātum [1]   *beat, whip*

verbum,-ī [n.]   *word*

vereor, verērī, veritus [2; dep.]   *fear, respect*

vērō   *indeed, really, certainly, for sure, yes*

versus,-ūs [m.]   *verse*

vertō,-ere, vertī, versum [3]   *turn*

vērum   *but, certainly, yes*

vērum,-ī [n.]   *truth*

vērus,-a,-um   *real, true, proper*

Vesta,-ae [f.]   *Vesta*

vester,-tra,-trum   *your* (pl.)

vestibulum,-ī [n.]   *hall, porch*

vestīgium,-ī [n.]   *trace, footstep*

vestiō,-īre, vestīvī (-iī), vestītum [4]   *clothe, dress*

vestis,-is [f.]   *clothing*

veterānus,-ī [m.]   *veteran*

vetus [gen. 'veteris']   *old, previous, longstanding*

vetustās,-tātis [f.]   *old age*

via,-ae [f.]   *road*

vīcīnus,-a,-um   *neigbouring*

vīcīnus,-ī [m.]   *neighbour*

victor,-ōris [m.]   *conqueror, winner*

victōria,-ae [f.] *victory*

vīcus,-ī [m.] *village, street*

videō,-ēre, vīdī, vīsum [2]   *see*

vīlis,-e *cheap, worthless*

vīlla,-ae [f.] *villa*

vincō,-ere, vīcī, victum [3]   *conquer*

vinc(u)lum,-ī [n.]   *chain, fetter*

vindex,-icis [m.]   *protector, enforcer*

vīnum,-ī [n.] *wine*

viola,-ae [f.] *violet*

violō,-āre,-āvī,-ātum [1]   *violate, outrage*

vir,-ī [m.]   *man, husband*

virgō,-inis [f.]   *girl, virgin*

virtūs,-tūtis [f.]   *courage*

vīrus,-ī [n.]   *poison, slime*

vīs [f.]   *force, power, violence*; [pl. 'vīrēs,-ium']   *strength, resources*

vīsō,-ere, vīsī [3]   *go to see, gaze on*

vīta,-ae [f.]   *life*

vitrum,-ī [n.]   *glass, woad*

vitta,-ae [f.]   *headband, ribbon*

vituperō,-āre,-āvī,-ātum [1]   *disparage, find fault with*

vīvārium,-ī [n.]   *pond, aquarium*

vīvō,-ere, vīxī, victum [3]   *live*

vīvus,-a,-um   *living, alive*

vix   *hardly, scarcely, with difficulty*

vixdum   *scarcely yet, barely yet*

vocō,-āre,-āvī,-ātum [1]   *call, summon*

volō, velle, voluī   *wish, want, be willing*

voluntās,-tātis [f.]   *wish, choice, inclination*

vomō,-ere, vomuī, vomitum [3]   *pour forth*

vōs   *you* (pl.)

vōtum,-ī [n.]   *promise, wish, desire*

vōx, vōcis [f.]   *voice, speech, sound*

vulgus,-ī [n.]   *crowd*

vulnus,-eris [n.]   *wound*

vultus,-ūs [m.]   *face*

English to Latin vocabulary

The English to Latin vocabulary is limited to words required for the exercises in this course.

abandon relinquō,-ere, relīquī, relictum [3]

able, be possum, posse, potuī

absent, be absum, abesse, āfuī

abundance cōpia,-ae [f.]

across trāns [+ acc.]; per [+ acc.]

after post [+ acc.]

all omnis,-e

also etiam, quoque

always semper

ambition ambitiō,-ōnis [f.]

amphitheatre amphitheātrum,-ī [n.]

and et, atque, ac, -que

any ūllus,-a,-um; quī (quis); aliquī (-quis)

appoint creō,-āre, creāvī, creātum [1]

army exercitus,-ūs [m.]

arrest dēprehendō,-ere, dēprehendī, dēprehēnsum [3]

arrogant superbus,-a,-um

as (coin) as, assis [m.]

ask (for) rogō,-āre,-āvī,-ātum [1]

bad malus,-a,-um

be sum, esse, fuī

bear ferō, ferre, tulī, lātum

beast bēstia,-ae [f.]

because quod, quia

become fīō, fierī, factus sum

bed cūbīle,-is [n.]; lectus,-ī [m.]

before ante [+ acc.]

beg (for) ōrō,-āre,-āvī,-ātum [1]

begrudge, cheat, envy invideō,-ēre, invīdī, invīsum [2; + dat.]

behind post [+ acc.]

blow ictus,-ūs [m.]

body corpus,-oris [n.]

book liber,-brī [m.]

both . . . and et . . . et

boy puer,-ī [m.]

bull taurus,-ī [m.]

but sed

by ā, ab [+ abl.]

captive captīvus,-ī [m.]

capture capiō,-ere, cēpī, captum [M.]

care for cūrō,-āre,-āvī,-ātum [1]

carry ferō, ferre, tulī, lātum

chariot currus,-ūs [m.]

chase fugō,-āre,-āvī,-ātum [1]

children līberī,-ōrum [m.pl.]

city urbs, urbis [f.]

come veniō,-īre, vēnī, ventum [4]

commend probō,-āre,-āvī,-ātum [1]

complaint querēla,-ae [f.]

concerning dē [+ abl.]

conquer vincō,-ere, vīcī, victum [3]

conspirator coniūrātus,-ī [m.]

consul cōnsul,-is [m.]

contrary contrārius,-a,-um

country (one's own) patria,-ae [f.]

courage virtūs,-tūtis [f.]

crazy dēmēns

cruel saevus,-a,-um

daughter fīlia,-ae [f.]

day diēs, diēī [m./f.]

decimate decimō,-āre,-āvī,-ātum [1]

decree cōnsultum,-ī [n.]

delighted laetus,-a,-um

despise contemnō,-ere, contempsī, contemptum [3]

dinner cēna,-ae [f.]

dismiss dīmittō,-ere, dīmīsī, dīmissum [3]

displease displiceō,-ēre,-uī [2; +dat.]

do faciō,-ere, fēcī, factum [M.]

drink bibō, bibere, bibī [3]

elephant elephantus,-ī [m.]

emperor imperātor,-ōris [m.]; prīnceps,-ipis [m.]

empire imperium,-ī [n.]

enter ineō,-īre, iniī, initum

escape fugiō,-ere, fūgī, fugitum [M.]

even etiam

ever umquam

face vultus,-ūs [m.]

farmer agricola,-ae [m.]

father pater,-tris [m.]

father-in-law socer,-ī [m.]

favour faveō,-ēre, fāvī, fautum [2; + dat.]

fear   timeō,-ēre,-uī [2], vereor,-ērī, veritus [2; dep.]

fear   metus,-ūs [m.]

field   ager,-grī [m.]

fight   pugnō,-āre,-āvī,-ātum [1]

find   inveniō,-īre, invēnī, inventum [4]

first   prīmus,-a,-um

flee   fugiō,-ere, fūgī, fugitum [M.]

flower   flōs, flōris [m.]

foot   pēs, pedis [m.]

forum   forum,-ī [n.]

free   līber,-era,-erum

freedman   lībertus,-ī [m.]

friend (female)   amīca,-ae [f.]

friend (male)   amīcus,-ī [m.]

from   ā, ab [+ abl.]; dē [+ abl.]; ē, ex [+ abl.]

gift   dōnum,-ī [n.]

girl   puella,-ae [f.]

give   dō, dare, dedī, datum [1]

gladiator   gladiātor,-ōris [m.]

go   eō, īre, iī, itum

go across   trānseō,-īre, trānsiī, trānsitum

god   deus,-ī [m.]

goddess   dea,-ae [f.]

good   bonus,-a,-um

great   magnus,-a,-um

grief   dolor,-ōris [m.]

grieve   doleō,-ēre,-uī, dolitum [2]

groan   gemō,-ere, gemuī, gemitum [3]

groan   gemitus,-ūs [m.]

ground   terra,-ae [f.]

hand   manus,-ūs [f.]

happen   fīō, fierī, factus sum

harsh   saevus,-a,-um

have   habeō,-ēre,-uī, habitum [2]

hear   audiō, audīre, audīvī (-iī), audītum [4]

help   auxilium,-ī [n.]

here   hīc

here (to here)   hūc

himself, herself, itself   ipse, ipsa, ipsum; sē

horse   equus,-ī [m.]; caballus,-ī [m.]

house   domus,-ūs [f.]

hundred   centum

hunt   agitō,-āre,-āvī,-ātum [1]

huntsman   vēnātor,-ōris [m.]

husband   coniūnx, coniugis [m.]; marītus,-ī [m.] ; vir,-ī [m.]

I   ego

if   sī

in, into   in [+ abl.], in [+ acc.]

in front of   ante [+ acc.]; prae [+ abl.]

in place of   prō [+ abl.]

in the presence of   cōram [+ abl.]

Italy   Ītalia,-ae [f.]

joy   gaudium,-ī [n.]

judge   iūdex,-dicis [m.]

kill   interficiō,-ere, interfēcī, interfectum [3]; necō,-āre, necāvī, necātum [1]; occīdō,-ere, occīdī, occīsum [3]

kind   benignus,-a,-um

know   sciō,-īre, scīvī (-iī), scītum [4]

lack   careō,-ēre,-uī,-itum [2; + abl.]

lady   domina,-ae [f.]; mātrōna,-ae [f.]

Latin   latīnus,-a,-um

Latium   Latium,-ī [n.]

laugh (at)   rīdeō,-ēre, rīsī, rīsum [3]

lavish   opulentus,-a,-um

law   lēx, lēgis [f.]

lead   dūcō,-ere, dūxī, ductum [3]

leader   dux,-cis [m.]

leave   relinquō,-ere, relīquī, relictum [3]

letter   epistula,-ae [f.]; litterae,-ārum [f.]

letter (of the alphabet)   littera,-ae [f.]

lie   iaceō,-ēre,-uī, iacitum [2]

live (in a place)   habitō,-āre,-āvī,-ātum [1]

live (be alive)   vīvō,-ere, vīxī, vīctum [3]

love   amō,-āre,-āvī,-ātum [1]

love   amor,-ōris [m.]

mad   īnsānus,-a,-um; dēmēns

make   faciō,-ere, fēcī, factum [M.]

make a mistake   errō,-āre,-āvī,-ātum [1]

man   vir,-ī [m.]; homō,-inis [m.]

master   dominus,-ī [m.]; magister,-trī [m.]

matron   mātrōna,-ae [f.]

mid, in the middle of   medius,-a,-um

mistress   domina,-ae [f.]; amīca,-ae [f.]

money   pecūnia,-ae [f.]

mother   māter,-tris [f.]

mother-in-law   socrus,-ūs [f.]

mountain   mōns, montis [m.]

much, many   multus,-a,-um

my   meus,-a,-um

neither … nor   neque … neque

never   numquam

no   immō, minimē, nōn

no (not any)   nūllus,-a,-um

noise   tumultus,-ūs [m.]

not   nōn

nothing   nihil

now   nunc

number   numerus,-ī [m.]

obey   pāreō,-ēre, pāruī, pāritum [2; + dat.]

on   in [+ abl.]

one   ūnus,-a,-um

one (of two) alter,-era,-erum

or aut

order imperō,-āre,-āvī,-ātum [1; + dat.]; iubeō,-ēre, iussī, iussum [2]

ornament ōrnāmentum,-ī [n.]

other alius, alia, aliud

other (of two) alter,-era,-erum

ought, owe dēbeō,-ēre,-uī, dēbitum [2]

our noster,-tra,-trum

out of ē, ex [+ abl.]

people populus,-ī [m.]

place locus,-ī [m.]

pleasing (it is) libet [+ dat.]; placet [+ dat.]

plunder praeda,-ae [f.]

poem carmen,-inis [n.]

poet poēta [m.]

porch vestibulum,-ī [n.]

portrait imāgō,-inis [f.]

praise laudō,-āre,-āvī,-ātum [1]

prefer mālō, mālle

prepare parō,-āre,-āvī,-ātum [1]

present, be adsum, adesse, adfuī

priest/priestess sacerdōs,-dōtis [m./f.]

prison carcer,-eris [n.]

prostitute meretrīx,-īcis [f.]

province prōvincia,-ae [f.]

queen rēgīna,-ae [f.]

read legō,-ere, lēgī, lectum [3]

receive accipiō,-ere, accēpī, acceptum [M.]

rein habēna,-ae [f.]

release līberō,-āre,-āvī,-ātum [1]

remain maneō,-ēre, mānsī, mānsum [2]

Republic rēs pūblica [f.]

reward praemium,-ī [n.]

river flūmen,-inis [n.]

road via,-ae [f.]

robber latrō,-ōnis [m.]

Roman Rōmānus,-a,-um

Rome Rōma,-ae [f.]

rose rosa,-ae [f.]

sacred sānctus,-a,-um

sad trīstis,-e

satisfied contentus,-a,-um

say dīcō,-ere, dīxī, dictum [3]

scorn contemnō,-ere, contempsī, contemptum [3]

sea mare,-is [n.]

see videō,-ēre, vīdī, vīsum [2]

seek quaerō,-ere, quaesīvī (-iī) quaesītum [3]; petō,-ere, petīvī (-iī), petītum [3]

senate senātus,-ūs [m.]

senator senātor,-ōris [m.]

send mittō,-ere, mīsī, missum [3]

shore lītus,-oris [n.]

shout clāmō,-āre,-āvī,-ātum [1]

shout clāmor,-ōris [m.]

show ostendō,-ere, ostendī, ostentum [3]

silver argentum,-ī [n.]

sing canō,-ere, cecinī, cantum [3]

sit sedeō,-ēre, sēdī, sessum [2]

slaughter trucīdō,-āre,-āvī,-ātum [1]

slave servus,-ī [m.]

so that ut

soldier mīles,-itis [m.]

son fīlius,-ī [m.]

song carmen,-inis [n.]

son-in-law gener,-ī [m.]

speak dīcō,-ere, dīxī, dictum [3]; loquor,-ī, locūtus [3; dep.]

speech lingua,-ae [f.]

story fābula,-ae [f.]

surely nōnne

surely not num

suspicion suspīciō,-ōnis [f.]

sweat sūdō,-āre,-āvī,-ātum [1]

sword gladius,-ī [m.]

table mēnsa,-ae [f.]

take capiō,-ere, cēpī, captum [M.]

teach doceō,-ēre,-uī, doctum [2]

teacher magister,-trī [m.]; praeceptor,-ōris [m.]

tear lacrima,-ae [f.]

tell dīcō,-ere, dīxī, dictum [3]; iubeō,-ēre, iussī, iussum [2]

tender tener,-era,-erum

that (person/thing) ille, illa, illud

thing rēs,-eī [f.]

third tertius,-a,-um

this (person/thing) hic, haec, hoc

three trēs, tria

threshold līmen,-inis [n.]

through per [+ acc.]

thunderbolt fulmen,-inis [n.]

time tempus,-oris [n.]

to ad [+ acc.]

together with cum [+ abl.]

trace vestīgium,-ī [n.]

tribune tribūnus,-ī [m.]

triumph triumphus,-ī [m.]

triumvir triumvir,-ī [m.]

Trojan Trōiānus,-a,-um

two duo

value aestimō,-āre,-āvī,-ātum [1]

victor victor,-ōris [m.]

victory victōria,-ae [f.]

villa vīlla,-ae [f.]

visitor salūtātor,-ōris [m.]

wander errō,-āre,-āvī,-ātum [1]

want volō, velle, voluī

war bellum,-ī [n.]

wave unda,-ae [f.]

we nōs

weapons arma,-ōrum [n.pl.]

weep fleō,-ēre, flēvī, flētum [2]

when cum, quandō, ubī

where ubī

whether num

whip flagellum,-ī [n.]

who, which, what quī, quae, quod; quis quae quid

why cūr

wide awake exsomnis,-e

wife coniūnx, coniugis [f.]; mulier-is [f.]; uxor,-ōris [f.]

wind ventus,-i [m.]

wine vīnum,-ī [n.]

wish volō, velle, voluī

with cum [+ abl.]

without sine [+ abl.]

woman fēmina,-ae [f.]; mulier,-is [f.]

wood silva,-ae [f.]

word verbum,-ī [n.]

wretched miser,-era,-erum

write scrībō,-ere, scrīpsī, scrīptum [3]

wrong, be errō,-āre,-āvī,-ātum [1]

yes certē, etiam, ita (vērō), sīc, sānē

you (pl.) vōs

you (s.) tū

your (pl.) vester,-tra,-trum

your (s.) tuus,-a,-um